WOMEN AND THE REFORMATIONS

WOMEN

AND THE

REFORMATIONS

A Global History

MERRY WIESNER-HANKS

YALE UNIVERSITY PRESS
NEW HAVEN AND LONDON

Published with assistance from the foundation established in memory of Oliver Baty Cunningham of the Class of 1917, Yale College.

All reasonable efforts have been made to provide accurate sources for all images that appear in this book. Any discrepancies or omissions will be rectified in future editions.

For information about this and other Yale University Press publications, please contact:
U.S. Office: sales.press@yale.edu   yalebooks.com
Europe Office: sales@yaleup.co.uk   yalebooks.co.uk

Set in Van Dijck MT by IDSUK (DataConnection) Ltd
Printed in Great Britain by TJ Books, Padstow, Cornwall

Library of Congress Control Number: 2024940499

ISBN 978-0-300-26823-2

A catalogue record for this book is available from the British Library.

10 9 8 7 6 5 4 3 2 1

MIX
Paper | Supporting
responsible forestry
FSC
www.fsc.org   FSC® C013056

*In memory of Miriam Usher Chrisman (1920–2008)
and Natalie Zemon Davis (1928–2023),
foremothers and friends*

CONTENTS

ILLUSTRATIONS AND MAPS

PLATES

IN THE TEXT

MAPS

PREFACE

The Year 2025 is the 500th anniversary of the wedding of the German noblewoman Katharina von Bora and the religious reformer Martin Luther, whose actions and writings sparked the Protestant Reformation, the movement that split Western Christianity. Will there be exhibits, lectures, plays, concerts, and special church services around the world, as there were in 2017 for the 500th anniversary of Martin's 95 theses, his arguments against the pope's sale of indulgences offering release from purgatory? I doubt it, though there will be a recreation of the wedding in Wittenberg, where Katharina and Martin lived, as there has been for several decades. This attracts tourists, who sometimes dress in costume and always spend lots of money. You can also buy bobbleheads and T-shirts of Katharina, just as you can buy dolls and T-shirts of another sixteenth-century woman famous in the realm of religion, the Spanish visionary and reformer St. Teresa of Avila, the first woman to be proclaimed a Doctor of the Church by the pope. Although the women and their ideas were very different, the dolls look remarkably similar. (See Plate I.)

What would happen if we put these two women, and the many others who shaped religious life in this era, in the middle of the story instead of at the edges? And we considered Protestant and Catholic women together, including women from outside of Europe who were important in the growth and transformation of Christianity as it became a global religion? This book does just that. It tells the story of women and religious change from the late fifteenth through the eighteenth century, taking in the full sweep of religious reform during this era when Western Christianity splintered and spread around the world. It includes the Protestant Reformation *and* the Catholic Reformation, the movement to reform and strengthen the Catholic Church in response to the Protestant challenge that began in the 1540s. That is why "Reformations" is plural in the title. The seventeenth and eighteenth centuries saw dynamic religious transformations that built on the Reformations, and these are here as well.

Along with the cultural shift of the Italian Renaissance and the European voyages of exploration, the Reformations have long been understood to usher in the "modern" world, so the period covered by the book, roughly 1450 to 1800, is usually called "early modern." Women were central to the making of the modern world, and this book tells the stories of some of them—261 named individuals, if my counting is correct, plus hundreds of thousands of unnamed others involved with religious change.

Both Catholic and Protestant Christianity contained strong elements of misogyny and were controlled by male hierarchies, with women instructed to be obedient and subservient. Christian teachings were used by men as buttresses for male authority in all realms of life, not simply religion. Most women did not dispute this, and many defended patriarchal teachings, viewing these as supported by the Bible and tradition. But others used the language of religious texts, the examples of pious women who preceded them, and their own sense of connection with the divine to subvert or directly oppose male directives and reform their churches and societies. Still others used their authority as the leaders of religious communities or the rulers of territories to maintain or dramatically alter the religious life of those under their control. Their actions stood as counterexamples to widely held notions of women's weakness. Networks of women related through family, marriage, and friendship shared religious convictions and communicated religious ideas, sometimes across vast distances.

This book features women from Britain and many parts of the European continent, as well as Asia, Africa, and the Americas. Some are women whose stories may be familiar to those in the faith traditions in which they are heroes: Katharina von Bora, St. Teresa of Avila, the English martyr Anne Askew, the Peruvian saint Rose of Lima, the Quaker leader Margaret Fell Fox. Others are women whose stories have only recently been recovered: the Dutch Anabaptist martyr Weynken Claes, the Spanish prophet María de Santo Domingo, the Kongolese visionary Dona Beatriz Kimpa Vita, the Ethiopian abbess and saint Walatta Petros, the Japanese convert and catechist Naito Julia, and the Afro-Caribbean Moravian missionary Rebecca Protten.

Some of the women have been made saints, have had schools, churches, and parks named in their honor, and are depicted in statues and stained-glass windows around the world. Most have been forgotten, or intentionally written out of the histories of the movements they shaped. A few have been made saints *and* are largely forgotten. I've been teaching the history of Christianity, the history of women, and the history of this era for more than forty years, but as I was writing, friends and colleagues kept introducing me to more and more women I had never heard of whose stories they thought absolutely had to be included. The book could easily have been twice as long.

I emphasize what made these women distinctive, as well as experiences they had in common, looking at them as individuals and as members of families and groups. One thing they shared is that their words and ideas were recorded far less often than those of men. In the sixteenth century, works by women made up less than 1 per cent of the total printed editions across Europe, a number that went up only slightly in the centuries that followed. There were far more books *for* women written by men, including religious works, guides for running a household, manuals on proper behavior, and biographies of exemplary women, as men thought it important to tell women and girls what they should do. Mansplaining did not begin in the twenty-first century.

Women published fewer works than men because they had lower levels of learning and less access to financial resources. Even more than was the case with men, works by women—and actually all documentation about their lives—skew toward the wealthy and socially prominent. Women's public speech was also linked with sexual dishonor in many people's minds, as a "loose" tongue implied other sorts of loose behavior.

Many women who did publish thus claimed that some external force had compelled them: divine inspiration, their duty as mothers, their loyalty to their husbands, the gravity of a situation. Or they published anonymously or used a pseudonym.

Hymns, letters, prophecies, pamphlets, and other writings by women *do* survive, however, in manuscript and published. As interest in women's history has grown over the last fifty years, more and more of these have been found, stuck in desk drawers and dusty attics, or overlooked on library shelves and in family archives. For other women, we have their words as recorded in trial testimony, Inquisition records, witness commentary, and other documents written by their friends and foes. For women who were rulers, there are thousands of documents. Recovering women's stories has involved both finding new sources and reading very familiar ones in new ways. Excerpts from these sources are included in my narrative, as these can give you more direct access to women's ideas and experiences than could my descriptions alone. Woodcuts, engravings, and paintings from the era provide further insights into the world in which these women lived, and more recent public artworks trace their legacy.

Another thing that links the women you will meet in this book is how young they were when they began actions that would have an impact. Rose of Lima started intense pious practices when she was a girl, as did the English prophet Anna Trapnel, the Mohawk convert Kateri Tekakwitha, and many others. The Protestant reformer Katharina Zell recounted toward the end of her life that she had been a "nurturer of the pulpit and school" since she was ten. Mary Stuart began her reign as Scotland's queen when she was eighteen, returning as a young widow from a childhood in France to handle complex political and religious conflicts. Many other women ascended to thrones when they were children or adolescents as well, first guided by regents (who were sometimes their mothers) but assuming personal rule when they were in their teens. Angélique Arnauld became the abbess of the French convent of Port-Royal when she was eleven, and at eighteen led the convent in a dramatic reform, bringing stricter observance of rules and better theological education. The Scottish Protestant Margaret Wilson was executed for attending illegal religious services and rebellion when she was eighteen, and girls even younger than this were martyred as well. Laws at the time facilitated young women's actions, with girls as young as twelve, or in some places even ten, often allowed to write a will, enter a convent, or make a marriage.

Every chapter in this book includes Protestants and Catholics, and some chapters include non-Christians whose lives were affected by institutions over which women held power. The chapter on migrants, for example, begins with the expulsion of the Jews from Spain in 1492, the first mass migration for religious reasons in European history. This resulted in large part from decisions made by a woman, Queen Isabel of Castile. Her policy—convert or leave—became that of nearly every political authority in Christian Europe. Jews were soon joined as refugees by German and Dutch radicals, English Catholics, French Protestants, and many others, in waves of religious migration and exile that began in the first decade of the Protestant Reformation and continued for centuries. Western Christianity was a unified Church under the pope when Queen Isabel sponsored Christopher Columbus on his first voyage, but by the time it really began to spread beyond Europe several decades later, it was divided. Missionaries spread various forms of Christianity, a story that has been well told, but so did people who moved, whether to the next town, a different country, or across the ocean.

Not surprisingly, the chapter on migrants is a long one, taking in the experiences of hundreds of thousands of women and girls, as is that on mothers, which includes spiritual mothers along with women who gave birth. The chapters on monarchs, martyrs, and mystics are shorter, as there were far fewer of these, but the impact of their lives and ideas outweighed their numbers. The chapter on missionaries focuses on women who spread some version of Christianity, or sought to do so, in Europe and around the world, along with those who responded to evangelization by adopting, rejecting, and transforming Christian beliefs and practices.

As you read the women's stories, you will learn about many other things: patterns of religious change, the ideas of male reformers, dynastic, national, and international politics, religious wars, education, public welfare and poor relief, family relations, art and music, notions of race, and much more. The standard way to tell the story would be to provide you with all this first, and then explain how the women fit in, a method that's sometimes sarcastically called "add women and stir." But we can also start with women's actions and ideas, and expand out from these, exploring other topics when necessary to gain an understanding of the broader picture. So the very first chapter is on women rulers, of which there were many in the Reformation era.

Putting women at the center of the story instead of at the periphery or added as an afterthought might seem like a newish idea, and in some ways it is. Only in the last fifty years have historians and scholars in other fields begun to examine the history of women as closely as that of men, who have been the primary focus of history writing for thousands of years. But more than 300 years ago, the German Lutheran theologian Gottfried Arnold spent hundreds of pages describing "blessed women" of the sixteenth and seventeenth centuries "who showed the way to the truth, or who suffered greatly, or who were amazingly gifted, enlightened or directed by God." Johann Feustking, Arnold's opponent in theological arguments that split the German Lutheran Church in the early eighteenth century, spent even more hundreds of pages attacking the same women as "false prophetesses, fanatics . . . and frenzied female persons through whom God's peace is disturbed."[1] They took these women seriously and recognized their impact, and so should we.

Arnold and Feustking had no doubt about whether the women they discussed were blessed or fanatics. Most of the other people you will meet in this book were also very sure in their views: their own beliefs and practices were correct and godly and those of others were not. We might be equally tempted to judge the women whose stories are in this book, as there is a strong tendency in women's history to "idealize, pity, or blame," as the medieval historian Barbara Newman put it.[2] There are many to admire, from a young Dutch radical Protestant who refused to recant her faith despite horrific torture to a middle-aged Portuguese Jewish woman who helped transport other Jews out of harm's way, to an aged Spanish nun who traveled around the world by ship and donkey to establish convents in new places.

But women also acted in ways we generally find less admirable today. They were not judges, inquisitors, or executioners, as these were official positions held only by men, but women rulers told judges, inquisitors, and executioners what to do, setting the policies that led to forced conversions, migration, and martyrdom. Women testified against those charged with heresy or witchcraft and were in the crowds watching those who were judged guilty die. Women's legacies were often mixed, just as were those of men. The world-traveling English Quaker Mary Fisher defied authorities to preach in Barbados and Boston and met with the Ottoman sultan in Turkey, but at her death in South Carolina, her property included an enslaved African.

Making ethical judgments about people of the past is inescapable, as we are living in a world that to some degree their decisions created. But we can also try to approach the past with a sense of historical empathy. This is not the same as sympathy, but instead involves seeking to *understand* why someone did what she did, not condone it. Historical empathy means trying to comprehend what someone experienced from within that person's frame of reference, by considering her thoughts, beliefs, and states of mind within the context of her times. Contextualizing the past can also help us come to be aware of our own position in history, what we might call contextualizing the present. Like the women (and men) in this book, we all have personal assumptions and values that consciously and unconsciously shape how we approach the world. I do, and despite my efforts at historical empathy, they influence the pages that follow. Yours will also no doubt shape how you feel and think about the women you meet in this book.

CHAPTER ONE

———✦———

MONARCHS

Although I am just a little Princess, God has given me the government of this country so I may rule it according to his Gospel and
teach it his Laws.

Jeanne d'Albret, Queen of Navarre

I will not make windows into men's souls.

Elizabeth I, Queen of England

The women who had the most impact on religious life in the era of the
Reformations were members of ruling families. Almost everyone in
Europe in this period—and in other agricultural societies around the
world—lived under a hereditary dynasty in which authority was handed
down through family connections. States governed by officials in the
Catholic Church were an exception, though even there, relatives of the
leader often became powerful figures. There were some cities that were
politically independent and led by a city council, but most were within
the realm of a monarch.

The primary duty for rulers in dynastic states was (and is) to have an
heir, preferably male and healthy, as rules of succession favored men.
Dynasties do not always work according to plan, however, which meant
women sometimes ruled in their own names as queens or empresses.
Between 1300 and 1800, thirty women had sovereign authority over

major European states, and many others led smaller ones. Women also ruled as regents during the minority of their sons, or when their husbands or other family members were absent or incapacitated. They were powerful queens consort—wives to kings—shaping the decisions of their royal husbands, and formidable queen mothers, influencing the decisions of their sons and daughters. Religious reformers recognized that royal and noble women had a great deal of power and made special attempts to win them over, in person and through letters.

Monarchs controlled religion as well as other realms of life. For those of us raised within a tradition of the separation of church and state (the phrase is Thomas Jefferson's), it may be hard to understand just how fully these two were joined before the eighteenth century. Christianity became the official religion of the Roman Empire in the fourth century and most of the states of medieval Europe in the centuries after that. It gradually split into two forms in Europe, now termed Catholicism and Orthodoxy, with Catholicism headed by the pope in Rome. (There were other forms outside of Europe.) Most people were baptized shortly after they were born and buried in a Christian funeral shortly after they died, with many rituals in between, making "Christian" an essential part of their identity. Non-Christians, primarily Jews and Muslims, lived in some parts of Europe, but were often viewed with suspicion and hostility because they were not part of the Christian community.

Before the Protestant Reformation, there were individuals and movements that disagreed with the Catholic Church or wanted reforms. Some of these movements came to influence church teachings, while others were declared heresies and were suppressed or went underground. What made the Protestant Reformation different from earlier reform movements is that Martin Luther and other sixteenth-century reformers convinced political authorities to break with the Catholic Church, or rulers decided on their own to do so. Individuals may have been convinced that Protestant teachings were correct by hearing sermons, listening to hymns, or reading pamphlets, but a territory became Protestant when the authority in charge, whether a dynastic ruler or a city council, decided this, and changed the rituals and institutions.

Once a ruler decided on change, residents of that territory were expected to more or less go along with it, at least in terms of outward behavior. If a later ruler became Catholic or a different form of Protestant, residents were expected to change again, because not following the wishes of the ruling authority put them outside the Christian community of that area. Nowhere was religion considered a private matter. Those who really objected moved, or were sometimes subject to arrest, imprisonment, exile, and perhaps death, as you'll see in later chapters.

Beginning with Queen Isabella of Hungary in the mid-sixteenth century, rulers in a few places allowed limited religious toleration, but this policy was usually short-lived and generally did not bring equal political and legal rights. Most of the British colonies in North America had state churches, though these were disestablished shortly after the American Revolution, and the First Amendment of the United States Constitution opens: "Congress shall make no law respecting an establishment of religion, or prohibiting the free exercise thereof." European countries gradually moderated the link between church and state as well, but even today in Europe, though people are free to worship as they choose, some countries have churches endorsed by the government. In Germany, a portion of people's income tax goes to support certain churches, unless they formally opt out. In Denmark, Norway, Finland, and Iceland, the Lutheran Church is the state church, and most people are officially members, though very few attend.

Women rulers made decisions about religion in ways similar to men, with political and dynastic concerns mixing with their religious convictions. Just as men rulers used paternal imagery to describe themselves, women rulers sometimes used rhetoric that emphasized their position as mothers of their territories when speaking to or about their subjects. In addressing the English Parliament in response to their petition that she marry, the thirty-year-old Queen Elizabeth I said, "I assure you all that though after my death you may have many stepdames, yet shall you never have any a more mother than I mean to be unto you all."[1]

Although Queen Elizabeth maintained her determination never to marry throughout her long reign, most women in ruling families did marry, and they also had children. The arrangements they made for their own children and other younger family members, especially their marriages, could have a dramatic impact on religious life, often in unexpected ways. Networks of royal mothers, daughters, daughters-in-law, grandmothers, granddaughters, aunts, and nieces communicated religious ideas and shared religious convictions. Many of these stretched across boundaries, as women often moved when they married.

THE QUEEN OF CASTILE AND HER HEIRS

The powerful impact of women rulers on religion in the era of the Reformations began before Martin Luther was born. In 1474, Isabel I (1451–1504) became the ruler of Castile, the largest state in the Iberian peninsula, after the death of her half-brother Enrique IV. (Later officials and historians, seeking to diminish Isabel's role, began to call her "Isabella"—little Isabel—but she always signed her name "Isabel the queen.") Five years earlier, she had married Ferdinand II of Aragon (1452–1516), prince of the second-largest state in Iberia, who became the king of Aragon in 1479. The two monarchs carried out similar policies but ruled largely separately, though under their heirs, their lands and other territories would become a more unified realm, Spain.

There had been women rulers in Castile's past, but most of these were regents for their sons, and in 1474 Isabel did not yet have a son. Thus she had to overcome doubts about whether a woman could rule effectively, which she accomplished through religious and political reforms, along with connecting herself with her dynasty and military conquest. (See Plate II.)

The religious situation in the Iberian peninsula provided Isabel and Ferdinand with unique opportunities to build up their power. Some Jewish families had been there since Roman times and some were more recent immigrants from England and France, from which Jews had been expelled around 1300. Initially both Christian and Muslim rulers welcomed them, but during the late fourteenth century attacks and riots against Jewish communities in Christian areas, stoked by preachers and church officials, became more common. Many Jews converted (or were forced to convert), becoming *conversos* or "New Christians." Others decided to convert throughout the fifteenth century because of the social and economic mobility this provided, because they were convinced of the truth of Christian teachings, or because they wished to marry someone who was Christian. (Or a mixture of these and other reasons.)

Particularly in Castile, *converso* men were often well educated, serving as lawyers and physicians, bishops and abbots, and local and royal officials, including to Isabel's predecessor Enrique IV. Their success enhanced popular resentment on the part of "Old Christians," and with the accession of Isabel this sentiment gained a royal ear. Isabel was very devout, and she also recognized that moving against *conversos* was a way to distinguish herself from the generally unpopular Enrique in people's minds. She and Ferdinand gained permission from Pope Sixtus IV to establish their own Inquisition in 1478 to ferret out what they saw as incomplete conversions or backsliding. Investigations, trials, and executions of *conversos* began several years later, with officials of the Inquisition charged to search out the least sign of Jewish practices, which they termed "Judaizing."

Trying to figure out what someone *really* believed from Inquisition records is nearly impossible; the consequences of many statements could be severe punishment or death, so people were careful about what they said. Thus we cannot know what share of the converts might have been the "crypto-Jews" that inquisitors accused them of being. But no matter how many converts actually maintained Jewish beliefs and practices, the focus on people being secretly Jewish led Spanish officials to develop a new type of anti-Semitism. Christian hostility toward Jews had existed throughout the Middle Ages, but Jews were defined primarily as a religious group, unacceptable because they did not believe Jesus was the Messiah. To the officials of the Spanish Inquisition and those they influenced, however, Judaism increasingly became not simply a religious adherence that could be changed through conversion, but an essential (and unchangeable) aspect of a person's nature, housed in the blood and heritable.

Thus along with investigating converts, Castile and Aragon passed laws requiring "purity of blood" (*limpieza de sangre*): that is, anyone claiming status as a noble—and ultimately other social privileges as well, such as entering a convent, joining a religious order, or migrating to the New World—must have no Jewish or Muslim ancestors. In some areas intermarriage between Old and New Christians had become common, so families sought to hide their ancestors, as the revelation of "tainted" blood could mean disaster. Individuals seeking to prove their purity of blood claimed that they were "without race," that is, without the *mala raza* (bad lineage) of Jewish or Muslim ancestry. Spanish Christians increasingly categorized those of other religions in racialized ways, as did Christians elsewhere in Europe.

Purity (*limpieza*) was also something expected of clergy, who were supposed to provide models of piety, devotion, and discipline. Isabel and Ferdinand gained papal approval to reform religious houses that did not live up to this standard. They particularly focused on women's houses, and ordered the nuns within them to be cloistered, that is, cut off from the world so that they could more easily maintain their virginity, chastity, and purity.

For centuries, every call for reforming the Catholic Church had emphasized the importance of the control of female sexuality in creating a Christian moral order and had tried to enforce cloistering for nuns. This became official policy in the papal decree *Periculoso*, promulgated in 1298 by Pope Boniface VII, which called for cutting women's convents off from the world physically, through walls and screens, limited or no family visits, and no travel outside convent walls. Enforcement of this decree waxed and waned, however, and had been lax, according to Isabel, under Enrique IV. She and Ferdinand sent dispatches to women's convents ordering stricter observance of cloister, with specific directions about walls, windows, curtains, and other issues. They then sent official visitors charged with making sure these instructions were followed.

Isabel was a married woman, and a mother—she eventually had five children, including one son—so she could not be physically pure in the way that nuns were supposed to be. But she and her advisers increasingly linked her with the purest woman of all, the Virgin Mary. Mary had also, of course, given birth to a son, but had done so, according to Christian teachings, after being impregnated by the Holy Spirit rather than a human man. Whether Mary was completely free of the sinfulness attached to human sexuality had been debated since the early Church, particularly after St. Augustine asserted in the fourth century that all humans carry the stain of Original Sin resulting from Adam and Eve's disobedience to God's command. This taint, he and others argued, was passed down through sexual intercourse so that all infants are born sinful. Medieval theologians debated whether the sex act that produced

Mary might have been free from this sin—an Immaculate (Latin for "without taint/stain") Conception—and many Spanish clergy became supporters of this doctrine. (It did not become an official doctrine of the Catholic Church until 1859, however, and is rejected by most Protestants.)

Isabel accepted the idea of the Immaculate Conception and encouraged its spread. She gave money for celebrations and written works that supported it, including a life of Christ written by a Spanish abbess, Isabel de Villena (c. 1430–1490). Written in Catalan, the local language, for the nuns in her convent, Isabel de Villena's work focused primarily on the actions of the women around Christ, especially Mary, whose birth and bodily assumption into heaven after her death are its opening and closing chapters. It is devotional literature, but also a defense of women, a contribution to a broad debate about women's character and nature that went on for centuries across Europe, which often goes by its name in French, *querelle des femmes*. Finished just before Isabel de Villena died, the book was published in Barcelona in 1497 with the support of Isabel of Castile.

Isabel also provided a building in Toledo for Beatriz de Menezes da Silva (c. 1424–1492), a Portuguese noblewoman who had been a lady-in-waiting at the Castilian court, to found a community of women dedicated to honoring the Immaculate Conception. The convent grew into the Order of the Immaculate Conception, which opened convents across southern Europe and later in the Spanish and Portuguese American colonies.

Isabel strengthened Catholicism through war as well as patronage and institution-building. Shortly after they took their thrones, she and Ferdinand began military action against Muslim-held territories in the south, continuing the centuries-long *reconquista*, the Christian conquest of Muslim Spain. Isabel did not lead troops into battle, but she did appear personally in areas where they were fighting. As a later Spanish chronicler commented, "By the solicitude of this Queen was begun, and by her diligence was continued, the war against the Moors, until all the Kingdom of Granada was won."[2]

In January 1492, Christian armies conquered the Emirate of Granada, the last Muslim state in the Iberian peninsula. Granada was home to many Jews, including families who had lived there for centuries and others who had migrated there more recently, but now it was no longer a safe haven. In March 1492, Isabel and Ferdinand issued the Alhambra Decree, ordering all practicing Jews to leave Spain in four months, without taking any of their property with them. Many converted, but tens of thousands left, about half going to North Africa and the rest dispersing throughout Europe and the Ottoman Empire. They included many women and children, some of whose stories you will find in Chapter 3. A decade later, Isabel banished Muslims from Castile as well, adding to the stream of migrants.

At about the same time as the Alhambra Decree, Queen Isabel decided to support Christopher Columbus, who promised to use the riches he gained from his voyage to fight Muslims. His three ships left in August 1492 on a voyage whose impact no one, including the queen, could have anticipated. Only nine months later, knowing that Columbus had found something (though no one was sure what), Pope Alexander VI gave Isabel and Ferdinand authority to claim any land not already ruled by a Christian king west of a line in the Atlantic Ocean. This "doctrine of discovery" became the basis of all European claims in the Americas, even among those countries that after the Reformation did not recognize the authority of the pope. Several years later the pope issued another papal bull, *Si convenit*, in which he gave the royal couple the title "King and Queen Catholic of all the Spains" in thanks for their conquering Granada, unifying the realm, expelling the Jews, and "zeal for the Catholic faith." Because of this, Isabel is sometimes referred to as "Isabel the Catholic."

Along with investigating *conversos*, the Inquisition also examined Christians charged with a variety of ideas and actions officials regarded as heresy. Its early targets included people charged with being *alumbrados* (illuminated ones), a Spanish term used to describe anyone who emphasized mystical union with God and mental prayer guided by the Holy Spirit more than church ceremonies. Many *alumbrados* were *conversos*, and many were women, including the person described by the Inquisition as the "true mother and teacher of all *alumbrados*," Isabel de la Cruz, a seamstress and devout single woman in Guadalajara. She began to practice and teach seeking God through interior prayer around 1509, gaining followers among Franciscans, university students, and others. Inquisitors developed a list of ideas associated with *alumbradismo*, and threatened

8

any person who held these with prosecution, imprisonment, and punishment. Isabel de la Cruz and several men were found guilty in the 1520s and went to prison for several years. The Inquisition also investigated people who criticized the power of church officials, swore at a priest, denied the Virgin Birth, made obscene comments about a saint, or otherwise engaged in actions it judged offensive.

After the 1520s, all these troublemakers were often lumped together as "Lutherans," a catch-all term that also included those who actually accepted Protestant doctrine. There were not very many of these, but Inquisition trials and executions put an end to what little Protestantism existed in Spain. Spain took its Inquisition around the world when it established colonies, so what Isabel and Ferdinand started became a global enterprise.

Isabel and Ferdinand were also marriage brokers extraordinaire for their children, and this, too, shaped the Reformations, though not always in ways they would have appreciated. They married their eldest daughter Isabel to a prince of Portugal, and when he died married her to his younger brother, who was by that time King Manuel I of Portugal. Isabel (the younger) herself died several months later immediately after giving birth, so Isabel and Ferdinand married their second daughter, Maria, to Manuel. (Yes, the Catholic Church had rules against marrying close relatives of former spouses, but only rarely were these enforced for rulers. Basically, every ruler of Europe was related, often along multiple lines, as were their younger siblings.)

As part of the marriage negotiations, Manuel agreed to establish a Portuguese Inquisition on the Spanish model, which also spread to Portuguese colonies, particularly under his son, John III. Isabel and Ferdinand's marital politics thus enhanced their religious policies in Portugal. When John died, his nine children were already dead, and the throne passed to Sebastian, his grandson. Sebastian led a crusade against Muslims in North Africa—another action Isabel of Castile would have approved of—but he was killed on the campaign and had not married, so the dynasty he was part of died out.

Sebastian had come to the throne when he was only three, and his grandmother Catherine of Austria (1507–1578) was named regent, effectively controlling the country. She was the granddaughter of Isabel of Castile and, like her grandmother, was determined to strengthen Catholicism. The Inquisition had been effective against Protestants within Portugal, but Catherine also worried about France. She wrote to one of her diplomats:

> Count, my friend, I the Queen send you many greetings. . . . From my ambassador in the court of the King of France, I have learned of the great role in that realm that the ministers of the Lutheran sect and their followers have, and the regard and authority enjoyed by very important persons in said realm, and how close it is there for the loss of our holy Catholic faith if our Lord [King Charles IX of France] does not deal with it. . . . I am obliged to take up the matter with the King of France, they [religious questions] being of the type that they are and that they very much affect the honor of Our Lord, peace and tranquility of all Christianity. . . . I want to resolve this thing immediately, since to delay could create great harm. Written in Lisbon, on the 22 of October of 1562. The Queen.[3]

Catherine was right that religious questions would upset "peace and tranquility." Open warfare between Protestants and Catholics broke out that year in France.

MANY MARYS, SEVERAL ANNES, AND ONE ELIZABETH RULE BRITANNIA

Isabel and Ferdinand's matchmaking supported their religious aims in Portugal, and initially did so in England as well. But ultimately dynastic marriages that did not work out as planned led England away from Catholicism, in what became the best-known story of queens and would-be queens in the early modern era. As is common in dynastic houses, many of these queens had the same name, so it is sometimes difficult to keep them straight. I've included their family names frequently in telling their stories to help in this, but at the time everyone would have known which Mary, or Anne, or Catherine, or Elizabeth you were talking about.

Shortly after her two older sisters were married to Portuguese princes, Catherine of Aragon (1485–1536), Isabel and Ferdinand's youngest child, was married to Arthur, the oldest son of Henry VII of England, the first ruler in the Tudor dynasty. Arthur died unexpectedly, and rather than lose this alliance and the dowry Catherine had brought with her, Henry VII wrangled a papal dispensation to allow Catherine to marry his second son, Henry. Marriage to a brother's widow was technically not allowed in canon law, but, as in the Portuguese case, the pope was persuaded through strong royal pressure and donations to the papal coffers. The marriage was about average for royal marriages—they neither especially hated nor loved one another—but it only produced one child who survived infancy, a daughter Mary Tudor (1516–1558). By 1527, Henry decided that God was showing his displeasure with the marriage by denying him a son and appealed to the pope to have it annulled. He was also in love with a court lady-in-waiting, Anne Boleyn (1504–1536), and assumed she would give him the son that he wanted.

Normally an annulment would not have been a problem, but the troops of Emperor Charles V were at that point in Rome, and Pope Clement VII was essentially their prisoner. Charles V was the nephew of Catherine of Aragon, and thus was vigorously opposed to an annulment, which would have declared his aunt Catherine a fornicator and his cousin Mary Tudor a bastard. (At that time, an annulment was generally understood as declaring there never was a marriage, making children of such a union illegitimate.) So the pope stalled. With Rome thwarting his matrimonial plans, Henry decided to remove the English Church from papal jurisdiction and make himself the supreme head of the Church in England. Henry's forces were in the process of conquering Ireland, so as king he became the official head of the Church there as well.

Theologically, Henry was conservative, and the English Church retained many traditional Catholic practices and doctrines, including clerical celibacy. Henry dissolved the English monasteries and convents primarily because he wanted their wealth. He executed people for heresy, for refusing to agree that he was the head of the Church, and for taking part in religiously inspired revolts, which he viewed as treason. This included women, some of whom became celebrated martyrs, both Catholic and Protestant, whose stories are in Chapter 4.

In 1533, Henry married Anne Boleyn, who later that year gave birth, although to Henry's great dismay, it was a daughter, Elizabeth

(1533–1603), rather than a son. When Anne failed again to produce a male child because of a miscarriage, Henry charged her with adulterous incest and in 1536 had her beheaded. His third wife, Jane Seymour, gave Henry the desired son, but she died a few days after childbirth. Henry went on to marry three more wives, one of whom he executed and another whom he thought was unattractive, so the marriage was annulled.

His last wife, Catherine Parr (1512–1548), smoothed over relations between Henry and his children and became particularly close to the young Elizabeth, overseeing her education. Catherine hosted readings of the Bible in English in her quarters of the palace and published several books of English translations of prayers originally written in Latin that suggested she was sympathetic to Protestant ideas. Some of Henry's officials wanted her arrested, but she convinced Henry that she was simply discussing Protestant teachings, not accepting them. Shortly after Henry died, she published a third book, *The Lamentation of a Sinner*, that was entirely her own work. A first-person narrative, it traces her moving from sinfulness to salvation through God's grace and through reading the Bible, key Protestant teachings. Catherine was clearly working on this before Henry died, but she recognized the risk it posed, and waited until England had a Protestant king before publishing it.

Henry VIII's marital woes are a story that no one seems to tire of telling, given all the novels, movies, plays, and television programs set at the Tudor court. What sometimes gets lost in all this is that the story, and the broader course of religious change, would have been very different had Mary or Elizabeth Tudor been a boy. There were many people interested in Protestant ideas in England in the 1520s and 1530s, but it was Henry's desire for a son, not dissatisfaction with the Catholic Church or new theological teachings, that directly caused the English Reformation. Mary and Elizabeth would both have an enormous impact on the Reformation through their actions, but they had already done so simply by being born girls. Gender matters.

Henry's son Edward VI (1537–1553) inherited the throne when he was nine and died six years later, after a reign that moved England in a distinctly Protestant direction. He worried about what would happen if his elder half-sister Mary Tudor inherited the throne, as she had remained Catholic, so he disinherited her, and Elizabeth too, declaring them both bastards—even though Henry VIII's will had left them in line to the throne. He named a teenaged distant cousin, Lady Jane Grey (1537–1554), a staunch Protestant, as his successor. This dramatic break with standard rules of succession was opposed by many. Mary Tudor rallied support and rode into London at the head of troops. Jane Grey was queen for nine days, then deposed when Mary was proclaimed queen. Jane Grey was convicted of high treason and beheaded half a year later in the Tower of London, along with her husband and father, after a rebellion against Mary's rule. Thus Jane Grey became a martyr in Protestant eyes and a romantic heroine for novelists and movie-makers.

This left Mary Tudor, the daughter of Catherine of Aragon and the granddaughter of Isabel of Castile, as queen, the first woman to rule England in her own right, and she became Mary I. She was a devout Catholic, loyal to the Church not only because of her personal feelings but also because, throughout Henry's marital escapades, the Catholic Church had maintained that she was his true heir. Mary rescinded the Reformation legislation of her father's reign and began to restore Roman Catholicism, although the pope agreed that most monasteries and other church lands could remain in the hands of their new owners. Some Protestant leaders were imprisoned, and other Protestants fled to the continent.

Only through marriage and having a child could Mary I make sure that Catholicism would continue and that the Protestant Elizabeth would never inherit the throne. (Murder was another option, and Mary did have Elizabeth arrested and sent to the Tower of London, but decided against executing her.) There had been marriage negotiations when she was a young woman, but these had fallen apart, and she was now thirty-seven, which in the sixteenth century was an advanced age for a first child. She tried anyway, marrying her widowed first cousin King Philip II of Spain (1527–1598), the son of the emperor Charles V, in 1554. Philip came to England for the wedding and stayed for a while; it seemed he had done his kingly duty, as Mary appeared to be pregnant, with a swollen abdomen, nausea, and no menstrual periods. The prospect of a Catholic heir on the English throne was celebrated in Rome, Vienna, Madrid, and other Catholic centers, and regarded with horror by Protestants, especially English Protestants who had fled to the continent. But Mary's condition was a false pregnancy, brought on by stress and her intense desire to have a child. (False pregnancy still happens, although medical imaging makes it easier to detect.) After nearly a year of rumors but no baby, Philip left. A brief visit several years later brought another false pregnancy, after which Mary fell into deep depression.

As this was happening, Mary I began to sharpen her moves against Protestants, reviving medieval acts against heresy. Several hundred Protestant preachers, church leaders, and ordinary laymen and women were arrested, imprisoned, and executed if they refused to recant, some by being burned at the stake. After Mary's death, stories about the martyrs circulated orally and in printed martyrologies with gruesome illustrations. Protestant writers vilified her, nicknaming her "Bloody Mary," but she was not much different from other rulers at the time, most of whom imprisoned and executed people whose religious beliefs differed from theirs. Harsh measures were not accompanied by much effort on the ground to reintroduce Catholic teachings during Mary's reign, however. Only seven monastic houses were reopened, just two of them for women. Mary died after ruling for only five years, too short a time to bring England back to Catholic practice.

Mary's death brought to the throne her half-sister Elizabeth, who had been raised a Protestant, and for whom remaining Protestant was also a political choice, as the Catholic Church considered her illegitimate. Elizabeth I's long reign, from 1558 to 1603, set England on a moderate Protestant path, steering between what Catholics wanted and the more extensive changes supported by some of her subjects. The English Parliament passed several acts establishing the Church of England as the official state church. Elizabeth required officials, clergy, and nobles to swear allegiance to her as the "supreme governor of the Church of England." She initially chose the word "governor" rather than "head" to provide a loophole for English Catholics to remain loyal to her without denying the primacy of the pope. She also realized that "head" might be viewed as inappropriate for a woman, for treatises about the family and proper gender relations always referred to men as the "head." Later the term "Anglican" would be used to describe the Church of England, but this word was not used during Elizabeth's time.

Elizabeth is quoted as saying that she "will not make windows into men's souls," that is, inquire too closely into what people believed, but her subjects were required to be members of the Church of England and to attend church. Anti-Catholic laws were initially applied unevenly, however, and those of high social status or who were useful to the political agenda of the monarch were not always actually penalized. Later in her reign, doubts about the loyalty of her subjects if there should be a joint Spanish–papal invasion led to increasing fines and imprisonment of those who did not attend church, termed "recusants" from the Latin word *recusare*, which means to refuse. Some English Protestants had fled to the continent during Mary Tudor's reign, and now some Catholics did, including English and Irish clergy and nuns. Both recusants and exiles included many women, whose stories you can find in Chapters 2 and 3.

Supporting the pope or priests was declared to be treason, and Elizabeth executed people for this, as well as for participating in plots against her. Men convicted were generally "hanged, drawn and quartered," which sounds better than being burned alive, but could actually be worse, as what this meant is that they were hanged until they were nearly dead, then cut open and their interior organs pulled out, and then cut into four parts, with their head and penis sometimes cut off as well. At some point in this process, they died. Women sentenced to be executed were usually simply hanged, though one was pressed to death. Mary got the reputation as "bloody," but her half-sister was not especially merciful.

Elizabeth's advisers and subjects expected she would marry, but she chose not to, and her status as the "Virgin Queen" became an essential part of her carefully constructed political identity. From early in her reign, authors and artists linked Elizabeth with heroic mythological and biblical virgins, and with the Virgin Mary. They used attributes associated with the Virgin Mary—Queen of Heaven, Bride of Christ, merciful intercessor, empress of the earth and seas—and Marian symbols such as the pearl, rose, or moon in their written and visual portraits of Elizabeth. John Aylmer, an exile during Queen Mary I's rule who later became the Anglican bishop of London, wrote that God had chosen Elizabeth, an untested woman "weake in nature," to accomplish the miracle of England's glorious Protestant destiny, providing a parallel with God's choice of the Virgin Mary. The poet Edmund Spenser proclaimed Elizabeth "the flower of Virgins," "free from stain . . . without spotte," using language associated with Mary's Immaculate Conception.[4] Elizabeth herself did not make these comparisons, and the most extravagant portrayals appeared after she died, but virginity was one part of the queenly persona she created and cultivated, along with other qualities generally seen as feminine, such as mercy and caring, and qualities associated with masculinity, such as bravery and brilliance.

Elizabeth's virginity meant she had no direct heir, of course, but shortly before she died she chose her distant cousin James Stuart (1566–1625), the king of Scotland, to be the next king of England as well. (James is referred to as James VI and I, as he was the sixth Scottish king named James and the first English one.) To understand how Elizabeth and James were related, we need some backstory, which also involves powerful queens who shaped the Reformation in Scotland and beyond.

James was the son of Mary Stuart, the woman usually known as Mary, Queen of Scots (1542–1587), who had succeeded her father James V as the ruler of Scotland when she was one week old. The actual government was in the hands of regents, one of whom was Mary's mother, Mary of Guise (1515–1560), a French noblewoman whose marriage to James V had been part of a long-standing Franco-Scottish alliance. Mary of Guise came from a firmly Catholic family, but during her regency Protestant teachings spread in Scotland. She initially tolerated this, but when Elizabeth I became queen of England and a group of Scottish Protestant nobles made an open declaration of their Protestant principles, she ordered Protestant preachers to appear before her. Among these were John Knox, the leader of the Scottish Reformation, whose fiery sermons had inspired mob violence and the sacking of religious houses. Knox had been influenced by the French reformer John Calvin (1509–1564), the most important of the second generation of Protestant reformers, while Knox was in exile in the Swiss city of Geneva, where Calvin led the reform.

Open fighting erupted between the armies of Scottish Protestant lords and Mary of Guise's French troops. Elizabeth sent an English fleet and English soldiers to support the Protestants, and Mary ordered the fortifications of the city of Edinburgh to be reinforced. Her actions won praise even from English observers, with the Protestant English bishop

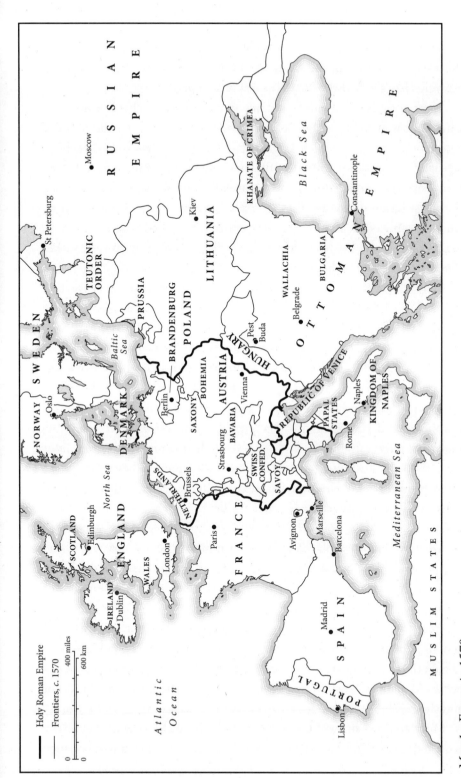

Map 1. Europe in 1570.

John Jewel praising her as "a woman with a man's courage," and the Protestant English ambassador in France, Nicholas Throckmorton, gushing that she had the "hart [heart] of a man of warre."[5]

Mary of Guise died quite suddenly in the middle of this conflict from what appeared to all at the time to be natural causes, and the war was ended by a treaty in which English and French troops agreed to leave Scotland. Scottish Protestant nobles and townsmen immediately assembled what became known as the Reformation Parliament and abolished the jurisdiction of the pope. A group of clergy and lay leaders, led by Knox, established a Protestant state church, the "Kirk" of Scotland, in which power was held by elected councils, called presbyteries, rather than by appointed bishops.

Mary of Guise had arranged for her daughter Mary to marry the heir to the French throne in what could have been a spectacular dynastic union, but he died when they were both still teenagers, just six months after Mary of Guise. The widowed Mary Stuart returned to Scotland as its young queen in 1561, to a tense political and religious situation. She was immediately confronted by John Knox, who opposed her because she was Catholic and had been raised in France, and also because she was a woman. In a treatise titled *The First Blast of the Trumpet against the Monstrous Regiment of Women* (1558), Knox had compared Mary Tudor with the Old Testament queen Jezebel, who incited her husband to worship other gods through her sexual allure. He included Mary of Guise and Mary Stuart in his attack, declaring that female rule was unnatural, unlawful, contrary to Scripture, and "monstrous." For Knox, nature and Scripture placed all women under male authority, with no exceptions, and subjects of female rulers needed no other justification for rebelling than their monarch's sex. (Knox had the misfortune to publish his work in 1558, the very year that Mary Tudor died and Elizabeth assumed the throne, making his position as both a Protestant and opponent of female rule rather tricky. He never apologized to Elizabeth, however, and she never allowed him to enter England.) Knox preached against Mary Stuart and she ordered him to stop; he did not and she had him arrested for treason, but he was acquitted and released.

Much to the dismay of Catholics across Europe, Mary Stuart officially accepted the religious situation in Scotland, and retained a royal council dominated by Protestants. This may have been because she was focusing primarily on her claims to the English throne, which were strong: her father's mother was Margaret Tudor, King Henry VII's daughter and thus King Henry VIII's sister, so she was Elizabeth's cousin. Despite her toleration of Protestants, Mary Stuart chose to marry a Catholic, her half-cousin Henry Stuart, Lord Darnley, another grandchild of Margaret Tudor. This decision led powerful Protestant lords to oppose Mary. She put down a first rebellion, but at the same time grew to hate Darnley, though she had a son by him. She may have been part of a plot that killed Darnley—there was no evidence, but she married the chief plotter—and in 1567 she was forced to abdicate in favor of her infant son James. The one-year-old James was raised by Protestant advisers, and Mary never saw her son again.

Mary Stuart fled to England, as she thought Elizabeth as a fellow monarch would help her regain her throne, but instead Elizabeth confined her to various houses and castles of loyal supporters. Elizabeth worried—quite rightly—that because of Mary's claims to the English throne she would become the center of Catholic plots to overthrow her. Mary was directly implicated in one of these when Elizabeth's spy network decoded letters written in cipher that called for the assassination of Elizabeth and a Spanish invasion. Mary was tried for treason and executed in 1587, as were several dozen conspirators.

While all this was happening, James was in Scotland, with a government led by a series of Protestant regents, then under his personal rule after he turned seventeen. He married Anna of Denmark (1574–1619), the cultured and vivacious daughter of the Danish king, in a ceremony conducted in French, a language they could both understand. Anna brought a Lutheran chaplain and many Danish ladies-in-waiting and artisans with her, and transformed the rather severe Scottish court into a place of music and dance.

When James became the king of England in 1603, both spouses moved to London, where Anna continued to patronize the arts, sponsoring lavish masques—performances involving acting, singing, dance, and elaborate scenery—and performing with her court ladies in many of these. Preachers in London criticized this as wasteful and sometimes scandalous, but ambassadors and other foreign visitors, Catholic and

Protestant, loved them. The masques also conveyed the prestige of the Stuart dynasty and its connection to Denmark and other Protestant powers beyond the British Isles. James wanted to further strengthen the Stuart dynasty by making England and Scotland a united kingdom rather than simply a personal union under a single monarch, though he was unsuccessful and this did not happen until 1707.

Some of the gentry and many urban residents in England thought that the English Church, with its hierarchical structure of bishops and elaborate ceremonies and outfits, was still too close to Roman Catholicism. They wanted to "purify" it of what they saw as vestiges of Catholicism, an aim that led them to be termed "Puritans." Other Protestants, dubbed "dissenters" or "sectaries" because their groups were seen as less official "sects" rather than "churches," did not want a state church at all. Puritans expected that, because James had been raised in Presbyterian Scotland, he would support them and get rid of bishops. Instead, he viewed the hierarchy of bishops as a key support for royal power, as did his son Charles I (ruled 1625–1649). They both formally required officials to be members of the Church of England and swear oaths acknowledging the king's authority over the Church, though they also tolerated Catholics at court as long as they were quiet about their faith.

Religious, economic, and political grievances against Charles I led to increasing opposition, centered in the English Parliament, then in 1640 to open civil war, and eventually Charles's execution. Many people shared far-reaching plans for change, orally and in print, during the English Civil War, including women you will meet in later chapters of this book. In the period after the execution of the king, England was led by Oliver Cromwell, a Puritan leader in the army and House of Commons. When he died, factions were divided about what to do next and Parliament backed the restoration of the Stuart monarchy. Charles I's older son was restored to the throne as Charles II in 1660. The Church of England, with its hierarchy of bishops, was also restored and religious dissent was repressed. Anyone holding an office in the Church or government, or a military position, or attending the universities of Oxford and Cambridge, was required to swear an oath to the Church of England, and exclusions were enforced more often than they had been earlier.

Queens re-emerged as important players in post-Restoration Britain, and religion continued to shape dynastic decisions and politics more broadly. Charles II had no legitimate heirs and, on his death in 1685, the throne passed to his openly Catholic younger brother James II, despite efforts by Parliament to prevent this. James appointed Catholics to important positions and suspended laws requiring religious conformity, decreeing that both Catholics and dissenting Protestants could worship freely, attend universities, and hold government offices. James's daughter Anne was the only member of the royal family who continued to attend Anglican services. James tried to force her to baptize her youngest daughter as a Catholic, but Anne refused, writing to her older sister Mary, who was at this point on the continent: "[T]he doctrine of the Church of Rome is wicked and dangerous, and their ceremonies—most of them—plain downright idolatry."[6] When James's second wife, the Italian Catholic Mary of Modena, gave birth to a son—thus assuring a Catholic dynasty—a group of leaders in the House of Commons offered the throne to James's daughter Mary and her husband, William of Orange, a Dutch prince who also happened to be a grandson of Charles I. In 1688 William invaded England with a small force, and James II and his wife and young son fled to France.

This coup, bloodless in England though not in Scotland and Ireland, was later called the "Glorious Revolution." William and Mary were named joint rulers by Parliament, he as William III and she as Mary II. Mary served as regent when William was on military campaigns abroad until she died from smallpox in 1694. She oversaw appointments to high positions within the Anglican Church and supported the establishment of the Society for Promoting of Christian Knowledge, an Anglican group organized to combat what it saw as immorality and to spread religious education in England and its colonies. Parliament passed acts allowing most dissenting Protestants their own places of worship and their own schools as long as they pledged an oath of allegiance to the monarchs, though dissenters were still not allowed to hold office or attend universities. The acts did not apply to Catholics or Jews, who continued to be excluded from many aspects of English society.

William and Mary had no surviving children, so were succeeded by Mary's sister Anne I (ruled 1702–1714), who continued Mary's support of the Anglican Church. Anne also had no surviving children, despite seventeen pregnancies and five live births. To prevent the throne from passing to a Catholic, in 1701 Parliament passed the Act of Succession, which limited the succession to the English and Irish crown to Protestants married to Protestants. This disqualified all the remaining descendants of Charles I except Anne, for all the others were Catholic.

Because Anne's children were already dead, the Act made Sophia (1630–1714), the granddaughter of James I, the heiress presumptive to the English throne. Sophia had inherited her right to rule through her mother, Elizabeth Stuart (1596–1662), the older sister of Charles I. Elizabeth Stuart had married a Protestant German prince, Frederick V of the Palatinate, who briefly became king of Bohemia before being ousted by Catholic forces in 1620 in one of the first actions of what became the Thirty Years' War (1618–1648). The couple went into exile in the Netherlands, from where Elizabeth raised funds and exerted political pressure to have English and Dutch troops sent to help the Protestant cause. Elizabeth Stuart had thirteen children, the youngest of whom was Sophia, who married another Protestant German prince, becoming the electress of Hanover. Sophia was seventy at the time of the Act of Succession, but she had five healthy living children and three living grandchildren, so it was an excellent bet there would be a Protestant to inherit the throne. She nearly became queen, dying at the age of eighty-three, only two months before the much younger Anne did. The crown went instead to Sophia's son George, who established a new dynasty, the Hanoverians, that provided six monarchs to England, ending with its second-longest ruling monarch, Victoria (ruled 1837–1901).

NEGOTIATING REFORM IN FRANCE

In contrast to Spain and England, women could not be queens regnant in France, where the Salic law excluded women from inheriting the throne. But here, too, female members of ruling families shaped religious life, supporting both Protestants and Catholics.

Many of those who favored Protestants in the sixteenth century were part of a dense network of interrelated women that stretched across several generations and reached beyond France. This began with the talented Louise of Savoy (1476–1531), the mother of King Francis I of France (1494–1547) and his sister Marguerite de Navarre (1492–1549). Louise served as regent for her son three times during his reign. During one of these, she negotiated the Treaty of Cambrai, ending a three-year war between France and the Habsburg rulers of the Holy Roman Empire. Often called "The Ladies' Peace," treaty negotiations were handled by a woman on the Habsburg side as well, Margaret of Austria (1480–1530), Louise's sister-in-law, whom she had known since childhood and who was serving as the governor of the Habsburg Netherlands.

Louise brought thinkers interested in new theological ideas and reforming the Catholic Church to the French court shortly after her son became king in 1515, so is sometimes seen as a foremother to the Reformation in France. Francis's sister, the charismatic and well-educated Marguerite de Navarre, had even more influence on religious change. She corresponded with reform-minded intellectuals and clergy and supported the translation of Luther's writings into French, even translating some herself. She took great risks to protect individuals who promoted new ideas and criticized Catholic practices, though some reformers thought she should have done more.

Marguerite also encouraged the education of the women at the French court, including not only prominent French noblewomen but also Mary Boleyn and her younger sister Anne, both of them future mistresses (and Anne also the wife) of Henry VIII of England. Louise married King Henry II of Navarre—a small independent kingdom on the border between France and Spain—and when Paris became too dangerous for individuals opposing Catholic teachings in the 1530s, she welcomed them in Navarre. Here she provided funding for schools, hospitals, and religious works in French, becoming a reformer in her own territory, though she never broke officially with the Catholic Church.

Marguerite's religious ideas emerge in her writings as well as her actions. These include the *Heptaméron*, a group of seventy-two stories, some light-hearted and others pointing to abuses of power, including women raped and threatened by priests. In her *Mirror of the Sinful Soul*, a long religious poem published in 1531, the speaker presents herself as a completely unworthy sinner who ultimately returns to God solely through His grace and connects with four women from the Bible—a daughter, mother, sister, and wife—who united with God as well. Condemned as heretical by French Catholic theologians for its emphasis on grace alone—a key part of Protestant teachings—the poem first circulated in manuscript.

One copy made it to England, perhaps with Anne Boleyn, where in 1544 (eight years after Anne had been beheaded), the eleven-year-old Princess Elizabeth translated it into English prose. She presented it, written in her own handwriting and with an embroidered cover that she herself had made, to her then stepmother, Catherine Parr, whose own writing she also translated, out of English into French, Italian, and Latin. Translating was seen as an appropriate activity for educated young women, as they were understood to be repeating the ideas of others, not conveying their own. But Elizabeth chose works by women, one of which—intentionally or not—linked the French network of elite women interested in religious reform with the English one.

The French network included Marguerite's daughter Jeanne d'Albret (1528–1572), who was exposed to the thought of reformers while a child at her mother's court. When Jeanne was twelve, her uncle, King Francis I, tried to marry her to a German prince with whom he was seeking an alliance, disregarding her firm opposition to the marriage. She wrote public letters to the king objecting to the marriage and refused to walk down the aisle when the wedding took place anyway, forcing a royal official to carry her. Marguerite had reluctantly gone along with this plan—Francis was her king as well as her brother—but after the ceremony she whisked her daughter away, claiming she was too young for sexual relations. Jeanne continued her opposition, politics changed, and the marriage was annulled. Marguerite and Jeanne's relationship was strained by Marguerite's initial agreement to the marriage, but toward the end of Marguerite's life the two were reconciled.

Jeanne's strength of character—and her stubbornness—thus emerged at a very young age, and it would be tested throughout her life. She married again when she was twenty; her husband was Antoine de Bourbon, a French duke, and the two became queen and king of Navarre, and of the nearby principality of Béarn, when her father died in 1555. Tensions had been building for decades in France between Catholics and Protestants, called Huguenots. The unexpected death of King Henry II in a jousting

1. Jeanne d'Albret, 1560s. This charcoal drawing of Jeanne d'Albret, by an artist in the workshop of the royal portrait painter François Clouet, was made in the middle of the French wars of religion. It shows the queen in fashionable but not flashy clothing, and with the serious demeanor befitting someone engaged in diplomacy and peace efforts.

accident in 1559 led to a power struggle between various factions, one led by Henry's widow Catherine de' Medici (1519–1589), a strong supporter of Catholics. Jeanne declared herself openly as a Huguenot in 1560, which made her the highest-ranking Protestant in France. She promoted the Protestant cause at the royal court, though it was becoming increasingly dangerous to do so, and her own husband wavered religiously.

Jeanne's husband was killed in the very first campaign of the religious wars that engulfed France in 1562. (For more on the French religious wars, see the section on French Huguenots in Chapter 3.) This left Jeanne free to carry out institutional changes in Béarn and Navarre on her own, which she did. She introduced Protestant services, closed monasteries and moved their funds to Protestant churches, built an academy to train pastors, and issued ordinances about baptism and marriage. The pope excommunicated her, and King Philip II of Spain threatened her, to which she replied: "Although I am just a little Princess, God has given me the government of this country so I may rule it according to his Gospel and teach it his Laws. I rely on God, who is more powerful than the King of Spain."[7] There was also pushback in her territories from those who wished to remain within Catholicism, and Jeanne responded with an edict saying she would not use force against her subjects or make them worship against their will, making her the second ruler in Europe to issue an official proclamation of religious tolerance. (The first was Queen Isabella of Hungary, about whom more below.)

Marguerite de Navarre and Jeanne d'Albret were among the most important supporters of the Protestant Reformation in France, male or female. Their extended family also included Renée de France (1510–1575), daughter of King Louis XII of France and related by marriage to Marguerite de Navarre, who moved to Ferrara in northern Italy when she married Ercole II d'Este, the duke of Ferrara. French and Italian scholars and religious reformers flocked to Ferrara, and Renée exchanged letters with many more. Her husband, the grandson of an earlier pope, Alexander VI, was firmly Catholic. Several Protestant sympathizers were arrested and executed, and Renée herself was arrested and charged with heresy. Her husband told her she would never see their daughters again unless she recanted, which she ultimately did, though she refused to attend Catholic services. After he died, she returned to France, and her estate became a refuge for Huguenots during the French religious wars.

Those wars dragged on, though Jeanne d'Albret met with Catherine de' Medici several times trying to negotiate a peace. In 1568 Jeanne joined other Protestant leaders in the port city of La Rochelle, a Protestant stronghold. Using a different metaphor than mother for women rulers, she wrote to her friend Elizabeth I of England, "I address you as one of the royal nurses of our church. . . . I would be ashamed if I did not join myself to the princes and lords, who . . . are resolved under the Lord God of hosts, to spare neither blood, life, nor goods to resist this horror."[8] In La Rochelle she took control of communication with foreign leaders, secured loans, provided funding, sponsored translations of religious works, and even visited the troops. She took the lead in negotiating a treaty, the Peace of St. Germain-en-Laye, that temporarily ended fighting. One of the conditions of the peace was a marriage between Jeanne's son Henry of Navarre and Catherine de' Medici's daughter Marguerite. The wedding took place in 1572, two months after Jeanne had died.

The wedding did not lead to peace, however, but instead its opposite. Several days after, there was an attempted assassination of the Huguenot leader Admiral Gaspard de Coligny in Paris, and Catholics feared that Protestants might take revenge. The royal council ordered the killing of prominent Protestants who had gathered in Paris for the wedding. This escalated into mob violence, whipped up by incendiary preaching that portrayed Protestants as evil and demonic. Thousands of Protestants from all walks of life were slaughtered in gruesome ways in Paris and across France, an orchestrated bloodshed that became known as the St. Bartholomew's Day Massacre.

The killing of Huguenot leaders appears to have been planned by King Charles IX and a group of advisers, but at the time Protestant writers blamed his mother, Catherine de' Medici. She had been the regent for Charles IX when he was a child, as well as for his older and younger brothers, and she did have a great deal of power. But she was also the perfect villain for the Protestant side in France—as a daughter of the wealthy Medici family in Florence, she was a foreigner, and one whose marriage to the French king had been arranged by her uncle, Pope Clement VII. And she was a woman in a country that officially excluded women from ruling. Unsurprisingly, Catherine was denounced in Protestant pamphlets as "the perfect picture and example of tyranny . . . who holds us between her paws" and who, "not satisfied with the bloodshed in this Tragedy," continued to plot "to attain her ambitious designs with masculine thoughts" and to "exercise and satiate her most devilish inclination."[9] Her reputation as a bloodthirsty Catholic fanatic who had caused the massacre lasted for centuries, just as Mary Tudor's reputation as "Bloody Mary" has.

INTERWOVEN DYNASTIES IN EASTERN
AND NORTHERN EUROPE

Mother–daughter links shaped the Reformations in northern and eastern Europe as well, most dramatically in the Jagiellon dynasty that ruled Poland-Lithuania and intermarried with the Vasa dynasty that ruled Sweden and Finland. The matriarch in this story was Bona Sforza (1494–1557), the only surviving child of the very wealthy duke of Milan who had married the Polish king Sigismund I, elected to office by Polish nobles. She and her husband increased the land holdings and power of the monarchy, and sponsored artists, architects, and musicians who brought Renaissance styles to Poland. They were not concerned about enforcing religious uniformity, and many Polish nobles, men and women, accepted one or another type of Protestant teaching and protected Protestants who had been persecuted elsewhere in Europe—even including radicals such as Antitrinitarians, who rejected the Christian doctrine of the Trinity.

Bona Sforza arranged for her eldest daughter Isabella Jagiellon (1519–1559) to marry the king of Hungary John Zápolya. He died a year after the wedding, leaving Isabella as regent for her infant son. Isabella spent the rest of her life fighting politically and militarily to preserve her son's inheritance from various powers that wanted to take over Hungary. The country was divided religiously, with Catholics, Lutherans, and other types of Protestants, and in 1557 Isabella decided the way to strengthen her realm was to grant freedom of religion to all Christian groups: "We and our most Serene Son have graciously consented to the urgent petition of the Lords of the realm that each observe the faith of his preference with new or ancient ceremonies, permitting freedom of choice to each according to preference, providing no harm be done to any."[10] She was the first European ruler to issue a law on religious tolerance, a policy her son confirmed when he became king after her death. In 1573, the Polish national assembly followed suit, officially granting religious tolerance to nobles and free persons in an act called the Warsaw Confederation.

Bona Sforza's second daughter Sophia married a German Catholic nobleman, though she converted to Lutheranism after he died, the only member of the Jagiellon dynasty to do so. The third daughter, Anna

(1523–1596), remained unmarried until she was required to marry when her brother, the Polish king, died, and the Polish nobles would not elect an unmarried woman as queen. She did so, and she and her husband were elected co-rulers in 1576, though she did most of the governing. The Jesuits—the most important new religious order in the post-Reformation Catholic Church, established by the Spanish former soldier Ignatius Loyola in 1540—had come to Poland about a decade earlier, as part of their plan to reconvert parts of Europe that had become Protestant and strengthen loyalty to the Catholic Church in areas that were religiously mixed. They established colleges for training noble boys and became preachers and confessors at the Polish royal court. Women and men responded to this effort, and loyalty to Catholicism grew.

Bona Sforza's youngest daughter, Katarina Jagiellon (1526–1583), married Duke John of Finland, who became King John III of Sweden in 1568 after a rebellion by Swedish nobles against his half-brother Eric XIV. Sweden had become officially Protestant but, as part of the marriage agreement, Katarina was allowed to keep her Catholic faith. Her sister Anna pressured Katarina to use her influence on John, to see if he would convert, and the couple's three children were all raised as Catholics. John showed some interest in Catholicism, particularly after several Jesuits came to Sweden, but he remained Protestant. The Jesuits were more successful with Katarina and John's son Sigismund, who was elected king of Poland-Lithuania in 1587. He repudiated the policy of toleration, repressing all religions other than Catholicism. Sigismund also inherited the throne of Sweden when his father died, but his attempts to enforce Catholicism there led to a bloody civil war. He was deposed and replaced by his uncle Charles IX. His aunt Isabella of Hungary could perhaps have advised him on the benefits of religious toleration.

Charles IX ruled only briefly, followed by his son Gustavus Adolphus (1594–1632), a brilliant military commander and innovator who expanded Swedish territory to make Sweden one of the great powers of Europe. He was killed in a major battle of the Thirty Years' War (1618–1648) that pitted Protestants against Catholics, leaving his seven-year-old daughter Christina (1626–1689) as the monarch of Sweden. Christina received an excellent education, studying philosophy, religion, and both ancient and modern languages. After assuming personal rule when she was eighteen, she sent her own representative to the peace negotiations that ended the Thirty Years' War. She invited scholars from all over Europe to her court in Stockholm, patronized painters and the theater, and established a large royal library of books and manuscripts, some of them taken from Catholic castles looted by Swedish armies. Following the example of Elizabeth I of England, whose biography she read, she decided not to marry, and in 1649 announced that her cousin Karl Gustav would be her heir.

Scholars who came to Stockholm included Jesuits trained in theology and the natural sciences, and Christina became increasingly convinced of the truth of Catholic teachings. She decided to convert and abdicate, and began to send books and other possessions abroad, knowing she would need ample funds to support the lavish lifestyle she wished to maintain. She abdicated in 1654 and left Sweden, first traveling to the Catholic southern Netherlands, and then in a triumphal journey to Rome, where she was received by the pope as a spectacular example of the successes of the Catholic Reformation. She assembled a stunning collection of art, became close friends with cardinals and courtiers, served as a patron for composers and poets, spent money wildly, traveled frequently, and put herself forward as a candidate for ruler in several places, including Sweden after Karl Gustav died. Her decision to convert had little effect on religious life in Sweden, but she became an iconic figure in the cultural life of baroque Rome and a model for later rulers who converted to Catholicism.

Christina's contemporaries commented that she sometimes wore masculine clothing or eccentric combinations of men's and women's garb, walked and rode a horse like a man, and had somewhat masculine facial features. This, plus her unwillingness to marry and passionate letters to one of her ladies-in-waiting, have led to speculation about Christina's gender and sexuality, so much so that in 1965 her corpse was dug up to see if her skeleton showed any signs of her being intersex. It didn't, but she is still often celebrated as lesbian, bisexual, or trans.

In Denmark-Norway, Protestant ideas began to spread in the 1520s, including to the crown prince, elected king as Christian III in 1536 after a civil war. Lutheran Protestantism became the state religion: Catholic bishops were removed from office and their land confiscated; monasteries and convents were forbidden to take in new residents; and church services were performed in Danish. Christian and his equally Lutheran queen, Dorothea (1511–1571), from a princely German family, were crowned king and queen in Copenhagen in 1537 by the German Protestant reformer Johannes Bugenhagen. In his coronation sermon, Bugenhagen outlined the role of the queen as "mother of her territory" (*Landesmutter*), whose duties included providing good teachers and schools so that all inhabitants of the kingdom would learn the proper religion. The University of Copenhagen was reopened as a Lutheran university the same year, and the royal couple supported lower-level schools as well.

Among those in attendance at Christian and Dorothea's coronation was the wealthy Danish noblewoman Birgitte Gøye (*c.* 1511–1574), one of Dorothea's ladies-in-waiting. Birgitte's father was among the earliest followers of Luther in Denmark, so she was exposed to Protestant teachings as a teenager. She was apparently influenced by the words of Bugenhagen at the coronation, as she and her husband Herluf Trolle— also a staunch Lutheran—gave money to several city schools and founded a boarding school for boys at their manor, which still exists. They also provided informal religious education to members of the household, which included children from other noble families as well as servants. At mealtimes someone read a chapter from the Bible and in the evening every member of the household participated in the singing of a hymn. The couple had no children of their own, but they were godparents to many. After she became a widow, Birgitte remained a much-loved and sought-after foster mother for young noblewomen, and thus instrumental in bringing up two generations of women in the Lutheran faith. Funeral sermons for Birgitte Gøye and Herluf Trolle, printed in Danish in small format that could be easily read anywhere, described their daily spiritual exercises, creating a role model for other nobles.

The Danish monarchs married their daughters to Lutheran rulers in north Germany, and their eldest son, the crown prince Frederick, to his much younger cousin Sophie of Mecklenburg-Güstrow (1557–1631), the daughter of a German prince and a Danish princess. Sophie was widowed at thirty-one, and during her forty-year widowhood she managed her estates so well that she became the richest woman, and perhaps the second-richest person, in Europe. She loaned vast sums of money to rulers and nobles across northern Europe, financing diplomacy and war.

Like Isabel of Castile and every other smart ruler, Queen Sophie also arranged her children's marriages strategically, thickening the web of ties among Protestant states. Along with marrying her daughter Anna to King James VI of Scotland, she arranged marriages for her three other daughters to princes and dukes in Germany, married her oldest son to a German princess, and sent her youngest son off to marry the daughter of the Russian tsar, though he fell ill and died before the wedding could take place.

To the east of Poland-Lithuania lay the vast territory of Russia, ruled by tsars in the sixteenth and seventeenth centuries and a series of empresses in the eighteenth. Tsar Peter I, usually known as Peter the Great (ruled 1689–1725), tried to modernize and westernize Russia to expand its borders, and make it more powerful and more centralized. He wanted to increase the Russian population, so forbade physically capable men and women of childbearing years from taking monastic vows and ordered priests to marry. He also limited the independent power of the Russian Orthodox Church, controlling appointments and funding. And he engaged in constant warfare, bringing in western European experts to advise him.

Peter's daughter, Elizabeth, was initially excluded from the succession and spent some of her childhood in a convent. But after a series of short-lived reigns of various other descendants, she seized the throne in a military coup in 1741 and ruled until 1762. She crowned herself empress, largely continued Peter's policies, and led Russia through two major international wars. She was supportive of the Russian Orthodox Church and ordered the building and expansion of churches and convents, including the magnificent Smolny convent in St. Petersburg, where she had stayed as a girl. Because she had never married and had no children, she declared her nephew Peter her heir, and arranged his marriage to a German princess from a tiny principality, whose mother was loosely related to Peter's Romanov family and to the rulers of Sweden.

On converting to Russian Orthodoxy, the princess took the name Catherine, studied Russian and French, and won powerful allies at court, including her noble lover, Gregory Orlov, and his officer brothers. Her husband became tsar as Peter III (ruled 1762), but when he called off a planned Russian attack on Prussia, Catherine and the Orlovs had Peter arrested. The Orlovs killed him, and Catherine became empress Catherine II, ruling until 1796.

Catherine—later, like Peter I, called "the Great"—issued a series of laws on all aspects of life, seeking to improve the economy, strengthen the power of officials, enhance civil order, expand education, and modernize everything. Like Peter, she regarded the Orthodox Church as simply a part of the government, so she nationalized church land, closed many monasteries, and placed the appointment of all offices of the Church under state control. Thus, without making any theological changes, she did exactly what Henry VIII had done. When Russia took over areas that were predominantly Catholic, including large parts of Poland, she did not prohibit people from attending Catholic services, but appointed the archbishops who oversaw them rather than leaving this to the pope. Late in her reign, she promised religious freedom to anyone who wanted to settle in Russia, seeing this as a policy that fit with her self-image as an enlightened ruler, and, more importantly, as a way to increase the Russian population. Religious dissenters and exiles from other parts of Europe did sometimes move to Russia, although the welcome they found there was often not as warm as they had anticipated.

THE EMPIRE AND BEYOND

In central Europe, what we call "Germany" was not a united country in the sixteenth century, but instead the Holy Roman Empire, a collection of hundreds of states of different sizes, including kingdoms, duchies, cities, prince-bishoprics, free imperial abbeys, and even tiny independent knightships. They were under the loose authority of an elected emperor but were largely independent and, after a series of religious wars that ended in the mid-sixteenth century, the territories could (with some restrictions) choose to be Catholic or Lutheran Protestant. Members of ruling houses intermarried with one another, and with the rulers of larger states outside the empire, in dizzying patterns that are difficult to follow, particularly because, as in the British Isles, many rulers had similar names. Women often agreed with their husbands in matters of religion, but religion could also be a flashpoint between spouses, just as it could be between generations.

As rulers and regents, women accepted Protestant teachings, brought in and supported reformers, issued new church ordinances, established institutions such as marriage and morals courts, and set up schools. Elisabeth of Braunschweig-Göttingen-Calenburg (1510–1558), for example, who served as regent for her son from 1540 to 1545, implemented the Protestant Reformation in her small state, releasing clergy and nuns from their vows, forbidding convents from taking in new residents, and participating personally in visits that tested the religious ideas of parish clergy and officials. She wrote treatises urging her subjects to greater piety and morality, describing herself as their "true mother who constantly worries about them," but also "their overlord by the grace of God."[11]

Elisabeth had been influenced by her mother, Elisabeth of Denmark (1485–1555), the daughter of a Danish king, who in the 1520s had become a Lutheran against the wishes of her husband Joachim I, the elector of Brandenburg, one of the larger states in the Holy Roman Empire. The son for whom Elisabeth (the younger) had been regent flip-flopped on matters of religion in the intricate and changing religious-political scene of sixteenth-century Germany, but ultimately ended as a Protestant. Her daughters (one named, of course, Elisabeth) generally married Protestant rulers and were active on religious issues.

In the seventeenth century, Countess Amalia Elisabeth of Hesse-Kassel (1602–1651), another small state in the middle of the Holy Roman Empire, took personal control of her territory's army after her husband's death during the Thirty Years' War. The Peace of Augsburg, a 1555 treaty that ended an earlier round of religious wars, had granted Catholic and Lutheran rulers in the empire the right to choose the religion that would be promoted in their territories. One of the issues in the Thirty Years' War was whether Calvinism would be a third option.

Amalia Elisabeth and many residents of Hesse-Kassel were Calvinist Protestants, so she strongly supported this, writing in 1639, when fighting had gone on for two decades, that "the land incurred the most extreme ruin and irrevocable damage, and the subjects spent their lives, limbs, and goods in order to assure freedom of thought and the free exercise of their traditional religion [meaning Calvinism], and to preserve the same for their children and their descendants."[12] She participated in the negotiations that finally ended the war, portraying herself at times as a vulnerable widow and at times as a strong ruler, changing her rhetorical strategy to influence peace talks in ways that would benefit Hesse-Kassel and her descendants. At the negotiations Amalia Elisabeth repeatedly demanded that Calvinism be recognized on an equal basis with Catholicism and Lutheranism, and she won, as the Peace of Westphalia that ended the war stipulated this.

Aemilia Juliana of Schwarzburg-Rudolstadt (1637–1706) explicitly identified herself as the "mother of her territory" in her published writings, and both wrote and publicly sang Protestant devotional songs. She understood herself—and had herself portrayed by the artists she supported—as a loving bride of Christ and also as the Old Testament figure Jonathan, wearing a sword and clasping the hand of her husband, who was portrayed as the Old Testament figure David. She and other rulers' wives and regents also used the term "pillar of prayer" (*Betsäule*) to describe themselves, emphasizing the fact that they provided strong support for the realm by interceding with God and encouraging greater religious devotion in their households and among their subjects. Piety and power were closely linked.

From 1440 to 1740 the emperor of the Holy Roman Empire was a member of the Habsburg dynasty, which also ruled huge territories outside of the empire, including Spain, the Netherlands, Austria, southern Italy, Hungary, Bohemia, other parts of Europe, and, beginning in the sixteenth century, a global empire. Female Habsburgs often served as governors and regents of specific territories, making political, military, economic, and religious decisions they thought would benefit their dynasty and their realm. These included many female governors of the Netherlands, beginning with Margaret of Austria, who negotiated the Peace of Cambrai with Louise of Savoy and served as governor of the Netherlands from 1507 to 1515, and again from 1519 to 1530. Margaret was succeeded as governor by her niece, Mary of Hungary (1505–1558), the sister of Emperor Charles V, who had also served as regent of Hungary after the death of her husband King Louis II. Mary was succeeded by Margaret of Parma (1522–1586), Emperor Charles V's illegitimate daughter (and thus Mary of Hungary's niece), who also served twice as governor of the Netherlands, from 1559 to 1567 and from 1578 to 1582.

It might seem odd to us that male rulers would choose women—including those born out of wedlock—to run territories, instead of male relatives or unrelated officials, but they saw these women as reliable family members and capable leaders. Women in ruling and noble families were expected to engage in political activity on behalf of their families, so were educated to do so. If you had asked them, Habsburg men would no doubt have said that of course women were inferior to men and should be subject to male authority, but at the same time their actions indicated they had full confidence in the capabilities of their female relatives. (This inconsistency is not limited to Habsburgs, of course, or to the past.)

All three of these regents confronted the Protestant Reformation in the Netherlands, which under Margaret of Parma became a full-blown revolt against Catholic Spanish overlordship. Although the Habsburgs remained Catholic, the three women were more moderate in their views than were most male members of the family, attempting negotiation and conciliation. King Philip II of Spain replaced Margaret of Parma as governor with a general, the duke of Alba, who was ruthless toward those he considered heretics, executing hundreds through a special court that became known as the "Council of Blood." Despite—or perhaps because of—Alba's harshness, the Netherlands split into two parts after a long war, a Protestant north, which became the independent United Provinces of the Netherlands, and a Catholic south, ruled by Spain, which ultimately became Belgium.

Habsburg women defended and promoted Catholicism in other parts of Europe as well. Mariana of Austria (1634–1696) married her much older uncle Philip IV to become queen of Spain. On the death of her husband, she became regent of Spain as her son Charles II was only three, and supported the Jesuits in their conflicts with other religious orders, at one point naming her Jesuit confessor the head of the Inquisition. She approved a Jesuit mission on islands in the Pacific, later renamed the Marianas in her honor.

Maria Theresa (1717–1780), the ruler of the Habsburg territories in central Europe for forty years, believed strongly in religious unity. She expelled Jews and Protestants from some parts of her realm, and imprisoned Protestants in others, releasing them if they agreed to Catholic statements of faith. She was wary of Catholic institutions that were not under her control, however. She selected high church officials rather than leaving appointments to the papacy. Although, like Mariana, she had been educated by Jesuits, she increasingly came to view them as a danger to her authority and limited their influence. When Pope Clement XIV suppressed the Jesuit order in 1773, she took over their property in Habsburg lands, using it to enrich the royal coffers or reward those she favored, just as rulers who became Protestant had done with church lands. She supported schools, orphanages, hospitals, and other institutions that addressed people's needs, and encouraged devout and moral behavior.

Maria Theresa was an actual mother as well as the mother of her realm, giving birth to sixteen children while she conducted wars and reformed institutions. She sometimes used her physical motherhood strategically. Immediately after she acceded to the throne, rulers of other European countries invaded parts of Austrian territory, using the pretext that, as a woman, Maria Theresa did not have the right to succeed her father. She skillfully kept her core domains intact in this war, and at one point she held up her infant son Joseph in a political assembly, promising that he, too, would fight on. In this dramatic gesture, she linked her physical and political motherhood.

Maria Theresa arranged marriages that sought to enhance Habsburg power for the nine children who survived to adulthood. This included marrying her youngest daughter, Maria Antonia, to Louis, the heir to the French throne. When she moved to France, Maria Antonia adopted the French version of her name, Marie Antoinette. She and her husband would be the last queen and king of France before the French Revolution, executed by guillotine in 1793, not an outcome Maria Theresa could have predicted.

From Isabel to Maria Theresa, the women rulers in this chapter shared many things. To some degree, their social standing trumped their gender. Hereditary dynasties always favored men—only in the late twentieth or early twenty-first century would some dynasties begin to allow daughters to inherit the throne on an equal basis with sons—but in Europe only France excluded women completely. Ruling families recognized that a daughter might become a monarch, and, if things went as the family hoped, would certainly be the wife of a monarch and the mother of a monarch who would need to be capable of serving as regent if needed. They educated women to be effective in serving family interests, whatever fate might bring. This did not mean that ruling families rejected standard patriarchal norms in which women were judged mentally, physically, and morally inferior; but, at the same time, they expected the women in their families to be capable, rational, and competent.

Because church and state were so tightly linked, their political position gave the women in this chapter authority over religion that no other woman had. Women you will meet in other chapters made decisions about their own religious beliefs and practices, oversaw the religious education of their children and households, and tried to influence others through actions, speech, and writing. If they were abbesses, they had authority over the people who lived in their religious communities and the lands they controlled. But the only women who could close monasteries and convents or reopen them, order clergy to perform a ritual or preach a sermon in this way or that, or arrest and banish people for their religious practices were ruling members of hereditary dynasties. That is why they are the subject of the first chapter in this book.

The authority of women rulers and regents over religion and other realms of life became a matter of public debate in the sixteenth and seventeenth centuries, in part because there were so many of them. The *querelle des femmes* came to include debates about women's rule. John Knox was not alone in declaring women's rule unnatural and an abomination in the eyes of God, for that sentiment was echoed in many other works. Defenders of women's rule, including the English Protestant bishop John Aylmer, countered that scriptural prohibitions of women teaching or speaking were only relevant for the groups to which they were addressed, and that a woman's sex did not automatically exclude her from rule, just as a boy king's age or an ill king's weakness did not exclude him.

As you have seen, powerful women themselves sometimes justified their authority, portraying themselves as chosen by God to be "true mothers" of their country and "royal nurses" of their chosen church. They saw themselves as distinct from other women, so, not surprisingly, did not extend their claims to authority into a general call for women's greater political voice, although by the sixteenth century a few less exalted women were beginning to argue for this.

Women who ruled or governed territories shaped religious change in many different ways, just as men who ruled or governed did. Assessments of their actions and impact have varied over time and continue to do so. Queen Isabel of Castile's measures to strengthen Catholicism were praised by conservative Spanish Catholics, with a group in the twentieth century even starting her on the road to sainthood. This process was stopped in 1991 after public outcry about her actions against Jews and Muslims, but Pope Francis has recently asked Spanish bishops to take up the cause again.

Mary and Elizabeth Tudor and Mary, Queen of Scots have tradition-ally been contrasted, with judgments falling into the "idealize, pity, or blame" categories I mentioned at the end of the preface: Mary Tudor is seen as the wicked "Bloody Mary" who sent Protestants to their death, or as a sad failure who desperately hoped to get pregnant; Elizabeth as the glorious monarch who defeated the dastardly Spanish, loved the theater, wisely chose never to marry, established a middle course in reli-gion, and reigned in triumph; Mary, Queen of Scots as a gullible failure who let pressure from scheming men overcome her training and judg-ment. You will probably not be surprised to hear me say that, in many ways, the three queens were more similar than different: all were highly educated; thought of themselves as no less rulers than their male pre-decessors; used royal symbols to establish their authority; appointed, worked with, and fired councilors, officials, and diplomats; engaged in foreign relations; set religious policy; and ordered the arrest and impris-onment of those who disagreed with them on religious matters.

Other women in this chapter have been similarly celebrated and censured, but some have also been forgotten until historians of women recovered their stories from the archives and libraries where they were hiding in plain sight. These have made us reassess key developments in religious life in this era and pay more attention to the women leaders involved. One of these is the gradual rise of religious toleration, which became official policy first under Isabella of Hungary and then Jeanne d'Albret in Navarre. It did not become permanent in either place, but their actions helped make toleration thinkable. Another is the conduct of religious and dynastic wars, in which women rulers hired and fired commanders, sent troops, raised funds, and also shaped the peace treaties ending them, as Louise of Savoy and Margaret of Austria did with the Treaty of Cambrai and Amalia Elisabeth of Hesse-Kassel did with the Peace of Westphalia. A third is the way Catholics and Protestants established networks of like-minded individuals, through which ideas, objects, and people flowed. Their hubs were not only Luther's Wittenberg, Calvin's Geneva, and papal Rome, but also Marguerite de Navarre's Paris, Queen Sophie's Copenhagen, Bona Sforza's Kraków, and Margaret of Austria's Mechelen, in Belgium. The Reformations were multicentric, and women in ruling families who shaped religion could be found everywhere.

CHAPTER TWO

—⟫·◆·⟪—

MOTHERS

If God has given grace to some good women, revealing to them by his holy scriptures something holy and good, should they hesitate to write, speak, and declare it to one another because of the defamers of the truth? Do we have two Gospels, one for men and another for women?

Marie Dentière, French Protestant reformer

Let us behave in a virile way, that we too, like holy Judith, having courageously cut off the head of Holofernes, that is, of the devil, may gloriously return to our heavenly home.

Angela Merici, Italian founder of the Ursulines

The Protestant and Catholic Reformations enhanced the authority of fathers, both actual fathers and spiritual fathers, whether these were Protestant pastors or Catholic priests. But mothers were also key, and motherhood was used as a metaphor for female authority and responsibility. Sermons, Bible commentary, and other types of written works outlined the duties of mothers. Images of good and evil mothers looked down from church walls and windows, and up from books, woodcuts, and even dishes.

Protestant reformers championed marriage as the "first order of God," and urged all women to marry. Catholic reformers reaffirmed that the worthiest life was one that was celibate and chaste, but they realized that most women would marry. People did not need reformers' advice on this—marriage was the clearest mark of social adulthood for both women and men, giving them authority over others. Although a significant proportion of the population did not marry, society was conceived of as a collection of households, with a marital couple as the core. Many households were blended families, with children from earlier marriages and sometimes other relatives along with the couple's own children, plus—for wealthier families—apprentices and servants, some of whom might be enslaved.

Women often expressed their religious convictions in a domestic setting. They prayed and engaged in religious rituals surrounding food, illness, childbirth, and death. They recited the catechism or rosary, read devotional literature if they were literate, and provided religious instruction for their children. Generally, such activities fit with the locally accepted religion, so were part of a continuum of devotional life that stretched from the household to the wider world. But sometimes they did not, as women created sacred spaces within their households in opposition to political authorities, holding services and teaching their children and servants ideas and practices regarded as heretical and dangerous. In this they might be supported by their husbands, but not always, as religious allegiance sometimes split family members apart.

Disagreement over matters of religion was not seen as a legitimate ground for separation or divorce and, by the seventeenth century, authorities in many areas prohibited their citizens from marrying those of different Christian denominations, just as they had long prohibited marriages between Christians and Jews or Muslims. Such laws were not always followed when it came to different kinds of Christians, however. Even for rulers, other concerns sometimes overrode religion on matters of marriage, with wealth or political alliances more important when making a match. In theory, the family was supposed to be a little church and a little commonwealth on which the larger Church and commonwealth were based, but in practice families could also challenge these larger institutions.

Women's domestic religion also took them beyond the household, for they gave charitable donations to the needy, cared for the ill and indigent, and established and supported almshouses, schools, orphanages, and funds for poor widows. Women taught in the girls' elementary schools that were established in some places, designed to teach them to be good mothers as well as good Christians. As one Protestant school ordinance read, schools were "to habituate girls to the catechism, to the psalms, to honorable behavior and Christian virtue, and especially to prayer, and make them memorize verses from Holy Scripture so that they may grow up to be Christian and praiseworthy matrons and housekeepers."[1] Women sometimes used the language of motherhood to support their larger role, declaring that God had given them a responsibility to their communities as well as their families. A few even called themselves "church mothers," with a role parallel to the much more familiar "church fathers."

Familial organization extended to women's religious communities, which were headed by an abbess or other type of leader whom the residents and others called "mother," a title of respect and authority. Abbesses in areas that became Protestant confronted challenges to their way of life that required adept leadership. Some responded by affirming the value of Catholic traditions, while others embraced Protestant teachings. Abbesses in areas that remained Catholic frequently led reforms within their convents that enhanced spiritual life and discipline. Devout women also created new types of women's communities devoted to education, care of the poor, and service to the world.

NEW ROLES

Marriage was at the heart of the Protestant Reformation. Martin Luther (1483–1546) first called for reforms and then broke with the teachings of the Catholic Church beginning in 1517, when he was a celibate friar and professor at the University of Wittenberg in the German territory of Saxony. Through studying Paul's letters in the New Testament, he gradually arrived at a new understanding of Christian doctrine. His understanding is often summarized as "faith alone, grace alone, Scripture alone." He believed that salvation and justification—moving from a state of sin to a state of righteousness—come through faith, and that faith is a free gift of God's grace, not the result of human effort. God's word is revealed only in the Scriptures, not in the traditions of the Catholic Church. Scripture should be available in the language people spoke, not just in learned languages like Latin and Greek. These ideas came to be shared by many other Protestants, a word that comes from a formal protest written by a group of German rulers in 1529, and which gradually became a general term applied to all non-Catholic western European Christians. (Luther never called himself Protestant or Lutheran, but "evangelical," from *euangelion*, the Greek word for gospel.)

Among the traditions without a firm biblical basis, Luther thought, were many related to marriage, including the idea that priests, monks, and nuns should not marry, that marriage was a sacrament, and that celibacy was superior to marriage. Luther preached sermons praising marriage beginning in 1519. Several years later he wrote his first formal treatise attacking the value of vows of celibacy and arguing that although marriage was not a sacrament, it was the best Christian life and a holy vocation. In 1525 he followed his words with deeds and married a nun who had fled her convent, Katharina von Bora (1499–1552). What started as a marriage of principle and mutual esteem became one of affection and deep emotional bonds.

Katharina von Bora, the daughter of minor nobility from the area of Saxony in eastern Germany, was sent to a convent after her mother's death when she was five, and later transferred to a different convent, Marienthron, where her aunt was a professed nun. She took vows when she was a teenager, and received a good education, even learning some Latin as well as reading and writing German. Religious literature circulated within convents and monasteries, and several nuns in Marienthron became dissatisfied with their life in the convent. They wrote to Luther for help and, in 1523, he arranged for a group of twelve nuns, including Katharina, to be smuggled out of the convent in the wagon of a merchant friend. The story was later told that the women were under or inside barrels of herring, a dramatic flourish in what was already a serious action, as removing nuns from convents was classified as kidnapping. It was punishable by death in some parts of Germany, including territory the women had to travel through.

The women reached Wittenberg, where Luther and his associates set about finding accommodation for them, as well as husbands for those who would not be returning home to their families. Several men were suggested as possible spouses for Katharina, but these matches all fell through for one reason or another, and she said she would marry only Nikolaus von Amsdorf, one of Luther's close associates, or Luther himself. Thus the impetus to marry came from Katharina, but Luther quickly agreed, and the two were married in a private and a public ceremony in 1525. The following year, she had the first of her six children, one of whom died as an infant and another as a child.

We know a lot about Katharina von Bora, because Luther talked a great deal about her, in letters to her, letters to other people, and in informal conversation at dinner, recorded by admiring students, colleagues, and friends seated around the tables (these are called the "table talk"). We also know that she wrote letters to Luther because his letters mention them, but not one letter from her to Luther survives, even in a later copy. The few letters of hers that *do* survive were primarily to wealthy nobles asking for financial help, especially after Luther died in 1546—he had been a monk, so never really worried about money matters, or who would pay for all those dinners.

The letter she wrote to her sister-in-law Christina von Bora shortly after Luther's death, which does survive, provides one of the few glimpses we have of her thoughts and feelings that does not come from the pen of a man. She expresses deep grief, in words about the death of a spouse that reach across the centuries: "I am in truth so very saddened that I cannot express my great heartache to any person and do not know how I am and feel. I can neither eat nor drink. Nor again sleep. If I had owned a principality or empire I would not have felt as bad had I lost it, as I did when our dear Lord God took from me—and not only from me but from the whole world—this dear and worthy man."[2]

The Luther family lived in what had been the Augustinian monastery of the Black Cloister, where Luther had lived before the Reformation. Its many rooms also housed students, boarders, refugees, and visitors, an ever-changing number of Luther admirers that could expand overnight from ten to eighty. (The building is now a museum and a UNESCO World Heritage Site.) Katharina managed the entire household, including its kitchen, brewery, stables, gardens, and fields. She purchased and ran an orchard, personally overseeing the care of apple and pear trees and selling the fruit to provide income for the household. She occasionally took part in theological discussions that went on after dinner and was teased by her husband for her intellectual interests. He sometimes called her "Professor Katie," but his letters are also full of affection and respect. One from 1545 addresses her as "my friendly, dear housewife Katharina of Luther, von Bora, preacher, brewer, gardener, and whatever else she can be," and many are signed "your little love."[3] Religious war forced Katharina out of Wittenberg the year Luther died and destroyed much of her property. She returned and rebuilt, only to be forced out of the city again by the plague in 1552. She died that year after a fall from a wagon when she was only fifty-three.

Clerical marriage was one of the most dramatic changes brought about by the Protestant Reformation, nearly as dramatic as the legalization of same-sex marriage in our own day. (In fact, in arguing their case, twenty-first-century right-to-marriage advocates have sometimes quoted the pro-marriage writings of sixteenth-century reformers.) Male clergy were no longer simply "fathers" in a spiritual sense, but actual fathers. They had to create a new ideal of clerical masculinity that included being sexually active and in charge of a household, and also had to face the practical problems this created. Supporting a wife and family cost more than supporting a priest alone, and communities often resented the expense. Protestant pastors preached and wrote defenses of their new married state to convince their congregations (and perhaps themselves) that it was respectable and godly.

Pastors' wives had an equally difficult task. Like Katharina von Bora, many of the wives of the early reformers had been nuns. They were crossing one of society's most rigid borders by marrying, becoming brides of men rather than brides of Christ. Nuns marrying priests or monks were accused of incest, because both bride and groom had taken vows under holy orders and were thus spiritual siblings. During the first few years of the Reformation, pastors' wives were likened to "priests' whores"—the women with whom priests often had sexual relations despite their vows of celibacy—in people's minds, and their neighbors closely watched their conduct.

Catholic opponents of Luther lost no time in attacking Katharina von Bora, in pamphlets, plays, and ever-longer biographies, in which they simply made things up, relating, as one title went, "the complete life of Katharina von Bora, the so-called wife of Martin Luther, in which all her pretended virtues, fictitious achievements, false visions, and pitiful miracles . . . are related at length."[4] In their writings, Protestants tended to mention her only briefly, if at all, a tendency that has continued into the twenty-first century, when massive biographies of Luther include very little about her.

But the Luther marriage had a visual promoter, the Wittenberg artist Lucas Cranach the Elder, who was one of the witnesses at the wedding. He painted a double wedding portrait—a common type of painting in the sixteenth century—an image that his workshop repeated, with minor variations, many times over the next few years. In these, Katharina von Bora looks like the biblical figures and noblewomen in most of Cranach's other paintings—tiny waist, sloping shoulders, slanting eyes—so we are not sure how much the portraits actually resembled her, and he never painted her later in life. (By contrast, Cranach and his workshop painted Luther over and over, from a gaunt tonsured monk in 1520, to a chunky, heavily jowled preacher with unruly hair in the 1530s, to a white-gowned corpse lying peacefully in his coffin in 1546.) But Katharina does wear slightly different clothing and head-coverings in the portraits, including black and gold hairnets and a white linen headdress with a chin wrap, so she may have had some say in how she was depicted. (See Plate III.)

The Saxon government sent the wedding portraits around Germany and beyond as diplomatic gifts, along with portraits of the leaders of Saxony. Initially the Luther double portrait was not very popular as a church or home decoration, as Protestants were still somewhat uncomfortable with Luther's marriage. By the nineteenth century, however, images of Luther the family man, singing and playing the lute with his wife and children around him, could be found in Lutheran churches, parish houses, and homes around the world.

In 1999, the city of Wittenberg placed a life-size bronze statue of Katharina by the German sculptor Nina Koch in the garden outside the house where the Luthers lived, one of very few statues to her anywhere in the world. In this, Katharina strides forward through a door, leading with her left hand, drawing attention to the wedding ring on her index finder. That ring has become part of newly invented Luther lore, as touching it is supposed to bring luck and a happy marriage. Judging by the lack of patina on Katharina's hand, plenty of visitors to the Lutherhaus have heard this rumor and touched the ring. At the same time, the city began to celebrate the anniversary of the wedding of Martin and Katharina in an annual festival, with a parade, music, dancing, a feast, and the standard trappings of a Renaissance fair. Onlookers are encouraged to wear costumes, and many do. Thus the Luther marriage has become fully embedded in heritage tourism for the city, something to be celebrated.

Reformers' wives were essential in the transformation of clerical marriage from scandal to model. Katharina von Bora and other reformers' wives created a respectable role for themselves largely by being models of wifely obedience and Christian charity, living embodiments of their husbands' views about the superiority of marriage to celibacy. They also demonstrated how a pastor's wife should interact with parishioners, as a representative of her husband and of the faith. Within a generation or so, these efforts were quite successful. Priests' concubines had generally been from a lower social class, but by the second generation of the Reformation, Protestant pastors in Germany had little difficulty finding wives from among the same social class as themselves, a trend that further aided the acceptance of clerical marriage. The activities and virtues of pastors' wives were described in funeral sermons preached by their husbands or sons that were then printed in collections. They were also inscribed in epitaphs on funerary monuments, proclaiming to all who heard or read them the women's stature as paradigms of piety and charity.

Katharina von Bora was not the first ex-nun to marry a reformer in Wittenberg, as a year before his marriage, Luther had presided over a wedding ceremony for Caspar Cruciger, one of his students, and his wife Elisabeth (1500?–1535), who had left her convent in the early 1520s. At about the same time, Elisabeth wrote a hymn in German, "Herr Christ, der einig Gottes Sohn" (usually translated in English as "Lord Christ from God, Forever"), which was included in the first Protestant hymnal in 1524, along with eighteen hymns by Luther and six by other men. The hymn proclaims Christ's divinity and humanity and conveys the key Protestant teaching that God alone "awakens us through grace." Hymns and songs were important means of spreading the Protestant message, meant to be sung by families at home as well as by congregations during worship services.

Elisabeth's hymn was translated into Swedish, Danish, and English in the sixteenth century. Her authorship was viewed as a sign that the Holy Spirit could speak through women as well as men, and that the end times predicted in the Bible, "when your sons and your daughters shall prophesy" (Joel 2:28–29) were at hand. By the later seventeenth century, these apocalyptic expectations faded, and hymnal publishers were not so sure that a woman could actually have written a hymn, or that anyone would be interested in singing it if she had. They attributed the hymn to a male author. Today the hymn is once again recognized as Elisabeth Cruciger's and included in several Lutheran hymnals in Europe and North America.

The very first biography of Luther, written in 1548 by his friend and colleague at Wittenberg, Philip Melanchthon, does not mention Katharina or any other nun who had married a reformer. He does mention Luther's mother Margarethe (1463–1531), whom Melanchthon had met several times, and portrays her as a model for other women: "Since all the other virtues of an honest Matron were seen coming together—modesty, fear of God, and prayer especially shown forth—the other honest women looked to her as an example of virtues."[5]

Luther's relationship with his father, a copper miner and mine owner from a peasant background who had high expectations that his son would have a brilliant legal career, has been plumbed for clues about Luther's personality and decisions. His mother, who came from a more middle-class background, also had high hopes for her son, and had the connections and the financial means to make sure he received a good education. Luther was close to his mother and named one of his daughters after her. She was also strict, as Luther later tells it, like his father giving him a thrashing when he misbehaved. Shortly before she died, in her final illness, Luther wrote to her. Embedded in his spiritual consolation was a clear Protestant message: "Dear Mother, you know now about God's grace . . . be thankful that He has not allowed you to remain stuck in papist error, according to which we were taught to build upon our works and upon the holiness of monks. . . . But now we know otherwise. . . . Be comforted and thank God with joy for such a great favor!"[6] To us, Luther's words may sound more appropriate for a pastor than a son, but he was both, and he wanted her to die confident of God's saving love for her.

Protestant teachings and institutions spread from Germany into Denmark-Norway, Sweden, England, France, and eastern Europe. Continental Protestants were firm in their support of clerical marriage, with a few even suggesting that all clergy *must* marry. English Protestants were more ambivalent, and more cautious. As you have read in Chapter 1, the English break with Catholicism was a decision made by King Henry VIII largely to solve his marriage problems. Henry rejected papal supremacy, but not clerical celibacy. A few English clergy married in the early 1530s, including Archbishop Thomas Cranmer, the highest official in the Church of England, who married the niece of the wife of a German reformer, whom he had met in Germany while he was the ambassador for Henry VIII at the court of the Holy Roman Emperor. But Henry clamped down in 1539 and ordered all married clergy to repudiate their wives and children or risk being executed. Thomas Cranmer did not repudiate his wife, but she and their daughter fled to Germany, and other pastors' wives also went back to their birth families or into hiding.

With Henry's death in 1547 and the accession of the more clearly Protestant Edward VI, the Church of England grudgingly allowed clerical marriage, though it still preferred that ministers "live chaste, sole, and separate from the company of women and the bond of marriage." Margarete Cranmer and her daughter came back from Germany and the couple had at least one more child. In some areas as many as a third of the clergy married in just a few years, although there was also hostility, as "people spoke slanderously of such marriages, and accounted the children begotten in them to be bastards."[7]

When England reverted to Catholicism under Mary I in 1553, she and her bishops ordered married clergy to give up their wives, declared their children illegitimate, removed married priests from office, and confiscated their property. She arrested Cranmer and other Protestant leaders for treason and heresy, and Margarete Cranmer went back yet again to Germany. Denying the supremacy of the pope or questioning Catholic doctrine were positions that could be recanted—which Cranmer in fact did, though he was still executed—but it was harder to deny that one had been married if there had been a public wedding. Faced with the attack on clerical marriage, some clergy hid their families, some went into exile in Protestant cities on the continent, and some renounced their wives and children, moving to a different parish and promising never to see them again.

Even the bones of women married to priests could be polluting. Catherine Dammartin (?–1553) was a German nun who left her convent in Metz and fled to Strasbourg, where she met Katharina Zell and other women active in Protestant reforms. She also met and married the Italian reformer Peter Martyr Vermigli. (She spoke no Italian and Vermigli spoke no German, so the two most likely initially talked to each other in Latin.) The couple moved to England in 1548 during Edward VI's reign, where Vermigli took a position at the University of Oxford. Vermigli was the first married priest at Oxford and hostility to clerical marriage was strong. Catherine was denounced as a "whore," the windows of their rooms were smashed, and the couple was forced to move to more secluded quarters. Catherine died in 1553 and was buried in Oxford, but in 1556, during Mary I's reign, her bones were dug up from the cemetery and thrown onto a dunghill.

With Elizabeth's accession to the throne in 1558, England returned to being Protestant. Catherine Dammartin's bones were dug up once again and reburied in the cathedral at Oxford, purposely mixed with the bones of the eighth-century abbess St. Frideswide so that neither Protestants nor Catholics would be able to sort them out if they wanted to desecrate the memory of one or the other.

Living pastors' wives fared worse than dead ones. Elizabeth was just as hostile to clerical marriage as her older sister and her much-married father had been, denouncing married bishops in crude language that made her courtiers squirm. She made it as difficult as possible for clergy to marry, requiring them to have permission from their bishop and two justices of the peace, and for the women to have their parents' permission, no matter how old they were. The widowed Margarete Cranmer chose not to marry another clergyman but instead married the publisher of Cranmer's major works. But Anglican priests and bishops kept marrying, and slowly their wives made clerical families acceptable. Their sons went to university, and then often became clergy themselves, and their daughters married into gentry families, or they married clergy. In England as well as on the continent, being a minister became an inherited occupation, just as being a shoemaker (or a monarch) often was.

Anglican clergy developed a model of marriage in which it was viewed as a "little commonwealth" on which the larger commonwealth of politics, society, and the created order rested.

SPEAKING OUT

Protestant women might become pastor's wives, but, just as in Catholicism, they could not be ordained as priests or pastors. Women's exclusion from ordination was based on widespread and deep-seated ideas about proper social roles for women and men. More specifically, it was also based on words ascribed to St. Paul (1 Timothy 2:11–15) which ordered women not to teach or have authority over a man. (Most biblical scholars today reject Paul's authorship of the Epistles to Timothy and the Epistle to Titus, as their style and words are different from those in the unquestioned epistles, and they refer to situations and types of church leaders that were not found in Paul's time. Until the nineteenth century, however, everyone regarded these as written by Paul.) Those same words were used throughout the Reformation era—and today—to attack women who spoke or wrote publicly on religious issues. Despite this, women did so, particularly in the early years of the Protestant Reformation or during periods of crisis. They often asserted that God had called them to do so, and that these were extraordinary times. A few described themselves as "church mothers," and maintained that their speaking out on religious matters was simply an extension of their role as mothers, responsible to their community as well as their families.

The boldest, such as Argula von Grumbach (*c.* 1492–*c.* 1564), a German noblewoman who published eight works in 1523 and 1524 defending Protestant teachings, commented that the situation was so serious that Paul's words should simply be disregarded: "I am not unfamiliar with Paul's words that women should be silent in church but when I see that no man will or can speak, I am driven by the word of God when he said, He who confesses me on earth, him will I confess and he who denies me, him will I deny."[8] Ursula Weyda (1504–1565), a middle-class German woman who attacked the abbot of Pegau in a 1524 pamphlet, agreed: "If all women were forbidden to speak, how could daughters prophesy as Joel predicted? Although St. Paul forbade women to preach

2. Title page of Argula von Grumbach's first 1523 pamphlet. The woodcut shows her using the Bible to debate with the male faculty, a scene imagined by the artist based on the title she gave her pamphlet: "Open letter well-grounded in Holy Scripture to the University of Ingolstadt from a Christian noblewoman in Bavaria." No such debate ever took place, of course.

in churches and instructed them to obey their husbands, what if the churches were full of liars?"[9]

Von Grumbach had no formal theological training but knew her Bible well and had read many of Luther's writings in German. She was inspired to pen the first of her publications when the faculty at the University of Ingolstadt, near her home in Bavaria, accused a student of Lutheran leanings and sentenced him to be executed. Her open letter to the university faculty challenged them to prove his heresy and to debate her, closing with a defense of her actions: "What I have written to you is no woman's chit-chat, but the word of God; and [I write] as a member of the Christian Church, against which the gates of Hell cannot prevail."[10] To no one's surprise, the university faculty did not bother to respond, and her Catholic husband was pressured to force her to stop writing. A few more of her letters were published over the next year, and she later corresponded with Luther, but other than that we have no idea how she spent the remaining forty years of her life.

Marie Dentière (c. 1495–1561) was a nun from an aristocratic family, who, like Katharina von Bora, became interested in Protestant writings in the 1520s, left her convent, married a former priest, and had several children. When her husband died, she married another reformer, and in 1535 the family moved from France to Geneva, a city in French-speaking Switzerland split by controversy over accepting Protestant reforms. She jumped into the conflict, marching into the convent of St. Clare with several others to encourage the nuns to accept Protestant teachings and leave the convent. Sister Jeanne de Jussie, one of the convent residents who became an abbess, later wrote of that day: "In their company was a monkess, false abbess, wrinkled and with a diabolical tongue, having husband and children, named Marie Dentière of Picardy, who meddled in preaching and in perverting people of doctrine. . . . The nuns were horrified by her false and erroneous words, and they spat on her with loathing . . . The wretched woman tried to charm the sisters, and others tried to drag some of them outside."[11]

Geneva had attracted a number of Protestant reformers, including John Calvin, who built on earlier ideas to develop his own theology and plans for institutional change. Like Luther, Calvin rejected the sacramentality of marriage, yet praised its God-given nature. He increasingly came to regard marriage as a covenant, a sacred contract like that between God and the church.

In 1538, several reformers, including Calvin, were banished from the city. Dentière published a long letter defending them to Queen Marguerite de Navarre, the French ruler with Protestant leanings. In her letter, Marie includes detailed theological discussions and gives ringing support for women's speaking out on religious issues:

Why is it necessary to criticize women so much, seeing that no woman ever sold and betrayed Jesus, but a man named Judas? Who are they, I ask you, who have invented and contrived so many ceremonies, heresies, and false doctrines on earth if not men? . . . Therefore, if God has given grace to some good women, revealing to them by his holy scriptures something holy and good, should they hesitate to write, speak, and declare it to one another because of the defamers of the truth? Ah, it would be too bold to try to stop them, and it would be too foolish to hide the talent that God has given to us, God who will give us the grace to persevere to the end. . . . I ask, didn't Jesus die just as much for the poor ignorant people and the idiots as for my dear sirs the wise and important doctors? Isn't it for all of us? Do we have two Gospels, one for men and another for women?[12]

The letter provoked a harsh reaction, with some leaders doubting that it could have been written by a woman, and most calling for all copies to be confiscated.

Calvin came back to Geneva in 1541 after the city reconsidered its expulsion. From that point he led the reform there, trying to transform Geneva into a well-disciplined Christian society in which church and state acted in unison. Geneva became the model of a Christian community for many Protestant reformers. Religious refugees flocked there from many parts of Europe, though there was also opposition to Calvin's measures. From Geneva, Calvinist Protestantism spread to parts of Germany, France, Scotland, England, eastern Europe, and ultimately to North America. (By the later sixteenth century, the Protestant Reformation had two main wings, those who followed Luther, often called *Evangelical*, and those who followed Calvin and other French and Swiss reformers such as Ulrich Zwingli, called *Reformed*, along with other smaller groups.)

There is very little mention of Dentière during the last twenty years of her life, though in one of his letters Calvin reports that she was preaching in taverns and street corners against pastors wearing long robes, which she viewed as akin to the scribes of the New Testament who opposed Jesus. He instructed her to stop, but, in his words: "She complained about our tyranny, that it was no longer permitted for just anyone to chatter on about anything at all. I treated the woman as I should have."[13] His derisive tone toward a woman who was not afraid to confront him or to preach publicly is clear. At the very end of Dentière's life there may have been a reconciliation, however, as she wrote a preface to one of Calvin's published sermons, on the need for modesty in women's dress, written to counteract Catholic charges that Protestants were immoral.

Calvin's exile from Geneva took him to Strasbourg for three years, where he encountered the most prolific of the early Protestant women reformers, Katharina Schütz Zell (1497–1562). Born into a middle-class family and trained as a tapestry-maker, Katharina Schütz read the Bible and later many of Luther's writings, becoming convinced that Luther's teachings about faith and grace were correct. She also regularly attended services at Strasbourg's cathedral church, where the priest was also preaching Protestant ideas. In 1523 she married that reforming priest, Matthew Zell. He was forty-six, she was twenty-five, about the same age spread as Luther and Katharina von Bora, who would marry two years later. The Zells' two children died in childhood, and her letters express her grief and pain.

Matthew was the first priest in Strasbourg to marry, and she was the first respectable woman in the city to marry a priest. Rumors began to spread about the couple and, in 1524, Katharina wrote and then published a short pamphlet defending her husband and clerical marriage in general. She recounts the arguments made in favor of clerical celibacy by Catholic authors and insults them in plain, but lively terms: one is "like a spoon that makes a lot of noise in an empty pot but is made out of such poor fir wood that one could not use it to stir a child's pap." Another is "a dog and evil worker who tramples God's vineyard with his feet and a rapacious wolf, yes, a father of all wolves, and a thief and a murderer who comes to strangle and kill." She asserts that clerical marriage "has indeed clear and bright—not faint—grounds in godly Scripture, in the Old and New Testaments, so that children and fools can read and understand." The Catholic Church prohibits clerical marriage, she argues—again in strong language about blindness and harlotry—because it wants to collect fines from priests who have concubines, and because priests do not want to limit themselves to one woman. She directly answers rumors that were being spread. Matthew had not married her for sex or money: "I can perceive in him no dishonorableness, no inclination toward lust or any other such thing—for I am not gifted with either overwhelming beauty or riches or other virtues that might move one to seek me in marriage!"[14]

Zell ends the pamphlet with a spirited defense of her own actions:

> Since I became his wife I want to defend him and risk my honor, body, and life for him. . . . I have placed myself and my husband in God's hand

with a joyous heart: may His will be done in us! . . . If someone says: "This is none of your business, it belongs to other folk than you . . . Paul says that women should keep silent." I answer, do you not know, however, that Paul also says in Galatians 3 "In Christ there is neither man nor woman"? And God in the prophet Joel says in Chapter 2, "I will pour out my Spirit over all flesh, and your sons and daughters will prophesy." And you know also that Zechariah became dumb, so that Elizabeth blessed the Virgin Mary. . . . I do not seek to be heard as if I were Elizabeth, or John the Baptist, or Nathan the prophet who pointed out his sin to David, or any of the prophets, but only as the donkey whom the false prophet Balaam heard. For I seek nothing other than that we may be saved together with each other. May God help us do that, through Christ His beloved son.[15]

Zell had no formal theological training, as this was available only at universities, which were closed to women, but in her defense of women's speaking out on religious issues she shows her familiarity with the Bible, as she easily quotes and refers to biblical texts to make her points.

Katharina Zell's deep knowledge of the Bible emerges in other of her writings as well. Several months before she published the defense of clerical marriage, she published another pamphlet, an open "letter to the suffering women of the community of Kentzingen," a small city near Strasbourg that had accepted Lutheran teaching but was being attacked by its Catholic overlord for this. Many of the men had been exiled and had left their wives and children behind. In this published letter, Katharina weaves together biblical texts to provide inspiration and consolation:

I beg you, loyal believing women, also to do this: take on you the manly Abraham-like courage while you too are in distress and while you are abused with all kinds of insult and suffering. When you may meet with imprisonment in towers, chains, drowning, banishment, and such like things; when your husbands and you yourselves may be killed, meditate then on strong Abraham, father of us all. . . . Consider the words of Christ, where He says, "Blessed are those who mourn, for they will be comforted."[16]

Strasbourg was one of the most tolerant cities in the Holy Roman Empire, welcoming Protestants of all kinds during periods when disputes among Protestants elsewhere about several issues were often vicious. The Zells hosted numerous visitors, including Ulrich Zwingli, John Calvin, and many other Swiss and French reformers, and they stayed with Luther in his home in Wittenberg in 1538. Katharina Zell took an active part in religious discussions and did not hesitate to criticize those she thought were incorrect. She wrote to Luther regarding the debate about the nature of the sacrament of communion—one of the most bitter disputes among Protestants—and he answered her with a very friendly letter. As with Katharina von Bora, Luther's letter was saved, recopied, and later published, and hers is lost. Katharina Zell also spoke publicly at Matthew Zell's funeral in 1548, and later wrote down the substance of what she said, which circulated in manuscript. This, too, was lost, but a single copy was discovered centuries later in private hands, and we can today hear her sorrow and her trust in God.

By the middle of the sixteenth century, Strasbourg was becoming less tolerant, and some church leaders attacked its earlier traditions of openness. The aging Katharina Zell again took pen in hand to answer those who were calling her deceased husband a heretic and her a troublemaker. In 1557, she published "A Letter to the Whole Citizenship of the Strasbourg," a long work with details about her long life, in which she had "diligently busied herself with His church and its household affairs . . . received refugees and the poor . . . and gladly served many with counsel and deed, according to my ability (as much as God has bestowed on me) . . . and as my husband commended to me." She uses the phrase "church mother" to describe herself: "Since I was ten years old I have been a church mother, a nurturer of the pulpit and school. I have loved all the clergy, visited many, and had conversations with them—not about dances, worldly joys, riches or carnival, but about the kingdom of God."[17] Here and in other of her writings, she saw the role of church mother as one of teaching and modeling faith, assisting in the physical and spiritual needs of the poor and ill and prisoners, and working with the clergy in their pastoral endeavors.

These responsibilities did not extend just to her own household, or only to women, but to the entire community. As part of her service to

Strasbourg's ill, Zell inspected the city hospital and was horrified at what she found there. The food was "only salted fish and tough, fatty meat that the healthy as well as the ill wouldn't want to eat." The house was "so Godless that when an 'Our Father' is said at the table it is done so quietly and secretly that no one knows if it's a prayer or a fart. . . . No one knows who Christ is, and no one is taught anything about him. . . . They sleep in horrible beds, like a sow in her own manure." She recommended the entire staff be dismissed, and instead "God-fearing women who will oversee things properly" be appointed.[18]

Zell's Letter is not simply autobiography, but also theology. She had just read the most famous sixteenth-century treatise on toleration, Sebastian Castellio's *De hereticis* (published in 1554 in German and French as well as Latin) as she cites it, and her arguments are similar to Castellio's. She asserts that the core doctrines of Christianity are very few, and that anyone who acknowledges Christ as the Savior should be regarded as a brother or sister in Christ. Following Christ's example is more important than dogma. She couches her arguments in terms of a defense of her husband's position, which both strengthens her portrayal of herself as a loving and obedient wife and gives her freer range to tackle theological topics not usually discussed by women. From the way she handles arguments, however, it is clear she is not simply repeating her husband's words, but expressing her own deeply felt convictions on such issues as the interpretation of the sacraments.

Zell draws her examples from the everyday world of ordinary believers, including women. She accuses younger pastors in Strasbourg of reintroducing the Catholic idea that infants who died before baptism would end up in limbo, that state outside of heaven and hell in the afterlife where the souls of those who were not baptized were consigned because of Original Sin. (Current Catholic teachings on limbo are somewhat in limbo themselves, with papal advisers stating that it is acceptable to believe in it or to hope that unbaptized infants will be saved through God's mercy.) Infant mortality was very high in this era, and stillbirths were common. Although anyone could conduct a baptism, this did not always happen. Zell recognizes that the idea that infants might be eternally cut off from God "had deeply pained so many poor mothers in their hearts, and even driven them into unbelief so that they completely forgot about the saving blood of Jesus Christ."[19] Luther would never have accepted this, she writes, as he had rejected the idea of limbo.

She ends the book with an image of the wise virgins waiting with their lamps for the Bridegroom, drawn from a parable in Matthew 25, and portrayed in Gothic sculptures that flank the door of Strasbourg's cathedral, which she and others in the city could see every day. The last acts of her life were also for women, as she preached at the burials of two women friends who were followers of a religious leader the clergy in Strasbourg did not support.

Argula von Grumbach, Marie Dentière, and Katharina Zell published all or most of their works in the first decades of the Protestant Reformation, a time of ferment when many individuals shared their ideas in print and tried to shape the religious institutions that were being created. Once Protestant churches were established and their structures set, published writings by women (and men who lacked formal theological training) decreased sharply.

Women's actions as well as their writings in the first years of the Reformation upset political and religious authorities, especially if the women were not from among the elite. The small south German city of Memmingen, for example, forbade "maids and other women" to discuss religion when they were drawing water at neighborhood wells. In 1543, during the reign of King Henry VIII, an Act of Parliament in England banned all women except those of the gentry and nobility from reading the Bible, and banned male servants and apprentices from reading it as well. Upper-class women could only read it privately, never aloud to others. Class as well as gender hierarchies were to be maintained, although from women's diaries and other sources, we know that this restriction was rarely obeyed.

By later in the sixteenth century such prohibitions had generally been lifted. Protestant clergy in England (and elsewhere) increasingly encouraged Bible reading for women and for men who lacked a university education. They provided directions in their sermons and in devotional manuals about taking notes, organizing material by subject (this is called "commonplacing"), and applying the Bible to one's own life. Ordinary Bible readers seized on this and copied, excerpted, and compiled material into what were termed "miscellanies," as well as more extended meditations and homilies, going beyond simply quoting to producing original devotional works. Some of these were hastily scribbled for their own use only, but others were "fair copies" transcribed with care and intended to be given to others, often as bequests for their children or circulated to friends.

The English noblewoman Grace, Lady Mildmay (*c.* 1552–1620), for example, left a 900-page fair-copy manuscript of meditations to her daughter when she died, along with a much shorter autobiographical account (which also has moral advice and Bible quotations), and papers and objects relating to her medical practice. Women's manuscript devotional writings tended to draw from a narrower range of sources outside the Bible than did men's, which is not surprising given their different access to published work, but writing provided both women and men with opportunities for self-understanding and spiritual authority.

Women's religious manuscripts were sometimes published posthumously by family members or sympathetic clergy. Generally these were men, but the Dutch Calvinist Protestant Susanna Teellinck (1551–1625) wrote an introduction to a confession of faith and religious poems by her deceased sister Cornelia Teellinck (1554–1576), edited these, and arranged for them to be published as a small book in 1607. Originally written during the 1570s, a time of Spanish invasions of the Netherlands, the poems urge repentance and provide consolation: "You need not fear sword or enemy for the Lord shall take up your case himself and show all that he is a God of vengeance over those who have persecuted the pious."[20] Such a message was welcome in 1607, when the Spanish were again attacking the Netherlands, which may account for the book's popularity, as it went through several editions. Crisis often provides women with increased opportunities to make their voices heard.

DEFENDING THEIR FAITH

The Catholic women who defended their faith in writing during the sixteenth century were primarily abbesses and other women religious, discussed later in this chapter. But there were many Catholic laywomen who defended their faith through their actions. They did not call themselves "church mothers," but their actions, and sometimes their statements as reported in court records, letters, and biographies written by their confessors, suggest they saw their role as similar to the one Katharina Zell set for herself.

The most celebrated—and best-documented—Catholic laywomen were in England and Ireland. As you have read in Chapter 1, during the reign of Queen Elizabeth, anyone holding public or church office was required to swear an oath of allegiance to her and attend services of the Church of England or pay a fine. Some Catholics left England, but most had to choose between following the law and refusing to do so. The majority chose the former, becoming what were termed "church papists," though they often attended private Catholic services as well. Those who did not swear the oath were termed "recusants."

Both sides hardened in the 1560s and 1570s. The pope forbade English Catholics to attend any Protestant services. He excommunicated Queen Elizabeth and released English Catholics from their duty to obey her. Catholic nobles led several revolts and plots to depose Elizabeth and replace her with Mary, Queen of Scots. Refusal to take the oath became treason in Elizabeth's eyes. Government policy toward recusants became harsher, with more and more men required to take the oath of allegiance or risk imprisonment, and ever-higher fines imposed on those who did not attend church. Further plots to depose or assassinate Elizabeth in the 1580s, plus England's wars with Catholic Spain, led to more anti-Catholic legislation, culminating in the colorfully titled 1593 "Act for the Better Discovery of Wicked and Seditious Persons Terming Themselves Catholics, but Being Rebellious and Traitorous Subjects."

Catholics were particularly numerous in the north of England and tended to marry one another, creating interwoven networks of Catholic families that also stretched to Ireland. Recusants included many women. A 1577 survey of known Catholics in the Diocese of York in northern England found that 64 per cent of them were women, ranging from "ladies" through "gentlewomen" through "inferior" women, some listed as widows or single women, but also as wives with and without their husbands. A similar count in 1604 found 60 per cent of the known Catholics were women. Some of this gender difference may be the result of Catholic husbands outwardly conforming and attending services, but it still means that wives were publicly disagreeing with their husbands on matters of religion and known to be doing so.

Women posed a special problem for royal officials. A single woman or widow found guilty of recusancy could be fined, but a married woman, according to common law, controlled no property. Imprisoning her would disrupt her family life and harm her husband, who might not even share her religious convictions. Recusant women were imprisoned, and a few were executed for their actions, but most men, including strong Protestants, were not willing to back measures that put the property of a woman's husband at risk.

Catholicism in England grew increasingly domestic, as women transformed their households into religious sanctuaries, making the image of the family as a "little church" used so often in sermons into a reality. They arranged for private Masses to be held in the home and built altars and chapels. They sheltered Catholic priests and Jesuits, who began sneaking into England illegally in 1580, having been educated in new seminaries set up on the continent specifically to train English priests. Those priests provided Mass and heard confessions, but otherwise women led prayers and devotions, recited rosaries and litanies, instructed children and other household members, and cared for the poor and sick. They established networks of hiding places (known as "priests' holes"), escape routes, and safe houses where priests could stay during government crackdowns. They smuggled their children abroad so they could attend Catholic schools or enter convents, and then sent funds to them. They operated secret presses in their homes, publishing Catholic works and selling them.

As stories were collected about the persecution of Catholics, a new type of Catholic heroine emerged—capable, benevolent, intelligent, and in many ways crafty in her dealings with authorities. This was an idealization, but one modeled on real recusant women, for Protestant judges and royal officials frequently complained about the influence such women had on their husbands, children, and servants. Stories about these women, written by priests the women supported and protected, were read by other Catholics in England and abroad, providing them with models to imitate.

Magdalen Dacre Browne, Viscountess Montague (1538–1608), for example, the widow of a wealthy Catholic nobleman, made her large household into what her biographer called "a visible Church or Company of Catholics . . . such was the number of Catholics resident in her house and the multitude and note of such as repaired thither, that even the heretics, to the eternal glory of the name of the Lady Magdalen, gave it the title of *Little Rome*."[21] She fasted according to the Catholic calendar, prayed and said the rosary many times a day, and protected several resident chaplains, who held daily Mass and weekly confession. She built a chapel that would house 120 worshippers, where priests held weekly services open to the community, with sermons that she hoped would deepen their Catholic faith.

Dorothy Constable Lawson (1580–1632) was raised in a Catholic family, with a mother who had been imprisoned for recusancy. She married a man who was at least outwardly Protestant and had fifteen children, but converted her husband to Catholicism, and after he died, arranged for many of her children to go to Catholic seminaries and convents on the continent. She was a midwife, and along with herbal remedies and her training, she made use of saints' relics to bring spiritual comfort to women giving birth. Mothers in labor reported that just her presence calmed them and made childbirth easier, viewing her as a living saint. She even conducted emergency baptisms on infants she thought might die, a role allowed to laypersons according to Catholic doctrine. "When any was to be reconciled [to the Catholic faith] thereabout," wrote her Jesuit biographer, "shee played the catechist."

Lawson built a new residence with each room named for an individual saint, and a chapel with several altars, open to her neighbors and also to any visitors who traveled on the nearby River Tyne, attracted by the word "Jesus" she had written on the side of the house. She hosted Jesuits, despite the laws that made it a felony to do so, and her daily religious practices included practices of meditation on the life of Christ drawn from Jesuit works. The Jesuits were so indebted to her that they decided "to impart . . . the privileges of the Society, and make her by communication partaker of their works, as if shee were a member thereof." In fact, they refused to allow her to withdraw to a more contemplative life when she requested this, but "to persevere as she had begun, not only in the study of her own perfection, but allso in the pursuance and acquisition of others." And she was successful: "Att her departure from thence . . . to heaven, there was not one heretick family, and six altars were erected for divine service."[22] Jesuits would not allow women members in their order but valued laywomen as assets to their mission.

English Catholics hoped that when James I became monarch in 1603 he might be more tolerant, but restrictions instead increased. For the first time, these specified punishments for married women, who were ordered to be imprisoned unless their husbands paid ten pounds a month (a huge sum) to keep them free. A widow who did not attend church risked forfeiture of the money or property her husband had left to support her, and could not act as executor of his estate nor claim any of his goods. Those found guilty of harboring priests could be executed, whether they were male or female. Again these laws were not always enforced, but the threat was there.

The sisters Eleanor Vaux Brookesby (1560–1626) and Anne Vaux (1562–1637?) and their sister-in-law, Elizabeth Vaux, born Roper (d. 1637?) were the center of a Catholic network that stretched across several counties. All three turned their family estates into Jesuit bases of operations, building quarters for priests and the boys who were their pupils, who sometimes numbered fifty or more. They were occasionally arrested and imprisoned for their activities, which included involvement in anti-government plots as well as harboring priests. Anne and Eleanor were most likely involved in the 1605 Gunpowder Plot, a plan by English Catholics to assassinate King James I and blow up the House of Lords, but they used stereotypes of women's weakness to their advantage when they were arrested. Elizabeth argued that no serious plotter would ever entrust secret plans to a woman: "I do assure your lordship that there are many that will receive such persons that will not put their lives and estates in the power and secrecy of a woman."[23] Her ploy was successful. She secured her release and immediately went to London and set up another secret safe house for priests.

Eleanor and Anne hosted annual meetings of Jesuit missionaries, one of which was raided by government agents. Seeking to hold off the early morning search party until the Jesuits had escaped, Anne reportedly referred to norms of women's modesty and harmlessness, chiding them: "Do you think it right and proper that you should be admitted to a widow's house before she or her servants or children are out of bed? . . .

Have you ever found me unwilling to open the door to you as soon as you knocked?" Once again the strategy worked, which led one of the Jesuits who had escaped to give words of strong praise: "though she has all a maiden's modesty and even shyness, yet in God's cause and in protection of His servants, *virgo* becomes *virago*."[24] Anne Vaux continued to be a virago—a strong, manly woman—for the rest of her life. She was convicted and imprisoned for recusancy when she was in her fifties and opened a school for boys from Catholic families when she was in her sixties, which the Protestant authorities shut down.

Most English recusant women came from extended families of Catholics, but some were converts. Elizabeth Tanfield Cary (1585/86–1639) came from a Protestant family that provided her with an excellent education, including learning Latin and Hebrew. Married at fifteen to Sir Henry Cary (later Viscount Falkland), she began to write, producing poetry, translations, prose works, and *The Tragedy of Mariam: The Fair Queen of Jewry*, the first extant tragedy written by a woman in English. The play tells the story of Mariam, second wife of the biblical figure Herod the Great, King of Judea. She rejects her husband's explanations for murdering several members of her family, refusing to show him the inner submission expected from good wives. Misinterpreting her disobedience as sexual infidelity, Herod has her beheaded, though at the end of the play regrets having done so.

This plot about the conflict between a wife's duty to her husband and her own loyalties prefigures Cary's own life. She became the mother of eleven children, but also began to read Catholic works and socialize with Catholics, particularly after she and her husband moved to Ireland, where he was lord deputy. The death in childbirth of her eldest daughter led her to openly declare her conversion to Catholicism, to the horror of her family. Her father disowned her, and her husband attempted to divorce her. He denied her access to their children, the youngest of whom was only three, and cut off all financial support, so that she lived precariously in poverty. She managed to spirit six of her children away from their Protestant older brother and convey them in secret to the continent, where they openly converted to Catholicism. Her four daughters ultimately joined English Benedictine convents in France, and one of her sons became a Catholic priest. Her daughter Lucy wrote *The Lady*

Falkland: Her Life by One of Her Daughters, a biography to which all the children added annotations. This portrayed her as a heroic figure who persevered despite opposition from family and state, and who even publicly objected to accusations of witchcraft directed against other women, as you'll see in Chapter 4. In contrast to Viscountess Montague, Dorothy Lawson, and the Vaux sisters, Cary never had the resources after her conversion to create a spiritual community within her own home, but the biography written by her children presents her as an example to the faithful.

Recusants were far more numerous in Ireland than in England. England had ruled part of Ireland since the twelfth century, and in the sixteenth century Tudor monarchs asserted their authority through military occupation and conquest. The Tudor monarchs established a Protestant Church of Ireland and, as in England, ordered people, particularly office-holders, to attend. The vast majority of people in Ireland, both Gaelic Irish and some Anglo-Irish—descendants of English families who had been in Ireland for centuries—refused, however, and continued to attend Catholic services. English officials noted that women were particularly likely to avoid Protestant services. Wrote one: "None of the women do come either to [Protestant] service or sermon."[25]

Even the wives of Protestant bishops in the official Church of Ireland generally remained Catholic, raising their children as Catholics, ensuring their servants were Catholic, and sometimes harboring priests. Most of those few people reported to have converted were wealthy young men, who, as one Catholic clergyman commented, "embrace the Lutheran leprosy to please the Lady Elizabeth [Queen Elizabeth I] rather than any other cause."[26] English officials recommended taking young nobles away from their families, as they "should not be allowed to live with their mothers or friends, who are recusants, but to be taught the principles of religion by which they may be made good citizens."[27] This did not happen, and instead Protestant converts were sometimes brought back to Catholicism by their wives when they married. Without Protestant women, no self-sustaining community of Irish Protestants could develop, and none did.

Seminary-trained priests, including Jesuits, began coming to Ireland in the 1560s, and were sheltered by women. An English commentator observed that "Jesuites and Roman priests swarmed in all places, filling the houses of lords, gentlemen and especially cittissens and domineering in them, as they might well doe, for howsoever the men grewe weary of them, they had the women on theire sydes."[28]

Women were also important in revolts against the English that combined political and religious grievances. English officials in Ireland reported that Dame Janet Eustace, from a leading noble family, was the "chief councilor and stirrer" of what became known as the Kildare Rebellion of 1534/35, a revolt that involved most of Ireland. She was imprisoned in Dublin Castle and tortured to implicate others. She refused, and died a year later, still in prison. Mabel Brown, Countess of Kildare (c. 1536–1610), an English Catholic noblewoman married to the Irish Earl of Kildare, was charged with encouraging her husband to maintain his Catholic faith and plot against the English. He was incarcerated in Dublin Castle and later the Tower of London on charges of treason, though she managed to stay safely at home in Ireland.

Anglo-Irish Catholics created interlocking networks through marriage, but there were also families in which there were both Protestants and Catholics. Elizabeth Fitzgerald (d. 1645), Countess of Kildare, married into a strongly Protestant family but remained a staunch Catholic. She harbored priests, especially Jesuits, and provided the funding for Kildare Hall, a Catholic college and chapel in Dublin that existed briefly in the late 1620s before it was suppressed.

Margaret Ball (c. 1515–1584), the wife and then widow of a prominent Dublin merchant and city official, was one of the few women in Ireland imprisoned for harboring priests. One of those enforcing anti-recusant measures was Ball's own oldest son Walter, Dublin's mayor and a prominent Protestant, who apparently thought it advantageous to take action against an open Catholic within his own family. Along with protecting priests, Margaret Ball taught women. These included, wrote her later biographers, servants who "went out like expert scholars from the finest school and won for Christ not only their fellow servants and maids but also sometimes and indeed very often their masters and mistresses and noble women [who] desired to send their daughters from near and far alike to be educated by her."[29] In their eyes, Ball was a "church mother" to be emulated. The elderly Margaret Ball died in prison, and later became revered as a martyr. Along with sixteen Irish men, she was beatified, that is, raised to the status of "blessed," often a step on the road to being canonized as a saint, by Pope John Paul II in 1992.

Irish recusants were sometimes exiled for their faith or chose to migrate. Many Irish Catholics moved around the British Empire, especially to the Caribbean. Social-climbing Irish men hoping to become members of the planter elite joined the Church of England and attended its services. But as with recusants in England and Ireland, Irish women in the Caribbean often continued to engage in Catholic practices (including baptizing infants) while their husbands went to Anglican services. They oversaw their husbands' burials in private ceremonies, thus having a say in the final destiny of their souls.

Along with maintaining Catholic practice in England, Ireland, and the Caribbean, the actions of laywomen were essential in re-Catholicizing parts of Europe that had become fully or partly Protestant, an important aim of the Catholic Reformation. New and reformed religious orders were key players in this effort, most prominently the Jesuits. But Jesuits and other religious orders worked with and through laypeople. For example, Jesuits came to multi-confessional Poland in the 1560s to strengthen and expand loyalty to Catholicism. Women responded to this effort, built and endowed churches, chapels, and altars, and established hospitals and orphanages. Wealthy urban women, especially widows, set up and joined religious confraternities, organizations of laypeople dedicated to specific aspects of devotion. Such groups both strengthened the Catholic Church and gave women opportunities for communal activities outside of the home.

In France, huge numbers of women joined confraternities in the seventeenth and eighteenth centuries. Some of these were dedicated to spiritual practices with special meaning for women, such as saying the rosary, the set of prayers focused on the Virgin Mary and the life of Christ assisted by a string of beads used to count the prayers. Membership in confraternities certainly contributed to women's greater loyalty to the Catholic Church in a period when much of France was becoming increasingly secular. During the French Revolution, women hid priests who refused to sign oaths of loyalty to the government, attended illegal worship services, and occasionally organized prayer meetings and processions. Like recusants in England and Ireland several centuries earlier, laywomen were essential to the maintenance of Catholicism in France, a fact more often recognized by the critics of the Church than by its clergy or supporters.

TEACHING AND PREACHING

The Protestant state churches established in the sixteenth century were powerful institutions controlled largely by rulers. Important preaching positions and chairs of theology at universities were often handed down from father to son, or from father to son-in-law, creating virtual clerical dynasties. Highly educated clergy and professors of theology developed rigid and complex theological systems in which the ideas of church mothers such as Katharina Zell—or any other person without university training—played no part. Sermons became occasions for pastors to show off their knowledge of obscure theological points rather than provide moral or spiritual guidance. A seventeenth-century Lutheran sermon on Matthew 10:30, for example ("Even the very hairs of your head are numbered"), did not focus on the larger meaning of this verse—divine concern for all aspects of human life down to the smallest detail—but on the origin and correct care of hair, other biblical references to hair, and the hairstyles proper to good Lutheran men and women.

By the late seventeenth century, many people thought that the services and rituals of state churches were not spiritually satisfying. They wanted to build meaningful religious fellowship through Bible study, prayer, moral discipline, and personal spiritual regeneration, a movement that came to be called pietism. Pietism originated as a term of ridicule and derision but was later used positively by people who had been so labeled. It began in Germany and then spread to the rest of Protestant Europe, across the Atlantic, and around the world to European colonies. Many pietists also had powerful millenarian aspirations, hoping to achieve what they termed "God's Kingdom" on earth and bring about Christ's Second Coming through universal conversion.

In the eighteenth century, pietism grew into a broader movement of evangelical Protestantism, in which personal spiritual awakening was often understood as being "born again." (This is now the normal meaning of "evangelical" in English; in German, *evangelisch* simply means Protestant, picking up Luther's usage.) This rebirth was sometimes confirmed by baptism, as some evangelicals adopted the practice of baptizing believing adults instead of infants and came to call themselves "Baptists." Pietism and evangelicalism often split established churches in Europe and European colonies, with leaders in official churches condemning evangelicals as "enthusiasts." Evangelicals did not dispute that emotions were important in their religious life but saw this as a good thing. Theirs was "heart religion," in which anyone could become a true Christian through heartfelt devotion and personal experience.

Pietism and evangelicalism grew and spread at the same time that many educated Europeans were developing a worldview that increasingly emphasized reason rather than revelation, a self-conscious intellectual movement its proponents called the Enlightenment. The "light of reason," they argued, could be used against the darkness of prejudice, blind belief, ignorance, tyranny, and injustice. By the mid-eighteenth century, groups discussing and advocating for enlightened ideas could be found in cities across Europe and the Americas, with ideas about freedom, liberty, and rights circulating in all directions. These intellectual currents were one of the factors in the political revolutions of the later eighteenth century, Haitian, American, and French. Most Enlightenment thinkers did not contemplate extending natural rights or civil liberties to anyone other than white male property owners, but women, along with men of lower status and non-white men, argued that notions of universal rights should truly be universal.

This questioning of received wisdom extended to the realm of religion, as Enlightenment thinkers challenged the cultural and institutional authority of the Christian churches and criticized many beliefs and practices as "superstition." The Enlightenment and evangelical Protestantism are often portrayed as opposites and opponents, with one emphasizing reason and knowledge and the other emotion and belief. That idea is supported by the trajectories of these movements since the eighteenth century, but at the time there were many overlaps. Both pietists and Enlightenment thinkers opposed state churches and official hierarchies. Both emphasized the individual. Both produced works that churches and governments banned and censored. Both inspired women to act and write, which made most men in both movements uneasy or hostile.

The history of pietism is often written as the history of its male leaders, but it was really a grassroots movement of laypeople who met in prayer circles and study groups called conventicles, among whom were many women. Pietists regarded personal religious devotion as more important than theological training or holding an official clerical position in determining who was properly called by God, so that women often played important roles in pietist groups, just as they do today in religious groups that challenge the power of institutional hierarchies.

Johanna Eleonora von Merlau (1644–1724) came from a noble family but rejected life at court as superficial and moved to Frankfurt, where she taught girls and organized several mixed-gender pietist groups. She led them in reading and discussing Scripture and religious literature, something that women in the official Lutheran Churches, or even in many other pietist meetings, were not allowed to do. The Frankfurt city council became alarmed at this and asked her to leave the city. She did not, but several years later she married a pietist pastor, Johann Wilhelm Petersen, despite objections from her family because of his lower social status. They moved to northern Germany, where she began to write as well as teach, ultimately publishing fourteen religious books.

Petersen also published her autobiography, the first by a woman written in German to appear in print. She directly challenged the biblical admonition against women's teaching, writing that Paul had also said that "God's grace cannot be dampened or suppressed in a woman (1 Thessalonians 5:19). Rather, all spiritual gifts whether they appear in a man or a woman are worthy to be presented and applied to the common good."[30] In her autobiography, she describes herself as a spiritually awakened "doer of the Word," called by God in a series of visions "to raise my voice like a nightingale." Her culminating vision was of the Trinity with a female element: "With this picture the secret of the Holy Trinity, of the Father, Son, and Holy Ghost, who in the Hebrew language appears in the feminine gender like a fruit-bearing mother and a hatching dove, has come into [the Book of] Revelation."[31] Petersen here points to the fact that the word for "spirit" in biblical Hebrew is grammatically feminine, which led other Christian thinkers as well, including Syriac theologians in the fourth century and feminist theologians in the twentieth century, to use feminine language and maternal imagery when talking about the Holy Spirit.

Most pietist women were not visionaries, but all were expected to engage in daily devotions, and very occasionally we can get a glimpse of these. In a letter written in 1750, Katherine Stolberg, the sister of an important German lawyer and poet, described the intensity with which her mother, Christiane Charlotte Friederike Stolberg, prayed, beginning when she was a child:

> My mother was a true pray-er. She did not start a trip or any under-taking without praying; she did not start reading a book or writing a letter without praying. Wherever she went, she took the first moment that she was alone to drop on her knees or sit down, and with closed eyes—she opened them only to cast devout glances at the heavens—and folded hand she prayed. The presence of her children or her servants did not bother her; I am also certain that few of her friends have not seen her in prayer; yet it occurred to no one to become annoyed at this or to wonder about it. Her whole demeanor was so open and so natural, with no doubts in her belief and with such joy in her prayer. Her whole being was so lively, so cheerful, that it was impossible to have any doubts about her. I do not know if she ever wished to have a miraculous sign of belief, but a child-like belief was her element. From childhood on she had a very special view of providence when-ever she listened to prayers, and she wished only that her dear Father would fulfill her requests, not give signs or miracles.[32]

Pietism was a movement of personal spiritual experience and growth, but it was also outward-looking, as pietists saw education, charity work, and missionary endeavors as essential to bringing about God's Kingdom on earth. Well-off pietist women supported schools and orphanages in Europe, North America, and India, extending their maternal responsi-bilities outward. Supporters included regents and consorts in princely states, high nobility, ladies-in-waiting, wealthy educated urban resi-dents, and the abbesses and other female officials in Protestant convents.

One of their projects was the mission to Tamil people in the tiny Danish colony of Tranquebar on the southeast coast of India, begun in 1707. Women in Europe sent money, subscribed to the mission news-letter, mentioned the mission in their daily prayers, created special endowments for widows and orphans, and organized the collection of funds. They became godmothers for newly baptized Tamil believers—whose names they learned in mission newsletters—and paid for the schooling of able Tamil pupils who could eventually become teachers and expand the global mission even further. Most of the Tamil teachers, catechists, and what were called "Bible-helpers" were men, but some were women, mostly widows who worked as teachers in girls' schools or as prayer leaders and "Bible women." They could not be ordained as ministers, but they did hold official positions, with a salary, long before this was possible for women in Protestant churches in Europe.

The women who organized prayer circles and study groups have generally left little record of their lives, but one who has was Susanna Annesley (1669–1742), the youngest of twenty-five children of a minister in England. She married Samuel Wesley, a deacon and then a priest in the Church of England, and had nineteen children, including several sets of twins, about half of whom died in infancy. Thus for twenty years of her life she was almost always pregnant, though she did get a short break when her husband left her and the children for over a year because of a disagreement between them about whether God fully approved of King William as the successor to Charles II. Samuel was clearly a man who took God's views (and his own) very seriously, as only a fire that nearly burned down the rectory where Susanna and the children were living brought him back.

Through all of this, Susanna taught her children to read, using the Bible as her textbook, and then other subjects as well, often for as long as five hours a day. A second fire that did burn down the rectory scattered the children temporarily into other people's homes, and Susanna began writing letters to them with interpretations of verses in Scripture, dialogues about God, and other original works meant to provide spiritual guidance, along with more conventional prayers and motherly advice. The family reunited once the house was rebuilt, but Samuel left again, this time to London for the annual meetings of Anglican ministers, appointing temporary curates to preach the Sunday sermons while he was gone.

While Samuel was away in the winter of 1711–12, Susanna had what she described as a revelation:

At last it came into my mind. Though I am not a man, nor a minister of the gospel, and so cannot be engaged in such a worthy employment as they were, yet . . . I might do something more than I do. . . . I might pray more for *the people*, and speak with more warmth to those with whom I have an opportunity of conversing. However, I am resolved to begin with my own children.

This is exactly what she did, gathering her children and servants to sing psalms and listen to her read and discuss printed prayers and sermons, especially on Sunday evenings, as the curates held only brief Sunday morning services. Gradually neighbors who heard about this joined them, as she wrote to her husband, "for I dare deny none who ask admittance. Last Sunday I believe we had above two hundred, and yet many went away for want of room." The curate wrote angry letters to her husband complaining about this, especially because only twenty or so people showed up at his morning services. Samuel scolded her and told her to stop. Susanna replied that evening services were bringing individuals and families back to the church and seemed to be improving their behavior. She deftly combined expectations of wifely obedience and individual responsibility to God:

> If you do, after all, think fit to dissolve this assembly, do not tell me that you desire me to do this, for that will not satisfy my conscience; but send me your *positive command*, in such full and express terms as may absolve me from all guilt and punishment for neglecting this opportunity of doing good when you and I shall appear before the great and awful tribunal of our Lord Jesus Christ.[33]

In other words, she says: I will stop these services if you tell me to because I am your wife, but the negative results will be your fault, and God will know. Samuel let the evening services continue while he was gone. (See Plate IV.)

Among those in attendance at these Sunday evening services was Susanna's son, John Wesley (1703–1791), who with several others, including his younger brother Charles (also at his mother's services, though he was a young child), went on to found the religious movement known as Methodism. John became an Anglican minister, and remained one until he died, but he also encouraged people to deepen their spiritual lives outside of normal church services through intensive Bible study, prayer, self-examination, and moral discipline. He preached in the open to large crowds of people, especially in the growing factory and mining towns that lacked churches or schools.

Wesley organized his followers into small groups called "classes" for weekly meetings of prayer, Bible reading, hymn singing, and religious discussion led by lay leaders, exactly as he had seen his mother do. This structure gave leadership opportunities to quite ordinary people, including women, and also kept members in line, as they had to give an account of their journey toward perfect Christian love to the group each week.

A few laypeople began to preach in public as well as lead smaller meetings. In London, Sarah Crosby (1729–1804) and Mary Bosanquet (1739–1815) led Methodist classes and worked aiding orphans and the poor. They also gave spiritual testimony to large groups, and some members complained, citing the biblical Epistle to Timothy as a reason women should not teach others in public. In 1771 Bosanquet eloquently defended what she and Crosby were doing in a letter to Wesley, providing the first defense of women's preaching in Methodism: "I understand that text to mean no more than that a woman shall not take authority over her husband. . . . I do not apprehend it means she shall not entreat sinners to come to Jesus." To those who said a woman could perhaps do this occasionally, but only if she felt an "extraordinary call," she answered: "If I did not believe this was an extraordinary call, I would not act in an extraordinary manner—I praise God, I feel near him, and I prove his faithfulness every day."[34] Like Susanna Wesley, Bosanquet set obedience to God as a woman's highest obligation, and like Susanna Wesley, she was successful. John Wesley reluctantly approved her preaching. During the 1770s and 1780s, other women preached as well. A group of female preachers in the city of Leeds called itself, without irony, the "Female Brethren."

Methodists were ridiculed for allowing female preaching, and often criticized in gendered language—as "silly women"—because of women's active role, and because male and female Methodists engaged in emotional pious practices such as weeping, which observers saw as too feminine. An English observer of a German Methodist service in Philadelphia, for example, commented that there was "a hue and cry from all sides, particularly from the wenches."[35] Methodists were also suspect because they supported romantically based marriages between "soul-mates" (a term they invented), even if these conflicted with family wishes.

Among those who heard John Wesley preach was Nathaniel Gilbert, an English colonist home for a visit from his plantation on the Caribbean island of Antigua, and two enslaved African women from his household, probably Mary Alley and Sophia Campbell. Wesley baptized the women, who, he reported, "appeared to be much awakened." On returning to Antigua, Gilbert began to hold Sunday prayer services for members of his household, just as Susanna Wesley had done. On his death the women continued this. As one contemporary reported, "Evening and Morning [they] would convene a little church in their humble habitation." Alley and Campbell also raised money and organized workers to build a church on Antigua, the St. John Methodist Society, which grew to over a thousand members by 1783, almost all of them Black women, who also "have good gifts in Prayer and hold prayer meetings." A visiting English Methodist minister commented that he was "astonished by their eloquence and notions. Their abilities far exceed those of most of the women I have heard speak or pray in England."[36] From Antigua, Methodism spread to other islands in the Caribbean.

Methodist preachers and other evangelicals brought their message to Britain's North American colonies in the eighteenth century, particularly during the evangelical revival of the 1730s and 1740s, called the First Great Awakening, in which itinerant preachers urged their followers to repent, pray, and be reborn in Christ. (You can read about the Moravians, another pietist group important in the evangelical revival, in Chapter 6.) Revivalists often traveled to frontier and thinly populated areas where there were few churches and people rarely attended services at the ones there were. The First Great Awakening and subsequent similar revival movements rekindled interest in religion somewhat, though, in contrast to the popular view of church-going colonial Americans, in the eighteenth century most people in British North America were not church members.

Women responded to the evangelical revival by giving testimony about their own experiences and exhorting others to deepen their spiritual understanding and change their lives. Sarah Osborn (1714–1796), for example, a poor schoolteacher in Rhode Island with a husband unable to work and four children to support, wrote a spiritual memoir and then thousands of pages of diary and hundreds of letters filled with the daily experiences that shaped her understanding of God. She experienced a spiritual awakening in the 1740s and began holding regular meetings of what she termed the Female Society in her own home that met for decades. In the 1760s she also began meeting with Black residents of Newport one night a week, a group that included men. Teaching men led to criticism, but she defended herself in person and in letters, with claims similar to those of Argula von Grumbach and many other women in this book: God has called me to do this. She also noted that she could run these meetings, teach school, and still care for her family and household. The meetings continued until she was too weak to run them, and after she died her pastor edited and published some of her writings.

Black women exhorted as well as listened in evangelical meetings, and, not surprisingly, encountered resistance. Elizabeth, born into slavery in Maryland in 1766, felt a call to preach when she was in her forties "not by the commission of men's hands [but] if the Lord has ordained me, I need nothing better." She started holding meetings at a widow's house in Baltimore, but she was "rejected by the elders and rulers [and] hunted down in every place where I appointed a meeting . . . for my holding meetings contrary to discipline being a woman." She left Baltimore for itinerant preaching that took her as far as Canada and Michigan, where she opened a school for "colored orphans," continuing her ministry into her eighties.[37]

Other women also gave testimony and preached the Gospel in the mid-eighteenth century, holding meetings outdoors and in houses, to listeners that included women and men, enslaved and free. Their message was generally conservative, urging individual repentance, not social change or women's equal political or legal rights. They did not demand that seminaries be opened to women, or that women be ordained, though they sometimes defied their fathers and husbands, leaving home to travel and preach. Their actions were more dramatic than their words.

The early nineteenth century brought a movement to silence women preachers, Black or white, no matter how traditional their message. After John Wesley's death in 1791, Methodists became increasingly hostile toward a female ministry and, from 1803, women were restricted to addressing other women and then only under strict conditions. Some women continued to preach anyway, however, particularly in rural, frontier, and mission areas, as Methodism grew into the largest Protestant denomination in the English-speaking world. But other evangelical groups also became less open to women's public ministry, viewing the proper role for women as teaching Sunday school, not traveling from town to town preaching the gospel. As they sought to transform themselves into respectable Protestant denominations, evangelical groups excluded women from preaching, and later wrote women preachers out of their histories and forgot about them. Pressure from women for a greater role never went away, however, and increasingly included demands for theological training and formal leadership roles. In the twentieth century, many Methodist groups began to allow female preaching again, and in 1956 the United Methodist Church in the U.S. ordained its first women ministers.

RESISTING AND SURVIVING

Laywomen were actual mothers and church mothers in the early modern world, and some women religious were called "mother" as well, of course, as this was a title for abbesses or prioresses of convents and often for the leaders of other types of religious communities for women. Abbesses were generally elected by the nuns themselves, a practice that had begun in the early Middle Ages, many centuries before any laywomen could vote for their leaders.

Abbesses could not say Mass or hear confession, because the Catholic Church ruled these were functions only for ordained priests, but otherwise they managed the internal and external life of the very large household that was the convent. They corresponded with the convent's patrons whose financial support was essential, and with parents who wished to place their daughters in the convent. (Because novices generally brought a dowry when they entered a convent, parents were also patrons.) They oversaw male officials, such as bailiffs and stewards. In large convents, abbesses appointed women to assist them, including a bursar who controlled money, a cellarer who handled food and drink, and an instructor of novices. Besides professed nuns and novices, convents also housed lay sisters and servants, poorer women responsible for the physical needs of the residents while the nuns concentrated on spiritual matters. Convents often controlled large amounts of land, with jurisdiction over many subjects, and sometimes minted their own coinage or lent money, functioning as banks. The abbess was thus a position with great social prestige.

In Eastern Orthodoxy, including in Russia, abbesses could also have significant power. Monasticism in the Orthodox world was different from that in the Catholic Church in that each individual house developed its own set of rules for organization and behavior rather than follow a uniform rule of a religious order. Monks and nuns were expected to be unmarried, although married persons could also enter monasteries with their spouse's approval. Many monastery residents were widows or widowers who entered monasteries late in life, rather than life-long celibates. Upper-class widows and, more rarely, unmarried daughters, regarded the establishment of a convent as the perfect way to demonstrate both their devotion and authority.

We often call any woman religious a nun, but technically this refers to a woman who had taken the monastic vows of poverty, chastity, and obedience and lived in a community. Like cloistered monks and some other male clergy, nuns spent much of their day (and night) reciting the canonical hours, also called the "Divine Office," fixed-time prayers, psalms, and readings that marked the hours of the day. These were actions designed to glorify God and assist the salvation of souls, the primary religious functions of monastic communities. (Today many nuns who have taken vows live outside of monasteries and work in education, health care, and other types of jobs.) There were also communities of women who took less formal vows, who might be called "canonesses" or some other title, but otherwise operated much like convents. Both convents and canoness houses sometimes functioned as schools, with some of the girls staying to become nuns and some leaving to marry.

Abbesses in areas that became Protestant faced serious problems. Nearly every Protestant reformer rejected the value of celibacy and monastic vows, often in scathing words. Katharina von Bora, Marie Dentière, and many other nuns agreed, and left their convents. But other women wished to stay where they were, which put them at odds with local authorities and often with family members who had accepted Protestant teachings. Family members tried a variety of tactics to make the women change their minds, beginning with letters and moving on to shaming tactics, pressure, and sometimes violence. Abbesses countered with letters, diplomatic missions, and sometimes enormous personal bravery.

Bernhart Rem, a church organist in the south German city of Augsburg, sent letters to his sister Katherina and his daughter Veronika, trying to convince them to leave the Dominican St. Katharine's convent in the city. He published their exchange of letters as a small pamphlet in 1522, without the women's permission, to which Katherina responded:

My brother Bernhart,

You have wished us the correct understanding of Jesus Christ. We thank you for that. We hope we have the correct understanding of God. God will fortify us because we praise and favor him. You have sent us two letters, which I am returning to you. We regard you as one of the false prophets that Jesus warned us against in the Holy Gospels when he said "Guard yourselves against prophets who come in the form of a sheep and are ravening wolves." Therefore you have also come with many good words and wanted to lead us astray and make us despondent. You should not think that we are so foolish that we place our hope in the convent and in our own works. Rather we place our hope in God. He is the true lord and rewarder of all things. Him do we serve more willingly in the convent than in the world, with the grace and help of God. . . . I certainly know that you have said that your daughter and I are to you more as if we were in a brothel than in a convent. You should shame yourself in your heart to think [such a thing] to say nothing of saying this. Whoever hears this from you cannot think very well of you. There we certainly see the brotherly love that you have for us. And that you allowed [the letter] from us to be printed! . . . God forgive you for everything. That is our angry message, [that] the bitter suffering of Jesus Christ press in your heart. . . . If you want to straighten us out, then we don't want your [message] at all. You may not send us such things anymore. We will not accept them. We also [already] have many good books.[38]

Despite Katherina's objections to her earlier letter being made public, Bernhart immediately published this letter along with his much longer answer, calling life in the convent a "human lie . . . godless error," and "worthless straw . . . practiced with the fine glitter of holiness." Lively pamphlets like this, from educated but not especially prominent people, sold well in the early years of the Reformation, when people were trying to sort out their own religious convictions. Katherina and Veronika knew their own minds and remained in the convent.

In response to pressure such as this from families, the prioress of St. Katharine's convent in Augsburg, Veronika Welser (?–1531), wrote to both the pope and the emperor asking them to confirm her authority, which they did. As Protestant ideas spread more widely in the city, a few nuns left the convent, but most stayed, as accepting reforms was still a matter of personal choice. This changed in 1534, when Augsburg became more clearly Protestant. The city council suspended Mass, Catholic sermons, confession, and the reciting of the canonical hours in the convent. It forced the nuns to listen to Lutheran sermons, said they should stop wearing the Dominican habit, and agreed to provide a dowry for any nun who wanted to leave to marry. When the nuns were not very enthusiastic about these changes, the city council moved in nuns from other convents who were more open to Protestant ideas and installed a new prioress it had chosen. It declared that the convent was no longer a religious community bound by solemn vows, but a secular institution devoted to pious purposes that women were free to leave when they chose. But the previous Catholic prioress did not completely stop her official duties, nor did she leave.

Thus living in the small convent of St. Katharine's in the middle of the sixteenth century there were Catholic nuns wearing habits, reciting prayers and rituals in Latin, saying their rosaries, and fasting according to Catholic tradition, alongside Lutheran nuns singing hymns in German, reading Luther's works, and wearing ordinary clothing. There were also probably women who mixed these practices together. The older of those Lutheran nuns may previously have been Catholic, while the younger entered the convent after the Reformation. It may be odd for us to think about "Lutheran nuns," and for centuries both Catholic and Protestant historians tried to ignore them, the Catholics because these women were Lutherans, and the Lutherans because they were nuns. (Or at least unmarried women who lived in communities with religious and charitable purposes, whether or not they were technically "nuns.") But this pluri-confessional convent provides an example of openness and some level of religious toleration in a century when much of Europe was torn apart by religious wars, which began in the 1520s and were not really over until the end of the Thirty Years' War in 1648.

St. Katharine's was unusual, but not unique. Catholic and Protestant women lived together quite peacefully for decades in convents in the German territory of Brunswick, and they mixed religious practices. The distinction between Protestant and Catholic that is so important in understanding the religious history of sixteenth-century Europe may have ultimately been less important to the women living in convents than the distinction between their pattern of life and that of laywomen.

This situation was not to last in Augsburg. The city became Catholic again in the later sixteenth century, and Catholic parents were encouraged to send their daughters to St. Katharine's. This included Anna Jacobäa Fugger (1547–1587), from Augsburg's wealthiest and most powerful family, who entered as a teenager. Twenty years later, in 1582, Anna fled the convent and publicly accepted Lutheran doctrine, testifying in a legal inquiry that she had entered as a "young, naïve, thirteen-year-old," who "deferred to my blessed mother, who was under the influence of the Jesuits." She had wanted to leave many times, she testified, first "because of physical ailments," and, after reading Protestant works on convent life, for "the salvation of my poor soul, which would not have happened in this [convent] life."[39] Her brothers tried to force her to return, but she resisted, and several years later she married a Protestant nobleman. The scandalous circumstances of her departure and the prominence of her otherwise firmly Catholic family led church and city officials to stop the flow of letters and books in and out of the convent and prohibit visits by family members and friends. St. Katharine's became an ordinary enclosed Dominican convent.

In the south German city of Nuremberg, the Franciscan St. Klara convent also became a site of high drama. Here Caritas Pirckheimer (1467–1532) was the abbess. Very well educated as a humanist alongside her brother Willibald and her other sisters, Caritas entered the convent when she was sixteen, held several offices, and was elected abbess in 1503.

Luther's ideas were being discussed in the city as early as 1517, including by the Pirckheimer siblings. Willibald supported Luther, Caritas did not, and a letter she had written to her brother criticizing Luther's views was published (without her knowledge) in a 1523 pamphlet. The Nuremberg circle of humanists included the city's most famous artist, Albrecht Dürer, who was personally acquainted with Caritas and dedicated his woodblock print book *Life of Mary* to her. (Caritas's connection to Dürer led an art forger in the twentieth century to paint a portrait of her in Dürer's style that sold for nearly £50,000. The forgery is currently owned by the Metropolitan Museum of Art in New York, which explains on its website that it is modern and was artificially aged, and that it is no longer on display in the museum. The charming portrait still shows up on many websites about Caritas as painted by Dürer or someone in his circle in the sixteenth century. It wasn't.)

This was a tumultuous time in Nuremberg, and the St. Klara convent was in the middle of it. The city's major churches began holding Protestant services in 1524, and two of the city's male monasteries disbanded and deeded their property to the city. Relatives of women in the city's two female convents and the city council applied pressure on nuns to leave, but none did so. Caritas had written a chronicle of the early history of her convent, and as she now saw her convent in danger, she once again put pen to paper, reporting what was happening. The handwritten chronicle was preserved and later published as *Denkwürdigkeiten* (literally "things worthy of being remembered").

The city council forbade Catholic sermons and confession and sent Protestant preachers into the convent, but Caritas refused to allow them to speak. The council ordered the nuns to put aside their religious habits and provide an inventory of convent property, with an eye to closing the convent and confiscating its property. Residents of the city gathered outside the convent walls, shouting and throwing stones. Mothers of three of the nuns entered the convent like "wild she wolves," demanding that the young women be released. The young women refused "with great weeping, crying, entreating, and imploring, but there was less pity for them than in hell . . . Katharina Ebner said to her mother: 'You are a mother of my flesh, but not of my spirit, because you did not give me my soul.' . . . Each mother argued with her daughter, for a while promising her much and for a while threatening her." The scene became increasingly violent:

> They heard the great fighting, tugging, and dragging accompanied by the loud crying and weeping of the children. Each of them was pulled by four people—two in front pulling, two behind pushing— so that little Ebner and little Tetzel fell on one another in a heap on the threshold, and the poor little Tetzel had her foot almost worn away. The wicked wives stood there and conjured their daughters out in the name of all the devils. . . . Then there arose an unbelievable crying, wailing, and weeping before they ripped off the clothing of the Holy Order and dressed them in secular clothes. . . . Ebner's wife had hit little Kathy in the mouth so that it had begun to bleed and bled the whole way. . . . Little Kathy got out in front of the Ebners' door at the fruitmarket; she clapped her hands together on her head and with great weeping complained to the people how it had taken place against their wills with violence and injustice.[40]

Luther's friend and associate Philip Melanchthon visited Nuremberg several months after this spectacle and advised the city council against any more forcible removal of nuns. The council questioned the nuns individually, hoping to convince some to leave, but ultimately only one of sixty nuns did so. The council decided instead to let the convent die out naturally by prohibiting the acceptance of new novices, and slowly confiscated its property. At Caritas's death, first her sister and then her niece became abbess, but neither of these women was the dynamic and vocal champion of convent life that Caritas was. The last nun died in 1591, the convent was closed and its church became a Protestant parish church.

Pressure to reform convents along Protestant lines came from outside the convents in Augsburg and Nuremberg and most other places, but sometimes it came from inside. At the convent of St. Mary Magdalene the Penitent in Freiberg, Duchess Ursula of Münsterberg (1491/1495–1534 or later), a member of the highest nobility who had entered the convent as a child, became convinced of the truth of Lutheran teachings. She attempted to reform the convent, securing a Lutheran preacher, encouraging nuns to read and discuss Lutheran works, and persuading them to stop reciting the hours and fasting. Because of Ursula's high social standing, the prioress of the convent, Katharina Freiberg (?–1529) was unable to stop these changes, but she was successful in preventing a full reform. Ursula left the convent in 1528, went to Wittenberg and met Luther, who arranged for the publication of a tract she had written against monastic vows, and then reprinted it with an afterword he had written. By this point, hundreds of women had left their convents, but Ursula was the most socially prominent of these. Prioress Freiberg answered her in a letter defending convent practices, though this was never published. The prioress's hopes were realized to some degree, however, as even though the territory in which the convent was located became Protestant, the convent itself remained pluri-confessional until the last nun died in 1580.

What happened in St. Katharine's, St. Klara, and St. Mary Magdalene happened in convents in many other areas that became Protestant as well, including Scandinavia and Germany. Nuns were forced to listen to daily Protestant sermons, denied confessors and Catholic ceremonies, and even dragged out by their families. The authorities hoped this would convince them to leave or disband, and in some cases it did. But many convents fought as long as they could. At the convent at Vadstena in Sweden, nuns stuffed wool and wax in their ears when they were forced to attend Lutheran services. Nuns at the north German convent of Lüne lit old felt slippers to drive the preacher out with smoke, sang during his sermons, and when ordered to be quiet recited their rosaries. Nuns in Medingen locked the convent door and took refuge in the chapel, forcing the Protestant duke who controlled the area to have a hole bashed in the chapel wall so that the preacher could speak through this. Convents were more vocal and resolute opponents of the Protestant Reformation

86

than were male monasteries, and their contemporaries recognized this. As a papal representative reported, "the four women's convents [in Magdeburg] have remained truer to their beliefs and vows than the men's monasteries, who have almost all fallen away."[41]

Protestant authorities in some areas gave up their direct attacks and allowed the women to stay, though they generally forbade the taking in of new novices so the convents slowly died out. In this more gradual process, they were sometimes supported by Protestant family members of women in convents, who suddenly realized the practical problems closing a convent would cause. As six noblemen who wrote to one of the dukes of Brunswick when he was contemplating closing the convents in his territory put it, "What would happen to our sisters' and relatives' honor and our reputation if they are forced to marry renegade monks, cobblers, and tailors?"[42] Although these men were Lutheran themselves, they were clearly not eager for their female family members to marry a "renegade monk" as Katharina von Bora had done. Becoming a pastor's wife was an enormous decrease in status for someone who had been an abbess, unthinkable for these noblemen or for women who had held convent leadership positions themselves.

In a few parts of Germany, Protestant authorities could not even accomplish a gradual closure. Led by their abbesses, the nuns' firmness, combined with family opposition and other religious and political factors, allowed many convents to survive for decades or even centuries as Catholic establishments within Protestant territories.

Other convents survived as religious institutions by accepting Lutheran theology except for its rejection of the monastic life. This was particularly true with what are termed "free imperial convents," convents or canoness houses within the Holy Roman Empire that had no secular overlord except the emperor. Some abbesses energetically intro-duced Protestant teachings into their territories. Elisabeth von Weida (1504–1576), the abbess of Gernrode in Saxony, sent a representative to the Diet of Worms in 1521, the imperial diet (a deliberative assembly similar to a parliament) of the Holy Roman Empire called by Emperor Charles V in the city of Worms. Charles had summoned Luther to attend and speak, and Elisabeth wanted a first-hand report about what Luther was saying. She began to name Protestant pastors to all the churches under her control in 1525, expecting the new teaching to bring a further deepening of the spiritual life in her convent and the territory she controlled.

Anna von Stolberg (1515–1574), the abbess of the free imperial abbey of Quedlinburg, governed a sizable territory, including nine churches and two male monasteries. When she became Protestant in the 1540s, she made all priests swear to accept Luther's ideas and turned her Franciscan monastery into an elementary school for both boys and girls, an interesting gender reversal of what was the usual pattern of male authorities transforming female convents into schools or using convent property to fund (male, of course) scholars at universities. Later abbesses of Quedlinburg continued to make religious changes. Abbess Anna Sophia issued a new baptism ordinance in 1680, and Abbess Anna Dorothea issued an "edict against the separatists"—that is, those who wished to leave the Lutheran state church—in 1700. Gernrode and Quedlinburg were joined by others. Fourteen convents in the territory of Brunswick/ Lüneburg that had been pluri-confessional into the seventeenth century became fully Lutheran, several of which remain Protestant religious communities of unmarried women today.

In England, King Henry VIII and his chief minister Thomas Cromwell dissolved the monasteries and convents in the 1530s as part of their measures to remove the English Church from papal jurisdiction. They transferred monastery assets to the royal treasury and later disbursed them to Henry's supporters. Some of the roughly 1,700 nuns received tiny pensions, while others fled to Catholic parts of the continent, as you will see in Chapter 3. Some abbesses did oppose the closures, though mostly through letters and diplomacy rather than the physical actions that were common in Germany. Margaret Vernon, for example, was the prioress of four different abbeys in succession from 1509 to 1538, and a friend of Thomas Cromwell, who sent his young son to her for schooling for a year. She wrote often to Cromwell as the process of closure was unfolding, hoping to avoid this or slow it down for the houses that she governed. Once it became clear this was impossible, she asked that she be allowed to sell off some of the convent lands "in order with the money to provide for her sisters instead of their pensions, pay off her servants, and buy for herself a living with such of her friends as will take her. If not, she begs that each of her sisters may have £4. a year pension, and herself £50. a year out of certain lands."[43] She was not allowed to sell convent lands, but the women from her house did receive a slightly larger pension than the average of £2 a year, and she herself received £40. Records show that she drew this pension at least until 1546, six years after Cromwell had been executed by Henry VIII on trumped-up charges of treason and heresy.

NEW ORDERS AND CONFRONTING THE JESUITS

Abbesses and other leaders of women's religious communities in Catholic areas were not threatened with violence or the closure of their houses, but they also confronted challenges. Medieval reform movements within the Catholic Church had always emphasized the importance of enclosure and strict standards of piety for women religious, but by the fifteenth century many houses were no longer following these rules. This is not surprising, as some convent residents were not there willingly but had been placed in a convent by their parents and had no religious vocation. This included women from wealthy families, who continued to live largely as they would outside the convent, entertaining visitors, eating fancy food, and leaving the convent to visit family and friends. Reform-minded abbesses, leaders of the orders with which the convents were affiliated, and sometimes secular political leaders attempted to prevent such behavior and enforce stricter rules of enclosure and higher stand-ards of spirituality. As you read in Chapter 1, Queen Isabel of Castile did exactly this in her drive to enhance devotion and piety among the Spanish clergy.

These fifteenth-century reforms had both positive and negative effects on women religious. On the negative side, decreased contact with the outside world led to fewer opportunities to get donations, especially as most benefactors preferred to give donations to a male house whose residents could say Mass. As a result, many women's houses became poorer. Not every nun agreed with the changes, and there were often bitter struggles over rules and leadership positions. On the positive side, the reforms often built a strong sense of group cohesion among the resi-dents and gave many nuns a greater sense of the spiritual worth of their lives, particularly if an abbess herself had led the reform. Because of their reinvigorated spiritual life, reformed convents were often the most vocal and resolute opponents of the Protestant Reformation in areas where it was introduced. (This can be confusing, as a "reformed" convent means one that followed stricter standards of Catholic observance, not one that became Protestant.)

The Council of Trent, the Catholic Church council that met between 1545 and 1563 to respond to the Protestant challenge and define what Catholic positions would be on matters of doctrine and discipline, re-affirmed the necessity of the cloister for all women religious, though enforcement came slowly. As they had in the fifteenth century, some abbesses and nuns supported reforms that brought more rigorous rules. The best known of these is St. Teresa of Avila, the mystic and reformer you will meet in Chapter 5. Other houses fought moves to wall them up. The nuns of the Venetian convent of San Zaccaria, for example, threw rocks at the bishop's men sent to weld shut their gateway. Still others thought new measures unnecessary. María de San José (1548–1603), a prioress in St. Teresa's Discalced Carmelite order, wrote in an advice manual to nuns that increasing the physical trappings of enclosure was far less important than improving internal spiritual discipline. "To reduce all reform to closing doors, bending bars [a reference to grilles on convent windows]," she wrote, "is nothing more than removing from our hands something that damages us, but what is damaged is not reme-died."[44] She noted that the rules already in place provided enough direc-tion for nuns on how they ought to behave.

Other women thought that the best devotional life was one connected to the world rather than cut off from it. In the 1540s, Isabel Roser (?–1554), a Catalan noblewoman from Barcelona, decided to seek papal approval for an order of religious women that would be out in the world engaged in charity and spiritual work. Roser had been an early supporter of Ignatius Loyola, the founder of the Jesuits, in Barcelona. After she was widowed, she traveled to Rome and helped the Jesuits establish a home for former prostitutes there, a very common form of charitable endowment. She saw her group as a women's order of Jesuits that, like the Jesuits, would devote itself to education, care of the sick, and assistance to the poor and, in so doing, perhaps win converts back to Catholicism.

Pope Paul III did allow Roser and two companions to take vows as Jesuits in 1545, but Loyola was horrified at this, and several months later he successfully petitioned the pope to release the women from their vows. (No woman has been a member of the Jesuit order since.) He also forbade the Jesuits from directing women's religious orders, the way the Dominicans, Franciscans, and other religious orders did. Despite this, Roser's group continued to grow in Rome and in the Netherlands, spreading Loyola's teaching with the Jesuit catechism. Her followers were still active into the seventeenth century, for in 1630 Pope Urban VIII published a bull to suppress them and reported that they were building convents and choosing abbesses.

Some women and the communities they established figured out ways to work around rules of enclosure. One was by remaining laywomen rather than professed nuns who took vows. During the Middle Ages, poor women who could not afford the dowry required for a convent sometimes chose to live communally in informal religious groups, supporting themselves by weaving, sewing, or caring for the sick. Some women who felt a special religious calling remained with their families, devoting themselves to helping others, fighting heresy, or prayer. Some joined Franciscan or Dominican third-order groups, laywomen affiliated with a religious order but who did not take formal vows. Such women are often called "tertiaries," from the Latin word for third. The Church sometimes regarded these women as suspect because they did not take formal vows and were not always under direct male supervision, but it generally allowed them to continue their lives as pious laywomen.

Angela Merici (*c.* 1474–1540), an extremely devout woman in Brescia, Italy, had lived much of her life as a Franciscan tertiary. When she was about sixty, she gathered a group of like-minded women around her, generally from artisan families, and founded what she termed the Company of St. Ursula in 1535, named after a legendary fourth-century saint who supposedly fled her homeland to escape an unwanted marriage and was eventually martyred, along with her 11,000 virginal companions. Merici identified with the biblical figure of Judith—the Jewish widow who cut off the head of the tyrant Holofernes to free the Jewish people from his power—as well as St. Ursula. In her rules for the Company, she wrote: "*Come on, valiant daughters*, let us all embrace this holy Rule. . . .

And *armed with its sacred precepts, let us behave in a virile way*, that we too, like holy Judith, having *courageously cut off the head of Holofernes*, that is, of the devil, may gloriously return to our heavenly home."[45]

Members of the Company of St. Ursula were laywomen who lived a life of prayer, penance, and devotion, engaging in charitable activities but not wearing distinctive clothing or taking vows. In Merici's plan, the Company was to be run entirely by women, under an elected General Mother. After Merici's death, the Company gained papal approval and, in the latter part of the sixteenth century, spread throughout the cities of northern Italy, as Ursulines conveyed their ideas personally and through their writing.

Reforming bishops in the era after the Council of Trent were intent on enclosing women monastics, but many of them saw the Ursulines as a way to enhance lay piety, both among the women who were its members and among those they served. Bishops approved Companies in the areas under their control and wrote new rules for them. These praised the Ursulines' role in the education of girls and moral reform of families, but also put restrictions on them, requiring them to wear distinctive clothing, take vows of chastity, and come under firmer control of male clergy. In the bishops' rules for the Company, they were no longer valiant daughters of Judith out to fight the devil, but weak women whose virginity was "a precious treasure in a fragile vase of glass," threatened from all sides. Some bishops required them to live communally, although they were still not fully cloistered.

From northern Italy, the Company of Ursulines spread throughout the rest of Italy and into France and began to focus completely on the education of girls. Some houses became part of a religious order of Ursulines, combining a contemplative life and teaching behind convent walls. They were so popular that noble and other wealthy families began to send their daughters to Ursuline houses for an education, including girls who were destined for marriage and those who intended to become nuns themselves. Merici's original idea of a group of uncloistered laywomen was not completely lost, however, as the Ursulines continued to found Companies as well as convents throughout Europe and beyond. (The Company still exists in more than twenty countries, now called the Secular Institute of St. Angela Merici, or Angelines, and the order in more than thirty, with most members in both involved in teaching.)

Other women also established groups that attempted to combine piety and an active mission in the world, though these were eventually restricted as well. Jeanne de Chantal (1572–1641), a noble French widow, and Francis de Sales (1567–1622), a Catholic bishop, established the Order of the Visitation of Holy Mary in 1610 in Annecy, a town in France near Geneva. The group combined spiritual devotions within convent walls and benevolent work assisting the sick and poor outside of them. They explicitly used the Virgin Mary as their model, naming their group the Visitation as a reference to Mary's visit to her cousin Elizabeth during Elizabeth's pregnancy with John the Baptist, which brought her comfort and revealed that both women would give birth to extraordinary sons. The order was to be open to older women and those who themselves were in poor health and could not endure the traditional monastic rigors of little sleep and fasting. Their public outreach lasted eight years, and then Visitation houses were ordered to accept cloistering or be closed. This cloistered form of the Visitation spread across France and beyond, though in the twentieth century some Visitation houses again began to operate schools and care facilities.

The Daughters of Charity (now often called the Sisters of Charity), begun in 1633 by Louise de Marillac (1591–1660), the illegitimate daughter of a French noble, and Vincent de Paul (1581–1660), a French priest, was more successful in resisting enclosure. Although both founders privately thought of the group as a religious community, they realized that outwardly maintaining secular status was the only thing that would allow them to serve the poor and ill. The Daughters took no public vows, did not wear religious habits, and constantly stressed that they would work only where invited by a bishop or priest. This subversion of the rules was successful, for the Daughters of Charity received papal approval and served as the model for other women's communities that emphasized nursing, educating girls, and serving the poor. As Louise de Marillac, whom the Daughters called "mother," wrote: "If the work to be done is considered political, it seems men must undertake it; if it is considered a work of charity, then women may undertake it."[46] The Daughters required only a small fee for women to join rather than the full dowry that convents required, which made them open to women of artisan and middle-class families.

Within a decade, the Daughters were staffing hospitals, prisons, hospices, and orphanages across northern France, negotiating with bishops and other church and state officials to maintain their ability to work freely out in the world. They served as the model for other women's religious communities, which together handled most of girls' education in France and staffed many of its hospitals. By 1700, numerous teaching and charitable congregations had been founded throughout Catholic Europe, often backed by larger women's religious confraternities that supported them financially. The Council of Trent sought to restrict women's options, but groups such as the Daughters of Charity enhanced women's physical mobility and vocational possibilities.

Measures to enhance spiritual observance within convents continued into the seventeenth century. Angélique Arnauld (1591–1661), the teen-aged abbess at the Cistercian convent of Port-Royal, decided in 1609 that the convent should become stricter in its observance of Cistercian rules. The nuns gave up private property and eating meat, wore simple clothing, did manual labor, observed strict cloister, and spent several hours a day in silent mental prayer and meditation. Nuns from Port-Royal became renowned for their piety, and their help was sought all over France for the reform of convent discipline. The abbey then became the spiritual center in France of what was known as Jansenism, a movement based on the ideas of Cornelius Jansen (1585–1638), the bishop of Ypres in the Spanish Netherlands. Jansen advocated greater personal piety, spiritual regeneration, lay reading of and meditation on Scripture, and scrupulous attention to morality, ideas that fit with those of Angélique Arnauld and also with the pietist movement among Protestants.

The pope condemned Jansenism in several papal bulls in the 1660s, asserting that it put too much emphasis on God's grace and downplayed the role of the Church, and thus was close to being Protestant. The Jesuits agreed, as did King Louis XIV, who ordered all members of the French Catholic Church to sign a statement indicating their adherence to the bulls. The Port-Royal nuns refused. Angélique's sister Agnés Arnauld (1593–1672) had taken over as abbess, and she responded: "I know it is not the place of nuns to defend the truth, but since bishops have the courage of nuns, nuns must have the courage of bishops."[47] (See Plate V.) The nuns also skillfully used stereotypes of women's weakness and duty of obedience, pointing out that, as women, they were clearly not capable of making judgments about theological matters on which learned men disagreed. The apostle Paul's letters in the Bible had ordered women to keep silent on matters of theology, they wrote, so they were simply obeying Paul rather than the king. The archbishop of Paris fumed: "These sisters are as pure as angels, but as proud as devils." In their use of gendered stereotypes to their advantage, they may have learned from the writings of Teresa of Avila, whose work had been translated into French and whom the Arnauld sisters greatly admired.

A truce with the papacy quieted the debate for several decades, but in 1705 the Port-Royal nuns were ordered to accept another anti-Jansenist papal bull. They again refused. Several years later Louis XIV sent soldiers to occupy the convent and banished the last seventeen old nuns to other houses. The soldiers demolished the convent, even scattering the bones in the cemetery so that it did not become a pilgrimage site. The writings of the Port-Royal nuns became part of a body of Jansenist literature that continued to circulate. Despite opposition from Jesuits, the pope, and the king, Jansenist women and men read the Bible and held underground prayer meetings. Women appear to have read and commented on Scripture at these meetings, and were imprisoned for distributing forbidden Jansenist literature. Despite its official prohibition, Jansenism continued to shape the religious life of many women in France, encouraging them not only to become literate but to become frequent readers, to develop their children's spiritual lives through family devotions, and to accept Catholic doctrine not simply as a matter of emotional commitment and habit, but also of intellectual conviction.

Angélique and Agnés Arnauld were not the only abbesses to oppose the Jesuits. At just about the same time in Ethiopia, a nun from a noble family, Walatta Petros (1592–1642), led opposition to the Jesuits that ultimately resulted in their being banished from the country. Christianity had come to Ethiopia in biblical times, and the Ethiopian Christian Church (officially the Ethiopian Orthodox Tewahedo Church) followed its own patterns, independent of Rome or the Orthodox Church in Constantinople. Intellectual leadership in the Ethiopian Church tended to come from monks and nuns, rather than priests or church officials.

In the late sixteenth century, Jesuit missionaries were sent to Ethiopia with orders to convert the king to loyalty to Rome. Interested in Catholicism and hoping for Portuguese military assistance, King Susenyos converted, first privately and then in 1621 publicly, dismissing all his wives except one as a sign of his new allegiance. He forbade the teaching of Ethiopian Christianity and attempted to forbid religious practices that deviated from Catholic ones. Most noblemen followed the king, but many women did not, perhaps because religious practices that were important to them, such as the circumcision of boys and traditions regarding food, were outlawed.

One of these women was Walatta Petros, who had married one of the king's commanders when she was sixteen and had three children, all of whom died as infants. When her husband converted to Catholicism, she left him and became a nun, despite his violent threats to harm her and others if she did. She traveled around the country protesting the abandonment of traditional Ethiopian Christianity, calling out the king and his advisers. According to a seventeenth-century biography written by one of her followers, "she exhorted the people of the town not to accept the filthy faith of Leo [that is, Roman Catholicism] and not to mention the name of the apostate king during the Liturgy since he was outside the true faith and accursed."[48] King Susenyos threatened her family and arrested and imprisoned her three times.

Walatta Petros resisted efforts to convert her to Catholicism, and was finally exiled to Sudan, north of Ethiopia, along with others. These included Eheta Kristos, a woman Walatta Petros had become friends with when she first became a nun and who became her life-long companion. As her biographer reported, the two "lived together in mutual love, like soul and body. From that day onward, the two did not separate, neither in times of tribulation and persecution nor in those of tranquility, but only in death."[49] Today we might interpret this as indicating a romantic or sexual relationship, but that was unlikely, as both women were devoted to celibacy and practiced strict asceticism, avoiding all pleasures of the flesh.

In Sudan, Walatta Petros set up a religious community for both nuns and monks. In 1632, King Susenyos reversed his opinion and restored the independent Ethiopian Church as the state religion. The Jesuits were expelled the next year. Walatta Petros returned from Sudan and established six more religious communities in northern Ethiopia, known for their rigorous discipline, which she headed until her death.

The nuns and monks in the communities Walatta Petros had established shared her life story orally, and thirty years after her death they ordered a young monk to write it down, which is how we know so many details about her life. The text, designed to assist in the efforts to make her a saint, was recopied many times. The campaign was successful, as Walatta Petros later became a saint in the Ethiopian Church.

Walatta Petros might seem very different from Caritas Pirckheimer or Angélique Arnaud, but all three women, and many other abbesses, confronted male authorities, including members of their own families, secular rulers, and religious leaders. They affirmed the value of their own religious traditions despite threats and violence, provided leadership to the women in their communities, and became models and inspirations to others at the time and since.

Through their words and actions, the biological and spiritual mothers in this chapter created long-lasting models for women. The first generation of Protestant pastors' wives supported their husbands' ministry, and also carved out a somewhat independent role for themselves in education, music, and charitable work. Protestant church mothers affirmed that God had called them to speak out and to write, giving them a responsibility to the larger community that extended to care for the ill, prisoners, children, and the poor. Recusant women defended their faith with inspired words and physical bravery, as did abbesses confronted by angry Protestant authorities and violent family members. Reforming abbesses deepened the spiritual life of their convents, and founders of new types of teaching and charitable congregations combined intense spirituality and an active mission in the world. Women created institutions that have lasted until today, including religious orders and communities within Catholicism and Ethiopian Christianity, and organizations with a variety of educational and charitable purposes within Protestant churches.

The women in this chapter were, as Johanna Petersen put it, "doers of the Word." At least in their writings and their statements recorded by others, they had little doubt about their responsibilities to God and to others. As Mary Bosanquet put it: "If I did not believe this was an extraordinary call, I would not act in an extraordinary manner." "[I write] as a member of the Christian Church, against which the gates of Hell cannot prevail," wrote Argula von Grumbach. They extended this to other women as well. "If God has given grace to some good women," wrote Marie Dentière, "it would be too bold to try to stop them, and it would be too foolish to hide the talent that God has given to us." Many of them understood themselves to be going beyond the normal expectations for women, to take on masculine roles. It was a time, wrote Agnés Arnauld, when "nuns must have the courage of bishops," when village women, wrote Katharina Zell, must "take on the manly Abraham-like courage." "Let us behave in a virile way," wrote Angela Merici to her followers, "that we too, like holy Judith . . . may gloriously return to our heavenly home."

This chapter is filled with actions as well as words that my students over the years have found surprising and inspiring: The nuns in Lüne lighting old felt slippers to drive away the Protestant preacher; Katharina von Bora brewing beer and pruning fruit trees during the day, and discussing religious issues at night; Argula von Grumbach challenging university faculty to debate with her; Dorothy Lawson providing Catholic rituals during childbirth to women who wanted them and writing "Jesus" in big letters on the side of her house; Margaret Ball harboring priests and teaching servants; Methodist "female Brethren" preaching in Leeds and building churches in Antigua; the Port-Royal nuns and Walatta Petros refusing to obey royal orders despite intimidation and banishment. As my students would put it: whoever expected nuns, or noblewomen, or Methodist ministers, or *Luther's wife* to be badass?

The women in this chapter deserve celebration, and some have received it. Angela Merici, Jeanne de Chantal, Louise de Marillac, and Walatta Petros are saints, and Margaret Ball is blessed. Though Protestants don't have saints, Katharina von Bora and Susanna Wesley practically wear halos in inspirational biographies written for girls. But their lives also deserve critical reflection. My students are generally less celebratory of women who chose to support or even enhance restrictions on their mobility rather than fighting them or figuring out how to get around them. So it is good to think about why the contemplative life, and even cloistering, might have been so appealing to the women who advocated for these. Pietist, Methodist, and Jansenist women all read and meditated on the Bible for themselves instead of depending on clergy to interpret it. But the message they took was largely one of individual repentance, not social change. The women in this chapter used their roles as actual or spiritual mothers to advocate for an expanded role in the larger community, a line of argument that many later women's rights groups around the world would use as well (and still do). Other women have seen limits in this emphasis on motherhood and instead based their calls for wider opportunities for women on ideas about individual human rights, rather than on actual or metaphorical female biology.

CHAPTER THREE

MIGRANTS

You have no power over my body, neither can you do me any harm—
for I am in the hands of the eternal Jehovah, my Saviour . . . and I do
verily believe that he will deliver me out of your hands.

Anne Hutchinson, New England Puritan leader

There is no such difference between men and women that women
may not do great things as we have seen by the example of many
saints . . . it seems that the female sex also in its own measure, should
and can undertake something more than ordinary in this great
common spiritual undertaking.

Mary Ward, English founder of the Institute of the
Blessed Virgin Mary

As the Protestant and Catholic Reformations unfolded, every political
authority in Christian Europe developed a policy of religious uniformity
and sought to purge ideas, objects, and people considered religiously
alien. The suppression of ideas judged religiously deviant, and the use
of violence to wipe them out, had not been unknown in medieval Europe,
but the extent of both increased significantly in the sixteenth century.
Those whose religious identity differed from that of those in power were
often given a choice: join or leave. Mass expulsions actually began in
1492, when first Jews and then Muslims were banished from Spain, and

hundreds of thousands left. They were soon joined as refugees by English Catholics, French Protestants, German and Dutch radicals, and a host of others, setting a pattern of religious migration and exile that continued for centuries, and came to stretch across the Atlantic. More than a million Europeans of different religious persuasions went into exile between the 1490s and the 1750s, some traveling only a short distance and some thousands of miles. They joined millions of other people on the move in the early modern world, an era marked by a rapidly increasing level of global interaction involving people, ideas, and goods.

In addition, the Reformations brought with them more than one hundred years of religious war, ultimately involving nearly all of Europe and further increasing the stream of migrants. What we might term "round one" of these wars, from 1529 to 1555, involved Catholics and several kinds of Protestants in Switzerland and Germany; round two, from 1560 to 1609, involved Catholics and Calvinist Protestants in France and the Netherlands; and round three, the Thirty Years' War from 1618 to 1648, involved nearly all of Europe. Added to refugees and war victims were those who chose to move for reasons that were often a blend of religious, economic, and familial factors. As the religious dissenters known as Pilgrims who came to Massachusetts in 1620 put it, their goal was to "serve their God and to Fish." The lines between different types of migrants were fluid and changing, as refugees became settlers, émigrés turned into permanent exiles, deportees became colonists and then deportees again.

Women and girls moved for religious reasons, on their own or as members of families or religious communities. Jewish and Muslim exiles from the Iberian peninsula included women and girls, traveling alone or with their families. Anabaptists and other groups that developed ideas most Christians viewed as radical (and thus dangerous) were forced to leave Switzerland, Austria, Germany, and the Netherlands, moving to Moravia in today's Czech Republic or further east. Sometimes only the men in these groups moved, hoping that this would be a temporary exile, while women kept farms and businesses going, but generally women and children moved as well. Quaker women chose to travel to places where they could spread their ideas and suffered banishment and exile when they did, as did other women who criticized the religious teachings of those in power. Migrants included nuns exiled from Protestant lands, nuns hoping to evangelize as the Jesuits did, and nuns who crossed the Atlantic and Pacific to establish convents and teach girls.

Travel in the early modern world primarily meant walking, with perhaps a cart to carry some goods along with very young children and the old and infirm. Roads and paths were unpaved and had few sign-posts. Cities and towns generally had inns for travelers, if you could afford these, although they were rough places for women traveling on their own, or even for families. Overnight stays might instead mean sleeping near the cart, under a tree, or in a barn or shed. Travel by sea involved going to a port, finding a willing captain and ship, and setting a price, or finding an agent who could arrange this. Ships might provide drinking water, firewood, and access to a communal cooking stove for their passengers. Everything else was usually up to the traveler, including bedding, clothing, cooking utensils, and all food, some of which went on board as live animals, especially chickens and sheep. The actual voyage—which could take months—brought storms, disease, seasickness, rats, spoiled food, brackish water, crowded accommodations, physical discom-fort, and, for women, childbirth while on board. Travel was not for the squeamish or the faint-hearted.

JEWS LEAVE SPAIN

The first mass migration for religious reasons resulted in part from deci-sions made by a woman, Queen Isabel of Castile, as you have read in Chapter 1. The Inquisition that she and King Ferdinand established targeted converts from Judaism, charging them with Judaizing, that is, being secretly still Jewish because they engaged in Jewish practices.

Converts did not dare attend Jewish schools or places of worship—which declined in number in any case—so activities in the home were particularly scrutinized, with household servants called in as witnesses and informers. As the home was traditionally women's domain, women were actually more often charged with Judaizing by the Inquisition than were men. *Conversas*—women converts—were accused of maintaining the Jewish Sabbath by cleaning the house on Friday, lighting candles on Friday evening, and avoiding cooking or spinning on Saturday. They were charged with following Jewish dietary regulations by not cooking or serving their families pork or rabbit, or by slaughtering animals or chickens following kosher practices. They were accused of not fasting on Christian holidays or sleeping apart from their husbands while menstruating.

Along with these domestic traditions, some were accused of actions that were more clearly religious, such as observing Jewish holidays with fasts or prayers, or throwing a bit of bread dough into the fire as a symbolic donation to the Temple in Jerusalem. Words as well as actions could get women in trouble: a woman named Constanza Díaz, for example, was charged with refusing to eat birds killed in a Christian manner, but also with publicly claiming that the Inquisition burned *conversos* not because of heresy, but because it wanted their property.

Women also invented new rituals, including "un-baptizing" children by washing off holy water or baptismal oil on the return home from the baptismal font. A young woman in late fifteenth-century Guadalupe, for example, reported that two women came to her mother right after her brother had been born, "and they brought a small pot of warm water and closed the door, and then this witness heard the child cry; and this was the day that it had been baptized, and she knows they washed the oil and chrism off of the baby. . . . And this witness also knows it, because she and her mother have discussed it, and her mother has confessed to her that it is true."[1] Washing off baptismal oil had no roots in Jewish traditions, nor was it seen as effective by Christians, for whom baptism could never be undone. But the women who washed the baby clearly thought it important.

Conversas responded to accusations in different ways, as the thousands of trial records reveal. When brought before the Inquisition, some argued that they were fully Christian and had been for generations, denying all charges. Others confessed to their actions but said these were the result of meticulous housekeeping or simply cultural traditions. Others confessed but said they had been misled.

After the conquest of Granada in 1492, many Spanish Jews and *conversos* went to Portugal, but within a year they were often arrested, enslaved, and sold. Several thousand Spanish children, aged two to twelve, were forcibly separated from their parents, enslaved, baptized,

and shipped off to the new Portuguese colonies on the largely uninhab-
ited islands of São Tomé and Príncipe off the coast of West Africa. Only
600 are reported as having survived. Those who grew to adulthood
intermarried with enslaved Africans, becoming a racially diverse population that grew and processed sugar for European landowners. At the end
of the sixteenth century, many of their descendants moved again, to
Brazil, where they established the sugar industry.

A few years later, Portugal's King Manuel I—negotiating marriage
with Ferdinand and Isabel's daughter—ordered Portuguese Jews to
choose expulsion or baptism. Knowing that the Portuguese economy
would benefit if they stayed, in 1497 he ordered children under the age
of fourteen to be seized and forcibly baptized. Parents who agreed to
baptism were promised reunification with their children, but many children could not be found.

Forced converts included members of the Mendes family of spice and
silver traders, one of whom was the widowed Beatriz (also known as
Gracia) Mendes Nasi (1510–1569). In 1536, after the Portuguese king
John III established a Portuguese Inquisition on the Spanish model,
worried *conversos* began to leave Portugal rather than risk arrest. Gracia
Mendes Nasi and her infant daughter moved to Antwerp in what is now
Belgium, the center of the world's spice and sugar trade. She ran the
family business from there, handling many types of goods and loaning
money to rulers. Among her "loans"—in quotation marks as most of
these were never repaid—was a huge one to the Emperor Charles V to
drop charges against her dead husband of secretly practicing Judaism,
which would have resulted in the confiscation of the family fortune.
Gracia Nasi helped arrange for *conversos* and Jews to get out of Portugal
and Spain, sometimes on Mendes ships that sailed from Lisbon to
Antwerp and from there to other parts of Europe.

Antwerp gradually became more dangerous politically and less stable
economically, so Gracia Nasi and her family moved to Venice in 1544, and
five years later to nearby Ferrara, whose ruler welcomed them and their
financial assets. Here she continued to do business and began to practice
her Jewish faith openly for the first time in her life. She patronized
learning and the arts, especially the publication of books by Jewish
scholars. They dedicated books to her, including the 1553 Ferrara Bible,

a translation of Hebrew scripture into Ladino (Judeo-Spanish), the language spoken by Iberian Jews that became common across the Mediterranean.

The Catholic Reformation made Italian cities less safe for Jews and *conversos*, so in 1554 Gracia Nasi and her immediate family moved again, this time to Constantinople, the capital of the Ottoman Empire. Other members of her extended family followed. She made an alliance with the Ottoman sultan Süleyman the Magnificent for trading and financial privileges, continued to aid Sephardic refugees from Spain and Portugal, and supported scholars, hospitals, and synagogues. She was one of the Jewish business leaders who organized a boycott of the port of Ancona, a town in Italy under papal rule that had been safe for Jews and *conversos* until the reformer-pope Paul IV (p. 1555–1559) sent in the Inquisition, which arrested and burned many at the stake. Toward the end of her life, she and her nephew organized a settlement of Jewish refugees in Tiberias in what is now Israel, though this did not last very long. Her daughter Reyna Mendes (*c.* 1539–1599), wife of another Sephardic migrant, Joseph Nasi, who served as a diplomat for the sultan, carried on her mother's tradition of subsidizing scholars. She established two printing presses for Hebrew books in suburbs of Constantinople, the first presses in any language in that city and the first presses run by a woman in the Ottoman Empire. Gracia Nasi's niece, also named Gracia Nasi (1540–1596), joined them in Istanbul, along with her husband, where they supported the growing Sephardic community.

After Gracia Mendes Nasi died, she slipped into obscurity, as have so many women, but lately has come back into the public eye, with festivals, websites, postage stamps, wine, museums, and street portraits in her honor. (See Plate VI.) She is praised by descendants of those she helped flee Spain, who now live all over the world, and she even has a Facebook page.

Dona Gracia moved from one part of Europe to another, but other Jewish women and *conversas* traveled much further. Blanca Méndez de Rivera, born in Seville to a New Christian family about 1590, was orphaned and sent to a convent for her education. She left the convent and, with the encouragement of relatives, began to practice Judaism, married and had five daughters, whom she also instructed in

Jewish practices and rituals. Some of her relatives were arrested for Judaizing, and she and her family emigrated to Mexico City, where her husband died. She and her daughters—who became known collectively as "the Blancas"—became important parts of the crypto-Jewish community, which had existed for decades. They were allowed to practice relatively freely for a time, but a crackdown began in 1641 when a new viceroy was appointed, and Blanca and her daughters were imprisoned by the Inquisition.

In a series of interrogations, Blanca first confessed to having learned about the "Law of Moses" only after coming to Mexico City, from her landlady who was now dead, and of only practicing some fasts. She used flamboyant language to confess her guilt—"my errors tear at my heart and cause streams of tears"—and thanked "Our Lord [who] through this imprisonment has delivered me from my errors and placed me and my daughters on the path to salvation."[2] But at the same time, spies sent to secretly listen to her conversations with her daughters heard them talk about concealing their actions and those of others. She was transferred from her cell to solitary confinement in the prison's torture chamber.

After a month Blanca broke down, and in interrogations over the next several years, she told a very different story of how she had first learned the "Law of Moses," now pointing to a female cousin back in Spain rather than to her Mexico City landlady. This cousin "taught me and told me how to keep Saturdays as a holy day, without working, putting clean clothes on and clean linens on the bed and the table," along with many other ritual practices.[3] She also described practices she had learned since coming to Mexico City, some of which were consistent with Jewish law and tradition, and some of which blended in Christian practices, such as eating only fish during periods of fasting. Some of these were inversions of Christian rituals, including Blanca's and her daughters' most serious infraction, taking a Christ figurine off a crucifix and flogging it with a small whip. In her confessions, Blanca identified many members of Mexico City's secret Jewish community, including those who had already been arrested and confessed to the Inquisition once, who would be burned at the stake as relapsed heretics if they were re-arrested.

The inquisitors judged Blanca and her daughters to be "proselytizing Jewesses, consummate rabbis, and dogmatizers," and described Blanca as "a great Jewish ceremony-maker."[4] Three of her daughters died in prison, and after four years in prison, she and one daughter were whipped, shamed publicly at a public ritual of penance termed an auto-da-fé, and banished from the New World. She returned to Seville, where she disappears from the historical record. By 1649, the Jewish community in Mexico City was gone, all the men and women either reconciled with the Catholic Church or burned in a series of autos-da-fé.

Spain and Portugal saw the largest expulsions of Jews in Europe, but other areas exiled Jews as well. England and France did so in the Middle Ages, and various German and Italian cities did so in the fifteenth or early sixteenth century, though they often let Jews settle right outside the city walls, so they could enter the city by day to work or trade. Some Christian authorities forced Jews to live in walled and gated enclosures within a city, which came to be called "ghettoes," a word derived from the area in Venice, established on an island where there were metal foundries (*geti* in Italian). Women were part of all these expulsions, forced to abandon their homes and sometimes their children, and begin life again somewhere else. Their exile set a pattern that women from many other groups soon experienced.

MUSLIMS ADAPT AND REBEL

The conquest of Granada brought more Muslims as well as Jews into Christian Spanish territory. Initially Isabel and Ferdinand promised Muslims they could practice their faith, but this toleration was short-lived. Isabel's zealous and intolerant confessor Francisco Jiménez de Cisneros led forced conversions and mass baptisms. Muslims responded with a series of revolts that began in 1499, which the Spanish monarchs countered with more forced conversions, burning Arabic books, and expulsions. Isabel banned Muslims from Castile in 1502, a ban that her grandson Charles V, the ruler of all Spain, extended to the whole country in 1525. Muslims who officially converted—termed "*Moriscos*" when referring to men or mixed-gender groups and "*Moriscas*" when referring to women—were forbidden to participate in any aspect of Muslim culture, including songs, dances, food preparation, reading Arabic books, bathing, and funeral practices. They were to live among, and, whenever possible, marry their sons and daughters to Old Christian families. In a move similar to the later establishment of boarding schools for Native Americans by the United States and Canadian governments, children between the ages of three and fifteen were ordered to be instructed in the Catholic faith, preferably in schools where they would be cut off from contact with their families.

The Inquisition expanded its investigations for incomplete conversions and apostasy from *conversos* to *Moriscos*, again using torture and isolation to force confessions. Punishments included whipping, autos-da-fé, confiscation of property, imprisonment, and occasionally execution.

As public expression of Muslim culture became more dangerous, practices moved into the home, just as they did with Judaism. Women gradually took over ceremonies and changed them. Rituals to welcome newborn babies, which had included readings from the Qur'an, now centered on bathing the infant to wash away the baptismal oil, dressing it in clean clothing, and perhaps giving it an Arabic name. Women hid writings in Arabic in their homes or clothing and taught their children— especially girls—food preparation methods, bathing practices, home remedies, clothing styles, and songs rooted in Muslim traditions. Inquisitors prosecuted *Moriscas* for all of these, relying on the testimony of witnesses who observed such suspicious activities as "bathing the arms, the hands, elbows, face, mouth, nose, ears, legs, and shameful parts."[5] (Christians did not generally wash their entire bodies or take off their clothes to bathe.) During interrogations, inquisitors tried to force the accused to implicate other family members or accomplices. Those who identified the person from whom they had learned Muslim traditions pointed most often to their mother, grandmother, or mother-in-law.

Increasing suppression of *Morisco* culture led to an armed rebellion that began in 1568 in the Alpujarra Mountains of Granada and involved fierce fighting before it was put down by Spanish forces. King Philip II responded by ordering all *Moriscos*, whether they had engaged in fighting or not, to leave Granada and be dispersed throughout Castile. Some 50,000 men, women, and children were uprooted from their homes. Many died along the way, "from work, weariness, burden, hunger, by violence of those same people who were to guard them, robbed, sold as slaves," wrote the Spanish diplomat Diego Hurtado de Mendoza, an eyewitness.[6] Women, he wrote, marched along, "their hands bound, tied to a rope, guarded by infantry and horse soldiers . . . so that they would not flee."[7] King Philip II offered special benefits of land and tax exemptions for Old Christians willing to settle in areas the *Moriscos* left, but provided little for *Moriscos* forced to move. Many of these were women whose husbands had been killed in the fighting, or children separated from their parents, some of whom were sold in the slave markets of Seville.

Moriscos from Granada were supposed to live dispersed among Old Christians in Castile, so that they and their children would forget Muslim traditions. Some certainly did, but others maintained them, despite surveillance from the Christian families among whom they lived. Women, often widowed, taught their children prayers, prepared food as their mothers and grandmothers had done, washed clothing and their bodies, maintaining a *Morisco* identity and creating domestic sacred spaces. Some also attempted to return to their original faith. Juana, for example, born in Alpujarras, had been enslaved as a child during the 1568 rebellion. In 1604, now nearly forty years old, she was accused by the Inquisition of attempting to cross from Gibraltar to North Africa "to live as a Moor," that is, to return to Islam. She was sentenced to appear at an auto-da-fé, renounce Islam, be whipped one hundred times, return to her master, and take instruction in "things of our Holy Faith."[8]

Spanish authorities were not only worried about the continuation and spread of Muslim traditions in the Old World, but in the New World as well. In the middle of the sixteenth century, they forbade Jewish or Muslim converts to travel to the Americas without a royal license and papers proving their "purity of blood." Wealthy emigrants obtained exemptions for their free and enslaved servants, however, and some women evaded or skirted the rules, particularly if they were married to Old Christians.

Among these was María Ruiz, a *Morisca* from Granada who had been resettled in Castile as a child, then married a Christian man and moved to Mexico City. In 1594, when she was fifty years old, under pressure from her confessor, María denounced herself to the Inquisition for having continued some aspects of Muslim practice when she first moved to Mexico. Perhaps she was worried someone else might reveal her background, or perhaps she was now a firm believer in Christian teachings (or both). She described the way her mother had taught her prayers in Arabic and central elements of Muslim faith. Probing what she had learned, the inquisitors asked whether she prayed to the Trinity, to which she said no, because "she did not believe in the Son or the Holy Spirit because she thought they were things of the air, and there was nothing to them."[9] She did confess and take communion when her husband told her to, but "in all the confessions she made, she confessed all her sins except this one of her belief in Muhammad."[10] She told the inquisitors that over the last three years she had become a good Catholic and wanted to be reconciled to the faith, and they gave her a light sentence—fasting, praying the rosary, further instruction from a local friar, and a renunciation of her previous errors in church. This was to be done in secret, however, so that her sentence would not deter others from coming forward and admitting to Muslim practices. None did, but there may very well have been other women and men who maintained some Muslim practices.

In 1609 the Spanish crown changed its policy toward *Moriscos*. Instead of trying to assimilate them by scattering them within the Christian population, King Philip III decided to expel them, first from Valencia (a province in eastern Spain) and then from all of Spain. He and his advisers debated what should be done with children who had been baptized and might be raised as Christians once they were away from their parents. Taking very young children away from their mothers meant having to find enough Christian wetnurses to feed them, noted some officials, which could be difficult. Ultimately Philip decided that *Moriscos* going to other Christian lands, such as Italy or France, could keep their children, but those going to the "infidel lands" of North Africa or the Ottoman Empire had to leave behind children under the age of seven. They were to live with Christian families, taking their name, and be educated in Christian schools, though boys were not to be taught any trade in which they would need to read or use weapons. Children of both sexes were to repent their religious errors to officials of the Spanish Inquisition, and some did. Thus, on the one hand *Morisco* children were supposed to be assimilated into Christian society, but on the other, no one was to forget that they were different.

Thousands of Valencian *Moriscos* resisted expulsion militarily, and the royal government paid a bounty to Old Christians who found and killed the adults and sold the children into slavery. Rather than meet this fate or leave their homeland, *Morisca* women at the village of Cortes de Pallás threw themselves and their children down from a mountain ridge. But the royal orders remained in force, and over the next five years, more than 300,000 *Moriscos* left Spain, usually traveling by boat from one of the Spanish ports. Some expulsion orders gave *Moriscos* three days to report to an embarkation point and allowed them to take only what they could carry. Women thus wore their best clothing and jewelry, though as one writer commented, this was also to "hide something of the sorrow of their hearts."[11] Philip III commissioned Valencian artists to portray the departures, which he viewed as a triumph, in huge dramatic paintings. (See Plate VII.)

The chaos at the docks often overwhelmed officials. Account records include payment to one Ynés Rodríguez of Huelves for the care of 300 small *Morisco* children left in Seville warehouses. The children who survived would be considered orphans, required to work for Old Christian families who took them in until they were twenty-five or thirty. Some *Moriscos* refused to give up their children, including a woman who gave birth on the docks and then "embarked with the infant in her arms on a harsh, windy and very cold day," according to a report by the Valencia Inquisition.[12]

Morisco migrants often established their own villages and cities, especially in North Africa. Here they could practice Islam freely, but many maintained a sort of hybrid identity, using Castilian as well as Arabic as their language.

Some *Moriscos* stayed in Spain. Free and enslaved servants in Christian households were exempt from the expulsion order, though officials worried about enslaved *Moriscos* "meeting together in streets or houses . . . speaking Arabic . . . sleeping or spending the night in any house except that of his master."[13] Enslaved people sometimes bought their freedom or were granted this by their owners, often when they became too old or sick to work. Some then petitioned the Inquisition to leave Spain for North Africa, arguing they had not been baptized so should be free to leave. Among these were women, details of whose lives emerge in the brief records of their case: "Ayamena, a female Moor, 31 years old, 'scarred [or branded] on the forehead'; her 5 year old son Amete, 'of white color'; Fatima, her 2 year old daughter; and Maymona, her daughter of 4 months."[14] Some were granted their petitions, some were not.

By the 1620s, Spain had largely become the purely Christian country that Queen Isabel had envisioned a century and a half earlier. The case for her sainthood stalled in the late twentieth century because of the role she had played in expelling the Jews and Muslims, but, as you have read in Chapter 1, Pope Francis has recently asked Spanish bishops to reopen it. The hundreds of thousands of women, men, and children whose lives these expulsions upended (or ended) are no longer able to provide testimony, but we can imagine what they might say about the pope's request.

ANABAPTISTS MOVE, AND THEN MOVE AGAIN

Along with Jews and Muslims, there were plenty of Christians on the move as well, almost as soon as the Reformation began. Isabel of Castile was not alone in thinking that every territory should have only one official Church: other Catholics agreed, as did Luther and most other Protestant reformers and leaders. Some Protestants disagreed, however, and sought to create a voluntary community of believers as they understood it to have existed in New Testament times. These groups also developed ideas about various Christian teachings that were considered radical by most Protestants and Catholics. Some denied the validity of infant baptism and baptized adults; for this, they were often called "Anabaptists" by their enemies, a word meaning rebaptizer. Some individuals and groups emphasized divine revelation and spiritual experiences instead of Scripture or university theological training. Both Catholics and the majority of Protestants saw voluntary church membership as dangerous and reacted very harshly to the radicals. Adult baptism was made a crime punishable by death in 1529 in Germany and soon after this in other places as well. Over the next century, thousands of

Anabaptists and other radicals were arrested, tortured, and often executed, including many women, whose stories are in Chapter 4.

Others chose to move. Anabaptists emerge in court records in the Austrian territory of Tyrol in 1527, and over the next several years, more than 200 women were named. Most were ordinary women from towns or the countryside, but they included Helena von Freyberg (1486?–1545), a noblewoman charged with turning her castle at Münichau near Kitzbühel into a center of Anabaptism. According to witnesses, she and all her household had been baptized as adults, thus undergoing a second baptism as they had been baptized as infants as well. She gave lodging to Anabaptist leaders who preached in the castle, provided financial support to Anabaptist groups, and even visited one group in prison. Her noble status protected her for a while, but in 1530 the order was issued for her arrest, and she fled to Bavaria and then to the city of Constance. Here she continued to shelter Anabaptists until the Protestant leaders of Constance confiscated her house and expelled her from the city to stop the "contagious Anabaptist evil," as they described it. She returned to Tyrol, where she officially recanted her Anabaptist faith. Officials had wanted this to be a public church ceremony because, as they commented, "she has been the primary cause of so many people joining the movement," but she succeeded in keeping it small and private.

Tyrolian officials hoped Helena would live quietly at home with her Lutheran husband, but instead she moved to Augsburg, where she continued to host Anabaptist gatherings in her home. (So much for her recantation!) She was briefly expelled from Augsburg—where she went is unclear—but in 1539 she returned to the city and continued to teach others about Anabaptism, including her tailor.

During these last years of her life, she wrote a "confession" to the Augsburg Anabaptist congregation about various spiritual failings and an unnamed sin, one of the very few writings that have survived from an Anabaptist woman of this era. "I barely grow and increase in the body of Christ, as an old woman in the faith [should]," she writes, "and am weak, miserable, lukewarm, and tired in my watching and praying." She mentions her impatience and swearing, pleads with God to forgive her, and asks the congregation "to forgive and pardon what I have done against them," especially her "forcefully want[ing] to retain the freedom that I thought I had." Most of her confession is couched in the language of complete dependence on God and the Holy Spirit, a position of humility common among religious writers of the time, especially women. To us, this sounds like self-denial, but it was also a way for women and for men who were not clergy to claim authority for their words: this is not me speaking, but God.

Helena also can't quite hide the willfulness that had clearly gotten her into trouble with the Augsburg Anabaptists. She repeatedly asks for forgiveness for wanting to "teach and discipline" others while not being "teachable or amenable to discipline" herself, but at the very end of the confession this pops out again: "I forgive (forget) and pardon from the bottom of my heart those whom I suppose have done things against me. I ask God also to forgive and pardon them, yes that God would give them grace to help them recognize their sin (as I have done through God's grace)."[15] It's humility, but with an edge: God, please help those who have done something against me to follow my example and ask for forgiveness.

Helena von Freyberg was not the only Tyrolian Anabaptist who migrated from place to place in Austria, southern Germany, and Switzerland. Anna Scharnschlager (1493?–1565), a middle-aged woman in the town of Hopfgarden, also near Kitzbühel, was baptized as an adult along with her husband in 1530. Fearing persecution and death—a reasonable fear, as more than one hundred Anabaptists were executed in her area in the 1530s—she sold the family estate to her brother-in-law, and moved with her husband Leupold and twenty-year-old daughter Ursula to the city of Strasbourg, more than 300 miles away. Here they stayed for several years. Ursula married a clockmaker who was also an Anabaptist, and the young couple decided to move to Moravia, in modern-day Slovakia and the Czech Republic.

Anna and her husband were expelled from Strasbourg, and settled in the town of Ilanz, in what is today eastern Switzerland. Leupold became the head of the Anabaptist congregation there, and Anna kept up a steady stream of letters to her widely dispersed family members, many of which have survived, which is how we know her story. These sometimes included the medicinal remedies that were an expected part of

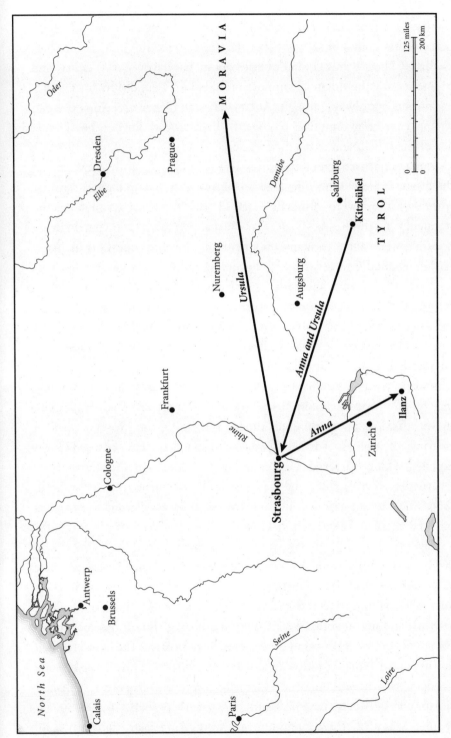

Map 2. *Anna and Ursula Scharnschlager's travels.*

women's care for their families, such as her recommendations of elder-berry leaves boiled in salt water or flax seed boiled in vinegar to reduce swelling. They also included queries about family property, debts, and payments, for the financial support provided for Leupold by his congregation was not always enough. At the very end of her life, Anna pleaded with her far-away daughter to come to Ilanz to care for her, but Ursula herself had died, and Anna died alone.

Anna Scharnschlager's daughter Ursula and her family were among the many radicals who migrated to Moravia in the sixteenth century. Although they were officially part of the territories ruled by the staunchly Catholic Austrian Habsburgs, Moravia and neighboring Bohemia were home to many opponents of Catholicism. This included Lutherans, and also Hussites, followers of the Czech reformer Jan Hus (c. 1372–1415), who had broken with the Catholic Church a century before the Reformation and been burned at the stake for heresy. Lutherans and Hussites included nobles with landed estates, who needed workers. They welcomed radicals as well as other Protestants, and thousands migrated. Among these was Jacob Hutter (c. 1500–1536), a Tyrolean hatmaker turned Anabaptist preacher who established communal sharing of property among his followers, adding this to adult baptism and pacifism as a core religious practice. In 1535, the Moravian diet, a meeting of nobles, turned against Anabaptists and ordered them expelled. Many scattered. Hutter and his wife Katharina (c. 1505–1538) returned to Tyrol, where he was tortured and burned at the stake in 1536. She was imprisoned and interrogated, escaped from prison, was arrested again and executed in 1538.

The expulsion of Anabaptists from Moravia turned out to be short-lived, as the nobles' need for farm workers and desire to assert their independence from the Habsburg government were stronger than their fears of those who rejected a state church. Back came Hutterites, along with Mennonites—followers of the Dutch Anabaptist pastor Menno Simons (c. 1496–1561)—and other types of radicals. In the late sixteenth century most radical groups dwindled away, but the Hutterites became stronger. Nearly one hundred Hutterite communities were established in Moravia between the 1550s and 1590s, with perhaps 20,000–30,000 people. Many of these communities were *Bruderhofs*, collections of buildings arranged around a village square, with the ground floor used for communal work and the upper stories with small private rooms for married couples. People did marry, but the choice of spouses was up to the community rather than the individual or the family, and men and women worked and ate separately. Children were cared for in large groups, taught to read and write, and trained in practical tasks.

Hutterites later remembered the late sixteenth century as a "golden age" of peace and prosperity, but it was not to last. Moravia became a key battleground in war between the Ottoman and Habsburg empires, which began in the 1590s. Both sides burned villages, killed people and animals, and took men, women, and children into captivity, sometimes enslaving them. Hutterites and Mennonites were pacifists, so did not resist. Some hid in underground caves and passages they had dug, while others fled. Moravia and Bohemia were also the first arena of conflict in the Thirty Years' War. As part of their moves against Protestants during this war, Habsburg authorities plundered Hutterite and Mennonite communities and then expelled them, giving them four weeks to either convert to Catholicism or leave.

Some radicals moved east to Hungary and Transylvania, but these were also under Habsburg rule, and in the eighteenth century, the Empress Maria Theresa supported stronger moves against radical Protestants. As you have read in Chapter 1, these were part of her efforts to make the Habsburg Empire more firmly Catholic, an aim strikingly similar to that of Isabel of Castile three centuries earlier. Just as *Morisco* children had been in Spain, Hutterite children were forcibly baptized or taken from their parents and placed in orphanages. Catholic officials seized and burned books, sealed meeting houses and workshops, and forced people to attend Catholic services. They arrested and imprisoned men, and other men went into hiding, leaving only women and children in the villages. Some refugees moved to Wallachia, in what is now southern Romania, and in the 1770s a small group moved to Ukraine (then part of the Russian Empire), where they flourished for a century. (To follow their story into the modern period: The introduction of a new Russian compulsory military service law in the 1870s led Hutterites and Mennonites to move further still, first to the United States. As pacifists and German speakers, they were persecuted in the patriotic fervor of World War I. Many moved to Canada, and ultimately to Central and South America.)

Radicals in eastern Europe included some who rejected the doctrine of the Trinity—the idea that God is made up of three persons, Father, Son, and Holy Spirit, who are co-eternal and share a single divine essence. Antitrinitarians instead thought of God as the singular creator of the universe, and Jesus as a prophet and moral teacher inspired by God, but not God himself. This idea spread among radical thinkers in northern Italy, some of whom were forced to move because of persecution, and in Transylvania (in modern-day Hungary) and Poland, where there were Antitrinitarian (known in Transylvania as Unitarian) congregations, schools, printing presses, and other institutions.

Well-educated noblewomen and townswomen were among the Antitrinitarians in Poland and Transylvania. They shared their opinions orally and occasionally in writing, and their opponents accused them of being firmer in their beliefs than men. As one Jesuit official sneered, "The ministers' wives and women preach openly to infidel Christians, Lutherans, Calvinists and others; women teach the ministers themselves, correct them, write sermons for them. St. Paul does not want such unrule."[16] With the reassertion of Catholicism in Poland, Antitrinitarians were ordered to be expelled from the country in 1658, but in some cases only the men left, while the women remained, keeping their property intact. Catholic members of the Polish parliament complained that Antitrinitarian women were preaching, teaching, corresponding with co-religionists elsewhere, and bringing up their children as Antitrinitarians. The new Polish constitution of 1662 specifically threatened Antitrinitarian women with confiscation of their property if they clung to their errors, and some moved to Transylvania, or further, to the Netherlands.

Those forced to move for opposing state churches included people who identified as members of certain radical or dissenting groups. They also included individuals who were not part of any organized group, but developed their own religious ideas through reading, prayer, and what they understood as direct communication with God.

One of these spiritual seekers was the German poet Anna Owen Hoyer (1584–1655), the daughter of a wealthy farmer who became the wife of a high official, with whom she had at least nine children. As an official, her husband was responsible for enforcing religious and secular laws in the Lutheran territory in Schleswig-Holstein in northern Germany where they lived, including prosecuting those opposed to the officially established Lutheran Church. While he was alive, Hoyer wrote literary poetry—and cared for the children—but immediately after his death in 1622 she opened her large estate to a small group that had been banished for their religious views. She also began reading widely and writing poetry criticizing the local Lutheran clergy for laxness, pride, greed, and empty formalism, calling them "devil pastors." She even blamed them for the recent renewal of religious warfare, what would become the Thirty Years' War. She advocated churches that did not have close relations with a state and called on laypeople to develop practices that met their spiritual needs better than the clergy did. Her social position protected her for a while, but the local pastors soon publicly charged her with maintaining a "secret church of religious enthusiasts" in her home.

Attempting to escape from war and avoid an outbreak of the plague, Hoyer and her children moved around the area, and in 1628 she wrote and published a poetic dialogue, *A Spiritual Conversation between a Mother and Child about True Christianity*. In this, she transforms a literary form normally supportive of traditional piety, the conversation between parent and child, into a bitter satirical poem. The mother first asks, "'What did you learn about salvation and the Bible in church today?' 'Nothing,' the child answers. 'About the prophets and Revelation?' 'Nothing.'" The mother then launches into a harsh critique of the clergy's monopoly of religious discussion despite their lack of spiritual understanding:

I know many, both men and women, among whom there is far clearer understanding of Jesus Christ, and more truth and spirit than in those who are supposed to teach you. Even though these others know more, they still must be quiet and listen, for the pastor alone has the word, as if it were his own. . . . No one is allowed to contradict him even if he says that crooked is straight and black is white. He must be right. So the peasants who listen only to their pastor don't understand much about right and wrong. Isn't that a pity![17]

Her enemies were equally harsh in their language, describing her and other women who criticized the Lutheran Church as false prophets and fanatics.

Hoyer's husband had left her many debts. She sold her estate to a sympathetic local noblewoman to cover these and moved to Sweden with her surviving five adult children. Here she lived in poverty, moving from place to place, at one point selling butter and other foodstuffs to support herself. Hoyer continued to write, with poems calling for an end to private property as God had made the earth for all to share. Other poems looked forward to a utopia where violence would be unknown. She tasted a bit of that utopia when Maria Eleonora of Brandenburg (1599–1655), the widow of the Swedish king Gustavus Adolphus, returned to Sweden at the end of the Thirty Years' War, and gave Hoyer a small house near Stockholm to live in. Her wanderings were over. A collection of Hoyer's religious and secular poetry was published in Amsterdam in 1650, praised by those who agreed with her and banned as heretical and shameful in her homeland of Schleswig-Holstein. She died five years later. Her critique of the established Church and her emphasis on individual spiritual regeneration were taken up in the eighteenth century by pietists, another movement in which women were central.

PREACHING AND PROVOKING

There were radicals who emphasized personal connections with the divine in England as well as on the continent, and they also moved, by force and by choice. These included members of the Society of Friends, or Quakers. The Quakers, founded in the 1650s by George Fox (1624–1694) and Margaret Fell (1614–1702)—who later became Fox's wife—stressed equality among Christians. They believed that there is "that of God in everyone," what they often referred to as an "Inward (or Inner) Light," akin to grace or the Holy Spirit. God could fill anyone with the gift of prophecy, charismatic spiritual power like that of the Old Testament prophets. Quakers had no ordained clergy or formal services but worshipped in silence until someone was moved by the Inward Light to speak or pray. Quakers refused to pay tithes, swear oaths, or show deference to their superiors. They dressed simply and addressed each other as "thee" and "thou," the older and less formal version of "you," to signify their rejection of hierarchy and their distinctiveness from others. Decisions were made communally, by discussing a matter until an agreement was reached.

Quakers advocated qualities for all believers like those that most Protestants stressed for women: humility, self-denial, piety, devotion, modesty. These were not to make one weak in the face of persecution, however, which came from the established Church of England and from the Puritans who left England before and during the English Civil War (1640–1660) and governed the British colonies in New England. Despite fierce opposition, early Quakers were intent to spread their message, and some traveled great distances to do so.

George Fox did not advocate women's social or political equality, but he did see women as spiritually equal to men. Margaret Fell was more radical. In 1666, while she was in prison for allowing Quaker meetings in her home and refusing to swear oaths, she wrote *Women's Speaking Justified*, arguing that the apostle Paul's prohibition of women's preaching in his Letter to the Corinthians in the Bible had only been meant for the "busie-bodies and tatlers" of Corinth. She provided a host of biblical examples of women who publicly taught and suggested that women should have the right to preach and minister to others if they had the spirit. They would be "mouthpieces of God," worthy vessels relaying his message. She advocated for separate women's meetings that would make decisions on moral and social welfare issues, which were established by some Quaker groups.

Quaker women preached throughout England and the British colonies in the New World, and occasionally elsewhere. In a few places they were welcomed, but more often they were whipped, imprisoned, and exiled, with no special treatment accorded to women for age, illness, pregnancy, or the presence of young children.

Mary Fisher (*c.* 1623–1698) and Ann Austin (?–1665) were the first Quakers to visit the British North American colonies. Fisher was a servant who met George Fox when he preached in the house where she worked and became convinced of the truth of his message. She was imprisoned for a year in York Castle for creating a disturbance in her church, where other imprisoned Quakers taught her to read and write. She then traveled south

QUAAKERS VERGADERING. · FRONTI NULLA FIDES. THE QUAKERS MEETING.

3. Made in London by the Dutch artist Egbert van Heemskerck and published in Amsterdam in 1678, this satirical etching conveys clear disapproval of the Quakers. In the middle a woman is preaching while standing on a tub; on the right a man fondles under a woman's skirts and a dog urinates on another woman's hem; and at the back people skulk around and cats snarl.

to Cambridge with Elizabeth Williams, an older woman. The two preached to the university students there, declaring them Antichrists and their college "a Cage of unclean Birds." They were arrested for preaching and vagrancy, with the city's mayor particularly incensed that when he asked them about their husbands, they answered that "they had no husband but Jesus Christ, and he sent them." He "said they were whores, and made a Warrant to the Constable to *whip them at the Market-Crosse until the blood came*," and ordered them driven out of town, the first time Quakers had been publicly flogged.[18] Scarred but undeterred, Fisher spent more time in York Castle prison for criticizing clergy and then boarded a ship across the Atlantic, with fifty-year-old Ann Austin, the mother of five children. Stopping first in Barbados, the two women preached to enslaved Africans and wealthy white people, beginning a Quaker community on this common stopping-point to the Americas. According to Quaker tradition, their converts included the lieutenant governor.

The women landed in Boston in 1656, where the response was quite different. Recognized as Quakers on the voyage because of their use of "thee," their luggage was searched. Quaker pamphlets and books they were carrying were confiscated and burned as "Heretical and blasphemous Doctrines, contrary to the Truth of the Gospel here professed among us." They were taken to prison, where they were forced to take off their clothes so that they could be searched for "witches' marks," the mark on the body of a suspected witch that people thought was the result of sex with the devil or where the witch's animal companion suckled. As the influential Quaker pamphleteer and chronicler George Bishop put it, in *New England Judged by the Spirit of the Lord*, "Two poor women arriving in your harbour, so shook ye, to the everlasting shame of you, and of your established peace and order, as if a formidable army had invaded your borders. . . . Is this your Entertaining of Strangers, your Civility, your Manhood to those who travel'd so many Thousands of Miles to Visit You in the Movings of the Lord?"[19] The women were imprisoned for five months, with little food or contact with others, and then deported back to Barbados. From there they went back to England. Continuing her ministry there, Ann Austin was imprisoned yet again in London, where she died in the Great Plague of 1665.

The Puritan authorities in New England feared—correctly—that Fisher and Austin would be followed by other Quakers intent on spreading their teachings. They prohibited ships' captains from bringing in any known Quakers or other "blasphemous heretics," ordered any Quakers who did make it into the New England colony to be imprisoned and whipped, and forbade the selling, publishing, importing, buying, or defending of any Quaker books or writings, with punishments that included fines, imprisonment, and banishment. All these punishments were carried out regularly, and in 1659 to 1661, four Quakers were executed, including one woman, Mary Dyer (*c.* 1611–1660). Mary Dyer was another migrant: she had immigrated with her husband to New England as a Puritan in 1635 and then returned to England, where she became a Quaker. When she returned to New England in 1657, she preached about the Inward Light and the idea that men and women were spiritually equal. She was imprisoned and banished three times, but kept returning to Boston, where she was ultimately hanged in 1660.

As news of these executions reached England, Elizabeth Hooton (1600–1672) decided she had to denounce the New England authorities personally, despite (or perhaps because of) the risks. Hooton was a middle-aged woman when she met George Fox in 1647 and became what is often described as the first convert to Quakerism. She immediately challenged religious and secular authorities and was imprisoned for preaching five times in different places in England. In 1661, she and another older Quaker woman, Joan Brooksoppe, sailed from England to Virginia, and then made their way to Boston, mostly on foot. They visited Quaker prisoners and were imprisoned themselves. Banishment followed, with the women driven out, as Hooton later described, by:

> men and horses armed with swords and staffs and weapons of war who went along with us near two days journey in the wilderness, and there they left us towards the night amongst the great rivers and many wild beasts that useth to devour and that night we lay in the woods without any victuals, but a few biscuits that we brought with us which we soaked in the water, so did the Lord help and deliver us and one carried another through the waters and we escaped their hands.[20]

The women sailed to Barbados, but quickly returned to Boston, where they were caught and placed on a ship back to England. There Hooton's adult son was arrested for attending a Quaker meeting and some of her cattle were confiscated. She decided she needed to tell King Charles II and his officials about the abuses she and other Quakers had experienced. First, she tried a letter-writing campaign, but there was no response, so she traveled to London and simply followed the king around, shouting and crying and running after him as he moved around the city. She finally annoyed him enough that he agreed to see her, but instead of restoring her cattle, he gave her a permit to purchase land anywhere in the colonies, including New England. He no doubt hoped this would get

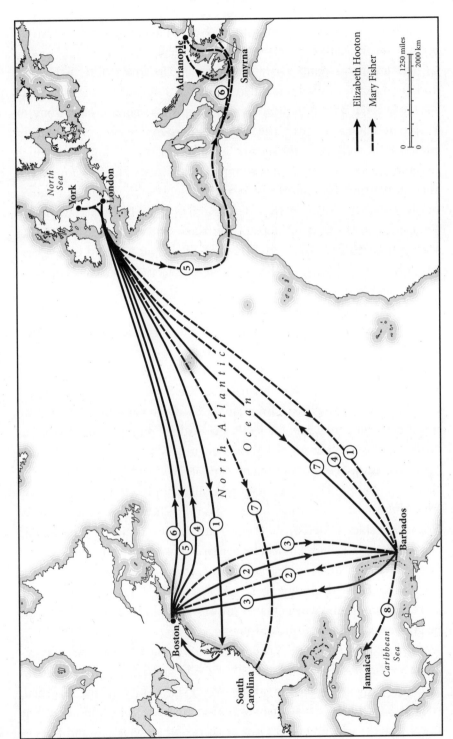

Map 3. *Elizabeth Hooton's and Mary Fisher's travels.*

rid of her, and would also indicate to New England authorities that he was the one in charge of policy toward Quakers.

Charles II was temporarily successful on the first count, as Hooton and her daughter sailed immediately to New England, but unsuccessful on the second, as nowhere in New England was she allowed to buy or even rent a house. Instead, the authorities ordered her to be whipped or imprisoned, following the newly issued Cart and Whip Act, which ordered Quakers stripped and whipped out of town the first four times they broke the law, and executed as "an incorrigible rogue and enemy of the common peace" if they did so a fifth time. Hooton returned to England, where she wrote letters, petitions, and pamphlets protesting the treatment of Quakers. In 1671 she sailed from England once again, this time to Barbados, in the company of George Fox, who hoped to boost the growing community of Quakers there. She continued on to Jamaica, where she became ill and died.

As Elizabeth Hooton traveled back and forth across the Atlantic provoking authorities, admonishing the king, and defending Quakers, Mary Fisher set off from England to Istanbul with five other Quakers, hoping to meet with the Ottoman Sultan Mehmed IV, whom they apparently hoped to convert to Christianity. The Ottoman Empire was at its most powerful, and Mehmed IV was widely regarded by European Christians as their most dangerous enemy. With five other Quakers, Fisher sailed in 1657 to Smyrna on the west coast of Turkey, where the British consul put them on a boat to Venice, hoping to keep them away from the sultan. The group separated, and Fisher and another woman, Beatrice Beckley, ended up on the Adriatic coast. From here they walked across Macedonia and Thrace, or perhaps took short boat trips around Greece, to reach Adrianople (now Edirne), where the sultan was camped with his army. At this point they had been on their way for about a year, and their simple and worn Quaker dresses stood in sharp contrast to the magnificence of the sultan's entourage.

Fisher badgered Grand Vizier Köprülü Mehmed Pasha—the sultan's highest official—describing herself as God's ambassador, until she was given an audience with the sultan. What she said was not recorded, though later Quaker historians reported that she told him about the Inward Light, which Quakers saw as accessible to Muslims and Jews as well as Christians. She answered his questions about Muhammad by commenting that all prophets could be judged by whether their prophecies had come true or not. Whatever she said apparently satisfied the young sultan, who offered her an escort to Istanbul. Instead, she walked on her own, and made her way back to England. Of her encounter, she wrote to three other Quakers:

> Now returned into England and many trials such as I was never tried with before, yet have I borne my testimony for the Lord before the King unto whom I was sent, and he was very noble unto me and so were all that were about him. . . . They do dread the name of God, many of them. . . . There is a royal seed amongst them which in time God will raise. They are more near Truth than many nations; there is a love begot in me towards them which is endless, but this is my hope concerning them, that he who hath raised me to love them more than many others will also raise his seed in them unto which my love is. Nevertheless, though they be called Turks, the seed of them is near unto God, and their kindness hath in some measure been shown towards his servants.[21]

Here Fisher comments that she was listened to, a far different experience than she had had in England or New England. Though she does not claim that she converted anyone, she predicts that at some point God will raise a "seed" among the Ottomans, and some will become Quakers.

After returning to England, Mary Fisher continued to defy authorities. She married a shipmaster and Quaker preacher whom she met in prison, and defended him physically when he was violently arrested, though she was pregnant at the time. After he died, she married a second Quaker husband, and the couple settled in South Carolina in 1682, where they acclimated to the local economy by purchasing at least one enslaved African. At the very end of her life, she was still witnessing, as a shipwrecked Quaker sailor wrote to his wife that he was being nursed back to health by an old woman whose "maiden name was Mary Fisher, she that spake to the great Turk."[22]

Quaker women who journeyed to preach were supported in their travels by women's monthly meetings, sometimes over the objections of the women's spouses. They often developed powerful bonds with one another. Katharine Evans and Sara Cheevers, for example, who were held captive together by the Inquisition on Malta between 1658 and 1662, emphasized in their joint account of their imprisonment the way their intense connection with one another and spiritual unity had allowed them to prevail over their captors.

Quaker women were not the only women imprisoned or forced to move for making their religious beliefs known in New England. Mary Dyer was executed in Boston in 1660 for proclaiming Quaker teachings and defying the order of banishment again and again, but decades earlier she had been embroiled in another religious dispute. This also included a woman among its major players, the Puritan Anne Hutchinson (1591–1643), who had immigrated to Boston with her husband and eleven children in 1633, following the popular preacher John Cotton. Hutchinson was a midwife, and this put her in contact with many women in the city. The daughter of an Anglican minister and well-versed in Scripture, she began holding meetings for women in her house, where they discussed recent sermons and other religious issues. These soon attracted men as well, including the colony's governor Henry Vane.

Along with several of the colony's ministers, including Cotton and her brother-in-law John Wheelwright, Hutchinson taught that salvation came only through God's grace and one's faith in Christ, not from good works, what became known as "free grace theology." She accused most of the ministers of Boston of what she termed a "Covenant of Works," that is, making salvation dependent on good works as well as faith, a theological position similar to Catholicism. They responded that good works were not a *means* of salvation but could be a *sign* that one was among those chosen for salvation, a demonstration that one was saved. Advocates of free grace, they thundered, were "Antinomians," who thought themselves bound by no laws, including the Ten Commandments. (Hutchinson and her associates did not agree with that characterization: this dispute is often termed the "Antinomian controversy.") Hutchinson argued that the assurance of salvation came from a mystical experience of grace, what she called "an inward conviction of the coming of the Spirit." She further claimed that she was receiving personal revelations from the Holy Spirit, which gave her the authority to interpret Scripture.

Religious differences led to public controversy, with arguments erupting in churches, market-places, government meetings, taverns, and homes. Ministers on each side preached sermons denouncing the other, there was a brief truce, and then Hutchinson and her supporters were accused of heresy. In January 1637 the General Court of Massachusetts Bay Colony called for a day of fasting and repentance, but this only led to more fiery sermons and the schism continued. In the spring, events began to turn against the free grace side. The sympathetic governor Henry Vane was replaced by the hostile John Winthrop, and other political leaders who had supported Hutchinson were voted out of office.

In November, John Wheelwright was banished, and Hutchinson was brought to trial in civil court, charged with slandering the colony's ministers, holding meetings in her own home despite being told to stop, and disturbing the peace of the community by supporting divergent opinions. Witnesses testified for and against her, and Hutchinson herself spoke to the court. John Winthrop's 1644 account of the controversy, *A Short Story of the rise, reign, and ruine of the Antinomians, Familists and Libertines, that Infected the Churches of New England*, presents her words:

> You have no power over my body, neither can you do me any harm—for I am in the hands of the eternal Jehovah, my Saviour, I am at his appointment, the bounds of my habitation are cast in heaven, no further do I esteem of any mortal man than creatures in his hand, I fear none but the great Jehovah, which hath foretold me of these things, and I do verily believe that he will deliver me out of your hands. Therefore take heed how you proceed against me—for I know that, for this you go about to do to me, God will ruin you and your posterity and this whole state.[23]

This bold statement declaring her independence and predicting that God would destroy the colony was too much for the authorities, and Hutchinson was banished, "as being a woman not fit for our society." Her husband and other family members left for Rhode Island to establish a new place to live, but Hutchinson was detained for four months in a house not her own, visited constantly by clergy seeking to change her thinking and gather evidence against her.

In March 1638, Hutchinson was put on trial again, this time in her home church, where the ministers charged her with various errors. Cotton had decided by this point that his protégée had gone too far and that continuing to defend her was dangerous. Instead, he picked up an argument made by her enemies, that denying the value of good works was simply a cover for adultery and immoral behavior:

> You cannot Evade the Argument . . . that filthie Sinne of the Communitie of Woemen; and all promiscuous and filthie cominge togeather of men and Woemen without Distinction or Relation of Mariage, will necessarily follow. Though I have not herd, nayther do I thinke you have bine unfaythfull to your Husband in his Marriage Covenant, yet that will follow upon it.[24]

He and other ministers wore her down, and she made a formal recantation of many of her opinions, but this was not enough. Instead, she was judged a liar and removed from the congregation, or in the fiery words of the sentence, "cast out" and "delivered up to Satan."

Despite Cotton's charge that she would surely be "unfaythfull to your Husband in his Marriage Covenant," Hutchinson joined her husband and others in a settlement on Aquidneck Island in Narragansett Bay, now in Rhode Island. The group included Mary Dyer and her husband, who were among the several dozen people who had moved to Rhode Island after being cut off from their communities and churches in Massachusetts because of the controversy. Hutchinson's husband died three years later and, when it appeared as if Massachusetts might annex the Narragansett Bay area, she and several of her children and other household members moved to New Netherland, the colony governed by the Dutch, settling in what is now part of New York City. At that point there was conflict between European settlers and the Siwanoy people who had originally lived in the area, and Hutchinson and almost all the household were killed in a Siwanoy raid in 1643. Unsurprisingly, the ministers of Boston interpreted this as God's judgment.

Other aspects of both Hutchinson's and Dyer's lives were viewed as divine retribution as well. Mary Dyer first came to the attention of Massachusetts authorities when she clasped Anne Hutchinson's hand at the end of Hutchinson's church trial, and Governor Winthrop learned that five months earlier Dyer had given birth to a stillborn infant with deformed features. Hutchinson was one of the midwives, and they had simply buried the infant quietly, the normal procedure for stillborn children. Winthrop ordered the infant dug up, a huge crowd gathered, and they declared it a "monstrous birth." From Winthrop's description, it appears that the infant was anencephalic—born without a major portion of the brain—a condition that results from neural tube defects during pregnancy. The Puritan leaders of Boston interpreted Dyer's baby not as an infant with a birth defect, however, but as a clear sign of the monstrosity of Hutchinson's beliefs.

This view was strengthened even further when, shortly after Hutchinson moved to Rhode Island, she delivered what is now termed a hydatidiform mole, a clump of fertilized tissue and uterine lining that contains small sacs of fluid that look like a bunch of grapes. The timing of this birth meant that she had been pregnant throughout her house arrest and church trial, which may account for observations that she was weak and ill. Viewing each of the sacs of fluid as an embryo, Winthrop wrote, "She brought forth not one, but thirty monstrous births or thereabouts. . . . see how the wisdom of God fitted this judgment to her sin every way, for look—as she had vented misshapen opinions, so she must bring forth deformed monsters."[25]

In comments such as this, we can see how ideas about women's proper place and role shaped the responses of men with whom they clashed, and how women's religious independence was linked with sexual deviancy. Helena von Freyberg, Anna Owen Hoyer, Elizabeth Hooton, Mary Dyer, and the others were not exiled or imprisoned because they were women, however, but because they held and communicated ideas regarded as so dangerous they needed to be rooted out and obliterated. Their opinions, and the actions they took to spread them, were taken seriously by their contemporaries, in fact much more seriously than they were by later historians, who tended to focus on male leaders and ignore women's actions. Only Anne Hutchinson became well known, and then only because the very influential John Winthrop made her the central figure in his telling of the events.

The authorities were successful in some cases in their efforts to eliminate certain teachings, as many radical Protestant groups did not survive the sixteenth or seventeenth century. But others did. Though their numbers are small, Hutterites, Mennonites, and Quakers can still be found around the world, continuing the migrations they began so long ago.

HUGUENOTS FLEE FRANCE

Anabaptists and Quakers were persecuted and exiled across Europe, but so were Protestants and Catholics who were not radical, as political leaders sought to enforce policies of religious uniformity. In central Europe, the first round of religious wars ended with the Peace of Augsburg in 1555, which gave the ruler of each territory within the Holy Roman Empire the right to decide whether to be Lutheran or Catholic. Inhabitants who disagreed with the official state church in their area kept quiet or left, creating streams of migrants going in all directions. As territories jockeyed for power, new rulers inherited from their fathers, or rulers themselves converted, religious affiliations changed, and people were often forced to move again.

Religious and political conflicts led to the outbreak of war in the Holy Roman Empire again in 1618, this time lasting thirty years, and ultimately involving most of the countries of Europe. As troops marauded across the land, people fled the destruction, and famine and disease killed many. In the southern and eastern Holy Roman Empire, the staunchly Catholic Habsburgs expanded their powers, and forced Protestant nobles and commoners to convert or leave. Hundreds of thousands left Bohemia and Austria, generally as whole families, leaving villages and districts virtually deserted. As a final act in this campaign of re-Catholicization, in 1731 the archbishop of Salzburg ordered all Protestants living within the territory he controlled to leave within six months: 20,000 did, leaving most of their possessions behind, and moving north to Prussia.

In France, King Francis I—the brother of Marguerite de Navarre, the queen you met in Chapter 1—initially generally tolerated Protestants but turned against them in the 1530s. He had some reformers executed, and others fled, including John Calvin, who headed just over the border to Strasbourg, Basel, and ultimately Geneva. Catholic theologians and pamphlet writers associated Protestants with negative qualities linked to women, such as gullibility, foolishness, and immorality, and referred to Protestant men as *femmelettes*, effeminate men who did not follow accepted standards of manhood. They also thought Protestant women meddled too much in religious matters for which they were intellectually and spiritually unfit.

But Calvinist Protestantism continued to spread in France, especially among nobles and city dwellers. French Protestants (called Huguenots) and their Catholic opponents used violent actions as well as preaching and teaching against each other, for each side regarded the other as a poison in the community that would provoke the wrath of God. This led to open warfare in the 1560s, with the French monarchy generally backing the Catholics. In August 1572 religious hatreds led to the St. Bartholomew's Day Massacre, the slaughter of thousands of Protestants, first in Paris and then elsewhere.

Charlotte Arbaleste (1548–1606), a young Huguenot noblewoman whose first husband had been killed in the wars of religion, recounted her escape from Paris in 1572. She hid in a neighbor's attic, from where she heard "the most disturbing screams of men, women, and children being massacred in the streets." She dressed as a servant and fled the city, traveling by boat and donkey, but still at risk of being discovered. As one of the boatmen commented: "By God she is a Huguenot who ought to be drowned, one can tell by the way she is terrified."[26] She made it safely to the Protestant stronghold of Sedan in northeastern France, where she met and married Philippe de Mornay, a leader and diplomat for the Huguenot side. Charlotte sometimes accompanied her husband on diplomatic missions, taking their young children along with her, and smuggled messages to and from him to other key Huguenots. Later their only son died leading Huguenot troops, and a grief-stricken Charlotte died six months later.

Charlotte Arbaleste was only one of many women who aided the Huguenot cause. Other women were also part of networks of information in the French wars of religion—actually on both sides—writing and exchanging coded letters with each other and with the men of their families, or slipping across enemy lines when it was too dangerous for men to do so. Armies on both sides often targeted wealthy estates for supplies, and women protected their families and belongings, sometimes brandishing muskets themselves.

Many Huguenots left France during the wars of religion, generally expecting to return from their exile soon, though sometimes this lasted the rest of their lives. Exiles included women as well as men, such as Ambroise Pithou, who fled the French city of Troyes twice in the 1560s and 1570s with small children in tow, hoping to meet up with her husband, who had left earlier. The first time she returned in secret to give birth to another child in her hometown, but her Catholic family rejected her and the midwife informed authorities about the birth. Soldiers came to arrest her and take the baby to be baptized as a Catholic, but she evaded them, and left town soon afterwards. She later commented on the distress this had caused her: "It has deprived me of the company of my husband, the presence of my daughter whom I was forced to abandon and all that is mine."[27]

French law required women whose husbands had left France to follow their husbands if the men were expected to be gone for a long time, reinforcing this by confiscating all the family goods so the women had nothing to live on. It also prevented women whose husbands had been exiled from marrying again unless there was clear proof the men had died, a situation that women today continue to face if their husbands disappear while migrating or fleeing persecution.

Despite the law, exile often separated spouses. In a letter to her husband in exile in England (discovered when the messenger smuggling a bunch of letters was apprehended by Catholic authorities in 1570), a woman named Marie Lengilon wrote that although "it has pleased God that we be far away from one another, he does not make us forget one another in our hearts . . . not a day goes by when my heart does not weep. I pray God that he gives you great patience." Other women reported their dire economic circumstances, plaintively or angrily asking for support from the men who had left. The wife of a man named Martin Plennart asked him to return home: "it is true that they confiscated the goods of some who were banished but there is no word about it at the moment. My desire is that you be near your wife and your children, for you would be as safe as the others who are coming back every day now." Exile separated other family members from one another as well. A man named Thomas Le Den wrote to his sister Jenne about their mother, "for since the hour and day that you went, her eye has never been dry and she is always crying, praying to God who watches over you to return you to her and us all."[28]

The fatal stabbing of King Henry III in 1589 left the Protestant Henry of Navarre as the king of France (he ruled as Henry IV, 1589–1610). The early 1590s saw widespread and intense fighting, and Henry IV realized that Catholics in France would never accept a Protestant king. He agreed to convert, and is later reported to have said "Paris is worth a Mass." Moderates on both sides accepted Henry as king and stopped fighting. Henry confirmed this truce in 1598 in the Edict of Nantes, which stated that Catholicism was the state religion of France but gave Huguenots the right to live and worship freely in certain defined areas, and the right to maintain about 150 fortified towns. Henry's toleration of Protestantism was too much for some, and in 1610 he too was stabbed to death, in the streets of Paris by a Catholic priest.

Henry IV's grandson Louis XIV (ruled 1643–1715) assumed the throne when he was only five, during a time of civil war and mob violence. He favored anything that encouraged order, unity, and uniformity, and that enhanced his own regal power. This extended to religion. Huguenots were increasingly deprived of their political rights, barred from many professions, ordered to quarter more troops in their households, and sometimes forced to undergo Catholic baptism. They were officially forbidden to emigrate, a policy that contrasted with that of England, where the rulers were happy to let religious malcontents such as Puritans and Quakers leave the country. Louis sent *dragonnades*, raids of mounted troops, into Protestant towns and homes throughout France to coerce Huguenots into converting. In 1685, Louis formally revoked the Edict of Nantes, ordering Protestant churches and schools closed and Protestant clergy to leave the country within two weeks, leaving behind any children over the age of seven. Protestant laypeople were ordered to convert and forbidden to emigrate, with threats that the men would be put on galleys as rowers or imprisoned and the women shut up in convents if they attempted to leave France.

Despite the prohibitions, perhaps as many as 150,000 Huguenots left France anyway over the next few years in a Huguenot diaspora known as the Refuge. Huguenots migrated to Switzerland, England, Germany, Denmark, and the Netherlands, and beyond to the Americas and South

Africa. They moved as individuals, as families or parts of families, and occasionally as whole neighborhoods or villages. Women and girls moved independently of husbands and fathers.

A few of the women who fled France after the revocation of the Edict of Nantes have left us records of their journeys. Anne de Chaufepié (1640–?) was the daughter, sister, and niece of Protestant pastors. Most of her family left France for the Netherlands in 1685 and 1686, but Anne was caught as she attempted to leave. She was locked away in a series of prisons and convents for two years and pressured to convert. Anne kept a journal of those years, naming people who treated her badly and those who treated her kindly, and commenting on her difficulties: "There, as in other places of my captivity, I was exposed to various temptations: the love of freedom, so natural to human beings; the fear of being imprisoned indefinitely, a reality with which I was constantly threatened; the sadness of the solitude in which I was forced to live eighteen or twenty hours of each day and night; the pain of being separated from those dearest to me." As a good Protestant, she followed this with a reflection on God's power: "On these occasions I often felt the weakness of the human spirit and the effectiveness of God's grace: flesh battled spirit, and grace always overcame and vanquished nature by far."[29] She tells her story as one of heroic perseverance, in which her suffering is similar to that of martyrs and a sign that she is among the elect, one of those who—in Calvinist theology—God has chosen for salvation. Finally, in 1688, she was released from the prison, and, as the relative of Protestant clergy, was expelled from France. She joined her family in the Netherlands.

Anne Marguerite Petit Du Noyer (1663–1719), from a middle-class Protestant family in Nîmes, also fled France in 1686. Much later, she recounted the story of her flight as part of her very long memoirs. Because she was short and young-looking, she cut her hair and dressed in boy's clothing. Meeting a priest and a judge in an inn, she related, "The judge was talking about people who had been arrested and the sorts of disguises they had used. All of this terrified me. But my fear was far greater when both the priest and judge turned to me and said, 'Here is a little rascal who could easily be a Huguenot.' I was very upset to see myself addressed that way. However, I responded with as much firmness as I could, 'I can assure you, sir, that I am as much a Catholic as I am a boy.' "[30]

Like Anne de Chaufepié, Du Noyer makes herself the hero of her own story, but one who was witty and observant rather than pious and reverent. She eventually made it to the Netherlands, but returned to Paris when she could not find a way to support herself. There she was briefly imprisoned and abjured her Protestant faith to marry a Catholic military officer. In 1701, she converted back to Calvinist Protestantism and fled to the Netherlands with her two daughters, leaving her husband and son behind. There she became the editor of a widely read newspaper, and the author of a popular novel as well as her memoirs, both of them published during her lifetime.

Family members often traveled separately. Following a route that became quite common, in 1687 six children from a noble Huguenot family made their way secretly on a ship from La Rochelle on the west coast of France to Devon in England and, later in the year, their mother and eldest brother did so too. The father left France later. Among the first group was the teenaged Suzanne de Robillard de Champagné (1668–1740), who later recorded her experience, as did her mother, Marie de La Rochefoucauld, dame de Champagné (d. 1730). Their memoirs have survived, the only story of exile for which there are two competing accounts from women.

Marie—the mother—wrote her account in 1690, when, after moving through a series of Huguenot refugee communities in England and the Netherlands, she had settled in the town of Voorburg in the Netherlands. She wrote it, as she comments, for her children, though she does not acknowledge that they actually left France before she did and knew much about what she was telling. She may also have recounted many of the events orally several times before she wrote them down, as Huguenots were expected to testify about their faith and the circumstances of their flight to their co-religionists whenever they came to a new community, a ritual called the *reconnaissance*. The memoir, embedded in the middle of family account books, is matter-of-fact rather than reflective or intimate. Marie makes only a few comments about religion, and instead focuses on the actions she carried out that made her a good wife and mother, including arranging the escape, taking care of the family finances, and securing her children's future:

I begin this book and promise sincerely to put nothing in it that I do not believe entirely true. I am pleased to put in it our departure from France so that those who come after me will know the pains I have had in order to save my family. . . . The departure of my children was very secret, and it would take too long to describe all the tricks I had to do in order to hide it. . . . We set sail and arrived at Falmouth eight days later, not without fear and many perils. . . . We felt as if we had left what is called purgatory and arrived in paradise. The liberty to worship God openly, no longer to fear the dragoons and churchmen, seemed to us a great happiness. . . . I remained there about two and a half months to recuperate from my exhaustion, which was great. . . . In May 1688 I went to stay with my nephew and my nieces at Voorburg near The Hague, where there was a French church served by the younger M Yver. I was the first French woman to take a house there, and six months later we were sixty refugees of good family.[31]

In her telling, Marie is an émigré, but one firmly embedded in French communities, with her social standing and to a great degree her economic position intact. Her husband joined them briefly in Voorburg, but took a position in a Huguenot regiment of the army of William of Orange (the Dutch prince who became the joint ruler of England with his wife Mary in 1688), went to Ireland and died shortly afterwards. Her eldest son also moved to Ireland with the military, and at the end of her life Marie joined him there.

Suzanne—the daughter—wrote her account later, after having read her mother's, in which she is barely mentioned. Her audience was the wider world, not the family, and the account circulated in manuscript after it was written, thus reaching some of the audience she intended. She is the center of her story, just as her mother was in her version. She is the one who arranges the voyage, cares for her siblings, finds food, and does other things that a good mother should, though she is only the oldest sister. She heightens her resourcefulness, in fact, by making herself only sixteen when the children left France, when in fact she was nineteen, and making her siblings younger than they actually were. As Suzanne tells it, she sacrifices herself for her siblings, which her mother never recognizes or appreciates. In fact, her mother does the opposite, marrying her off to a much older émigré friend of Suzanne's father and transferring some of what Suzanne expected to inherit to one of the sons. Leaving France had dramatically lowered Suzanne's social position, and she writes of herself with anger and loss as an exile. She left Voorburg long before her mother did, shortly after her own husband died, and moved to the Huguenot community in Celle in Germany, where she lived in the household of the duchess of Zell, herself a Huguenot émigré. As she tells it:

I was at La Rochelle, capital city of the Aunis and a seaport, in 1687, the eldest of the children of my father and my mother, and in their absence mistress of the household they had there, and of five of my youngest brothers and sisters, of whom the oldest was ten and the youngest two. I had gotten permission from this dear father and mother to try to take advantage of opportunities that might arise for leaving the kingdom, with all or part of the family. . . . [She made an agreement with a captain, and they boarded a boat.] The wind, which was favorable to us, carried us by eleven or twelve o'clock in the morning out of the sight of all the enemies of truth. . . . Our captain and three or four of his crewmen, for they were not more numerous, treated us quite cordially, gave us as many biscuits, peas, and salted meats as we could eat. Our seasickness did not allow us to cost him much. . . . Several of his men to keep busy set up fishing lines. I asked them to give me one, to which they agreed, I had the good fortune after dinner to catch seven large fish called mackerels, excellent fish to eat. . . . [They reached the English town of Exeter.] I kept my little household without a maidservant with my little family, to whom I acted as a mother for the whole time we were deprived of our own, who only came to join us three months later. . . . I instructed as best I could the brothers and sisters who could learn, the two oldest responded once a week to the catechism. . . . [I] kept them orderly besides, made all their clothing—even my brothers' jerkins—in order not to spend too much, having no idea whether our father and mother would one day be in a position to furnish us with what we needed, or be able to put money in our hands. . . . [They moved to different cities in the Netherlands, and finally to Voorburg.] In

Voorburg we found numerous refugees of our nation and acquaint-
ance who, like us, had come there to live for reasons of economy,
being able to live there more cheaply than in the big cities.[32]

The women who left some written record of their journeys from
France were only a tiny minority of the thousands who left, each with
her (or his) own set of experiences. For some, family bonds enhanced and
supported their religious choices, while for others, religion tore families
apart. Some who moved established expatriate communities and maintained their French culture, while others integrated into the new host
society, becoming immigrants rather than exiles. Others hovered
between these two, losing their sense of original identity but not really
assimilating to their new location.

ESTABLISHING NEW COMMUNITIES

Women who chose or were forced to move for religious reasons
included Jews, Muslims, and Protestants, and also Catholic laywomen,
who—alone or with their families—became religious refugees, including
English and Irish recusants. They also included women from the group
that Catholic male authorities most hoped would stay put: nuns. Nuns
in areas that became Protestant sometimes fought to stay in their
convents, but often this was impossible, so they moved to convents in
Catholic areas, generally trying to maintain some semblance of the
cloister when they were on the road. Many monks in areas that became
Protestant moved as well, of course, transferring to another monastery
if they remained Catholic or moving into the secular world if they
converted. Only a very few lucky ex-monks, like Luther, were given the
monastery in which they had lived as their family household after
the Reformation, but positions as clergy in Protestant churches—an
opportunity open to no woman, of course—often included some type of
housing.

Moving was more disruptive for nuns than it was for monks. Women
generally entered religious houses in their hometowns and then stayed
there, whereas monks and friars were more likely to enter a religious
house further from home. Convents often held close-knit family groups

of sisters, cousins, aunts, and nieces that could not always stay together when they were exiled, so moving to a different convent might involve stressful separation from family as well as home.

What happened to nuns varied across Protestant Europe. In many cities of the Dutch Republic, the convents were closed, their assets liquidated, and the women given their dowries and a pension. Some returned to their families, while others continued to live together or near one another in small, informal domestic groups of what were termed *kloppen* or *geestelijke maagden* (holy maidens). Many were members of wealthy and prominent upper-class families who had only slowly accepted the Reformation, so were supported by their families in their decisions to remain unmarried and devote themselves to religious activities.

In England, where monasteries and convents were taken over by the crown, most nuns received very small pensions and were expected to return to their families, although not all did. Many English nuns fled to religious communities on the European continent or continued to fulfill their religious vows in hiding while they waited for the chance to emigrate. Beginning with the Benedictine abbey in Brussels in 1598, convents were opened on the continent specifically for English Catholic women and girls. Eventually there were twenty-one established across the southern Netherlands and parts of France, which housed a total of about 4,000 nuns, the vast majority of them English, as well as hundreds of English Catholic girls, who attended for an education and then returned to secular life.

Irish nuns actually began to migrate to the continent *before* the Reformation, starting with a group of Dominican nuns who traveled from Galway to Bilbao in the Basque region of northern Spain in 1499 to establish a convent and school for girls there. They joined an existing Dominican convent, and, as more Irish nuns followed their path, they joined other Dominican or Poor Clare convents across Spain that had an educational mission. These convents were supported by Irish and Spanish patrons, and later also by the Spanish crown.

Irish religious houses were officially dissolved in the 1530s and 1540s by the Protestant Tudor rulers of Ireland. Some of their residents tried to maintain a more informal religious life in Ireland, including a group of women in Limerick in the 1560s called Mná Bochta. They ministered to poor women until they were forced to disband by English Jesuit missionaries, who insisted that religious women be enclosed. Other Irish nuns fled to the continent. Here they generally joined local convents or the ones established for English nuns, though in 1639 a separate Dominican convent was established in Lisbon for Irish nuns.

In 1641, a Catholic-led rebellion in Ireland led to the creation of a Catholic Irish state, and some nuns trickled back to Ireland. Other women took their vows in Ireland in a small group of new convents. British troops reimposed control over Ireland in 1653, with harsh repressive measures against Irish Catholics. Irish nuns fled to Europe again. Those who left included Mary Bonaventure Browne (*c.* 1610–*c.* 1694), the abbess of a Franciscan convent of Poor Clares in Galway founded in 1642. Fluent in English, Irish, and Spanish, Browne wrote a long history of the Irish Poor Clare order, in Irish, while she was in exile in Spain, and a shorter memoir of her experiences in the Galway convent.

In their letters, reports to their superiors, chronicles, memoirs, and appeals for financial support, English and Irish nuns emphasized the persecution they and their families had suffered and linked their exile to exiles in the Bible. These were enclosed convents, so the nuns were officially cut off from the outside world as well as separated from their homelands and families, but the convent enclosure also provided them with a relatively safe space from which to challenge the Protestant English state. That challenge included activities the Catholic Church judged acceptable for enclosed nuns, such as prayers and rituals for the conversion of England, which the nuns themselves saw as part of the mission to their homeland. When taking their vows, members of the Paris Benedictine convent promised "to offer myself and all my actions for the Conversion of England, in union with our Fathers' labour of the mission; and as they promise and swear to go and return as they are commanded, so will I live and die, in this my offering, in this Convent."[33]

But challenging Protestants could also include direct political action, particularly after the execution of King Charles I in 1649 during the English Civil War and the exile of his son Charles to the continent. Nuns in English convents on the continent became convinced that the best way to end their exile and bring back Catholicism or, at the very least, toleration of Catholics to England and Ireland was to return the Stuart monarchs

1. The bobblehead of Katharina von Bora is sold by Old Lutheran, an online store that describes its mission as providing "unique products and services that help customers express their Lutheran identity." The doll of St. Teresa of Avila is sold by Shining Light Dolls, whose mission is "passing on the Faith through proven play-based learning."

II. This 1490 oil painting by an anonymous artist shows Isabel of Castile wearing a jewel she received from her father, connecting her with the dynasty. It was painted in northern Europe from drawings or sketches, as Isabel herself never left Spain, and is now in the Prado in Madrid, a museum that was largely endowed by royal women.

III. The Wittenberg artist Lucas Cranach the Elder painted this double wedding portrait in 1526 shortly after the Luther marriage, and members of his workshop painted more. All later depictions of Katharina are based on this, as it was the only one made during her lifetime.

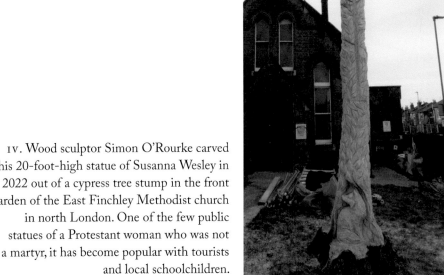

IV. Wood sculptor Simon O'Rourke carved this 20-foot-high statue of Susanna Wesley in 2022 out of a cypress tree stump in the front garden of the East Finchley Methodist church in north London. One of the few public statues of a Protestant woman who was not a martyr, it has become popular with tourists and local schoolchildren.

v. Philippe de Champaigne's oil painting from 1662 depicts what was understood as a miraculous healing of Sister Catherine de Sainte Suzanne, the painter's daughter, from a paralyzing illness through the prayers of Mother Agnès Arnauld. The artist, himself a Jansenist, gave the painting to Port-Royal in gratitude and in hope that the healing would aid the Jansenist cause.

vi. This postage stamp, issued by Israel in 1992, shows Dona Gracia at several points in her life. In the background is a bronze portrait medal made by the Italian artist Pastorino in 1558, long thought to be of Gracia Nasi. It's actually her identically named niece, and is the earliest known example of a portrait medal with a Jewish subject and a Hebrew inscription.

VII. In the foreground of this 1612 painting, *Departure of the Muslims from Valencia*, the Valencian artist Pere Oromig shows a Muslim father kneeling to say goodbye to his young daughter, who is standing with a Christian family. Light breaking from the clouds shines directly down on the Christian women, conveying Oromig's and Philip III's view.

VIII. From a series of fifty paintings referred to as *The Painted Life* portraying the major events of Mary Ward's life, this scene shows well-dressed women listening to her ideas in London in 1609, and then sailing to St. Omer with her. The series, painted by several different unknown artists in Germany after Mary's death, was most likely commissioned by her followers, for whom writing her biography would have been risky.

ix. The young Diego Velázquez captured Sor Jerónima's likeness in 1620 in a full-length oil portrait, staring intently at the viewer and holding a book and a large crucifix, both essential to her for the task ahead. The inscription at the top reads (in Latin), "It is good to await the salvation of God in silence," a verse from the Book of Lamentations and a reference to her Poor Clare order's practice of not speaking excessively.

x. This seventeenth-century watercolor painting, made by an unknown artist who may have been an eyewitness, depicts the Great Martyrdom of Nagasaki in 1622, when fifty-five Japanese, Korean, and European Christians were executed. Missionaries are in a fire pit in the middle, while samurai cut off the heads of convert families, including women, in the foreground. The crowd watching includes Japanese, Chinese, Africans, and Europeans, both women and men.

XI. This magnificent white marble sculpture, created in 1647–1652 by the Italian sculptor Gian Lorenzo Bernini for the burial chapel of a Venetian cardinal in a Discalced Carmelite church in Rome, shows Teresa in a swoon of ecstasy as a smiling young angel opens her robe and points an arrow toward her heart. Based loosely on Teresa's own description, Bernini's sculpture makes the saint young and beautiful and heightens her sensuality in a way that was popular in the baroque art of the time. On the side walls of the chapel, life-size statues of male members of the cardinal's family sit in boxes as if they were in a theater, gaze at Teresa, and converse, an element of voyeurism that more recent visitors to the chapel have found slightly creepy.

XII. In this painting by the Mexican artist Cristóbal de Villalpando from the late seventeenth century, María de Agreda and St. John the Evangelist look heavenward to a vision of the Virgin Mary, Christ, the pope, and angels, with Mexico City's Plaza Mayor hovering below. Villalpando, Mexico's foremost artist at the time, uses intense color to highlight the connection between the Virgin Mary and the "lady in blue."

XIII. In this portrait from the late seventeenth century by the French artist, poet, and musician Élisabeth Sophie Chéron, Madame Guyon looks calmly out at the viewer, not betraying the turmoil of her life. The artist, the Catholic daughter of a Protestant painter father and a Catholic mother, published a book of Psalm paraphrases as well as producing paintings, drawings, and etchings.

XIV. The Mexican artist Luis de Mena depicts the Virgin of Guadalupe with various mixed-descent families, known as *castas*, and scenes from everyday life in 1750. Both *casta* paintings and images of the Virgin of Guadalupe were common genres in colonial Mexico, but Mena's painting is the only one to combine them, suggesting that he shared the view of Guadalupe as an intercessor for Mexico's *mestizo* population.

XV. This large bronze statue, made in 2003 for the cathedral in Santa Fe, New Mexico, by the sculptor Estella Loretto, a Jemez Pueblo, portrays Kateri Tekakwitha wearing turquoise jewelry and holding eagle feathers, elements that come from Pueblo and Sioux traditions, not Mohawk or Algonquin. Loretto thus continues the process of cultural mixing that Tekakwitha herself had begun.

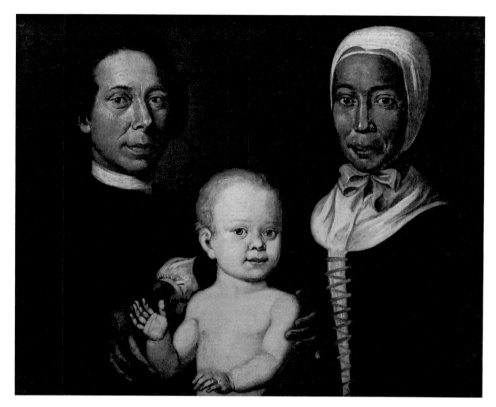

XVI. This portrait of the Protten family by the Moravian artist Johann Valentin Haidt was made around 1751 when the Prottens lived in Herrnhut, shortly after the birth of their daughter Anna Maria. Haidt shows Rebecca in the gown, head-covering, and blue ribbon of a married Moravian woman, with a peaceful gaze. The artist may have purposely painted the family with very different skin tones to emphasize the universality of the gospel, but as both parents were of mixed descent, Anna Maria may actually have had light skin.

XVII. This larger-than-life bronze statue of Mary Dyer at the Massachusetts State House in Boston was made by the American sculptor Sylvia Shaw Judson, herself a Quaker, in 1958. She used another woman in her Lake Forest Illinois Friends Meeting as the model for Dyer.

to the throne. They had already established networks that stretched across the Channel and to other Catholics in exile, through which they secured money, recruited novices and pupils, and obtained patronage. They now extended these networks to royalist diplomats, officials, and Charles himself, who visited convents many times during his exile.

Abbess Mary Knatchbull of the Ghent Benedictines, for example, arranged loans for Charles, transmitted messages to and from his advisers, and passed along news. She forwarded coded letters, which were generally ignored by government spies because they thought that women's letters would not contain anything political, and she also paid bribes to make it even more certain they were not intercepted. The restoration of Charles II in 1660 did not bring the toleration the nuns had sought, however, and Charles reneged on his promise to Mary Knatchbull to support a royal convent in Dunkirk on the north coast of France, which was then still English territory.

The accession of the Catholic James II in 1685 looked to be (literally) the answer to the nuns' prayers, but his reign lasted only three years. It was ended by the Protestant-led coup known as the "Glorious Revolution" that made William and Mary rulers of England. The nuns continued their allegiance and assistance to James's family, the Stuarts, who tried several times to regain the English throne militarily. The nuns compared their own exile to that of the monarchs, who were now often nearby in France and Belgium. As Mary Rose Howard, the abbess of the Brussels Dominican convent, wrote to James II's son James Francis Edward Stuart in 1724, "Not that I complaine, wee glory to suffer with yr Magesty & as banished from our country for our religion, to all losses wee redily conforme and are perfectly easy in."[34]

William and Mary banished Catholic clergy from Ireland but made no mention of women religious. Most Irish convents officially closed, but after a discreet interval Irish nuns were sometimes able to emerge from hiding and begin their communities again. Many Irish and English nuns also remained in continental convents until the French Revolution, when almost all of these were closed. At that point the nuns sought refuge in what had become a more tolerant England and Ireland.

The English and Irish convents on the continent were important nodes in Catholic political networks, but they carried out all their actions from behind convent walls, as these were contemplative convents that followed strict rules of enclosure. In this, they accepted—and indeed championed—rules for women religious that had been affirmed at the Council of Trent. The English nuns viewed their commitment to physical separation from the world as a positive choice and a means to connect with the broader movement of Catholic religious reform.

Not every exiled English nun agreed that enclosure was desirable, however. Mary Ward (1585–1645) was born into an English Catholic family in Yorkshire whose house had been burned down during anti-Catholic riots. Her grandmother and several other women relatives had been imprisoned for their faith, as had other recusant women, providing Ward with models of strong pious women. With a sense of religious vocation that began when she was a child, Mary Ward left England and became a lay sister at the convent of the Poor Clares at St. Omer in present-day Belgium, and then a nun at the new convent of English Poor Clares at Gravelines on the north coast of France. Here she had a revelation that the contemplative life was not what God had called her to. In 1609 she returned to London, where she began to help the poor and sick and visit those imprisoned for being Catholic. She gathered a group of like-minded young women around her and they moved back across the Channel to St. Omer, where they opened a school for the daughters of English Catholic émigrés (see Plate VIII). Ward thought that the survival of Catholicism in England depended on women's actions, so educating girls was essential.

Ward was contemplating what the organization of her small community of women should be when she had another revelation, which told her that she should take the Jesuits as her model, just as Isabel Roser had attempted to in the 1540s. Ward drew up a plan for an order of women religious that, like the Jesuits, would have an active apostolate in the world, answer only to the pope and not to bishops, be free of the requirement to recite the canonical hours so that they could be more flexible in their work, and focus primarily on education. She knew that she would need papal approval so, in 1621, she and some of her companions walked to Rome and presented their petition for what they termed the Institute of the Blessed Virgin Mary to the pope. They opened a school in Rome, and over the next few years Ward traveled extensively, founding communities in Cologne, Trier, Naples, Perugia, Munich, Vienna, and Pressburg (Bratislava), even though she was in constant pain from gallstones. These communities often operated free schools for both boys and girls, teaching them reading, writing, and a trade.

The Institute needed steady donations, for which Ward and her associates corresponded with secular and church authorities. She realized that this sort of public role for women was something new in Catholicism, in her words, "a course never thought of before," but she stressed that there "is no such difference between men and women that women may not do great things as we have seen by the example of many saints."[35] She also wanted women in her Institute to return to England as missionaries, for "it seems that the female sex also in its own measure, should and can . . . undertake something more than ordinary in this great common spiritual undertaking."[36]

Mary Ward's enemies were just as active. At the point that she requested papal approval, secular priests in England—that is, priests who were not members of religious orders—were in a quarrel with the Jesuits over who should lead attempts to reach some accommodation for Catholics with the English state. They saw Ward's group—whom they contemptuously called "Jesuitesses"—as useful ammunition in their fight. They attacked them, telling the pope they were "idle and garrulous women" who "gad about," and noting that "it was never heard in the Church that women should discharge the Apostolic Office."[37] For their part, the Jesuits refused to agree to any formal role or link with Ward's group. Thus the Institute was attacked for its connections to the Jesuits, but there really weren't any.

Ward appealed to cardinals and the pope by letter and in person but, beginning in 1628, houses of the Institute began to be forcibly closed, and in 1631 Pope Urban VIII issued a formal Bull of Suppression, a year after he had issued a similar bull against the houses established in Roser's tradition. The bull described the Institute in vicious language, as "poisonous growths in the Church" and commanded "all the Christian faithful to regard and repute them as suppressed, extinct, rooted out, destroyed and abolished." Ward and her associates had attempted "works which are most unsuited to their weak sex and character, to female modesty and particularly to maidenly reserve," and were not to be tolerated.[38]

The Inquisition placed Ward herself under house arrest in a convent in Munich, and then summoned her to Rome to face charges of heresy. She appeared before the pope, and declared she was not a heretic. He agreed not to have a formal trial and allowed Ward and her companions to continue their charity and educational work, though as laywomen, not women religious. They were forbidden to leave Rome. In 1639, the pope allowed Ward to return to England for reasons of health, and she did, arriving in London right before the outbreak of the English Civil War. As London became too unstable, she and her community moved to York, where she died in 1645.

Despite the lack of papal recognition and fierce opposition, women in Paris, Rome, and Bavaria kept a few Institute schools and houses open, sometimes with the support of local bishops, who valued the education they provided. Generally known as the "English Ladies," with the restoration of the English monarchy in the 1660s a few women returned to England, where they opened schools and charities. These included a school in York in 1686, which became Bar convent, now seen as the oldest surviving Catholic convent in England. The women were prohibited from recognizing Ward as their founder, however, with a second papal bull issued in 1749 emphasizing this. Many of her letters and documents were destroyed.

OCEAN-CROSSING NUNS

Protestant suppression of convents and women's desire for active service in the world were not the only reasons that nuns traveled. They also quickly followed Spanish and Portuguese overseas conquests as part of colonial ventures.

The first convent in the Americas, the Convent of Our Lady of the Conception, was founded in Mexico City in 1541 by the Conceptionist order, founded by Beatriz da Silva and supported by Isabel of Castile. Most of the founding mothers were from Spain, though they did not come from a convent there, but took their first vows in Mexico. More convents followed, especially in Mexico City, which had eleven by 1630. By 1700, there were fifty-seven convents in New Spain, with one or two even in small cities. The first convent in South America was founded in

Cuzco, Peru, in 1558, again relatively soon after the Spanish conquest, so the nuns were migrants to Peru, born in Europe or in parts of the Spanish colonies other than Peru.

For some Spanish nuns, simply crossing the Atlantic was not enough. In 1620, a group of nuns left their cloistered convent of Los Isabel de los Reyes in Toledo, Spain, to establish the first women's convent in East Asia, in Manila on the Philippine Islands. Their Toledo convent had direct connections to Spain's "most Catholic" queen: it had originally been a Moorish palace when Toledo was part of Muslim Spain but had been confiscated by Queen Isabel in the late fifteenth century and given to the Franciscans. The convent was affiliated with the religious order of the Poor Clares, the order for women founded by Clare of Assisi (1194–1253), one of Francis of Assisi's first associates. Its best-known resident in the early seventeenth century was Sor Jerónima de la Asunción (1556–1630), born into a fairly wealthy noble family, who had gained a reputation for intense piety through strict fasting, wearing a shirt embedded with sharp combs for carding wool next to her skin, and other acts of bodily penance. Noblewomen who supported her convent, including members of Spain's royal family, prayed with the saintly nun, and asked for her blessings, advice, and healing touch.

Franciscan friars who had been in Asia and her noble supporters decided Sor Jerónima would be perfect to lead the nuns, even though she was in her sixties and very thin and ill from decades of fasting. She enthusiastically agreed, welcoming the predicted hardships. The group of ten nuns assembled and headed first to Seville, Spain's principal port for trade with the Americas, where people flocked to see or touch her, hoping for miraculous cures. Among these was Diego Velázquez, then a young painter, who would go on to become the leading artist of the Spanish court and an influence on scores of other painters, but at the time was far less famous than Sor Jerónima. (See Plate IX.)

Sor Ana de Cristo, one of the group, recorded much about the journey in her long biography of Sor Jerónima, written when the group was in Manila with an eye to promoting Sor Jerónima as a saint. Sor Ana left Spain as a nun able to read but not write, and learned this skill while on the journey from a Franciscan friar who accompanied the group. The nuns traveled first across the Atlantic to the Caribbean, and then on to the east coast of Mexico, in a tiny space cordoned off from the rest of the ship to maintain a partial cloister. From there they traveled on foot or by mules to Mexico City, crossing flooded rivers and sleeping in huts, churches, or in the open. As Sor Ana reported, "we rode the mules like wet chickens, but all in a good mood as we crossed the river, our mother in the lead like a flagship."[39]

Along the way, they met Indigenous, African, and *mestizo* (mixed-heritage) people who had been baptized as Christians and had heard about Spanish holy women with spiritual powers. Sor Jerónima's reputation had not yet spread to Mexico, but that of another Spanish nun, Mother Juana de la Cruz (1481–1534) had. Juana de la Cruz was a mystic whose public visionary experiences included trances during which she spoke in a voice that identified itself as Christ, and whose rosary was supposedly taken to heaven by her guardian angel, where it was blessed by Christ. (This is a different Juana de la Cruz than Sor Juana Inés de la Cruz, the brilliant Mexican nun and writer you will meet in Chapter 6, who is much better known today.) Consulted by powerful leaders during her lifetime, including Emperor Charles V, Juana's body was reported to have not decayed after she died. Her life story was published in the early seventeenth century by supporters attempting to have her declared a saint, and copies were shipped around Europe and to the Spanish colonies. (These often referred to her as a saint, though the campaign for her canonization was ultimately unsuccessful.) The beads from her rosary were held to have miraculous powers, as were any beads that touched these. They could heal the sick, ward off the devil, and calm or raise winds for ships. Wherever they went, Sor Jerónima and the nuns in her group distributed the beads for people to carry or ground them and mixed them with water as medicine against fevers, skin ailments, and dysentery.

The nuns also stopped in what is today one of the most-visited religious sites in the world, the shrine for the Virgin of Guadalupe, now within Mexico City. The shrine marks the site where the Virgin Mary is said to have appeared in 1531 to Juan Diego Cuauhtlatoàtzin, an Indigenous farmer and Christian convert. Speaking in Juan Diego's Nahuatl language, the apparition told him that a church should be built at this site, and her image miraculously appeared on his cloak. Shortly afterward a church dedicated to the Virgin of Guadalupe was begun, named after a royal monastery in Spain where various miracles associated with the Virgin Mary had been reported, including some involving Christian victories over Muslim forces.

The Mexican Virgin of Guadalupe soon far outstripped her Spanish counterpart in significance. Preachers and teachers interpreted her reported appearance as a sign of the Virgin's special protection of Indigenous people and *mestizos*. Pilgrims from all over Mexico began to make the trek to her shrine to view the image on the cloak, which became a symbol of Mexican Christianity. A group of local Christian women took over care of the chapel and its revered contents. (Many aspects of the Virgin of Guadalupe are disputed and controversial, from whether the events actually happened to whether she most strongly symbolizes *mestizo* Christianity or the destruction of Indigenous culture.)

Sor Ana was clearly taken with the Virgin of Guadalupe, providing the first description of the church and cloak written by a woman:

> The next day's journey in New Spain was to a chapel that they call Our Lady of Guadalupe; we spent the night there. It is a paradise and the image is one of much devotion. It was manifested when Mexico was won and dust was being thrown in the eyes of the enemies. She appeared to an Indian in that place where [the chapel] is now, that is, between two boulders, and she told him to have a church built for her. A little fresh water sprang from the ground where her feet had touched. We saw it when we passed by the spot and it is boiling as if over a very large fire. We were given a jug and it tasted salty. Also, some laywomen (*beatas*) who were taking care of the chapel told us that the Virgin herself asked the Indian for his cloak made of cloth, which measured from head to toe. Her image was imprinted on it and then she gave it back to the Indian, telling him to put it in that place, where it would make many miracles.[40]

Here detailed knowledge about what would become the most venerated miracle in the Americas passed directly from local women to European women, who carried it personally to Asia and in their writings to the wider world. Devotion to the Virgin of Guadalupe connected women, as it would so often in the future.

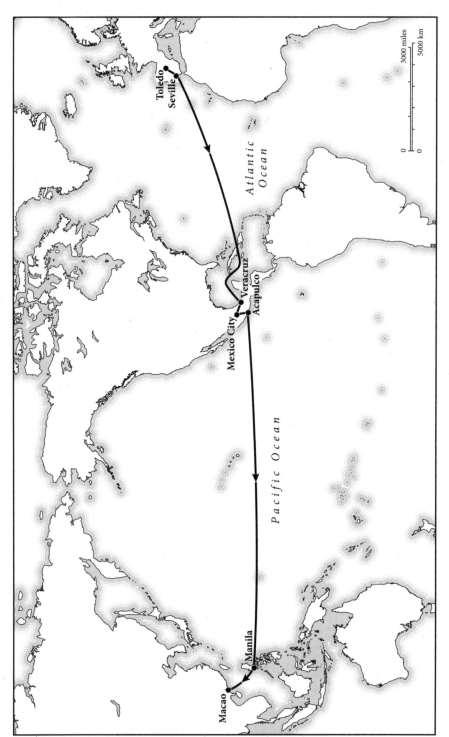

Map 4. *The nuns' journey from Toledo to Manila and Macao.*

After staying for five months in Mexico City, the nuns took to their mules again, traveling through tropical forests and harsh terrain to Acapulco on Mexico's west coast. From here they boarded a Manila galleon, one of the large, sturdy cargo ships that crossed the Pacific, for the three-month journey to the Philippines, arriving there fifteen months after they had left Spain. One of the nuns died of dysentery on the way and was buried at sea, but Sor Jerónima made a miraculous recovery from the same illness, proof, to the nuns and sailors around her, that she was a saint, or nearly one.

In busy and crowded Manila, the nuns converted the house of one of their patrons into their convent and began accepting new novices from creole families, that is, from the locally born Spanish population. Sor Jerónima also wanted to accept *mestiza* and Indigenous nuns, but local elite families opposed this, and she was ordered to allow only creoles. But social class could sometimes trump ethnic background. Among the first group of novices was Naito Lucia (?–1629), the daughter of a wealthy Japanese nobleman (*daimyo*), who, along with other members of his family, had converted to Christianity and then been forced to move to the Philippines. Naito Lucia was accepted as a novice, though she died only a few months later.

How did a Japanese Christian woman happen to be in Manila in the early seventeenth century? Christian missionaries first came to Japan in 1549 under the leadership of the Jesuit Francis Xavier. They gained converts, especially in the southern Japanese island of Kyushu, where Portuguese traders and Jesuit missionaries congregated in the bustling port city of Nagasaki. Here Jesuits built churches and preached, converting ordinary people and elites, including one of the local rulers. By 1610 there were perhaps as many as 300,000 Christians in Japan, a higher percentage of the Japanese population at that time than during any later period. Some historians put the number even higher. Some of these converts were in fact Koreans who had been brought to Japan as prisoners or servants during the Japanese invasion of Korea in the late sixteenth century.

Japanese converts—termed Kirishitan—included many women, who sometimes learned Latin and Portuguese to better study Christian literature. The women persuaded women and men to convert, disputed with

Buddhist priests, translated and wrote religious works, preached sermons, and taught catechism. They even baptized children and women, which Catholic canon law allows laypeople to do in an emergency.

One of these converts was a woman who came to be known as Naito Julia (1566–1627). As expected for a noblewoman, she had married quite young, but her husband died when she was twenty-two, and she became a Buddhist nun and then the abbess of a Buddhist monastery. She converted to Christianity about 1595, taking the Christian name "Julia." She founded a community of women catechists in Kyoto called the *Miyako no bikuni*, whose "principal work," wrote a seventeenth-century Jesuit historian, "was teaching Christian Doctrine to pagan ladies and exhorting them to convert to the holy faith." Such work was especially needed, he commented, "because in Japan it was the custom for upper-class ladies and their daughters not to go out to see men, even clerics."[41] In Europe the Jesuits were hostile to women having an active religious role, but in Japan they apparently supported Naito Julia, as the head of the Jesuits in the Philippines later reports:

> Usually she taught non-Christians Christian doctrine, catechizing them so that they would be converted to our holy faith and be baptized, and at the same time, she attended to the teaching of Christians, instructing them so that they would be ready to confess and receive the holy sacrament. And she was so busy with these holy ministries that regardless of her deep desire to retreat so as to make the [spiritual] exercises of our father Saint Ignatius, she was seldom able to obtain them from the fathers of our Society because they were continuously sending her to evangelize in various kingdoms, cities, and private houses where our own could not go.[42]

But just as Christianity was expanding in Japan, the political situation changed, and leaders attempting to unify Japan became convinced—in part through the arguments of Protestant Dutch and English traders opposed to Portuguese or Jesuit influence—that Christians were intent on military conquest and overthrowing the government. Edicts were passed in 1587 expelling Jesuit missionaries and restricting Japanese Christians, and in 1612 forbidding the propagation of the faith by anyone and ordering the destruction of churches. The 1612 edict was enforced by gruesome torture and executions designed to force Christians to recant, executions that included women, as you will see in Chapter 5. The Spanish nuns on their way to Manila knew about this, as they used the miraculous rosary beads of Juana de la Cruz as protection against being forced to land in Japan as well as against storms and illness.

After the second edict, authorities in Kyoto destroyed Christian churches in the city and the house where Naito Julia and her community were living. They arrested and tortured the women, stripping them and exposing their naked bodies in public. Naito Julia and fourteen other women catechists from Kyoto were expelled from Japan and deported to Manila in 1614, becoming another group of ocean-crossing nuns. One of these women, Marina Pak (1572–1636), was already a migrant in Japan, as she had been an enslaved war captive from Korea before becoming a Christian and joining Naito Julia's group. Another was Naito Lucia, who was Naito Julia's niece and lived briefly in Sor Jerónima's convent as a novice.

In Manila the Japanese and Korean women lived in an enclosed community, adopting the contemplative life of prayer that Naito Julia had wished for earlier. They took in no new members, and the last of the women died in 1646. Meanwhile, Japan continued to ban interactions with Europeans. Finally, in 1641 contact with outsiders was limited to small numbers of Dutch and Chinese merchants who remained on tiny artificial islands in the Nagasaki harbor. The perceived threat of Christianity was one factor in Japan's decision to implement a "closed door" policy, which lasted until the 1860s. Perhaps Japanese leaders were also afraid of the power of women such as Naito Julia, who had been crucial agents in Christianity's spread.

Despite the dangers posed by the Japanese and other local powers, for some Spanish nuns, Manila still wasn't far enough. Sor Magdalena de Cristo (1575–1653) came to the Philippines with Sor Jerónima when she was forty-five. Thirteen years later, in 1634, she crossed the South China Sea from Manila to Macao with seven other women to establish another Franciscan convent there, the first Franciscan convent in continental East Asia. Sor Magdalena and her sisters built up the new community in Macao until she and several others were expelled from the island in 1644, a result of Portugal's split from Spain, which led to the expulsion of many Spanish residents from Macao.

They ran into a terrible storm that almost caused the boat to capsize and were forced to land in Vietnam—then termed Cochinchina—where they were taken prisoner by the local ruler and transported to today's Da Nang. Portuguese and French Jesuits were already there as missionaries, and they reported that the king and queen were quite taken with the women. Members of the court were especially impressed that the women had cut their hair, verified when a court lady reached under a nun's habit to touch her head: "The lady touched the head of the oldest one and finding no hair on it exclaimed loudly that it was certainly true. This was considered a very great wonder."[43]

The queen had a private meeting with the nuns, and although women were not supposed to engage in active missionary work, the Portuguese Jesuit who wrote about this voyage repeatedly emphasized the nuns' role in "showing them the way to heaven," commenting that "in the ten days that the *madres* and two friars were at court and in the aforementioned house, 54 men and women were baptized."[44] Sor Magdalena clearly impressed the local ruler, who eventually allowed the entire group to return to Manila, where Sor Magdalena felt inspired to write her autobiography and *Floresta Franciscana* (*Franciscan Grove*), a three-volume mystical treatise glorifying the Franciscan order.

About the same time that Sor Magdalena was establishing a convent in Macao, French women religious were establishing religious houses in New France, what is now eastern Canada. The first official French settlement was Quebec in 1608, and in 1639 the first nuns immigrated. These included several Augustinian nursing nuns, and also Marie Guyard, a French widow later called Marie of the Incarnation (1599–1672), who founded the first Ursuline convent and school in North America, at Quebec in 1641. (This is often seen as the first girls' school in North America.) She learned several Indigenous languages and took in young women from various groups, including Hurons and Algonquins. In her letters, published first by Jesuits and separately after her death, she reports on the activities of Native American women in her convent, sometimes describing them as effective missionaries. Cécile Gannendaris, for example, a Huron, "was so solidly instructed in our mysteries and so eloquent in explaining them that she was sent new arrivals among the Savages who were asking to embrace the faith. In a few days she had them ready for baptism."[45] Marie wrote thousands of letters to her son, acquaintances, and supporters, some published during her lifetime and many after she died, which form an importance source for our knowledge of life in New France. Marie was declared venerable—the first major rung on the ladder to sainthood—in 1875, beatified by Pope John Paul II, and declared a saint by Pope Francis in 2014.

Marie left a strong immediate legacy as well. Ursuline and Augustinian houses for women grew to seven by the eighteenth century, which meant there were more religious houses for women in French Canada than for men. By 1725, one of every hundred European residents in New France was a nun.

In the 1650s, another French woman, Marguerite Bourgeoys (1620–1700), established a school in the frontier town Montreal—the first European one there. She went back to France twice to recruit more women and set up a teaching congregation modeled on those being founded in Europe by the Ursulines. This took in Canadian-born and immigrant French girls, and later Native American and mixed-heritage girls were admitted as well, both as temporary residents before marriage and as full members. Declared venerable in 1878, she was canonized in 1982, the first woman saint of Canada.

On one of her trips to France, Bourgeoys met with Louis XIV, successfully seeking his support in her efforts to defend her community from being cloistered. She described the Virgin Mary's uncloistered life as her model, writing:

> We are asked why we prefer to be vagabonds rather than cloistered, the cloister being a protection for persons of our sex. Why do we not make solemn vows which are conducive to greater perfection and which draw women to religious life? Why do we go on missions that put us in danger of suffering greatly and even of being captured, killed or burned by the Indians? . . . The state we embrace and to which we commit ourselves in this uncloistered community is the same as that of the Blessed Virgin, our foundress, our mother and our queen. Having received from God this country as her domain in accordance with the prayers of the first settlers, she planned to have

the little girls taught to be good Christians so that they would later be good mothers of families. For this she chose the poor women of the Congregation without brilliance, skill, talents or goods; just as Our Lord chose men who were not refined or held in high esteem by the world to teach everyone his doctrine and his Gospel.[46]

Today we might cringe at Marguerite Bourgeoys' comment that the Virgin Mary "received from God this country as her domain in accordance with the prayers of the first settlers," as if no one was living on the land before the French arrived. The communities that she started did take in Indigenous and mixed-heritage women and Sor Jerónima wanted to, but most convents did not. The first convent especially for Indigenous women in the Philippines was not founded until 1721 and in Mexico City not until 1728. As you will see in more detail in Chapter 6, in European colonies, individual women and women's groups operated within the context of conquest and enormous power differences. Nuns could cross oceans, but they did not leave the social, religious, and racial hierarchies of Europe behind. Instead they helped replicate them in the places they went.

Some of the women in this chapter were willing travelers, but many moved or migrated because they were forced to, sometimes by women rulers. Jews, Muslims, and converts from both groups left Spain because of Isabel of Castile's policies, Protestants left England because of Mary I's and left Austria because of Maria Theresa's, Catholics left England and Ireland because of Elizabeth I's. Women rulers as a group were neither more nor less tolerant of religious difference than men rulers. It is important to remember that women caused expulsion and exile as well as experiencing these.

Migration was wrenching. Jewish and Muslim women exiled from Iberia were leaving places where their families had lived for centuries in vibrant communities, and often had to travel great distances to completely different physical and cultural environments before they could begin to establish a community again. Protestant and Catholic laywomen whose religious allegiance was unacceptable to the rulers of their homelands could generally find a place that would tolerate them not quite so far away, but toleration did not necessarily mean acceptance and was not always permanent. Authorities sometimes intentionally separated parents and children, or threatened to do so to force agreement with their policies. Many families moved again and again, within a single generation or over several. Nuns whose convents were closed were leaving places that might have housed generations of family members, and still housed their bones, though convent cemeteries were sometimes demolished as well. Migration also shaped the experiences of women who did not move, as they took over the responsibilities of those who had left and created new ways of practicing their faith.

Migration provided opportunities for ingenuity, kindness, wit, independence, and bravery. This chapter is full of women who demonstrated all of these: the wealthy Jewish merchant Gracia Nasi, who transported her poorer co-religionists out of harm's way; the teenaged Huguenot Suzanne de Champagné, who caught mackerel for her younger siblings to eat and made clothing for them to wear as they were exiled from France; the aged Quaker troublemaker Elizabeth Hooton, who forced the king to hear her concerns; the abbess Mary Knatchbull, who passed along secret messages for royalists in her attempts to restore England to Catholicism. The museum and historic site dedicated to Marguerite Bourgeoys in the heart of Montreal captures these positive qualities, describing her admiringly on its walls and website as "a key figure in the origins of Montreal—Montreal's foremost educator, pioneer, entrepreneur, founder and great advocate—a woman of character whose values are still relevant today."

Together with men who moved, women took their traditions and beliefs with them and recreated meaningful religious life in new homes and places of worship. Many bonded with other women on their travels, both those they traveled with and those they met. Some established expatriate communities and maintained their original culture as much as they could, while others created new hybrid identities or ultimately integrated into their new place of residence. Their opportunities to do so were shaped by their gender, but also by their wealth, social status, race, and many other factors. In moving, they sometimes displaced the people who had long lived in some areas, aided in colonial settings by violence and disease.

A few women commented that moving could bring opportunities. Mary Ward hoped that the women in her Institute could return to England as missionaries, for "it seems that the female sex also in its own measure, should and can . . . undertake something more than ordinary." More described the hardships travel and migration brought. "It has deprived me of the company of my husband, the presence of my daughter whom I was forced to abandon and all that is mine," wrote the French Huguenot Ambroise Pithou. Those who left no record of their thoughts may also have wished that the opportunities to demonstrate resourcefulness and courage or call on God for help and deliverance had been fewer.

———⟫•⟪———

CHAPTER FOUR

MARTYRS

I have been commanded to speak, and I have been called to that, so I may not remain silent about it. . . . If they were to burn me tomorrow, or drown me in a Sack, that's all the same to me: as the Lord has ordained it, so it must be.

Weynken Claes, Dutch Protestant martyr

I am sentenced to die for harbouring a Catholic priest, and so far I am from repenting for having so done, that I wish, with all my soul, that where I have entertained one, I could have entertained a thousand.

Anne Line, English Catholic martyr

Migration was one result of authorities' opposition to religious dissent, and martyrdom was another. Catholic leaders imprisoned and executed Protestants, while Protestant leaders imprisoned and executed Catholics. Protestants and Catholics executed Anabaptists and other types of radicals and dissenters whose ideas they regarded as unacceptable or threatening, along with Jewish and Muslim converts accused of returning to their original faith. Outside of Europe, missionaries, members of religious orders, and laypeople were arrested, tried, and sometimes executed for teaching or espousing Christian doctrine. Religious opposition was sometimes mixed with political rebellion, particularly in the minds of authorities, who could then execute people for what they portrayed as treason or revolt rather than simply for dissent.

Women made up a significant share of those arrested, tried, tortured, punished, and ultimately executed because of their religious beliefs, perhaps 20 per cent in total. If we understand martyrdom to mean dying because of your religion, most women martyrs in sixteenth-century Europe were the Jewish, Muslim, *conversa*, and *Morisca* women and girls from Spain and Portugal who were killed directly for their religious practices or who died through exile or in rebellions. But Christian authorities also tortured and killed Christian women. If we understand martyrdom to mean dying because of *someone else's* religious ideas, most women who did so were those accused of witchcraft.

When questioned about their religious beliefs, most people told authorities what they wanted to hear. Officials also generally tried to get people to recant and thus avoid death—sometimes many times over months or years—as a repentant heretic provided better support for prevailing religious ideas than a dead one. So martyrdom was rare— perhaps 3,000 Christians were killed outright for religious dissent across all of western Europe in the sixteenth and seventeenth centuries, fewer than died in a single outbreak of the plague.

The stories of martyrs came to have an impact far greater than their number, however. Accounts of martyrs' steadfastness in the face of torture and death circulated orally, in songs, and in print. They were often gathered into large collections called martyrologies, illustrated with woodcuts and engravings. These were designed to both outrage and comfort, and to stimulate those who read them into similar heroism if confronted on their faith. Martyrologies shaped religious identities, first in Europe and then beyond when European Christians traveled, moved, and migrated. The oral stories of martyrs also traveled, and became the basis for songs, plays, and poems far from the place where the individual had died.

It may be difficult for us to read martyrologies, with their gruesome accounts of torture after torture, but they were very popular reading material in the sixteenth and seventeenth centuries. They might be the only book that families in which people could read owned, other than the Bible. When I teach about the Reformations I warn those in the class that I will be talking about suffering and pain, but at the time stories of martyrdom—especially those involving young people—were regularly given to schoolchildren and novices in convents as examples they should follow.

Those arrested and tried for their faith included educated women and members of the elite, and also poor city dwellers and villagers. Records of their trials and witness testimony are some of the few sources we have for the religious ideas of ordinary people. Their voices are not unfiltered. Trial records were written by the hostile male authorities who were questioning and sometimes torturing them, often in a language different from the one spoken by the accused. Witness testimony might come from people who spoke their language and agreed with them in matters of faith, but it was often recorded long after the events and written with specific aims in mind. Despite their limitations, through these sources we learn that many women (and men) who could not read or read very well had memorized large parts of the Bible by heart and could argue complicated theological concepts. They often looked back to martyrs of the early Church, whose stories they had heard or read about, for inspiration and guidance.

Contemporaries recognized the power that women's martyrdom could have. The Catholic polemicist Florimund de Raemond, describing Protestant women martyred in France, wrote how "simple weak women seek out torments to prove their faith. Going to their death they cry out only 'Christ, Savior,' and sing some Psalm. Young virgins march most gaily to their execution, as if they were going to their marriage bed . . . in a word, to die smiling, like those who eat the Sardinian herb [a poisonous plant]." The women's actions, he wrote, "cast confusion not only in the souls of the simple, but also in those of the greatest."[1] He saw this clearly as a bad thing, but for those who shared the martyrs' beliefs this was the pinnacle of faith.

The authorities who imprisoned and executed religious dissenters sometimes also investigated, arrested, imprisoned, tortured, and executed people for witchcraft. The numbers were much higher, however. Between 100,000 and 200,000 people were officially tried, and between 40,000 and 60,000 were executed for witchcraft from the late fifteenth through the seventeenth century in Europe; 80 per cent of these were women, roughly the opposite of the gender balance among martyrs.

The witch-hunts occurred at the same time as the Reformations, but their histories are entangled rather than fused. Those accused of witchcraft might be charged with heresy, but only a few religious dissidents were accused of witchcraft, as these were generally separate categories in the minds of the authorities. Protestants and Catholics, laymen and clergy, all hunted witches. Skeptics about the power of witches included people from all Christian denominations. Those accused of witchcraft are better seen as victims rather than martyrs, but in the eyes of persecuting authorities both dissenters and witches were enemies to be eradicated.

MARTYRS IN SONG AND STORY

The first Protestant woman martyred in Reformation Europe was Weynken Claes, burned at the stake at The Hague in the Netherlands in 1527 after being imprisoned for half a year. She denied the validity of core Catholic teachings, including transubstantiation—the idea that, when consecrated by a priest, the bread and wine in the Eucharist become the body and blood of Christ—and the Church's power to forgive sin. When shown a wooden crucifix during her lengthy interrogation, she is reported to have said, "This is not my God, I have been saved through a different Cross. That is a wooden God, throw it into the fire, and warm yourselves with him." Asked about sacrificial oil, she said, "Oil is good for a salad, or for greasing your shoes." Asked about the sacrament of the Eucharist, she answered, "I hold your Sacrament to be bread and flour, and if you people believe it to be a God, so I say it is your Devil." Authorities brought in one of her female friends, who asked, " 'Dear Mother, couldn't you just think what you wanted, and remain silent about it? Then you wouldn't have to die.' Weynken answered by saying: 'Dear Sister, I have been commanded to speak, and I have been called to that, so I may not remain silent about it. . . . If they were to burn me tomorrow, or drown me in a Sack, that's all the same to me: as the Lord has ordained it, so it must be, and not otherwise; I will remain steadfast in the Lord.' "[2]

Weynken Claes was burned, in the words of the authorities, "so that no memory would remain of her."[3] Their aim was not fulfilled. A lengthy pamphlet with her interrogation and a grisly description of her execution was printed immediately in Dutch and then translated into German, though efforts were made to trace and destroy all copies. Her views about the sacraments were shared by many Protestants, and Lutherans and Calvinists later claimed her as one of their martyrs. They were also key teachings of Anabaptists, who later added a denial of the validity of infant baptism and a rejection of other practices they saw as un-biblical to the mix. Anabaptists came to view her as one of their own as well.

People not only read about martyrs, but also sang about them. Singing in German, Dutch, English, and other vernacular languages was an important part of Protestant worship, melding a group of individuals into a community of believers. There were prayer songs, songs of consolation, songs of advice, rhymed psalms, and songs that told dramatic stories from the Bible, many sung to secular melodies that people would know. And there were songs about martyrs, often with many, many verses that told the story from start to finish. Most of these were written after a martyr's death, but a few by martyrs themselves. Anna Jansz, executed by drowning in Rotterdam in 1539, penned the apocalyptic "Trumpet Song," proclaiming: "Arise O Zion, gird your loins, Prepare yourself for battle. . . . The Lord will come to repay, To avenge the blood of us all!" Martha Baerts, a domestic servant who was beheaded along with three other women in Ghent in 1560, told in her song of long attempts to convince her and the other women to recant: "The tempters torment me so much / To separate me from God's creed; / But yet, believe them I will not, / For to ruin me they seek." She ended with a call to others: "I pray all who hear this Song. / Pray, do not be frightened off / From taking on the cross; / God can help us endure."[4]

Song was especially important for Anabaptists, who used it to witness to the world. Anna Jansz was initially arrested when people heard her singing an Anabaptist song while traveling. When waiting to be executed in Antwerp, Lijsken Dircks "spoke boldly and valiantly to the people, and sang a beautiful hymn, so that people were greatly astonished."[5] The authorities moved her to a place where fewer people could hear her, but she kept singing.

The hymn "Six Women of Antwerp" highlights six women imprisoned and executed in 1559, comparing the pains of torture to those of childbirth: "They started to torture two of the maidens; / Little did those Tyrants consider that we all emerge on this earth in pain, / Brought forth through women." But God "reveals himself in his weak vessels," and the women were "in their faith strong, as men might be."[6] Songs were passed from person to person, written down and shared as manuscripts, and then printed in songbooks, often with a note about the melody, and the scriptural references noted in the margin. Multi-versed songs detailing women's "manly courage" were included in printed Anabaptist songbooks, and in those of groups in the Anabaptist tradition such as Mennonites and Hutterites, from the sixteenth century to today.

Couples were sometimes arrested at the same time, though physically separated in prison. For a few, consoling letters they wrote to one another have survived. Lijsken Dircks exchanged letters with her husband Jeronimus Segersz, full of biblical references she hoped would inspire him:

> I wish us both the crucified Christ as a Protector and Shepherd of our Souls. He himself will keep us in all righteousness, holiness and truth to the very end, and he will also keep us as his sons and daughters, if we keep our [Heb 3:14] Devotion to his being until the very end, indeed, as the [Zech 2:8] apple of his eye. . . . The Lord is faithful (says Paul), he will not let us be tested beyond our ability. [2 Cor 1:3] . . . My dearly beloved husband in the Lord, you have prevailed through some trials; in those trials you have remained steadfast, the Lord be given eternal praise and glory for his great mercy. And I also pray the Lord, with weeping, that he will make me, too, fitting for that, to suffer for his name's sake.[7]

The original did not include the chapter and verse citations, as Dircks assumed her husband would recognize them anyway, but a later editor was not so sure of his readers, so put them in.

Dircks and Segersz were both executed, though six months apart, as she was pregnant at the time of her imprisonment, and the authorities waited until after the child was born to drown her. Worried about her supporters, they did this in the middle of the night, but witnesses still reported "that she went boldly unto death," and that husband and wife had, indeed, "remained steadfast."

Husbands were not the only family members to whom women directed their last thoughts. Along with writing the "Trumpet Song," Anna Jansz wrote a lengthy testimonial to her infant son Isaiah the day she was executed, filled with biblical allusions. She provided him with spiritual advice: "My son, hear the instruction of your mother, and open your ears to hear the words of my mouth. Watch, today I am travelling the path of the Prophets, Apostles, and Martyrs, and drink from the cup from which they have all tasted. . . . Let the light of Scripture shine through you. Love your Neighbour; with an effusive, passionate heart deal your bread to the hungry."[8] Mayken Boosers of Doornik, burned in 1564, also left a testament to her children: "Let a heartfelt and affectionate greeting be written to you, my dear children, from your mother who is now imprisoned for the sake of upright truth. . . . My children, act according to the Lord's will. I, your mother, hope to travel this road before you: note in what way, and what manner, I go before you, and do not attend to the honor of this world, but consider it an honor to suffer for the name of our God."[9]

Maeyken Wens, burned in Antwerp in 1573, wrote to her oldest son Adriaen, in the only handwritten letter by a female Dutch martyr for which the original survives:

Oh my dear son! Although I have been taken from you here, if you will turn yourself to the fear of God from your youth, you will have your mother again in the new Jerusalem up above; there will be no more parting. My dear son, I hope now to be going before you (follow me in this if you, all of you, love your souls), for there is no other path to salvation than this one. And now I want to commend all of you to the Lord. The Lord will be the keeper of you all; I entrust this to the Lord, that he will do this, if you will indeed seek him. Love one another all the days of your lives that you are with one another. Do sometimes take Hansken [her three-year-old son] in your arms for me; and if your father should be taken from you, take care of one another. The Lord keep you all of you, my dear children; kiss one another for me as a remembrance of me. Farewell my dear children, all of you. My dear son, there is no need to fear this suffering, for compared to that which remains eternal it signifies nothing. The Lord takes away all fear; I was almost beside myself with joy when I was sentenced. Therefore never cease fearing God on account of this timely death; I cannot thank God sufficiently for all the [mercies] which God has shown me. Here is yet another goodbye, my dear son Adriaen, be kind to your sorrowing father all the days of your life, and do not cause him any pain. I ask all of you the same thing, for that which I say to the eldest, I mean also for the youngest. With this I want to commend you once again to the Lord.

I wrote this after I was sentenced and when I was about to die for my testimony for Jesus Christ, the 5th day of October in the year of our Lord Jesus Christ, 1573.[10]

Trial testimonies, songs, and letters of these women, along with those of other Dutch radicals, were included in martyrological collections. In the sixteenth century these culminated in *Het Offer des Heeren* (*Sacrifices for the Lord*), first published in 1562 and seeing ten editions before the century's end. *Het Offer* formed the core of the most famous Anabaptist martyrology, the Dutch Mennonite Thieleman van Braght's *Martelaers Spiegel* (*Martyrs Mirror*), first published in 1660 in Dutch, in the eighteenth century in German, and in the twentieth century in English. The original Dutch version was expanded in an ornate second edition in 1685, lavishly illustrated with 104 copper engravings by the Dutch engraver Jan Luyken. These were often included in later editions and sometimes published on their own, with the martyrs displaying visually the qualities related in the text: bravery, piety, trust in God, concern for others. Luyken often chose the most agonizing detail of a martyr's experience for his engravings. Often this was the death itself, so there are people being crucified, burned alive, pierced with pitchforks, buried, and drowned. But sometimes this was emotional rather than physical pain. The engraving of Maeyken Wens shows her son Adriaen, who watched the execution, searching the ashes for the iron screw that was screwed into her tongue so she could not testify at the stake, and that of Anna Jansz shows her saying goodbye to her infant son.

In *Het Offer*, about 20 per cent of the attention goes to women, and in *Martyrs Mirror* about 30 per cent, a proportion far higher than in the literature of other persecuted groups. (And far outweighing the amount of text devoted to women in every recent history of the Reformation or

4. Martyrs Mirror *etching of Anna Jansz. On her way to be executed by drowning, Anna Jansz gives her infant son Isaiah to an impoverished baker to raise him, along with a bag of money. The martyrology reports that her son later became mayor of the city of Rotterdam, so he would have easily been able to read the court records of his mother's trial, although we don't know if he did.*

of martyrdom.) Of the fifty-four etchings in *Martyrs Mirror* that depict sixteenth-century martyrdoms, twelve include or are only of women. Martyrologies are clearly partisan—their purpose is to portray the heroism of the martyrs and the cruelty of those who killed them. Their editors certainly made choices, modifying language and adding biblical references. But the editors also felt a strong sense of responsibility to get the account right, and most scholars today see the texts as idealizing, but reasonably authentic. Court records that still exist have generally backed up the accounts of the martyrologies, though their authors sought to demonize the martyrs rather than venerate them. They have also revealed new information, which helps us learn more about what happened.

Most Anabaptists stressed that every believer, male and female, was to search Scripture and share their understanding with others, and that all were equal before the eyes of the Lord. But women's experiences of martyrdom were different than men's. None of their interrogators, torturers, judges, or executioners were women. For some women, the thought that unrelated men would be seeing and touching their bodies was worse than the thought of torture. Elisabeth von Leeuwarden, who had left a convent and joined an Anabaptist group, said to her inquisitors: "O my Lords, do not shame me, for never yet has a man touched my naked body."[11] Many married women were pregnant while in prison, which delayed their executions, but also created extra costs for their family because of the longer imprisonment, as prisoners generally had to provide for their own upkeep. Women also worried about who would care for their new infant after they were dead, as well as the children they already had. Anabaptists who were fathers sometimes mention their children in their testimony or letters, but Anabaptists who were mothers almost always do.

The last Anabaptist martyr in the Netherlands was a woman, Anneke van der Hove, a domestic servant buried alive outside Brussels in 1597. Several songs and pamphlets describing her bravery and grim fate appeared in print shortly after her death, their details picked up and expanded in the *Martyrs Mirror*, with an engraving.

Persecution of radicals continued in the seventeenth century, though not in the Netherlands. The seven northern provinces of the Netherlands won their independence from Spain through warfare in the late sixteenth and early seventeenth centuries, becoming the Republic of the United Provinces of the Netherlands. (This long official name is shortened in various ways: the United Provinces, the Netherlands—which means "low countries"—and the Dutch Republic all refer to the same political entity; "Dutch" is a variant of the word "*Deutsch*," meaning German.) This political independence facilitated amazing commercial prosperity, as did broad policies of religious toleration unique in Europe. English Puritans and Catholics, French Huguenots, and Iberian Jews were welcome in the Netherlands, as were those fleeing religious or political persecution in other parts of Europe. They brought their money, but more importantly their talents and hard work, as immigrants always do, providing a basis for economic prosperity that was the envy of the world. When van Braght published *Martyrs Mirror* in 1660, his primary aim was to remind his readers of the heroism of the past and make sure that the stories of martyrs were not forgotten, not to warn Anabaptists and Mennonites about present dangers.

DYING FOR THEIR FAITH

The fluctuating politics in the British Isles in the sixteenth century meant that what was regarded as religious dissent changed as the aims of the monarch did. Under Henry VIII, both people born in England and immigrants from the continent were executed under heresy laws for holding and teaching Protestant beliefs and smuggling Protestant books. This would continue as Henry VIII himself rejected the authority of the pope and dissolved some Catholic institutions. Henry also executed Catholics, officially for treason, but actually for rejecting his title as supreme head of the Church of England. Protestants and Catholics were sometimes even taken to their executions together. The vast majority of those executed for heresy or dissent during Henry's reign were men, many of them clergy or government officials, but there were also a few women.

The first—and ultimately most famous—woman executed for acting on Protestant beliefs in England was Anne Askew (*c.* 1521–1546), questioned, tortured, and killed at the very end of Henry VIII's reign. Askew was from a prominent landowning family in Lincolnshire. Her father was a gentleman at Henry's court and had been one of the jurors in Anne Boleyn's trial. Forced into a marriage to a Catholic against her will, Askew began reading the Bible and other religious texts publicly, though the Act in Advancement of Religion in 1543 allowed women of the nobility and gentry to read the Bible only in private. (Ordinary women, servants, apprentices, and other lower-status people were not to read the Bible at all.) Anne's husband threw her out, and she responded by seeking a divorce, arguing on biblical grounds that this was allowed because he was an "unbelieving partner." She left her husband and went to London, where she again spoke publicly about her religious ideas. She was imprisoned on suspicion of heresy in 1545 and interrogated by Edmund Bonner, the bishop of London, and other officials.

Very quickly after her death, Askew's accounts of her two interrogations, titled her *Examinations*, were edited and printed, with added commentary, by the English Protestant propagandist John Bale, who was in exile on the continent. Bale claims that she wrote them herself and smuggled them out of prison, but no manuscript survives, so it is impossible to tell how accurately they represent what she actually said. They do reflect what an intelligent, well-educated, biblically knowledgeable woman *might* have said, and they were regarded as her words for centuries, by both her opponents and her supporters. So we can view them as what we might call the textual Anne Askew, recognizing that this is not exactly the same as the historical person.

During the interrogation, Bonner questioned Askew about her ideas about confession, the sacraments, private masses, and other matters. To the annoyance of her interrogators, she often replied simply, "I believe as the scripture doth teach me," not giving them what they wanted to hear. Sometimes she said nothing at all: "My Lord Mayor sayde one thing unto my charge . . . and it was whether a mouse eating the host received god or no. This question did I never aske, but indeed they asked it of me whereunto I made them no answer but smiled." Her questioners brought up the issue of women speaking publicly about religion several times:

Then the bishops chancellor rebuked me, and said that I was much to blame for uttering the scriptures. For S. Paule (he said) forbode women to speke or to talke of the word of god. I answered him that I knew Paules meaning so well as he, which is I. Corinthians xiv, that a woman ought not to speke in the congregation by way of teaching. And then I asked him, how many women he had sene, go into the Pulpit and preache. He saide, he never saw none. Then I said, he ought to finde no fault in poor women, except they had offended the law.

She defended her silence—perhaps somewhat mockingly—with references to biblical teachings about gender: "Then he asked me, why I had so few words. And I answered God hath given me the gyfte of knowledge but not of utterance. And Solomon saith, that a woman of few words is a gift of God. Proverb XIX." And later: "it was against S. Paules learning, that I being a woman, should interpret the scriptures, specially where so many wise learned men were." After twelve days of this, Bonner released her and told her to go back to her husband in Lincoln. She did go back to Lincoln but stayed with her brother.

Askew was arrested again the following year and asked repeatedly about the bread in the sacrament of the Eucharist. She maintained that this "was left to us to be received with thanksgiving, in remembrance of Christ's death," a position that fit with what many Protestants were teaching. Along with biblical texts, she also used everyday experience in her arguments:

> Yea, for the same Son of God that was borne of the Virgin Marye is now glorious in heaven, and wyll come againe from thens at the latter day like as he went up, Acts 1. And as for that ye call your God, it is but a piece of breade. For a more proof thereof (marke it when ye list) Let it lie in the box but three months, and it will mold and turn to nothing that is good. Whereupon I am persuaded that it can not be god.

She was threatened with burning if she did not recant, and then tortured by a group of high-ranking secular and religious officials. Torture was very unusual treatment for a woman of high social standing, but Askew's social position may, in fact, have been part of the reason for this. Henry's court was divided between religious conservatives, who favored an alliance with Catholics, and reformers, who wanted England to take a more Protestant direction. Henry was at this point married to Catherine Parr, his sixth and final wife, and there were suspicions that the queen and some of the women in her circle were pushing for more clearly Protestant measures.

During the second interrogation, Askew was specifically asked about certain of Catherine's ladies-in-waiting, as interrogators hoped she would implicate them, or perhaps the queen herself. She refused, and, as she tells it, "then they dyd put me on the racke bycause I confessed no ladies nor gentyll women to be of my opinion, and thereupon they kept me a long time." Her clothes were taken off, other than her shift, and she was pulled on the rack so hard that her shoulders and hips were yanked from their sockets and her elbows and knees were dislocated. Asked again "if I wolde leave my opinion . . . I sent him again word that I wold rather die rather than break my fayth."[12] Several weeks later, she was carried to execution in a chair, as she was unable to stand. When she was burned at the stake she had to be held upright with chains.

Included with her accounts in Bale's printed version are some of her letters, prayers and meditations, and a ballad she ostensibly wrote and sang in prison:

> Like as the armed knight
> Appointed to the field,
> With this world will I fight
> And Faith shall be my shield. . . .
> I now rejoice in heart
> And Hope bid me do so
> For Christ will take my part
> And ease me of my woe.

Bale's *Examinations* were printed in 1546 and 1547, somewhere in continental Europe, and then smuggled into England. It would have been impossible to print them in England, as immediately after her death, in a proclamation naming Askew specifically, King Henry VIII had made it illegal for "any man, woman, or person, of what estate, condition, or degree soever" to "receive, have, take, or keep in his or their possession" any Protestant works. They were reprinted in England once it became safe to do so. They were also included, with long added commentary, in John Foxe's *Acts and Monuments*, the most influential English Protestant martyrology, first published in 1563.

Bale and Foxe present Askew as virtuous and heroic, but Catholic commentators seized on the fact that she had left her husband to portray her as immoral and disruptive. The English Jesuit Robert Parsons wrote of Askew in 1604, "she was a coy dame, and of very evil fame for wantonnesse: in that she left the company of her husband Maister Kyme, to gad up & down the countrey a ghospelling & ghossiping where she might, & ought not. . . . [She] did follow the liberty of the new ghospell, going up and down at her pleasure, to make new ghospellers and Proselits of her religion." Parsons ignores her beliefs, and instead focuses on her independence and her wit: "And the proud and presumptuous answers, quips, & nips, which she have both in matter of Religion & otherwise, to the Kings Councill, and Bishops, when they examined her and dealt with her seriously for her amendment, do well shew her intolerable arrogancy."[13] Sixty years after her death, Askew's "quips and nips" still upset her Catholic opponents. Today they can be found on online quotation sites and inspirational posters: "God has given me the bread of adversity and the water of trouble."

Askew is unique in having (most likely) left a written legacy. Joan Bocher, who came to the attention of authorities in the 1530s and 1540s, is much more typical. Bocher lived in Kent in southeast England, where she apparently encountered Dutch Anabaptist refugees, from whom she learned a slightly different view of how Christ could be both human and divine than that accepted by most Protestants. (The standard view was that Christ received his human flesh from Mary, but some radicals taught that God imparted human flesh to Jesus directly from heaven.) With Henry VIII's death and the accession of Edward VI in 1547, England took a more Protestant turn, but holding certain ideas of radical Protestants still left one liable to persecution.

Bocher was arrested and released, then arrested again and imprisoned for over a year as various people, including the archbishop of Canterbury Thomas Cranmer, tried to convince her to recant her ideas. She would not and was burned at the stake in 1550. Joan Bocher left no writings herself, and the sources about her are vague and contradictory.

Henry VIII executed Catholics as well as Protestants, ranging from powerful and prominent government officials such as Sir Thomas More to ordinary monks and laymen. There were only two women executed, also from opposite ends of the social scale. Elizabeth Barton (1506–1534) was a teenaged domestic servant in Kent, who began to see visions, claimed she could prophesy the future, and urged people to honor the Virgin Mary and resist Protestant teachings. Some of her prophecies appeared to come true and her fame as the "Holy Maid of Kent" spread. Church authorities assessed her orthodoxy and placed her in a Benedictine convent. She also met with high officials, and even with King Henry, all of whom supported her, as her visions fit with their aims at that point. But Henry's decision to annul his marriage to Catherine of Aragon and declare himself the head of the English Church changed the situation: Barton prophesied that if the king remarried he would die quickly and go to hell. She was arrested, forced to confess she had made up her visions, and charged with being at the center of a treasonous conspiracy against the king. She and five of her male supporters were hanged and her head was put on a spike at London Bridge, the only woman in history whose actions were seen as serious enough to warrant this.

Margaret Pole, Countess of Salisbury (1473–1541), was a member of the Plantagenet dynasty that had ruled England before the Tudors and a distant relative of Henry VIII. She was a lady-in-waiting to Catherine of Aragon, and governess to Princess Mary, to whom she remained loyal. Her sons and other male relatives were involved in several revolts and alleged Catholic conspiracies against Henry, and Margaret Pole may have been as well, though much of the evidence against her appears to have been fabricated. She was arrested, held in the Tower of London for two and a half years, and ultimately executed in 1541 when she was nearly seventy, denying to the end that she had done anything wrong. Her younger son Reginald was by this point a cardinal in the Catholic Church and declared his mother a martyr to the faith. Three hundred and fifty years later, in 1886, Margaret was beatified by the pope, often a step on the road to being made a saint, though Margaret never was.

Edward's death in 1553 left his older sister the Catholic Mary Tudor as queen. She revived medieval acts against heresy, and hundreds of wealthy and middle-class Protestants fled into exile. Many who proclaimed their beliefs publicly were arrested and imprisoned, and, beginning in 1555, executed if they refused to recant, some by being burned at the stake. Trials were presided over by bishops, who excommunicated those found guilty and turned them over to secular judges for execution. Roughly 280 people were executed for heresy during Mary's reign, 56 of whom were women. Most of these were quite poor. Some were executed alone and others with family members or in small groups.

One of the Marian exiles was John Foxe, a Protestant author and deacon, who, while he was living in various European cities, began to compile a book of Christian martyrs beginning with the early Church. As reports of the executions in England reached the continent, Foxe added these, publishing a 700-page martyrology in Latin in Basel in 1559. With Mary's death, Foxe returned to London, where he gathered materials— trial records, bishops' reports, eyewitness testimony, pamphlets—and in

1563 published in English an 1,800-page martyrology, *Acts and Monuments*, which made him immediately famous. (The book is often called "Foxe's Book of Martyrs," not its official title.) The book included martyrs from the early Church and Middle Ages but focused particularly on Protestants who had been killed during Mary's reign.

Acts and Monuments was one of the most extensively illustrated works of its time, with 57 woodcuts in the first 1563 edition and 153 in the even-larger 1583 edition, of which 77 were of Mary's reign. The wood-cuts allowed even those who could not read to share some of the experience of the executed and witnesses, and were widely reproduced beyond the text as well. *Acts and Monuments* shaped Protestant identity in England and cemented Mary's reputation as "Bloody Mary." Foxe was, of course, highly partisan in his presentation, but the rough outlines of what he presents are accurate, and he often included documents verbatim. For some of the events, *Acts and Monuments* is the only source available.

Acts and Monuments is full of women in both text and illustrations, from well-known martyrs such as Anne Askew, whose account of her ordeal and beliefs—based on Bale's *Examinations*—is the longest entry on a woman, to women who are given only a line or two and identified only by place. Women are the subjects of small woodblocks that show a single individual or a group in flames. These are generic in terms of style and reused throughout the text, sometimes with the number and sex of the martyrs in text and image not matching each other. But there are also large woodcuts of individual female martyrs, with the women highly individualized in terms of visual appearance.

The most horrific image of women in *Acts and Monuments* is that of three women of Guernsey, one of the islands in the English Channel off the coast of Normandy. Katherine Cawches, her younger daughter Guillemine, and her elder daughter Perotine Massey were charged with not attending Catholic services and unspecified other acts of heresy, and condemned to be burned:

> They were first strangled, but the rope brake before they were dead, and so the poor women fell in the fire. Perotine, who was then great with child, did fall on her side, where happened a rueful sight, not only to the eyes of all that there stood, but also to the ears of all true-hearted

Christians that shall read this history. For as the belly of the woman burst asunder by the vehemence of the flame, the infant, being a fair man-child, fell into the fire, and eftsoons being taken out of the fire by one W. House, was laid upon the grass. Then was the child had to the provost, and from him to the bailiff, who gave censure that it should be carried back again, and cast into the fire. And so the infant, baptized in his own blood, to fill up the number of God's innocent saints, was both born and died a martyr.[14]

Hand-coloring of these woodcuts, which began in the sixteenth century, only added to the gruesomeness. The images were so violent, in fact, that by the late nineteenth century editors replaced them with new

5. *In this stylized woodcut from* Acts and Monuments, *the three women martyrs from Guernsey are surrounded by flames and smoke, while some soldiers look on and others pay little attention. A Catholic critic later blamed Perotine Massey for her son's death, arguing that she should have "pleaded the belly," that is, revealed that she was pregnant, which would have delayed the execution until after the birth.*

illustrations more suited to a Victorian sensibility. These show the moment *before* violence occurs rather than the reality of execution, as showing bare-breasted women in extreme agony was no longer acceptable.

In the text, Foxe portrays the women with qualities that were widely accepted norms for female behavior: piety, humility, charity, cheerfulness, generosity. Margary Polley, the first woman to be executed, was a widow "in the prime of her life, pious, charitable, humane, learned in the Scriptures, and beloved by all who knew her," writes Foxe. Cecile Ormes was thirty-two, "a very simple woman, but yet zelous in the Lordes cause." A woman identified only as "Prestes wife," "about 54 years of age," had a "chearefull countenance, so liuely, as though she had bene prepared for that day of her mariage to meete the Lambe: most pacient of her wordes & answeres, sober in apparel, meat & drinke, and would neuer be idle: a great comfort to as many as would talke with her: good to the poore."

But some of the women also acted in ways that subverted expectations for proper female conduct. Anne Askew left her husband, sought a divorce, and answered her interrogators cleverly with Scripture. Agnes Potten and Joan Trunchfield (d. 1556), the wives of artisans in Ipswich, were arrested and imprisoned for bringing food to a jailed married clergyman; executed together, they remained "ardent and zealous" and publicly urged those watching "to lay hold on the Word of God, and not upon man's devices and inventions." Agnes Prest (d. 1557) left her Catholic husband and during her examinations declared that she had renounced her earthly spouse for the sake of Christ, her heavenly spouse. Alice Driver (1528?–1558), also burned at Ipswich, likened Queen Mary to Jezebel, for which her ears were cut off. Comparing herself to her judges, she proclaimed: "I was an honest poor man's daughter, never brought up in the University, as you have been, but I have driven the plough before my father many a time (I thank God): yet, notwithstanding, in the defence of God's truth, and in the cause of my Master Christ, by His grace I will set my foot against the foot of any of you all, in the maintenance and defence of the same." Foxe does not suggest that religious devotion gave all women a justification for opposing patriarchal authority—these women were martyrs, after all, thus clearly exceptional—but they do provide models for those who wished to follow this path.

With Queen Elizabeth's accession to the throne in 1558, execution for religious reasons initially stopped, but as Catholicism was increasingly identified with hostility to Elizabeth's reign, arrests and imprisonment of recusants—English Catholics—increased. As you saw in Chapter 2, wealthier female recusants sometimes made their homes into religious sanctuaries, sheltering priests, building altars, and arranging for services.

Three Catholic women were executed during Elizabeth's reign for just such actions. Margaret Clitherow (1556–1586), a middle-class married woman from York, converted to Catholicism, refused to attend the established Church, and sent her oldest son abroad to be trained for the priesthood. Her husband was sympathetic and paid her fines, though he remained a member of the Church of England. She set up two hiding places for priests, one in her own home. These were discovered, and she was arrested for harboring priests. She refused to enter a plea—doing so would have made her children liable for questioning—and was subjected to what was termed *peine forte et dure*, a common law method of extracting a plea that involved being pressed with heavier and heavier weights. The door from her own house was placed on her, with a huge pile of rocks on it, and she died in fifteen minutes. Margaret Ward (1550–1588) was charged with helping a priest to escape from prison. As was standard, she was offered a pardon if she would recant and attend Protestant services. She refused and was hanged along with five men.

Anne Line (1563–1601) was born into a Protestant landowning family in Essex. She and her husband and brother converted to Catholicism; their property was confiscated, and her husband fled to the continent. After he died, Line ran a house for harboring priests in London, where she also instructed Catholic girls. They were able to avoid discovery for several years until neighbors alerted authorities that a large number of people were holding a Catholic service there. Line was arrested and, although no priest was discovered in the house, she was sentenced to death by hanging. At her execution, Line is reported to have said: "I am sentenced to die for harbouring a Catholic priest, and so far I am from repenting for having so done, that I wish, with all my soul, that where I have entertained one, I could have entertained a thousand." Friends accompanying her to the gallows "insisted that she should leave them some memento of her; and she gave them what she had. And having given everything, when she was at the gallows, she asked the executioner for a knife and cut off the lace on her petticoat and gave it to a friend."[15] Line had already been described as a "living saint" by Jesuit priests in England, who also sought physical objects associated with her, relics that gave them a tangible connection to this revered woman.

Line's contemporaries saw her as a saint, and ultimately the Catholic Church did as well. With Clitherow and Ward, she became an officially approved saint in 1970, along with thirty-seven men as part of the Forty Martyrs of England and Wales canonized by Pope Paul VI. (Normally, saints are required to have a miracle associated with them, but exceptions are made for martyrs.) Schools and churches are named after the three women, who became models for future generations of English Catholics, especially women. They share an official feast day, August 30. That is also their feast day in the contemporary Anglican Church and Episcopal churches around the world, denominations that, along with Catholicism, venerate saints and other spiritually worthy people. Thus the institution that declared them heretics and ordered their execution now sees them as saints, an ironic twist in the story.

Catholics continued to be executed in England until 1681, though all of these were men, predominantly priests or laymen charged with treason after actual or invented conspiracies. More than 250 of the men executed by English monarchs have been beatified by the pope, though not yet raised to sainthood. Margaret Pole remains the only woman so honored, and a Catholic church in Dorset has been dedicated to her.

Female martyrs shaped religious identity in Scotland as well as England. The Stuarts, who were rulers of Scotland and England in the seventeenth century, favored a hierarchical Church with bishops rather than the Scottish Presbyterian church structure. Charles I and his archbishop of Canterbury tried to introduce changes to the Church of Scotland in 1640, but the Scots revolted and invaded England. This was one of the factors leading to the English Civil War, and ultimately to Charles's execution. During the war, individual church congregations in Scotland signed agreements known as covenants, sometimes in blood, supporting the establishment of a Presbyterian Church in both Scotland and England.

With the restoration of the monarchy under Charles II in 1660, individuals—men, women, and children—were expected to take an

Oath of Abjuration, swearing allegiance to the king as the head of the Church and the bishops he appointed. Many people did so, but those known as Covenanters refused, saying that they were loyal to King Jesus, not King Charles. Covenanters worshipped in secret meetings outdoors called conventicles rather than in churches, and occasionally engaged in political violence, including assassinations of officials and clergy and resistance to the royal army. Not surprisingly, the English viewed them as political rebels, and they were subjected to waves of suppression and banishment. Many ended up in the Netherlands or the colonies of Jamaica, Barbados, and Virginia. But some stayed, despite a royal order in 1685 decreeing that anyone who even attended an outdoor meeting would be punished by death and a confiscation of their goods.

The year 1685 marked the height of what later Presbyterians called the "killing times," in which hundreds of people died. Among these were Covenanters in the town of Wigtown, including two women, the eighteen-year-old Margaret Wilson and the sixty-year-old Margaret Lachlane, charged with taking part in a rebellion, attending conventicles, and refusing to take the oath. The women were officially reprieved on the plea of Margaret Wilson's father, but were executed anyway, tied to stakes on the shore and drowned when the tide rose. Both women were depicted in Presbyterian martyrologies and in funeral monuments erected later. They left no direct records, but another Covenanter, Helen Alexander (c. 1653/54–1729), who comforted a convicted leader in prison and barely escaped execution herself, attributed her own perseverance and that of other Covenanters to God's intervention: "my Lord, that many a time brought me through, brought me through at this time, for which I bless the Lord. It was for his sake I suffered that and many other things; but my soul had cause to bless the Lord that he was aye with me in all my trials."[16]

Charles II was succeeded by his Catholic brother James II, which led to the coup that brought in the Protestant William and Mary as rulers in 1688. Scotland and England were officially united in 1707 and declared the "Kingdom of Great Britain," though opposition to English rule in Scotland simmered and several times led to open rebellion. The Church of Scotland was re-established with a Presbyterian structure, and most Covenanters were readmitted. The "killing times" were over in Scotland, though stories of brave Covenanters and their trauma and loss would survive for generations for communities that stretched across the Atlantic.

JAPANESE CHRISTIANS PERISH AND SURVIVE

Executions for holding religious beliefs unacceptable to those in power were not limited to Europe but happened in mission areas as well. One of these was Japan. Jesuit missionaries first came to Japan in 1549, slowly gaining converts, especially around the port of Nagasaki on the southern island of Kyushu, the center of trade with the Portuguese. By the end of the century there were several hundred thousand Christians in Japan, some of them actually Koreans who had been brought to Japan as war captives and servants from the Japanese invasion of Korea. There was also repression, but this was sporadic.

More stringent suppression began in 1587, as you saw in Chapter 3, when Jesuits were banished and Christianity restricted. Government officials targeted both foreign missionaries and Japanese Christian (Kirishitan) leaders, portraying both groups as disloyal. Leaders of religious confraternities were arrested in several areas during the early 1600s, including women, and some were executed.

The government took decisive measures to suppress Christianity beginning in 1612. It issued a ban on Japanese conversion to Christianity under penalty of death, again ordered missionaries expelled, and executed a prominent noble who had converted on the charge of treason. It arrested and deported missionaries and Japanese Christian leaders, including Naito Julia and her group of women catechists to Manila. The few remaining church buildings were destroyed, and Christian assemblies began to meet in secret. Beginning in 1619, there were several mass executions, including what were later termed the Great Martyrdoms of Kyoto (1619), Nagasaki (1622), and Edo (1623). Women in prominent Christian households—including Japanese and Korean servants as well as wives, widows, and children—were tortured and executed alongside the men. (See Plate X.)

The government established a neighborhood watch system, promising rewards for anyone who turned in a missionary or reported suspicious activity. People were required to take part in public ceremonies desecrating Christian images and to register in Buddhist temples. There were regional and national campaigns to search for hidden Christians, in which many women were arrested and executed for harboring priests or refusing to renounce Christian beliefs. Sometimes wives and husbands were arrested together, but married and unmarried women and widows were also arrested and executed on their own, often in horrific ways, such as being lowered upside down into pits of manure, crucified, or thrown into volcanoes or freezing water. Some women executed were leaders of women's confraternities or members of religious orders, while others were simply believers. About 4,000 people were executed as Christians after the 1612 ban, roughly 10 per cent of whom were women. For many of these women, the only thing we know about them is their original or baptismal name and their place of execution, and for some we do not even know that, as proper names of women were often left out of the records, and they were simply identified as "women and girls."

Most of the writings of Japanese Christians were destroyed, including all of the original writings by women. What have survived are letters by European missionaries that mention or sometimes even quote women, along with martyrologies and translations of European texts produced through collaborations between Jesuits and Japanese Christians. These were written in a script preferred by ordinary readers, including women, rather than the more specialized script used by male elites. They would have been accessible to literate women, just as the *Martyrs Mirror* and *Acts and Monuments* were accessible to European women who could read their own language but not necessarily read Latin.

Women may very well have influenced the way certain passages were translated or interpreted. A 1592 Japanese translation of a work by the Spanish Dominican friar Luis de Granada, for example, amplifies the emphasis in the original on God choosing the lowliest beings to demonstrate his power, and applies this explicitly to women threatened with martyrdom. It reads:

These women, despite their physiques, so beautifully dressed that the moon and flowers might envy them, and easily blown away by a rough wind, are not afraid of the humiliation, slander, or assaults of torture. Forgetting the affectionate relationship with their fathers and mothers, disregarding others' tears, even when finally [the torturers] grind their bones and tear their bodies in half by pulling them apart by two wheels, they surely maintain their faith. . . . Women are naturally weak, and they shake and quiver at a sword's shadow. Yet in regard to their faith they run to win first place, competing with a single horse-riding warrior whose might is worth that of one thousand warriors.[17]

The "single horse-riding warrior" comes from a Japanese saying about male battle valor, here applied to weaponless women.

Just like *Martyrs Mirror* and *Acts and Monuments*, Japanese martyrologies often include examples from the early Church that were held up as models. St. Catherine of Alexandria, for example, who according to tradition was a beautiful and learned virgin princess tortured and executed in the early fourth century by an evil Roman emperor, makes an appearance in several martyrologies. In these, she eloquently argues for Christianity in front of large crowds, converting many, including the empress and many of her court ladies, who then become martyrs as well. St. Eugenia of Rome, a third-century noblewoman who dressed as a man to join a men's religious community, is also in Japanese martyrologies, described as so wise that she almost became an abbot. She converted many, reverted to female clothing, and was ultimately beheaded.

St. Catherine's story resonated with female converts, including Julia Ota, taken as a war hostage from Korea, who served as a lady-in-waiting in the households of several Japanese nobles. Baptized in 1596, Julia Ota had a secret chapel in her living quarters, maintained a vow of chastity, and refused to renounce her faith when interrogated. Beginning in 1612, she was banished to ever more remote islands, where she seems to have continued teaching. She wrote a letter to the Jesuits, asking them to send her stories of martyrs and virgin saints, as she was determined to suffer for her faith. She was allowed back to Nagasaki, where she took care of Christian girls, but was forbidden from preaching. Exactly what happened to her is unknown, though she is viewed as a martyr and the small island where she was last exiled has an annual festival in her honor.

St. Eugenia's story of cross-dressing also fit with local cultural traditions for women. In Japanese Buddhism as in Christianity, women were seen as spiritually, intellectually, and physically weaker than men, and as sources of pollution through menstruation and childbirth. A valiant few might overcome their limitations, however, through courageous actions, virginity, and intellectual power. In doing so, they might even miraculously become men. Eugenia is described in just such terms in the Japanese martyrologies—as looking like a strong man, passing as a man, or even becoming a man. Kirishitan writers describe her and Catherine as learned despite the fact that their bodies were female, and as having goals like those of men.

European observers of the executions of Japanese Christians praised the women among them in similar terms, as showing strength understood as masculine. As one wrote: "Most of the Kirishitans endured these tortures and other such torments, even the tender, chaste, and pure women bearing them with stouthearted fortitude." This despite treatment designed to shame the women, just as was true with the handling of women accused of heresy in Europe: "And the women had their thighs thrust apart: and then with tongs and hooks they pried into their private parts."[18] Among the various accusations hurled at female martyrs is that they refused to marry, using vows of virginity to oppose their families' wishes, and thus not living up to traditional Japanese expectations for women.

Accounts of valiant Japanese female martyrs circulated among Christians in Japan and were included in reports of the Japanese mission published in Europe. Many of the women remained nameless members of groups of martyrs, but for others detailed stories spread. Among these was that of Hosokawa Tama Gracia (1565?–1600), the daughter of one powerful lord and wife of another. Though her husband ordered her to remain in the house while he was away fighting in Japan's civil wars, she surreptitiously visited the Jesuit mission in disguise and debated religious issues with several missionaries. She corresponded regularly with Jesuits and, in 1587, right after the initial edict ordering the Jesuits to leave Japan, she was baptized (by her female servant, who was also a convert) along with much of her household. She recognized the danger of doing so, as she wrote in a letter to Gregory de Cespedes, a Jesuit missionary still in Japan: "All the Christians whom I have with me are strong, and I work in exhorting them to martyrdom, if perchance we may be found worthy of so great a thing."[19] She had read accounts of early Christian martyrs and saw the possibility of torture and death as following in their footsteps. Tama Gracia wrote to the Jesuits that she wanted to leave her abusive husband, but they urged her to stay, writing that she might be able to convince him to convert and that her leaving would put the Christian community in greater danger.

Tama Gracia's own fate turned out to be similar to what she hoped for, although not for the reasons she expected. While her husband was away on a military campaign in 1600, soldiers from a rival faction in the civil wars surrounded the house, demanding her as a hostage. She sent her servants and court ladies away, and then (depending on the source) was either killed by the soldiers, killed herself, or ordered her husband's samurai to kill her rather than allow her to be captured, the behavior expected of a noblewoman and proper wife according to the moral code of *bushido*. Ladies-in-waiting who claimed to have witnessed her suicide also reported, however, that she composed and recited a death poem with martyrological overtones in its acceptance of death:

Because they know when
Their time to perish is come
In this world of ours
Blossoms fall as blossoms will
And people as people will.[20]

Jesuit missionary accounts and Japanese chronicles initially portrayed Tama Gracia as an ideal wife dutifully obeying her husband even unto death, downplaying her resistance to her husband's orders that she remain secluded. Her remains were scattered at several different burial sites, including a Christian cemetery and a Zen Buddhist temple, and the anniversaries of her death were celebrated with elaborate memorial ceremonies for at least a decade.

With the final expulsion of the Jesuits from Japan and reports circulating in Europe about the gruesome executions of missionaries and converts, Tama Gracia's story was too good to leave as it was. It became the basis of a didactic play in Latin, *Mulier fortis* (*Brave Woman*), first staged at the Jesuit college of St. Ignatius in Vienna in 1698, in front of the Habsburg emperor and his family. In this play, the character that represents her husband links Christian faith with marital infidelity: "You are a Christian: That is crime enough. If a woman be unfaithful to the gods, how can I trust that she be faithful to her husband?" She refuses to honor a statue taken from a temple, proclaiming, "God forbid that I should do this thing . . . Christ alone is the true god."[21] He orders her flogged, and she ultimately dies from this, though her death occurs offstage. The first interpreters of Tama Gracia's life had made her an ideal obedient wife, and in this play the authors transform her into an ideal Christian martyr, perfect for emphasizing the global reach of the Jesuit mission. An ideal Tama Gracia is exalted in both versions, though the historical one gets flattened.

By the time *Brave Woman* was performed in Vienna, the Japanese mission was a memory. The Shimabara Rebellion of 1637–1638, in which peasants protested their conditions, involved many Japanese Christians in Kyushu. National leaders sent a huge army and, after their victory, captured and beheaded perhaps 35,000 of the rebels and their sympathizers, including women and children. (Counts of Japanese Christian martyrs sometimes include those from this rebellion, so are much higher than those that count people executed for Christian practices alone.) This revolt resulted in a final exclusion order of 1639, banning any further visits by Portuguese ships or interaction with Catholic lands. In 1641, contact with Europeans was limited to a small island in Nagasaki harbor run by the Dutch East India Company.

Japanese rulers assumed they had obliterated Christianity but, despite the extensive system of surveillance with monetary rewards offered for the exposure of Christians, Christianity survived as an underground religion in remote farming and fishing villages of Kyushu and some smaller islands. These "hidden Christians" had no clergy, but lay leaders secretly taught, kept records, and baptized. They maintained their community by marrying within the group, and gradually developed a distinctive version of Christianity. When Japan was reopened in the 1860s, these Japanese Christians contacted Catholic priests, who were astounded to learn of their existence. Half of the Catholics in Japan today are descendants of the "hidden Christians." Nagasaki again became the center of Catholic Christianity, with a larger percentage of

Christians than any other city in Japan. The Urakami Cathedral in northern Nagasaki, completed in 1914, was the largest Catholic cathedral in East Asia, though it was completely destroyed in the U.S. atomic bombing of Nagasaki in 1945.

FEAR, MISOGYNY, AND WITCHCRAFT

As I said in this chapter's introduction, the upsurge in trials and executions for witchcraft occurred at the same time as the Reformations, and sometimes involved the same authorities as investigators and judges. Like the trials of religious dissidents, witch trials can give us access to the ideas and emotions of women—and men—who otherwise leave no trace in the records. There are thus important parallels and intersections with the story of the Reformations, but the witch trials are also their own extremely complex story. I always teach them separately, and here I just touch on a few of the most important connections with other religious transformations.

Most people you have met so far in this book, and indeed most people in Europe (and elsewhere in the world), believed in witches—people who used magical forces to do evil deeds and cause harm. They believed this long before the era of the witch-hunts, and many continued to do so for long afterward. But other than a handful of cases, only between the fifteenth and the seventeenth centuries were there large-scale hunts and mass executions. Why?

The most important reason is a change in ideas about the core of witchcraft among many educated Christian theologians, lawyers, and officials in the fifteenth century, which then spread to ordinary people. For them, the essence of witchcraft became making a pact with the devil, a pact that required the witch to do the devil's bidding. Witches were no longer simply people who used magical power to do bad things (called *maleficia*) or get what they wanted, but people used by the devil to do what *he* wanted. (The devil is always described and portrayed visually as male.) Witchcraft was thus not a question of what one *did* but of what one *was*, and proving that a witch had committed *maleficia* was no longer necessary for conviction.

This demonological or Satanic idea of witchcraft was fleshed out, and witches were thought to engage in wild sexual orgies with the devil, fly through the night to meetings called sabbats which parodied the Mass, and steal communion wafers and unbaptized babies to use in their rituals. Some demonological theorists also claimed that witches were organized in an international conspiracy to overthrow Christianity.

Ideas about the activities of the devil, demons, and witches can be found in many types of writings from the fifteenth through the seventeenth centuries. They appear in their purest form in the hundreds of works specifically dealing with witchcraft and demonology that were penned—and then often published—by learned men, which circulated around Europe. Most of the authors of demonological works also wrote other things, and many were active as pastors, officials, university professors, lawyers, physicians, and a few even as rulers, including King James VI/I of Scotland and England. Some were also witch-hunters, judges, or officials involved in actual trials. They brought their ideas with them to the trials, framing questions based on their readings, and then used their experiences as the basis for their demonology. The upsurge in trials is often called the "witchcraze," but it was not the result of hysterical superstition involving ill-educated villagers and fanatical clergy. The authors of important works on witchcraft included leading philosophers and scientists, who saw the power of witches as part of the natural world they were seeking to understand and explain.

Europeans took their notions of witchcraft with them to the New World. In Spanish colonies, Indigenous women and women of mixed heritage were sometimes charged with witchcraft and idolatry, and in the British New England colonies a few people, most of them women, were executed for witchcraft, most notoriously at Salem in Massachusetts. Some European thinkers even blamed witchcraft on the explorations, asserting that demons had decided to return to Europe from the Americas once Christian missionaries were there, and so were possessing and seducing many more people than they had in the Middle Ages.

The earliest trials involving this new notion of witchcraft as diabolical heresy were in the 1430s in the area around Lake Geneva in Switzerland and France, and in 1484 Pope Innocent VIII authorized two German Dominicans to hunt witches in nearby areas of southern Germany. One of these, Heinrich Krämer (c. 1430–1505), oversaw the trial and execution of several groups—all of them women—but local authorities objected to his use of torture and his extreme views on the power of witches, and banished him. While in exile, he wrote a justification of his ideas and methods, the *Malleus maleficarum* (*The Hammer of [Female] Witches*), published in 1486 in Latin. The *Malleus* pays particular attention to the sexual and gendered nature of witchcraft:

> As for the first question, why a greater number of witches is found in the fragile feminine sex than among men . . . the first [reason] is, that they are more credulous; and since the chief aim of the devil is to corrupt faith, therefore he rather attacks them . . . the second reason is, that women are naturally more impressionable . . . and the third reason is that they have slippery tongues, and are unable to conceal from their fellow-women those things which by evil arts they know. . . . But the natural reason is that she is more carnal than a man, as is clear from her many carnal abominations. . . . To conclude. All witchcraft comes from carnal lust, which is in women insatiable.[22]

The *Malleus* also provided practical advice for future witch-hunters, advising them how to recognize and question witches, and recommended that secular authorities work with inquisitors in prosecuting witches.

Later demonological works were not as deeply misogynistic as the *Malleus*, but witchcraft was increasingly associated with women, for witches were now understood to be dependent agents of a powerful male devil rather than independently directing demons themselves, which fit general notions of proper gender roles. Women were viewed as weaker and so more likely to give in to the devil's charms, or use scolding and cursing to get what they wanted. They were associated with nature, disorder, and the body, all of which were linked with the demonic. Women also had more contact with areas of life in which bad things happened unexpectedly, such as preparing food or caring for new mothers, children, and animals.

This new notion of witchcraft spread. Secular rulers north of the Alps passed witchcraft statutes authorizing the death penalty if witches harmed people through magic. These civil witchcraft laws, such as the criminal code of the Holy Roman Empire from 1532 or the English and Scottish witchcraft statutes of 1563, tend to focus more on *maleficia* and less on pacts with the devil, though in actual trials the influence of *Malleus* and other works of demonological theory is evident. Witch trials died down somewhat during the first decades after the Protestant Reformation, when Protestants and Catholics were busy fighting each other, but they picked up again more strongly than ever in about 1570.

The testimonies of accusers, witnesses, judges, and accused witches themselves generally contain a kaleidoscope of beliefs that come from various sources, learned and popular, local and foreign. Though witch trials were secret, executions were not. They were public spectacles witnessed by huge crowds, with the list of charges read out for all to hear. Illustrated pamphlets and posters portrayed witches riding on goats or pitchforks to sabbats where they engaged in anti-Christian acts such as spitting on the communion host and sexual relations with demons, ideas that first emerged in learned demonology. Conversely, accusations that witches entered cellars and storerooms to steal food and wine, changed straw or mud into living animals, danced with elves or fairies, made love charms, or shot magical arrows emerged first in local accusations and then later showed up in formal demonological treatises.

Along with new witchcraft statutes, other legal changes also played a role in causing, or at least allowing for, massive witch trials. One of these was a change from an accusatorial legal procedure to an inquisitorial procedure. In the former, a suspect knew the accusers and the charges they had brought, and an accuser could in turn be liable for trial if the charges were not proved; in the latter, legal authorities themselves brought the case. This change made people much more willing to accuse others, for they never had to take personal responsibility for the accusation or face the accused's relatives. Inquisitorial procedure involved intense questioning of the suspect, often with torture. Areas in Europe that did not make this change saw few trials and almost no mass panics.

The use of inquisitorial procedures did not always lead to witch-hunts, however. The Inquisitions of southern Europe had no trouble ordering people they judged heretics or Jews whose conversions they doubted to be put to death. They executed very few witches, however. Officials in the Inquisition firmly believed in the power of the devil and were no less misogynistic than other judges, but they doubted very much whether the people accused of doing *maleficia* had actually made a pact with the devil that gave them special powers. They viewed them not as diabolical devil-worshippers, but as superstitious and ignorant peasants or city dwellers whose main crime was undermining the Catholic Church's monopoly on supernatural remedies by claiming they had special powers. They generally sent the accused home with a warning and a penance, or at most with a whipping.

Though there were "witch-hunters" like Krämer or the self-proclaimed English witch-finder Matthew Hopkins in the 1640s who came into areas specifically to hunt witches, most hunts began with an accusation of *maleficia* in a village or town. Individuals accused someone they knew of using magical words or ritual actions to spoil food, make children ill, kill animals, raise a hailstorm, or do other types of harm. This might be a person who had a reputation for doing magic or it might just be a family member or neighbor with whom one had quarreled. The *Malleus* warned that midwives were prone to witchcraft, but actual accusations against them were not especially numerous. Women who took care of infants and new mothers were more common targets, charged with killing the child or drying up the mother's milk. The women first accused of witchcraft in a trial were often poor, older, and socially marginal, with stories about the devil that revolved more around food than sex or power. As Bessie Martin, a Scottish woman, confessed: "And then the Devil said, 'Thee art a poor overworked body. Will thee be my servant and I will give thee abundance and thee shall never want.'"[23]

Accused women were sometimes argumentative, willful, independent, and aggressive. As the indictment of Margaret Lister in Scotland in 1662 put it, she was "a witch, a charmer, and a libber."[24] The last term carried the same connotation and negative assessment of "liberated woman" as it can today. Doritte Nippers, convicted and executed for witchcraft in 1571 in Elsinore in Denmark, despite refusing to confess even when tortured, was the leader of a group of women traders who would not stop doing business when ordered to by the town council.

Sometimes the woman accused actually did perform magic for herself and others, using words, gestures, and substances to find lost objects, attempt to heal an illness, attract desirable suitors, harm enemies, or other useful tasks. A reputation as a person who could perform magic, or even as a witch, could protect a woman for many years. Neighbors would be less likely to refuse assistance, and the food or wood the woman needed to survive would be given to her or paid as fees for her services. This can help explain why women sometimes confessed to being witches without the application or even threat of torture. After decades of providing magical services, they may have been as convinced as their neighbors of their own powers.

Women number very prominently among accusers and witnesses as well as those accused of witchcraft not only because of misogyny, but because the actions witches were initially charged with, such as harming children or curdling milk, were generally part of women's sphere. Women also gained economic and social security by conforming to the standard of the good wife and mother, and by confronting women who deviated from it. The records of witch trials thus contain women's voices, but their comments were always in response to leading questions posed by men. The same was true for the trials of religious dissidents, of course, but Anabaptist or recusant women were generally not coerced into confessing something they did not do or that in some cases no human body could do.

After an accusation, the suspect was brought in for questioning by legal authorities, as were family members, neighbors, and witnesses. Assorted experts might also be consulted, including physicians, clergy, lawyers, university professors, exorcists, and midwives, to help determine evidence, motive, and proof. They might carry out various tests, such as "pricking" the accused with a needle to see if she had a place that did not feel pain—regarded as a sign from the devil—or "swimming" her to see if the pure water rejected her so that she floated or accepted her so that she sank. Suspects were stripped and shaved in a search for a "witch's mark"—often simply a mole or wart—left by her sexual contacts with the devil or an animal familiar. These investigations were carried out by a group of male officials—judges, notaries who recorded the witch's answers, the executioner who did the actual pricking or other types of torture—gathered around an accused who was often partially naked. Sexual sadism may certainly have played a role.

Courts often kept meticulous records, chilling to read. At the trial of Suzanne Gaudry in Valenciennes in 1652, for example, the accused first confessed to being in service to a devil named Petit-Grignon for twenty-five years, who had "known her carnally three or four times" and took her to "nocturnal dances." When she later reversed herself and said "that what she had said was done by force . . . that she retracts it, crying Jésus-Maria, that she is not a witch," the trial records report that "being more tightly stretched upon the torture-rack and urged to maintain her confessions," she (unsurprisingly) "said that it was true that she is a witch." A physician affirmed that a mark on her body was "not a natural mark but a mark of the devil," and the judges "legitimately condemn the aforesaid Suzanne Gaudry to death, tying her to a gallows, and strangling her to death, then burning her body and burying it there in the environs of the woods."[25] Those sentenced to be executed for witchcraft knew they would not be given a proper funeral or buried in consecrated ground, and thus had little chance for salvation.

No woman wrote a demonological treatise, and only a tiny handful wrote anything on witchcraft at all. One of these was Margaret Cavendish, the duchess of Newcastle (1623–1673), a poet, essayist, playwright, historian, biographer, philosopher, and scientist. Cavendish was from a royalist family loyal to the monarchy during the English Civil War, and accompanied Queen Henrietta Maria on her exile in France after the execution of King Charles I. She was also a materialist, who argued that the occurrences allegedly caused by witches were either tricks or had natural causes that just weren't understood yet, "for Nature is so full of variety that she can and doth present sometimes such figures to our exterior Senses, as are not familiar to us." In her *Philosophical Letters*, published in 1664, the height of the witch-hunts, Cavendish argues:

[If] by reason we cannot assign any Natural cause for them, [we] are apt to ascribe their effects to the Devil; but that there should be any such devilish Witchcraft, which is made by Covenant and Agreement with the Devil, by whose power Men do enchaunt and bewitch other Creatures, I cannot readily believe. Certainly, I dare say, that many a good, old honest woman hath been condemned innocently, and suffered death wrongfully, by the sentence of some foolish and cruel Judges, merely upon this Superstition of Witchcraft, when as really there hath been no such thing; for many things are done by slights or juggling Arts, wherein neither the Devil nor Witches are actors.[26]

Cavendish was a member of the high nobility and did not come under suspicion herself. But as a self-taught woman interested in science and philosophy who did not know Latin—the learned language of the day— she was generally regarded as eccentric and odd, and her ideas were trivialized by learned men.

Another of the very few references to a woman speaking out against a witch accusation comes from the biography of the English recusant Elizabeth Cary whom you met in Chapter 2, written by her daughter Lucy. When she was only ten, wrote Lucy, Cary had cleverly saved a woman accused of bewitching several people to death who was brought before Cary's father, a judge in Oxfordshire:

She falling down before him trembling and weeping confessed all to be true. . . . But the child, seeing the poor woman in so terrible a fear, and in so simple a manner confess all, thought fear had made her idle [incoherent], so she whispered her father and desired him to ask her whether she had bewitched to death Mr John Symondes of such a place (her uncle that was one of the standers-by). He did so, to which she said yes, just as she had done to the rest, promising to do so no more—if they would have pity on her. He asked how she did it; She told one of her former stories; then (all the company laughing) he asked her what she ailed to say so? Told her the man was alive, and stood there. She cried, "Alas, sir, I knew him not, I said so because you asked me." Then he, "Are you no witch then?" (says he) "No, God knows;" says she, "I know no more what belongs to it than the child newborn." "Nor did you never see the devil?" She answered, "No, God bless me, never in all my life." Then he examined her what she meant to confess all this, if it were false? She answered they had threatened her if she would not confess, and said, if she would, she should have mercy showed her—which she said with such simplicity that (the witness brought against her being of little force, and her own confession appearing now to be of less) she was easily believed innocent, and [ac]quitted.[27]

This is, of course, family lore designed to portray Elizabeth Cary as caring and intelligent even at a very young age, but the false confession easily coerced by fear that it recounted was a standard part of witch trials.

Accused witches were always pressured to reveal other names, and small hunts sometimes grew into large-scale witch panics in which the accused could number in the hundreds. The worst of these were in Germany and eastern France in the 1570s, 1590s, 1610s, and 1660s, the last spreading as far north as Sweden. These were also decades of particularly cold weather, and some historians have seen a link between witch panics and severe weather. Much of the heartland of the witch-hunts consisted of small governmental units along the Rhine River and within the Holy Roman Empire, which were jealous of each other and, after the Reformation, divided by religion. The rulers of these small territories often felt more threatened than did the monarchs of the large states of western Europe. They saw persecuting witches as a way to demonstrate their piety and concern for order. They consciously used patriarchy as a model, describing themselves as firm but just fathers, ruling their subjects for their own benefit. (King James VI/I did so as well, writing treatises on the divine right of kings and on demonology.) A campaign in which most of the accused and convicted were women, and many of them women who did not conform to male standards of female behavior, fit their aims very nicely.

Women continued to be the majority of those accused in such mass panics—in 1585, two villages in Germany were left with one female inhabitant each after such an outburst—but when such large numbers of people began to be accused, they ranged beyond odd, older, and marginal women. Wives of honorable citizens were taken in, and the number of male suspects increased significantly. This expansion to a wider group of people is perhaps the primary reason any mass panic finally ended. It suddenly or slowly became clear to legal authorities, or to the community itself, that the people being questioned or executed were not what they understood witches to be, or that the scope of accusations was beyond belief. Some from their community might be in league with Satan but not this type of person and not as many as this. This realization generally did not cause them to give up their ideas about witches and their power, but rather simply to become skeptical about the course of the hunt in their village or town and to call for it to be stopped.

Similar skepticism slowly led to the gradual end of the witch-hunts in Europe. Although in the sixteenth and early seventeenth centuries, most judges and other members of the learned elite firmly believed in the threat posed by witches, there were a few doubters. Margaret Cavendish was in the minority, but not alone. These doubts gradually spread among the same type of religious and legal authorities that had so vigorously persecuted witches, and they increasingly regarded the dangers posed by the people brought before them as implausible. By the end of the sixteenth century, prosecutions for witchcraft were already difficult in the northern Netherlands. The last official execution for witchcraft in England was in 1682, just about the same time as the last execution for treasonous heresy. Witchcraft trials were prohibited in France in 1682, England in 1736, Austria in 1755, and Hungary in 1768. Sporadic trials continued into the late eighteenth century in other areas, with the last execution for witchcraft in the Holy Roman Empire in 1775. At the popular level, belief in the power of witches often continued, but this was now sneered at by the elite as superstition, and people ceased to bring formal accusations when they knew they would simply be dismissed.

In their words and even more in their actions, women martyrs conveyed a sense of determination and strength that their contemporaries and later commentators often viewed as both masculine and praiseworthy. They went beyond their gender to show "manly courage" and "stout-hearted fortitude," to be like "single horse-riding warriors" who were "in their faith strong, as men might be." In the ballad attributed to Anne Askew, she compares herself to an "armed knight appointed to the field" who will fight "and Faith shall be my shield." Women put themselves in a line of those who suffered for their faith that stretched back to Christ and included earlier martyrs, both male and female. "Watch, today I am travelling the path of the Prophets, Apostles, and Martyrs, and drink from the cup from which they have all tasted," wrote Anna Jansz in her testament to her infant son. After being exiled, Julia Ota asked for even more stories of martyrs and persecuted saints. Women also viewed themselves as showing a path to salvation to the wider community as well as to their own families, something that was more often the province of men.

Women accused of witchcraft were also portrayed as not fulfilling the expected social roles for women, but this was condemned rather than praised. Instead of being supportive wives and loving mothers, wrote the sixteenth-century scientist and physician Theophrastus Paracelsus, witches were always "turning away from men, fleeing men, hiding, wanting to be alone, not attracting men, not looking men in the eye, lying alone, refusing men."[28] The *Malleus* argued the opposite, that "all witchcraft comes from carnal lust, which is in women insatiable." The learned men who wrote demonology saw this not as a contradiction, but as simply more evidence of a witch's ability to deceive.

Martyrs knew what their interrogators wanted them to say but refused to do so. Women accused of witchcraft generally knew that nothing they said would make the "foolish and cruel Judges" they stood before let them go.

CHAPTER FIVE

＊＊＊

MYSTICS

Lord of my soul, you did not hate women when You walked in the world; rather you favored them always with much pity and found in them as much love and more faith than in men. Is it not enough, Lord, that the world has intimidated us . . . so that we may not do anything worthwhile for You in public?

St. Teresa of Avila, Spanish mystic and reformer

There came many to see me, some out of goodwill . . . and others came to gaze, and others to catch me at my words, so as to reproach me; but the Lord taught me how to speak before them all.

Anna Trapnel, English prophet

In most Christian churches after the Reformations, authority came primarily through a position in an official hierarchy, obtained through appointment, election, theological training, familial connections, force of personality, or some combination of these. Most people with church offices were men, but in the Catholic Church women held positions as abbesses, prioresses, and other positions in convents. Catholic and Protestant women rulers and noblewomen also held power *over* Christian churches, though not *within* them.

But from the early history of Christianity, some people also asserted spiritual authority in a different way, through direct experiences of the divine: seeing visions, hearing voices, entering trances, or going into ecstasy, through which they lost themselves and united with God. Such people were sometimes described as mystics, or as prophets, visionaries, ecstatics, or seers, and can be found in many other religious traditions as well as Christianity. They designed their own plans for a more intensive spiritual life, sometimes within religious institutions and sometimes outside of these. Mystics and prophets were often sought after by their neighbors and others to heal, provide advice, predict the future, and serve as intermediaries with the world beyond.

The late medieval period saw an upsurge in mysticism in Western Christianity, including among women, a few of whom were later made saints. The most influential of these was Catherine of Siena (1347–1380), who refused her middle-class parents' plan for her to marry and lived in seclusion at home, fasting so intensely she later found it difficult to eat anything other than the Eucharist, and practicing other bodily austerities. She also saw visions, including one of a mystical marriage with Christ in which she received Christ's foreskin as her wedding ring. (This built on the widespread notion that nuns were "brides of Christ," and the more unusual idea that the marriage linked her to Christ's physical body, not simply his spirit.) When she was twenty-one, Catherine became a Dominican tertiary. She worked with the poor and plague victims, gaining a reputation for sanctity and attracting followers.

Along with her adviser and confessor Raymond of Capua, Catherine traveled to Avignon in southern France in 1376, where the popes had been living for almost seventy years. They tried to convince the pope to return to Rome, which he did, but he died a year later, regretting that he had listened to what he called "meddling women." Instead of solving problems, however, the pope's return only led to a split in the Catholic Church—later called the "Great Schism"—a twenty-five-year period during which there were two and later three popes. Through writing hundreds of letters and speaking to anyone who would listen to her, Catherine tried to heal the schism, reform problems in the Church, and convince warring Italian city-states to make peace with one another. She failed at all of these.

Catherine also founded a convent in Siena, though she herself remained a lay tertiary. Here she dictated her major theological work, a conversation between God and a soul called the *Dialogue of Divine Providence*, in which she sees Christ as the bridge to union with the divine, experienced most intensely in consuming the Eucharist. She died in Rome when she was only thirty-three, unable to eat or drink. Devotion to her memory developed quickly, and she was made a saint in 1461. Her *Dialogue* was published in Italian in the late fifteenth century, very shortly after the invention of the printing press, and in the early sixteenth century Cardinal Cisneros, Queen Isabel's confessor and the most powerful church official in Castile, ordered a translation made into Spanish.

Catherine set a pattern followed by other Italian women, some of whom were also canonized, including three other Catherines: Catherine of Bologna (1413–1463), Catherine of Genoa (1447–1510), and Catherine de' Ricci (1522–1590). All these women were venerated as mystics and for their work as teachers or with the poor.

Mystics became figures of popular devotion, and sometimes acquired large numbers of followers and fans, both during their lifetimes and after their deaths. Because of this, institutional churches were sometimes skeptical or hostile toward those who claimed mystical links with the divine, charging them with being "false saints" or "false prophets" who faked their visions or misinterpreted demonic visions as divine. Political authorities were also often wary or aggressive toward visionaries whose prophecies related to them. As you saw in Chapter 4, Henry VIII had Elizabeth Barton, "The Holy Maid of Kent," hanged and her head put on a spike when she began asserting that her visions foretold his death.

Women mystics were particularly likely to be doubted. As the Spanish Catholic clergyman Gaspar Navarro wrote in 1631: "More credit should be given to the revelations of men than those of women: because that feminine sex is weaker in the head, and they mistake natural things or diabolic illusions for those of heaven and God; they dream more than men and think their dreams are complex truths . . . they are more imaginative than men, and thus less judicious and reasonable and still less prudent, and so the Devil is more likely to deceive women."[1] Most Protestants agreed. Among the worst "errors, heresies, blasphemies and pernicious practices" of those who wanted to do away with the official state church in England, wrote the Puritan preacher Thomas Edwards in his polemical treatise *Gangraena* (1646), was the fact that they thought "tis lawfull for women to preach" if the women felt themselves inspired by the Holy Spirit.[2]

Visionaries themselves often downplayed their own role, describing themselves as mouthpieces of God or as "impregnated with the Holy Spirit." If they spoke publicly or wrote about their visions, they claimed to be doing so on the advice of a male confessor, family member, or associate. But many also highlighted Old Testament and classical precedents for what they were doing, putting themselves in a long line of female prophets and seers. Whatever the sources of their experiences, the women in this chapter had an impact on their societies, and many continue to do so. Their writings, available in multiple languages, provide inspiration and guidance in prayer and spirituality, as do their images—as statues, stained-glass windows, paintings, devotional cards, candles, and many other types of objects, and in films, television programs, and online media.

HISPANIC VISIONARIES GAIN FANS AND FOES

The best-known early modern female mystic, and arguably the most important woman in sixteenth-century Christianity overall, is St. Teresa of Avila (1515–1582). Teresa was the granddaughter of Jewish converts in Toledo on her father's side. Her grandfather had come before the Inquisition because of suspected Jewish practices and been forced to endure a public ritual of penance before being reconciled with the Catholic Church. The family moved to Avila, where her father became a successful merchant and bought a knighthood. The family changed their name to that of Teresa's mother and hid their Jewish roots, so it is not clear whether Teresa knew about this part of her family history. Teresa's mother read her stories of Christian martyrs and chivalric romances, and the little girl decided to act these out in real life. She persuaded her brother to leave their house to seek martyrdom fighting Muslims, though their uncle spotted them on the road and brought them home. This event is often used as demonstration of her early path toward piety, though it seems more like an attempt at adventure beyond the bounds of a strict Spanish home, just like those of knights in the stories she was reading.

Teresa's mother died when she was fourteen and her father, worried that she was becoming too interested in her hair and clothes, sent her to an Augustinian convent for an education. She initially resisted family pressure to become a nun, but in 1535, when she was twenty, she entered a Carmelite monastery in Avila. The convent housed many women from the city's wealthier families, some professed nuns and some not, and was not strictly cloistered, so Teresa was able to visit her family and friends as she wished. She spent the next twenty years in relative obscurity, reading works on contemplation and asceticism, and engaging in rituals of mortification common in many convents and monasteries at the time, including self-flagellation and fasting. She went through great spiritual turmoil with extremes of exaltation and melancholy, suffering physical effects such as illness, trances, and paralysis. During one of her spells of paralysis, her family members thought she had died.

In 1555 she had a radical conversion experience and began having mystical experiences. She saw angels and demons, heaven and hell, Jesus and Joseph. On the advice of her confessors, she tried to resist these, using holy water, a crucifix, and the physical discipline of her body, but she said that then God seized her ever more relentlessly. Her most distinctive vision was of an angel piercing her heart repeatedly with a flaming spear, causing both pleasure and pain. As she later described it:

In his hands I saw a great golden spear, and at the iron tip there appeared to be a point of fire. This he plunged into my heart several times so that it penetrated to my entrails. When he pulled it out, I felt that he took them with it, and left me utterly consumed by the great love of God. The pain was so severe that it made me utter several moans. The sweetness caused by this intense pain is so extreme that one cannot possibly wish it to cease, nor is one's soul then content with anything but God. This is not a physical, but a spiritual pain, though the body has some share in it—even a considerable share. So gentle is this wooing which takes place between God and that soul that if anyone thinks I am lying, I pray God, in His goodness, to grant him some experience of it.[3]

Artists have often portrayed this piercing of the heart—called the transverberation—as a moment of physical and emotional ecstasy, most famously in the sculpture by the Italian artist Gian Lorenzo Bernini, made shortly after Teresa was raised to sainthood. (See Plate XI.)

At other times or places, even these dramatic visions might not have merited much notice, but this was Spain during the sixteenth century, when the Spanish crown was using its own Inquisition to stamp out any sign of *alumbrado*, Lutheran, or other deviant ideas, as well as what it saw as incomplete conversions from Judaism or Islam. Other nuns and *beatas* (devout laywomen who felt a sense of religious vocation) had been accused of heresy and questioned, so Teresa's confessors ordered her not only to describe her mystical experiences in writing but also to reflect on them and try to explain why she thought these were happening to her. Although Teresa complained about having to do this, she also clearly developed a sense of passion about her writing, for she edited and refined her work, transforming it into a full spiritual autobiography, known today in English as *The Life of Teresa of Jesus*.

Teresa describes the stages of mystical prayer that she experienced as her soul ascended to God: first withdrawal from the world through meditation, reading, and mental prayer; then quietude and peace, as God granted her greater awareness; then surrender of reason to God as she became conscious of her absorption in the divine; and finally, ecstatic union, in which her consciousness of her body and senses disappeared. She writes: "The soul is then so suspended that it seems entirely outside itself. The will loves; the memory is, I think, almost lost, and the mind, I believe, though it is not lost, does not reason—I mean that it does not work, but stands as if amazed by the many things it understands."[4] She describes herself as a weak woman in the face of divine power, but concedes women's powerlessness and inferiority so often that this almost appears ironic, an intentional manipulation of stereotypes of femininity. She also uses informal language to deflect charges that she was teaching theology, and, in later editions, to appeal to a wider audience.

Teresa's confessors and Inquisition officials decided that her visions were genuine and her ideas acceptable. Copies of her *Life* were passed hand to hand among her supporters and others who had heard about her, and it was published only six years after she had died, edited by the poet and friar Luis de León. The *Life* was translated into several languages, including French, English, and Italian, in the seventeenth century, and since then it has become a classic, available in many editions and languages. Teresa went on to write *The Way of Perfection* and *The Interior Castle*, guides to stages of becoming closer to God through prayer, asceticism, meditation, and making oneself open to divine gifts. In *The Interior Castle*, she envisions the final two stages as spiritual engagement and marriage, a transforming union of the soul with God. She addressed the book to women only, in the hopes that this might protect her from charges of trying to teach men, though the Carmelite official who oversaw her restricted access to the book to educated men who might serve as women's confessors.

Like Angela Merici and Mary Ward, Catholic women you met in earlier chapters, Teresa also yearned for some kind of active ministry and explicitly chafed at the restrictions on her because of her sex. "Lord of my soul," she wrote in *The Way of Perfection*, "you did not hate women when You walked in the world; rather you favored them always with much pity and found in them as much love and more faith than in men. Is it not enough, Lord, that the world has intimidated us . . . so that we may not do anything worthwhile for You in public?"[5] In part, she solved this by interpreting her prayers and those of other nuns as public actions: "we shall be fighting for Him [God] even though we are very cloistered."[6]

When she was fifty-two, Teresa also began to reform her Carmelite order, attempting to return it to its original standards of spirituality, enclosure, and poverty, just as abbesses had reformed convents in the fifteenth century. Houses were not to require women to bring a dowry, and nuns were to be discalced, that is, to wear sandals instead of shoes as a symbol of their rejection of material goods. She established the first house of Discalced Carmelites in Avila in 1562, over opposition from many people in the city, who objected to its rules of absolute poverty. Five years later, the head of the Carmelite order gave her permission to establish other Discalced Carmelite houses. To do this, she traveled all around Spain, founding new convents and writing meditations, instructions for monastic administrators, and hundreds of letters. Along with Carmelite friars who supported her reforms, she founded several houses for men as well. (From that point on, religious houses in Spain and the

Spanish colonies were divided into "calced," houses in which residents did not have to give up their possessions or servants, and "discalced," houses in which they did.)

Teresa's actions provoked the wrath or annoyance of some church authorities. A papal nuncio called her a "restless gadabout, a disobedient and obstinate woman, who invented wicked doctrines and called them devotion . . . and taught others against the commands of St. Paul, who had forbidden women to teach."[7] The leaders of the Carmelite order commanded her to stop founding new houses and go into retirement. They also brought serious charges against Teresa and some of her associates with the Inquisition, asserting that they held various ideas judged heretical or at least associated with people who did. She was accused of *alumbradismo* (illuminism), that term used to describe those who taught that interior prayer and a personal relationship with the Holy Spirit were more important than outward forms of devotion. By the mid-sixteenth century, *alumbradismo* had come to be associated with rejection of the authority and traditions of the Catholic Church, so was used against people who had all sorts of ideas.

Along with being an *alumbrada*, the Inquisition also accused Teresa of hearing confessions of nuns, an action limited to priests, and even listened to charges of lurid sexual crimes brought by her enemies. It conducted several formal investigations, though it never brought her to trial. She enlisted both the pope and the king of Spain in her support, and was able to resume her reforming activities, founding more convents in the last years of her life. She ultimately founded seventeen, many of which housed poorer women, who otherwise had few opportunities to be part of the Church. After her death, Discalced Carmelites were given permission to separate from the Carmelites and found a new order. Women founded houses in France, Italy, Austria, Poland, and elsewhere in Europe. In the early seventeenth century, the order spread to Mexico and then into California.

Teresa's success in reforming the Carmelites ultimately won her more supporters than critics within the Catholic Church, for—unlike Angela Merici and Mary Ward—she did not advocate institutionalized roles for women outside of the convent. Her frustration at men's alterations of Christ's view of women did not lead her to break with the Church hierarchy, and the words from *The Way of Perfection* expressing that frustration quoted above were expunged from the book by church censors. The version of Teresa that was presented for her canonization proceedings, held in 1622, was one that fit her into the acceptable model of woman mystic and reformer, assuming a public role only when ordered to do so by her confessor or superior. Her own ideas were recognized a bit more when she was named a "Doctor of the Church" in 1970, the first woman to achieve what is Catholicism's highest honor. But only recently have we begun to understand that Teresa thought of herself as a warrior in the Catholic Reformation, viewing the new religious houses she established as answers to the Protestant takeover of Catholic churches elsewhere in Europe.

It is easy to view Teresa as an anomaly, but in many ways she fits into a pattern of women's religious experience that began in late medieval Italy with Catherine of Siena and became quite common in Spain, Portugal, and the Spanish and Portuguese colonies. Other nuns also had visions, composed spiritual autobiographies, and shared them with others. Other nuns and some *beatas* acted as reformers and social critics, combining mysticism and activism. Such "holy women," as they were known at the time, were often revered by people in their neighborhood and beyond. Their confessors and other churchmen wrote biographies detailing their trials and triumphs, hoping to raise them to the status of blessed or even to sainthood. The women resolved local conflicts and were sought for advice on personal, political, and religious matters. They sometimes gained power over political leaders all the way up to the ruler of the territory, who in turn used the approval of such women as an endorsement of their policies and an enhancement of their prestige. A few women gained an international reputation, such as Juana de la Cruz, the nun whose beads were carried by Sor Jerónima and her group to the Philippines.

Others were not so sure about the source of the women's visions and ecstatic trances, however, and they were sometimes investigated by the Inquisition or other church courts, charged with heresy, fraud, pretending to be saints, and often with being unchaste. Diego Pérez de Valdivia, a professor at the University of Barcelona, complained that some holy women had "much freedom and little modesty" and were easily tempted by "the devil, the world, and their own flesh."[8]

Many visionary *beatas* had both supporters and detractors, just as Teresa did. María de Santo Domingo (*c*. 1485–*c*. 1524), the illiterate daughter of peasants in Castile, began pious practices and intense prayer as a child. As a teenager, she joined the third order of the Dominicans, just like Catherine of Siena. She lived first at a house for *beatas*, and then at a house for friars, highly unusual for a woman. At both, she criticized the residents for lax practices of their religious rule, not a popular message, especially coming from the daughter of peasants. She also began to see visions, hear voices, fall into trances, and experience bodily raptures that seemed like dancing, which she and some of those around her understood as coming from God. These led her to begin making political predictions, and in 1507 she was ordered to come to the royal court of King Ferdinand of Aragon. She impressed many at the court as genuine, but the head of the Dominican order in Rome, Thomas Cajetan, was worried that her call for stricter observance might split the order. He convinced the pope to order an investigation, which resulted in a series of four trials over several years.

Things might have gone badly for María, but her prophecies worked to the advantage of powerful men as well as herself. The wealthy lord of the territory in which she lived, the duke of Alba, was cultivating his reputation as a pious supporter of religious houses. One of the things she had predicted, according to her defender at the trial, "many years before, when she knew no king or grandee, and it did not seem that she would ever know one . . . [was] that in Aldenueva a grand convent would be built and that in it many women would live together in the service of God." She also predicted that King Ferdinand would conquer Jerusalem from the Muslims and become emperor, neither of which happened, but which fit well with Ferdinand's own ambitions to keep expanding the Spanish realm after the conquest of Granada in 1492. (Monarchs are always much happier with predictions of triumph than of death.) One of her military predictions did come true: Spanish armies were victorious over Muslim forces in Oran, in North Africa, a campaign planned, paid for, and led by Cardinal Cisneros, the archbishop of Toledo and Inquisitor General, who saw this as part of a continuing crusade against Islam. The duke, the king, and the cardinal all interceded in her trial, and she was ultimately held to have an "exemplary life and doctrine" that were "very useful and highly recommended."[9] The duke of Alba also did just what María prophesied, founding a large convent in Aldenueva, her hometown. He then named her prioress. María's mystical experiences provided her with spiritual authority that led to contact with the wealthy and powerful, and ultimately to a position in the church hierarchy that brought official authority as well.

Francisca de los Apóstoles (c. 1541–?), a visionary *beata* in Toledo, was less fortunate than María, and her story is a more common one for female mystics. Poor harvests and rising prices had made life difficult in sixteenth-century Spain, and some women had turned to selling sex for survival. As Francisca commented in a letter, "There are many young women and widows who would have occasion to offend God out of [economic] necessity," a situation that church officials were not taking seriously as they "spend their incomes on their own enjoyment and . . . let the poor perish and the young women be lost." She attempted to found a *beaterio*, or house for *beatas*, that would both provide poor women with a safe haven and, through its prayers and penance, work for more general salvation. She sought endowments for her house from wealthier women in the city and official approval from the Catholic Church.

Initially there was enthusiasm, and about a dozen women moved into the house, but two women made accusations against Francisca to the Inquisition, stating that she claimed to have visions from God telling her how to set up the *beaterio*. Inquisition officials imprisoned her, charging her with being "spiritually arrogant" and an *alumbrada* because she said she had visions. They were particularly disturbed by two visions in which God, Christ, and the Virgin Mary asked her and the women in her movement to take on a redemptive role for others, experiencing the torments of demons to appease God's wrath. Such an intercessory role was fine for priests, in the eyes of the inquisitors, but not for women, unless they were saints. Over and over they asked her how she knew these visions came from God rather than the devil. At first she was confident that they came from God, explaining that she had experienced them right after communion and that they left her soul sweet and peaceful. But after months of imprisonment and repeated questioning, she began to doubt herself.

The inquisitors brought formal charges against Francisca, suggesting that she be burned. In response, she agreed that she would "believe everything" the inquisitor said, "because he is a person who has more illumination from God to understand such things." This was still not enough for the inquisitors, who left her in prison for a year, and then added accusations of sexual misconduct with another prisoner to the list of charges against her. She denied this, and retreated even more strongly from her visions: "So I have decided to ignore my understanding of what I have experienced and only to believe what the Holy Office [the Inquisition] has taught me, and if an angel were to tell me the opposite, I would not believe it."[10] Her sentence was reduced to one hundred lashes and three years' banishment from Toledo. With that she disappears from history.

All three of these Spanish mystics were investigated by the Inquisition, but the results were very different: Teresa of Avila was declared a saint and later a Doctor of the Church and is widely venerated today; María de Santo Domingo was praised by powerful men and got a position within her religious order; and Francisca de los Apóstoles was imprisoned, forced to deny her visions, and banished from her home.

No other European mystic achieved the level of fame that Teresa did, but into the eighteenth century other Spanish and Italian visionaries and aspiring saints shared the fates of María and Francisca—esteem and shame. Many experienced both. Luisa de la Ascensión (1565–1636), for example, a Franciscan abbess at Carrión de los Condes, had raptures in which she levitated, and her face glowed like that of a young woman. Her rosary beads and bread she had touched were reported to heal the sick, as did wooden crosses that were touched to her head. High-level church officials, nobles, and royalty visited her convent and requested her prayers and miraculous interventions. These included supernatural appearances simultaneously blessing the Spanish fleet in the West Indies and Spanish troops in the Netherlands, examples of the phenomena of spiritual bilocation that was sometimes ascribed to mystics. One of her crosses was reported to have restored the sight of a blind Moqui boy in today's New Mexico, after which 10,000 members of this Indigenous tribe instantly converted to Christianity. Despite these and many more reported miracles, when she was seventy, Luisa was imprisoned and interrogated by the Inquisition. She died shortly afterward, and although her name was eventually cleared, the veneration of objects and books associated with her was prohibited. Her reputation faded.

The reputation of another Spanish bilocating nun, María de Agreda (1602–1665), has remained strong, despite an Inquisition investigation and her own disavowal of her most spectacular visions. A devout child, María convinced her mother and father to turn their home into a convent, part of the Order of the Immaculate Conception founded in Spain with Isabel of Castile's support.

María began to fall into trances and see visions, in one of which angels transported her to settlements of the Jumanos people in New Spain, what is today Texas and New Mexico. Missionaries there reported that the Jumanos also had visions, of a "lady in blue" who urged them to be baptized. Letters sent to Mexico City with reports of María's visions led missionaries to connect these two, and one of the missionaries traveled to Spain in 1631 to speak with her. He became convinced that María was this "lady in blue," a conviction he communicated to King Philip IV, who also visited her several times and with whom she exchanged hundreds of letters providing spiritual and political advice. She became convinced of it herself and sent encouraging letters to Franciscan friars in New Mexico. Ever skeptical of visionaries' claims, the Inquisition opened an investigation, but found nothing suspicious, which further enhanced her reputation on both sides of the Atlantic.

María's trances continued and she wrote a long treatise, the *Mystical City of God*, a book of revelations about the life of the Virgin Mary that María said was dictated to her by the Virgin herself. In the 1650s, María disavowed her accounts of bilocation and said that the Franciscan missionary and her confessor had pressured her into affirming their version of the events. That disavowal never became widely known, however, and the "lady in blue" (*la Dama Azul*) became an important figure of devotion in colonial New Spain. (See Plate XII.) Although the Inquisition condemned the *Mystical City of God* after her death and forbade people to read it, that decision was never implemented in Spain or the Spanish colonies, and her works spread widely. New stories were added to her legend, and today the lady in blue appears in artwork, literature, plays, and devotions, especially on the U.S./Mexican borderlands, although the historical María has somewhat disappeared from view.

As the example of María de Agreda shows, Spanish patterns of women's holiness spread to the colonies through letters, printed books, personal travel, and migration. Lima, the capital of the Viceroyalty of Peru, became the center of intense Catholic culture in the seventeenth century, filled with churches, monasteries, convents, and shrines to saints. Church bells tolled every hour, and processions wound through the streets every day. City residents engaged with sacred objects in their homes and on their persons, looking at a portrait of the Virgin Mary, wearing a badge with a religious image, or carrying a relic from a saint or other holy person. About a fifth of the women in the city lived in religious institutions, as nuns, the lay sisters known as *beatas, donadas* (religious servants), students, or free and enslaved servants. Here they prayed, listened to sermons, made their confessions, carried out penitential acts, taught and learned, sewed clothing and adornments for statues of the Christ child, and embroidered banners for processions. For some women, their spiritual pathway included mystical experiences of the divine.

Of these, the model was the woman who became known as Rose of Lima (1586–1617). Born Isabel Flores de Oliva, the daughter of a Spanish soldier and partly Indigenous mother, she gained the name "Rose" when a servant claimed to see her face transform into a rose, and she then took that name officially at her confirmation. When she was a child, she heard about Catherine of Siena and began to emulate her, engaging in intense pious practices and severe bodily penance. Rose fasted for days on end, slept little, whipped herself, hung herself from her hair, and wore a spiked crown, harming her health in the process. Her parents wanted her to marry, and her confessor wanted her to enter a convent, but she wanted to do neither. Instead, she persuaded her parents to allow her to live as a recluse in a hut in their yard, as Catherine had lived at home.

Extreme asceticism has been part of Christian religious practice at various times and places, though today it may be hard for us to understand. Women engaged in every kind of self-mortification but seemed particularly attracted to practices involving food. They were often very devoted to the Christian Eucharist, which in Catholic theology actually becomes Christ's body at the moment it is consecrated. Some women tried to live by eating only that and giving up all other food, transforming their own bodies into divine vessels. Both Catherine of Siena and Rose of Lima did this at times, which became part of their reputation for sanctity, though other young women who did so were denounced as frauds or charged with what was termed "pretense of holiness."

For us, intelligent and intense young women choosing not to eat is generally interpreted through a medical lens as the eating disorder anorexia nervosa, which has a range of psychological, physical, social, and cultural causes in the contemporary world. We also view other types of self-harm, as well as seeing visions and hearing voices, primarily as psychiatric matters or mental disorders, again with multiple causes. This response was not unknown in the sixteenth and seventeenth centuries. The Inquisition and other courts sometimes found visionaries and "holy women" to have mental disorders and ordered their relatives to take them home and care for them. Confessors and other church officials, as well as family members, sometimes tried to convince or force young women to stop behavior that they regarded as extreme and knew was life-threatening. Young women sometimes hid what they were doing, just as those with eating disorders do today. Thus there are parallels in restricting food intake and other types of asceticism across the centuries, but for the women in this chapter who chose not to eat, food had a religious meaning that it generally does not today. To their societies as well as to them, severe asceticism and the resultant poor health were signs of holiness, of the women's being willing to suffer in imitation of Christ's suffering, atoning for the sins of others as well as their own.

Rose followed Catherine of Siena's model in other ways as well. She joined the third order of the Dominicans, and ministered to the sick and poor, sometimes taking them into her parents' house to care for them. She had regular visions, often while praying and meditating, during one of which she experienced a mystical marriage with Christ, though she did not receive Christ's foreskin as her wedding ring. As her reputation for holiness grew, Rose gathered a group of spiritually devout women around her, including married women who gave up sexual relations with their husbands. Dominican and Jesuit friars came to her for advice, and people in all social groups, including people of Indigenous and African descent, asked for her prayers and intercessions.

At her early death in 1617 Rose was viewed by many as a saint. Women who had known her well in Lima immediately provided testimonials for her beatification, describing her heroic asceticism, frequent prayers, and ecstatic experiences. Some were visionaries themselves, including Luisa Melgarejo de Soto (1578–1651), a well-off married woman whose home was a place where people of different social classes and races gathered to discuss spiritual matters. But in 1623, Luisa and five of Rose's other supporters were arrested, charged with being *ilusas* (deluded visionaries) and *alumbradas*, and imprisoned. The notebooks in which they had written about their mystical experiences were confiscated and burned. Luisa Melgarejo was ultimately released, but the other women, who were of lower social standing, were whipped and forced to participate in an auto-da-fé, the public ritual of penance often imposed by the Inquisition.

Criticism of her supporters did not dent Rose's great public following, however. Stories spread in both Peru and Spain about her miraculous intercessions, with even the king of Spain claiming to have experienced this. Rose was beatified in 1667 and canonized in 1671, the first person born in the Western hemisphere to be made a saint. She was named the patron saint of Peru, the Americas, and the Philippines, and since then, countless parishes, churches, and festivals have been named in her honor. Her feast day, August 30, is a public holiday in Peru, with large processions in Lima. Her skull, wearing a crown of roses, is on display in the huge baroque Convent of Santo Domingo in Lima. In 2015, forensic anthropologists used CT scanning to reconstruct her face from the skull and found her to be more attractive than traditional portrayals had showed. A life-size statue based on that reconstruction is now on display in Lima and has become part of the pilgrimage circuit for devotees of the Peruvian saint.

Women of all social classes came into Rose of Lima's orbit. Ursula de Jesús (1604–1668), a woman of African descent born into slavery, worked as a servant while she was a child in Luisa Melgarejo's household. She then went to work for a woman who entered one of Lima's many convents, attending to her needs and laboring alongside other enslaved Afro-Peruvian women in the convent kitchen and infirmary. At this point, half of Lima was Black, both free and enslaved. One of the convent residents purchased Ursula's liberty when she was in her forties and she became a *donada*, a pious woman working in a convent who took simple vows. (Spanish law prohibited someone of African or Indigenous heritage from becoming a professed nun, and Ursula did not have the money the convent required as a dowry in any case.) There were hundreds of *donadas* in Lima's convents during the seventeenth century, whose lives involved both manual and spiritual labor.

Ursula thus shared many aspects of her life with other Afro-Peruvian women, but she also began to see and hear visions. Many of these were of free and enslaved convent servants she had known who were trapped in purgatory, the place where, according to Catholic doctrine, the souls of sinners go after death to make up for their sins before going to heaven. Catholic doctrine also taught (and teaches) that the living can help those in purgatory through prayer, penance, and purchasing masses or indulgences for them. (An indulgence is a piece of parchment or paper, signed by a church official, that substitutes a virtuous act done by a holy person for time in purgatory of someone else. The vigorous sale of these in Martin Luther's part of Germany was what led to his first public objection to Catholic teachings, the 1517 "Ninety-five Theses on the Power of Indulgences.") Purgatory was often portrayed as a place of purifying fire, and the souls who spoke to Ursula asked her to intercede on their behalf with God to make their time in purgatory easier and shorter. These visions disturbed her, however, and she began to compose a spiritual journal, most likely dictating this to one of the nuns and justifying it by claiming that her confessor had commanded her to do so. As she described one of her visions:

Monday, as soon as I had gone to the choir and prostrated myself before the Lord, I saw two black women below the earth. In an instant, they were beside me. One of them said to me, "I am Lusia, the one who served Ana de San Joseph, and I have been in purgatory for this long, only because the great merciful God showed compassion toward me. No one remembers me." Very slowly, she spoke of God's goodness, power, and mercy, and how we should love and serve Him. Lusia had served this community in good faith, but sometimes they had accused her of certain things, and at times she suffered her penance where she tended to cook. For the love of God, would Ursula please commend her spirit to God. Before Lusia died, she endured awful hardships. . . . I said to God that if He sent the suffering, I would commend them to Him and offer whatever I could for them. . . . I see that the flames do not come out of the top of her head as they did before, now they only reach to the middle of her forehead.[11]

Ursula became widely known in Lima as a holy woman, but her journal also reveals the limits of fame for an Afro-Peruvian, as her everyday duties interfered with her spiritual life:

> On Thursday of Holy Week, I had spent the entire night in front of the holy altar without being able to do anything but sleep. At dawn I said to the Lord: "Hello, I have been lazy all night long." The voices said that I would see what I could do and a weak nature needs to rest. The entire night before I had prepared food for this day in the convent. The voices said, *Why does that cooking matter to you? What matters is that you should look toward God.*[12]

Ursula sometimes complains about idle and gossipy nuns who neglect their spiritual obligations and force her and other servants to work, and there are hints that she found solace from racial inequality in her spirituality, but her primary concern is her interaction with God and the dead souls who sought her out.

Ursula's spiritual journal is the only autobiographical text by an African woman that has survived from the Spanish American colonies in the early modern period, but she was not the only non-white female visionary. Catarina de San Juan (1607?–1688) lived in Puebla de los Angeles, the second-largest city in New Spain—what is now Mexico—and spent the last half of her life in seclusion, prayer, asceticism, and penance. According to the biographies written shortly after she died, she saw visions of God and other heavenly figures, made prophecies about important leaders, bilocated to help Jesuit missionary ventures, and even intervened with God to assure that the queen of Spain would have a healthy child. At her death, huge crowds gathered to view her body and perhaps tear off a bit of her clothing to have a relic that would also bring them divine favor. She was buried in the large Jesuit church, in a ceremony attended by the highest-ranking city and church officials. The room where she had lived was made into an altar and portraits of her were sold for people's personal devotions.

Details about her death can be confirmed, but trying to learn about Catarina's life is far more difficult, as the only sources that we have are the sermon preached at her funeral and two biographies written by her supporters. These make her life into an adventure story, with the evidence of divine favor and piety needed for candidates for sainthood. They relate that she was born into a pagan royal family in India, but was kidnapped by Portuguese slave traders, who took her to Manila in the Philippines. Here she converted to Christianity after meeting Jesuit missionaries. In 1619, she was taken across the Pacific to New Spain, where she was enslaved by a couple in Puebla. After they died, the local priest forced her to marry one of his slaves, even though she had taken a vow of chastity. She prayed to be made to look ugly, so that her abusive husband would leave her alone, which apparently worked. By the 1640s both her husband and the priest had died, and she began her life as a secluded holy woman.

How much of this is true is impossible to say, but there were many enslaved and free Asians in Mexico by this point, brought across the Pacific in the cargo ships known as the Manila galleons. In fact, Catarina would have been sailing from Manila to Acapulco just a few years before Sor Jerónima and the other ocean-crossing nuns from her convent sailed in the other direction. All people from Asia in Mexico were known as *chinos*, a word derived from China, and Catarina came to be referred to as the *china poblana*—that is, the Asian woman who lived in Puebla. (*China poblana* is also a traditional style of dress for women in Mexico, with a white embroidered slightly lowcut blouse, brightly colored full skirt, lace-edged slip, and shawl. This developed in the nineteenth century and was then linked to Catarina de San Juan, but she had nothing to do with it and would most likely have disapproved.) Asians intermarried with other groups, adding to the complex cultural and ethnic mixture that was colonial New Spain. Catarina's popularity in Puebla came in part because people wanted a hometown saint who would bring divine favor to their community, and also perhaps in part because whoever she was, she was decidedly not purely Spanish.

That local enthusiasm led to suspicion, however. The papacy was making the process of becoming a saint more centralized, rigorous, and legalistic, and promoters of any candidate would get into trouble for venerating them too fervently before they were officially canonized.

Within a few years of Catarina's death her portraits were prohibited, the altar was boarded up, and one of the biographies was banned as blasphemous. The Jesuit biographer had gone too far in his tales of heroic tests of her virtue, the inquisitors decided, particularly in describing her struggles withstanding the temptation of a nearly naked Christ:

> On one occasion, the Lord showed himself to her in that same form of a child, but almost naked, much as we are accustomed to dress his image on the feast of his Resurrection, or of his Nativity in the manger. . . . The charity and love of this, his beloved and dear Spouse, grew with this vision, almost to the point of causing a rapture, and rendering violent her impulse to clasp the Child God in her arms, to no longer be held back by the shackles of her virginal reserve, being frightened by the nakedness of her only and divine Lover. . . . Catharina responded with new, greater, and more ample refusals of his loving purity, that he should leave her alone, go away, disappear; for this nakedness of his humanized divinity frightened and unnerved her, and she could not find the strength to embrace him.[13]

Like other holy women, Catarina was understood to be a bride of Christ, but even in the exaggerated, baroque style popular in the seventeenth century, describing this in such an eroticized way was unacceptable.

Teresa of Avila and Rose of Lima were the only mystics from the Hispanic world who were made saints before 1800, despite the hundreds of women who followed their examples, and the dozens of spiritual biographies written by clergy as evidence of women's holiness. In fact, this was not a good era for women saints overall. No women were made saints in the sixteenth century, only six in the seventeenth century, and only six in the eighteenth century. Along with Teresa and Rose, these twelve included five Italian mystics—Catherine of Bologna, Catherine of Genoa, and Catherine de Ricci, mentioned above, plus Mary Magdalene de' Pazzi (1566–1607) and Agnes of Montepulciano (1268–1317). (Catherine of Siena had been canonized in the fifteenth century.) The twelve also included four medieval women raised to sainthood for various reasons—Queen Elizabeth of Portugal (1271–1336), venerated for her piety and service to the poor; the Catalan tertiary Mary de Cervellione (1230–1290), venerated for rescuing ships at sea; the Italian servant Zita (1212–1272), venerated for aiding servants and assisting in finding lost keys; the Italian tertiary Margaret of Cortona (1247–1297), venerated for establishing a hospital for the poor. Of all the other women in this book, only Jeanne de Chantal, the French founder of the Order of the Visitation of Holy Mary you met in Chapter 2, was canonized before 1800. (Other women have been canonized since, and there are also many more who were beatified.) Thus, being a mystic was not a great way to become a saint in the early modern period, but, given their small numbers, mystics were still over-represented among the saints, especially among women.

FRENCH CONTEMPLATIVES INSPIRE

Teresa and other Hispanic mystics drew on the writings and accounts of the life of Catherine of Siena, and Teresa's writings in turn became important in France, where they were published in translation in the seventeenth century. Jeanne de Chantal and Francis de Sales used them extensively in establishing the Order of the Visitation of Holy Mary, as did others seeking to create groups that combined spiritual devotions within convents with assistance to the poor and ill outside them.

Teresa often stressed the importance of mental prayer in becoming closer to God, that is, prayer that did not involve reciting set prayers aloud. The Spanish theologian Miguel de Molinos (1628–1696) went further, writing in *Spiritual Guide* (1675) that any visible religious activity, including attendance at services, meditative rituals, or even ascetic discipline, should be avoided. These took one away from passive contemplation and inner peace, through which one could lose one's individual soul in God. These contemplative practices, dubbed "quietism" by church leaders who opposed them, were condemned as heresy by the pope in 1687. Molinos was arrested by the Inquisition, which argued that his teachings were leading people to neglect morality and reject the authority of the Catholic Church. At his trial, Molinos refused to defend himself, which his followers interpreted as quietism in action and his opponents as a sign of his guilt. The pope decided not to make a martyr out of Molinos, however, and imprisoned him for the rest of his life instead of executing him.

Similar ideas that one could reach God simply through quiet prayer and contemplation developed in France, advocated especially by Jeanne-Marie Bouvier de la Mothe Guyon (1647–1717), a wealthy French widow who read both Teresa and Molinos. She became the center of a group of intensely religious individuals and had several mystical experiences. Madame Guyon felt herself called to spread a contemplative method of turning inward like that advocated by Molinos. In 1685 she published (in French) *A Short and Easy Method of Prayer*:

Everyone is capable of inward contemplative prayer, and it is a terrible shame that almost all people have it in their heads not to do it. We are all called to this prayer as we are all called to eternal life. Contemplative prayer is nothing more than heartful affection and love. . . . [It] can be done at any time, and does not depend on any particular walk of life. This includes princes, kings, clergy, priests, lawyers, soldiers, children, craftsmen, workers, women, and the sick; indeed, everyone can perform this type of worship, my friend. This is not a prayer stemming from the mind, but a prayer stemming from the heart. . . . Those who cannot read are not deprived of the chance for contemplative prayer. Jesus Christ is the great book, written on both the inside and the outside, which will teach all things. They must learn this fundamental truth, which is that "the kingdom of God is within you" (Luke 17:21), and that it is there they must look. . . . Let them begin with a deep act of adoration and emptying themselves before God, and, after that, let them attempt to close the eyes of the body and to open the eyes of the soul as they focus inward. . . . In this way let them pray the Our Father, perhaps understanding little of what they are saying, but thinking that God is with them and wants to be their Father.

. . . If they feel inclined to peace or silence, let them not continue [saying the Our Father] but remain in this state as long as they are so moved, after which they continue on to the second request, that "your will be done as it is in heaven." Thus they will desire that God's will be done in them and through them.[14]

Madame Guyon's ideas attracted women and men, including high church officials such as archbishop of Cambrai François Fénelon, who wrote that he had learned more from her than from any theologian. Through Fénelon, her ideas reached the French court, where they were taken up by the Marquise de Maintenon (1635–1719), initially the governess to some of King Louis XIV's children and later his (secretly married) second wife. Madame Maintenon had been educated by Ursulines and was in the process of founding a school for poor but honorable aristocratic girls at Saint-Cyr, near the royal palace at Versailles.

Despite support for her from some highly placed people, however, the king and most French churchmen opposed Madame Guyon's ideas, dubbing them "quietism," and her published works were condemned. She was imprisoned several times, once in the Bastille in Paris for seven years, on the orders of Bishop Bossuet, the most powerful cleric in France. Fénelon was silenced and exiled from Paris. Bossuet was particularly incensed about Madame Guyon's ideas that everyone's prayers were equally valuable and that external forms did not matter. If such ideas spread further, wrote Bossuet, they would lead to an intolerable lack of respect for authority. He and others called her mad, dangerous, seductive, and ignorant. Released from the Bastille in 1703, Madame Guyon was ordered to leave Paris. She spent the last years of her life in a village in western France, writing letters and poetry and meeting with a steady stream of supporters. (See Plate XIII.)

Madame Guyon's writings were placed on the Papal Index of Forbidden Books, though she always asserted she was submissive to the Catholic Church. Despite (or perhaps because of) the prohibition, her autobiography was published shortly after her death and immediately translated into several languages. Her ideas became better known among Protestants than Catholics, becoming especially popular with pietists, Methodists, and other dissenters who opposed state churches. They are now widely available in paperback versions, online, and as audiobooks, advertised for their guidance in prayer and spirituality, not as historical documents.

Madame Guyon was not alone among French mystics in attracting Protestants to her ideas or developing a far-flung network of supporters. Antoinette Bourignon (1616–1680), from a wealthy merchant family in Lille, felt a sense of spiritual calling from an early age. She read the Bible, but then stopped, as she later wrote, "because God taught me inwardly all that I needed. To me the (inward) guidance of God and the reading of the Bible were the same thing." She refused marriage twice and left her home to start a community of what she viewed as "true Christians," who would be saved at the Last Judgment, which God had told her was coming soon.

Bourignon began to draw followers, but also detractors, particularly because she criticized all forms of organized religion, Catholic and Protestant. She refused to be associated with any group, saying that the divisions within Christianity were signs of the coming end of the world. What mattered was not a particular doctrine, she wrote, but that one was guided by the Spirit of Justice, Truth, and Love, which she saw as a new sort of Trinity replacing that of Father, Son, and Holy Spirit. This spiritual rebirth was more important than baptism, so that Jews and Muslims might also be saved and resurrected.

Bourignon was firm in her conviction that she was among the most blessed, and unsurprised at her critics, writing in *The Testimony of Truth* (*Le Temoignage de Verité*) that "Nowadays men are less disposed to receive divine illuminations than are women because in their pride their hearts are puffed up to apply all the glory and authority to themselves instead of referring it to God; and they cannot endure that a simple woman, such as I am, speaks of divine matters." Responding to those who challenged her authority to teach, she commented, "I have experienced great displeasure that God created me a woman, but since he let me know that I was pleasing to him thus, I have been content therewith."[15] In contrast to the Quaker Margaret Fell Fox, who thought that God spoke to many women, giving them a voice on religious matters, Bourignon thought that God spoke directly to only a few, including, of course, herself.

The middle of the seventeenth century was a point at which many people were dissatisfied with the established churches and seeking spiritual answers outside them. In Chapter 3 you met the German poet Anna Owen Hoyer, forced to move from Germany to Sweden because of her critiques of the official Lutheran Church. Many of these spiritual seekers moved to the Netherlands, the most tolerant place in Europe, where they could also often find printers willing to publish their works. Bourignon joined the stream, moving to Amsterdam in 1667. Here she met other critics of organized religion, which included some of Europe's most important scientists, such as the English chemist Robert Boyle and the Dutch biologist Jan Swammerdam. She also came into contact with Anna Maria van Schurman (1607–1678), a Dutch scholar, artist, and philosopher widely regarded as the most highly educated woman in Europe in the seventeenth century. When she was a young woman, van Schurman had argued in print that advanced education for women was perfectly compatible with Christian teachings, as it would lead to stronger faith, moral improvement, better guiding of their children, and "a more tranquil and free life." By the 1660s, van Schurman had rejected her earlier learning and argued that reading the Scriptures while guided by the Holy Spirit was all the education any Christian, man or woman, needed. She joined a splinter religious group and exchanged ideas with Bourignon in letters.

Bourignon and a small group of followers moved to several different places on the North Sea coast, where they set up a printing press and began printing Bourignon's works to sell at fairs and markets. Lutheran authorities were particularly incensed that her followers included married men who had left their wives, whom Bourignon described as her "spiritual sons." They confiscated her press and forced her to move again. She bounced around various north German cities and died while trying to return to Amsterdam.

Bourignon's works—all nineteen volumes of them—were quickly published by her followers and translated into other languages, including German and English. They were influential enough that the Catholic Church and many Lutheran churches forbade people to read them, and in the early eighteenth century the Scottish Presbyterian Church ordered its ministers to denounce the "dangerous errors of Bourignonism [that] do abound in some places of this nation." That order continued until the late nineteenth century, by which point most Scottish ministers had no idea what Bourignonism was or that its founder was a woman. In contrast to Madame Guyon, Antoinette Bourignon is completely unknown today.

SEEING AFRICAN SAINTS

Catholic visionaries could be found in Africa as well as in Europe and the Americas. Portuguese missionaries had accompanied merchants setting up trading posts and making treaties with local rulers along the west coast of

Africa beginning in the late fifteenth century. Missionaries had the greatest success in the Kingdom of the Kongo, a powerful state that included parts of what is now the Republic of Congo, the Democratic Republic of Congo, and Angola. After a series of apparitions interpreted as the Virgin Mary and other saints, there were many converts, including the king Nzinga Nkuwu (ruled to 1506), who took the Christian name João I. The next king, Nzinga Mbemba, whose Christian name was Afonso I (ruled 1506–1543), was raised as a Christian, sent his son and others to be ordained as priests in Europe, and worked to convert his subjects to Christianity, as did other members of the political elite. He wrote a series of letters to the king of Portugal complaining about the quality of priests sent to him, and also complaining about Portuguese slave traders who enslaved and exported Kongolese citizens in ways that were contrary to Kongolese law.

Many of the ideas of Christianity—an unseen realm of divine figures and spirits that revealed itself through visions, priests with special powers, an initiation ritual involving water and signifying rebirth—paralleled religious ideas already present in the Kongo area, and many people were baptized as Christians. Afonso and his successors created a Kongolese version of Christianity, over which the king had significant control, just as rulers did in Europe. Kongo's most important religious holiday, St. James Day (July 25), was also a celebration of King Afonso's military victory over his half-brother. All Saints' Day was also important, a time when Kongolese could visit the graves of their ancestors, as they traditionally did, while still celebrating a Christian holiday. Churches and chapels were built in all Kongolese provinces in the sixteenth century, each dedicated to a saint who was often chosen through revelation and linked to an otherworldly being already venerated in the area. Schools instructed children in Christian teachings, using a catechism in the local language, KiKongo, after 1624. Women and men formed and joined religious confraternities.

The later sixteenth and seventeenth centuries saw frequent warfare in Kongo between rival claimants to the throne, often involving the Portuguese and Dutch as well. Refugees fleeing the conflicts were sold to European slave traders. The Kongo capital Mbanza Kongo (also known as São Salvador) was abandoned, the kingdom broke apart, and people thought longingly of past unity and strength.

In this volatile setting, Dona Beatriz Kimpa Vita (1684–1706), the daughter of an elite army commander, began to see visions in 1704 after a serious illness. (Like many Kongolese at the time, she had two names, a Portuguese one, Dona Beatriz—the honorific Dona, which means "lady" plus her saint's name, Beatriz—and a KiKongo one, Kimpa Vita, the name more commonly used for her today.) These told her that she was possessed by the spirit of the thirteenth-century Franciscan friar St. Anthony of Padua, who had been born in Portugal and was a popular saint there. As a child, Kimpa Vita had dreams of playing with angels, and she had trained as a *nganga marinda*, a traditional healer and spirit medium who communicates with the supernatural world, an accepted role in Kongolese Christianity. Channeling St. Anthony thus fit with her other spiritual inclinations, and also with the central role of saints in Kongolese Christianity. She began singing "Salve Antonia," a prayer to the saint in KiKongo reworked from the Marian hymn "Salve Regina."

Kimpa Vita's revelations told her that the Virgin Mary, Jesus, and St. Francis were Kongolese, and that Jesus had been baptized at Mbanza Kongo. Other saints were also African. She accepted the authority of the pope, but not that of European missionaries, whom she saw as corrupt. She taught that Kongolese Catholicism was the true faith and could stop the cycle of civil wars and make the country united again, a message that attracted followers, known as Antonians. These included male and female peasants who hoped for a better life and women of all social classes, but also contenders for the throne, who thought she could help them defeat their enemies.

Most of what we know about Kimpa Vita's life and ideas comes from an Italian Capuchin priest, Bernardo da Gallo, who spoke with her and drew her portrait. He reported that every Friday she had a revelation in which she ritually died and ascended to heaven, where she spoke to God about the Kongo, Jesus, the saints, and other topics. Bernardo asked her, "Tell me, in Heaven are there blacks from Kongo, and if there are, do they still have their black color in Heaven?" To which she replied, "There are black Kongolese up in heaven."[16] Bernardo also reported that she levitated and healed the sick, including women who were unable to have children. Like holy women in the Hispanic world, she came to be regarded by her followers as a saint in the making.

Kimpa Vita gathered her followers in the ruined former capital Mbanza Kongo, a place of great symbolic significance, from where she sent missionaries to spread her teachings. She allied with one of the contenders to the throne, but in late 1705, she discovered she was pregnant and traveled to her parents' home to have the baby. This was in territory controlled by another, more powerful contender, Pedro IV Nusamu a Mvemba, and she was captured. She was tried and executed for heresy and witchcraft under Kongo law. Pedro IV's forces attacked her followers, selling many of them into slavery. Stories spread among the Antonians that she had not really died, however—a common story with messianic leaders—and only when Pedro's forces took Mbanza Kongo in 1709 was the force of the movement broken.

Some of her ideas lived on, evident in visual objects such as crucifixes showing Jesus with African features and wearing cloth with Kongolese designs that continued to be made for more than a century after her death. Her words endured as well. Enslaved Kongolese Christians who participated in the 1739 Stono Rebellion in South Carolina chanted the word "*kanga*" (meaning salvation) from her "Salve Antonia," and used their experience in fighting the Kongolese civil wars as they acquired arms and killed slave owners. Enslaved Africans in Haiti—many of them from Kongo, where civil wars that resulted in captives sold into slavery had continued throughout the eighteenth century—also chanted the word "*kanga*" on the eve of the Haitian Revolution in 1791. Several new Christian movements that developed in the twentieth century in the Democratic Republic of Congo, including Kimbanguism and Bundu dia Kongo, see themselves as heirs to her message.

Kimpa Vita's identity as an embodiment of the spirit of St. Anthony and a mystic with a messianic vision of salvation was central to her followers, though in the twenty-first century she tends to be celebrated primarily as an African leader who challenged colonial powers. A school of higher education in Uíge, Angola was renamed Kimpa Vita University in 2009, and the 2016 documentary by the Congolese filmmaker and actor Ne Kunda Nlaba, *Kimpa Vita: The Mother of the African Revolution*, focuses mostly on her opposition to slavery.

PREDICTING DEATH AND DESTRUCTION

The best-known mystics and seers from the early modern period are Catholic, but visionaries could also be found among Protestants. In 1700, the German Lutheran pietist Gottfried Arnold published (in German) *Impartial History of the Church and Heretics from the Beginning of the New Testament until 1688 AD*, a 1200-page sympathetic history of "churches and heresies" that included a long list of "blessed women who showed the way to the truth, or who suffered greatly, or who were amazingly gifted, enlightened or directed by God."[17] Although most of Arnold's biographical entries are brief, a few are quite long. Antoinette Bourignon gets more than twenty pages.

Protestant mystics included in Arnold's book often have life histories like those of Catholics. Many began to see visions when they were children. Johanna von Merlau Petersen, the pietist leader you met in Chapter 2, saw visions from an early age of God calling her to teach and write, which continued throughout her long life. Rosamunde Juliane von der Asseburg (1672–1712), from an impoverished noble family, began to see visions of Christ and the Virgin Mary when she was seven, thought of herself as the prophet Samuel reborn, and made predictions of the coming end of the world. She did not levitate, but observers reported that her face shone so brightly one could see it through cracks in the wall. She lived with Johanna Petersen and her pastor husband, who published her visions in his letters, much as Catholic women's confessors did.

From 1618 to 1648, Germany suffered in the Thirty Years' War, which ultimately involved Catholic and Protestant armies from all over Europe. There were no clear lines of battle, so armies indiscriminately burned crops and villages, slaughtered animals, and terrorized and killed people. Sexual violence, long a standard part of conquest, was common, but women were actors as well as victims in the war. Until the development of systems of provisioning in the late eighteenth century, during actual campaigns troops were accompanied by men and women who pillaged the countryside for food and other provisions, as well as food for horses. The undisciplined troops and plundering mob that accompanied them acquired its own name—*Soldateska*, a word that came from the Italian words for "unbridled soldiers." Hunger and disease, including dysentery, plague, and syphilis, accompanied the troops and the refugees who fled from place to place, killing far more of them than did battle wounds. Some historians estimate that at least one-quarter and perhaps as much as one-third of the population of Germany died during the war, though total devastation was localized. Such civilian losses would not be matched again until the wars of the twentieth century.

Unsurprisingly, many of the visionaries Arnold discusses were caught up in the war, and their visions and predictions involved death and destruction. Christina Poniatowska von Duchnik (1610–1644) was the daughter of a Protestant Polish nobleman and pastor, whose family was driven into exile by Catholic forces. She began to see visions involving the Bohemian nobleman Albrecht of Wallenstein, the general of the Catholic armies fighting for the Holy Roman Emperor. One of these saw him walking through a bloody valley with poison pouring out of his heart. When in 1634 the emperor accused Wallenstein of conspiracy and had him assassinated, her visions seemed vindicated and her status as a prophet grew, particularly when her prophecies were published after her death. Sophia Lotterin, a young Bohemian Lutheran, saw a glowing angelic child who showed her an army that would conquer Bohemia and the burning villages left in its wake.

Anna Vetterin (?–1660) was a blacksmith's daughter whose father was killed by mercenaries when she was a child. Her mother wandered from place to place with her children, supporting herself by buying feather-beds people had died on, carrying them many miles away and selling them again. Anna began to see visions of Christ in heaven and local pastors and officials in hell. She made political predictions and wrote letters to various rulers, nobles, and city leaders, urging them to repent. In the early 1630s, Swedish troops under the leadership of King Gustavus Adolphus fought Catholic forces in southern Germany. The decade saw an upsurge in young women prophesying, many of whom were war refu-gees and some of whom claimed to see visions of the Swedish king.

Young visionaries emerged in other situations of religious conflict as well. In 1688, a fifteen-year-old uneducated shepherdess in the Cévennes region in southern France, Isabeau Vincent, began to pray out loud, sing psalms, and prophesy, first in the local language, and then in French. This was right after Louis XIV had revoked the Edict of Nantes and ordered Protestants to convert, when Huguenots were fleeing France. Vincent's father had converted, but her visions told her that Catholic teachings were wrong, and that faith was the only thing that mattered: "Stand firm and may your faith always be founded on Jesus Christ. . . . Because he who perseveres to the end will receive eternal life, you must suffer to defend God's word." She also urged personal repentance: "Repent! . . . Seek his word and you will find it through repentance."[18] One of the literate men who came to hear her wrote down her statements and they were published in French in Amsterdam and then in English translation. She was arrested and questioned but continued to preach. She was imprisoned, transferred to a hospital and then a convent, where she disappears from the records.

Her story also circulated orally and her words in handwritten copies, which inspired other young women from the region. They also began to prophesy over the next several decades, a movement later called the "Minor Prophets." The Cévennes was an area of intense Protestantism, which grew even stronger when French troops burned churches, forced conversions, massacred villagers, and closed the borders to prevent people from leaving France. Adult Protestant men, mostly peasants and artisans, began to preach and prophesy as well, leading to an armed rebellion in 1702 known as the Revolt of the Camisards. Fighting continued off and on for several years, and then gradually died out, as did reports of young women prophesying.

Arnold views some of the more extravagant visionaries a bit skeptically and suggests that illness might have contributed to their visions and trances, but in general he judges women's actions positively, as heroic signs of God operating through the least of his creatures. He notes that local pastors often listened to women visionaries without interrupting them, surely a sign their visions must be real! And that learned clergy sometimes published their sayings and life stories—more proof of their authenticity. Arnold equates the Lutheran theologians who forced Bourignon to flee with the Spanish Inquisition and describes Vetterin's attempt to feed her family by sewing and selling bread as brave.

In 1704, Arnold was answered by the prolific German Lutheran theologian Johann Feustking in *Gynaeceum Haeretico Fanaticum* (*Women's*

Quarters of Fanatic Heretics), a 700-page denunciation of, as his full title reads, the "false prophetesses, Quakeresses, fanatics, and other sectarian and frenzied female persons through whom God's church is disturbed."[19] He began with women in the Bible and early Church who had led men astray and included a few medieval abbesses and nuns who were vision- aries. He then worked alphabetically through a long list of women from the sixteenth and seventeenth centuries, mostly Protestants, beginning with the English Quaker Alida Ambrosia, who had founded several meet- ings despite persecution, and ending with the Dutch Catholic activist Helena Wouteria, who had hung crosses and rosaries around people's necks and urged them to return to allegiance to the pope. In between were about a hundred Anabaptists and enthusiasts, millenarians and mystics, prophets and pietists, quietists and Quakers from all over Europe, and even a few from the American colonies, including Mary Dyer. In some cases, Feustking is the only published historical source that mentions the women's names and actions, for he regarded the obscure and prominent alike as dangerous.

Feustking was furious at the well-placed and educated men who were influenced by these women and published their works, and even more furious at the women themselves. It was clear they were *not* divinely inspired, he fumed, because they criticized ministers and rulers, "actions entirely alien to them and nothing any pious woman would do." A few of their prophecies might have come true, but this was accidental. Their inspiration was more likely to be demonic than divine, as Satan often approached "curious, ambitious, thoughtless, misguided little women," especially those who wanted to be seen as more pious than men. The argument that there was much good in these women's writings is misguided, he wrote, as there was also good in the Qur'an, and Christians shouldn't read it. Besides, whatever *is* good in the women's words or writings, they just took from men. (An argument that Feustking was not the first or last to make, of course.)

Most of the women Arnold mentions are also in Feustking— along with many others—but viewed very differently. To Feustking, Rosamunde von der Asseburg was a melancholic fantasist who just wanted to be someone special and whose revelations came straight out of works by men she had read. Christina Poniatowska was lucky with her

6. *The title page woodcut from Johann Feustking's* Gynaeceum Haeretico Fanaticum *depicts the "frenzy" he thought would result if women preached. Women swoon in the foreground, while men and an angel push over a pulpit where a woman is preaching. The pulpit banner reads, in Latin: "Women should remain silent in church."*

foretelling of Wallenstein's death but had far more false predictions than true ones. Anna Vetterin was insane. He sums them all up: "All prophecies of women today are in general suspicious, because like Eve, women have itchy ears, and always want to know more than what they can or should."[20]

Arnold and Feustking both include a number of English women in their lists, as seventeenth-century England was particularly fertile ground for prophecy. Religious, political, and social ferment culminated in the English Civil War (1640–1660), during which the monarchy was overthrown, and the government run by the leaders of Parliament, headed by Oliver Cromwell. Many who opposed the king were Puritans, including some who wanted a state church, but one with no bishops and simpler ceremonies, others who wanted each congregation to be separate (these were called "Independents" or "separatists"), and others who wanted other types of church structures.

There were also individuals and groups with much more radical ideas. You have already met the Quakers, who stressed equality among Christians, going so far as to suggest that women should have the right to preach and minister to others if they had the spirit. The Ranters preached that God was in everyone, so that people should listen to the Jesus Christ inside themselves rather than to ministers in church buildings. The True Levellers called for an end to private property and demonstrated their aims in a sort of street theater, tearing down hedges and digging up fields that had previously been held in common by villages but were now owned by gentry. (Their enemies mockingly called them "Diggers.") The Fifth Monarchists, inspired by a prophecy in the biblical book of Daniel, believed that the execution of King Charles I would usher in a Fifth Kingdom, that of the Saints. This would lead directly to the millennium, that is, the Second Coming of Christ. These ideas were spread by word of mouth, as Quaker preachers and Leveller orators spoke on street corners and town squares, and also communicated through posters, pamphlets, and cheap books.

Radicals often claimed to be directly inspired by God, but more mainstream Puritan groups also encouraged individualized religious reflection. Puritans drew on the ideas of John Calvin, the French reformer so influential in Geneva, who taught that God is infinite in power, humans are completely sinful, and salvation comes only through Christ as a gift of God. Original Sin involved a loss of free will other than to sin. God has determined who will be saved and who will not, an idea called *predestination*. One's own actions could do nothing to change one's fate, but many Calvinists came to believe that hard work, thrift, and proper moral conduct could serve as signs that one was among the "elect" chosen for salvation.

Having a particularly powerful experience of religious conversion was another indication that one was among the "saints," the term some Puritans used for God's chosen. Puritan thinkers and clergy in England and the English colonies taught that all believers, male and female, should engage in spiritual introspection and, in particular, focus on their experience of conversion. An especially dramatic conversion could give one a certain amount of power, especially if it resulted in the healing of an illness or a continuing experience of divine revelation. Women and men related their conversion experiences orally—in New England, this became a requirement for joining a Puritan congregation as a full member—and some wrote them down, or others wrote them down for them.

Puritan women's conversion narratives are often very personal and physical, and some involved fasting and other types of asceticism or self-harm. In this they are like the accounts of Catholic candidates for sainthood. A few also involved mystical and ecstatic experiences, which became more common during the English Civil War era. The teenaged Sarah Wight (1632–?), for example, saw herself as sin-laden and abandoned by God. She attempted suicide several times, suffering a concussion after launching herself off a roof, and in 1647 went into a trance during which she became paralyzed and comatose. She heard God's voice, giving her assurance of grace, and woke up. Those around her encouraged her to eat, but she refused, saying, "I cannot. I am so full of the Creator, that I now can take in none of the Creature. I am fill'd with heavenly Manna." Sounding much like Catarina de San Juan, she spoke about her desire for Christ and about his nakedness: "Now I have my desire; I desired nothing but a crucified Christ and I have him . . . a crucified Christ, a naked Christ. . . . I have him and nothing else."[21] In contrast to Rose of Lima, she even refused to eat the bread and wine of the Eucharist.

Wight might have been dismissed as a troubled adolescent, but during this tumultuous time, as news about her fast and visions spread, people instead flocked to her bedside. These included pastors, physicians, government officials, army officers, nobles, and many women, listening as she spoke "speeches of grace" and provided what they understood was advice for their own troubles and spiritual doubts. Among these was a woman listed among the visitors as "Dinah the Black," a "Moor not born in England," thus most likely one of the many enslaved Africans then in London. She told Wight she was tempted to suicide because "I am not as others are, I do not look so as others do." Wight does not mention her own attempts to kill herself, but instead refers to the woman's skin color:

Sarah: When Christ comes and manifests himself to the soul, it is black in itself, and uncomely; but he is fair and ruddy, and he clothes the soul with his comliness.
Woman: He may do this for some but not to me.
Sarah: He doth not this to one only, nor to one Nation only; for many Nations must be blessed in him. . . . He is a free Agent; and why should you exclude yourself?[22]

The printed version of this exchange reports that this woman, like most of those who came to Wight, was comforted, though we might wonder just how comforting the idea that Christ would make her soul attractive by making it "fair and ruddy" actually was to "Dinah the Black."

Wight's pastor, Henry Jessey, stayed by her side, and recorded her trials, conversations, and utterances, writing these up as *The Exceeding Riches of Grace Advanced by the Spirit of Grace, in an Empty Nothing Creature, Viz. Mris* [sic] *Sarah Wight*. The book appeared right as Wight broke her fast, after eleven weeks, printed for the Puritan bookseller Hannah Allen, who had taken over her husband's printing and bookselling business at his death and was known for printing books by radical religious thinkers and visionaries. It became a bestseller and went into multiple editions over the next several decades, apparently succeeding in its efforts, as the title page read, to "refresh poor souls."

Wight's visions revolved around a personal assurance of grace, but those of other women were more political. Anna Trapnel (1630s–?) also began to see visions when she was a child, after her mother said "Lord! Double thy spirit upon my child" three times before she died.[23] In despair about her own sinfulness, Trapnel thought about suicide and sought solace in several different congregations. In 1654, she fell into a months-long trance during which she recited prophecies in verse, often against Oliver Cromwell and his government. The public attention led to an invitation to travel from London to Cornwall, where she again fell into prophetic trances, speaking to large crowds about the fate of the Parliamentary government. Reflecting on this later, she wrote: "There came many to see me, some out of goodwill . . . and others came to gaze, and others to catch me at my words, so as to reproach me; but the Lord taught me how to speak before them all."[24] She was arrested for being an impostor and a vagabond, and accused of witchcraft. "Some would fain have that witch-trier woman of that town . . . come with her great pin which she used to thrust into witches, to try them," in search of a spot that felt no pain, she wrote later. "But the Lord my God in whom I trust, delivered me from their malice" and no witchcraft charges were brought.[25] She was taken back to London and sent to Bridewell prison. Trapnel published several books with her life story and prophecies—one with the evocative title *The Cry of a Stone*—and joined the Fifth Monarchists, who allowed women to speak and vote, though not to preach.

Mary Cary (*c.* 1621–1653), another Fifth Monarchist, prophesied that the victory of the Parliamentary army was foretold in Daniel. That victory would lead, she hoped, to a utopian society with no poverty or famine and where:

> No infant of days shall die; none shall die while they are young; all shall come to a good old age. They shall not be afflicted for the loss of their children; for they shall live till they be an hundred years old. . . . The streets shall be full of boys and girls playing . . . and old men and women shall live till they come of good old age, till they walk with a staff in their hand for age.[26]

In a society where half the children died before they were five, this was a utopia indeed.

Most of the prophecies by English women that made it into print did so during the Civil War, when the established system for approving works for publication had broken down. Some appeared illegally before this, including those of the noblewoman Lady Eleanor Davies Douglas (1590–1652). Just after Charles I had become king in 1625, Lady Eleanor heard a voice that she interpreted as the Old Testament prophet Daniel, telling her the millennium would begin in nineteen and a half years. She took this message personally to the archbishop of Canterbury—the highest religious official in England—and published her visions illicitly as *A Warning to the Dragon and All His Angels*. This was the first of what would be some sixty pamphlets, filled with allusions to the Bible and the prophetic messengers who visited her, and with anagrams and complex word play. She made no attempt to hide her authorship, though her pamphlets were burned, and she was frequently arrested and imprisoned for sedition, debt, and smuggling illegally printed works into England from Amsterdam.

Lady Eleanor gained fame when she accurately predicted the death of her first husband and of several prominent nobles and officials. She interpreted the execution of Archbishop Laud in 1645 by Parliament as the fulfillment of her first vision, even though it was (sadly, for her) not followed by the Second Coming. She gained notoriety through her pamphlets, and even more when she protested changes Laud had ordered making church furnishings and services more elaborate by pouring hot tar and wheat paste on the hangings of an altar in Lichfield Cathedral. For that, she was sent to Bethlehem Hospital, the hospital in London commonly known as "Bedlam" that specialized in the treatment of the insane.

Even that did not silence her or convince her to tone down her words. Her very last published pamphlet, from 1652, *Bethlehem, Signifying the House of Bread: Or War*, justifies her earlier actions at Lichfield as a protest against those who had "in execrable manner Crucified the Oracles of God" by hiding the Ten Commandments with an embroidered "coarse purple Woollen altar cloth." She rails against those who had shut her up "in *Bedlems* loathsome *Prison*, infected with those *foul Spirits* day and night blaspheming," and ties her imprisonment to the outbreak of war between England and Scotland in 1639.[27] Lady Eleanor did not join any of the groups that advocated radical social change—she was a noblewoman, after all—but she did meet with other women to discuss religious issues.

NEW SEXUAL AND GENDER IDENTITIES

The restoration of the English monarchy in 1660 dramatically curtailed the publication of political prophecies but did not end English women's direct experience of the divine. Some of the Quaker women you met in Chapter 3 heard voices telling them to preach or travel and had ecstatic visions while they were imprisoned. The most prominent English female visionary at the end of the seventeenth century was Jane Lead (1624–1704), who, like Sarah Wight and Anna Trapnel, had first heard a voice calling her to a spiritual life when she was a teenager. Despite this, she married and had children, but after her husband died in 1670, her visions began again. As she later relates, she saw:

An overshadowing bright cloud, and in the midst of it the figure of a woman, most richly adorned with transparent gold, her hair hanging down, and her face as terrible as crystal for brightness, but her countenance was sweet and mild. . . . Immediately this voice came, saying, Behold, I am God's eternal virgin, Wisdom, whom those hast been enquiring after. I am to unseal the treasures of God's deep wisdom unto thee. . . . Behold me as thy Mother.[28]

Lead's visions are full of female and maternal imagery. The biblical personification of Divine Wisdom (or Sophia, to use the Greek word for Wisdom) was a mother figure from whom she obtained knowledge and sustenance: "My Spirit still attended eagerly longing to lay my Mouth to Wisdom's Breast, from which the Word of Life so sweetly did flow."[29] Wisdom was her "true Mother" out of whose womb she would be spiritually reborn and whose milk transmitted divine knowledge and salvation, in contrast to the more common focus on Christ's blood. The Virgin Mary, to Lead, was an emissary of Sophia who took on human form. Divine Wisdom would also restore all souls at the end of time, so that all would be saved and would return to a genderless androgyny that Lead saw as God's original plan.

Lead began publishing her ideas in 1681 and developed a circle of followers in London and on the continent. They called themselves the Philadelphian Society, after a city in what is now Turkey mentioned in the Book of Revelation whose name means "city of brotherly love." (The English Quaker William Penn named the city he founded around the end of the seventeenth century Philadelphia for exactly the same reason.) The Philadelphians described Lead as their "spiritual mother," and adopted her ideas, especially that of universal salvation and an imminent end of the world. The group fell apart quickly after she died, though her ideas remained influential with other utopian groups in Europe and North America.

Other mystics were also viewed as spiritual mothers by their followers. Jane Wardley and her husband were Quakers near Manchester when, in 1747, she began to have visions telling her that Christ would return soon, but in the form of a woman. She communicated this to her Quaker meeting, often shaking or trembling as she did so, a practice the group adopted, becoming known as the "Shaking Quakers." Ann Lee (1736–1784), the illiterate daughter of a blacksmith, joined the group when she was in her twenties, and quickly became its leader. She married a blacksmith and had four children, all of whom died as infants. She also had visions of Adam and Eve having sex and became convinced that sexual relations had caused the fall of humanity and were the source of sin in the world. This was not that different from the widely accepted notion of Original Sin, but Lee went further. Only by giving up sex, she argued, could people bring about the kingdom of God on earth. Her visions also told her that she was the Second Coming of Christ the group had anticipated, and they named her their "mother in spiritual things." Some swore themselves to celibacy and chastity.

Mother Ann Lee shared her visions widely and loudly, disrupting Sunday services in other churches by shaking and shouting about sinful depravity and divine messages. She was arrested several times for breaking the Sabbath and blasphemy, as were some of her followers, and in 1774 she led eight of them to the American colonies. Persecution continued and she died as the result of beatings. There was fluidity in leadership for a while, but the person who emerged as the primary leader was another woman, Lucy Wright (1760–1821). Wright herself was not a visionary, but she was a gifted leader, and under her guidance the group expanded, despite—or perhaps because of—their advocacy of celibacy. They formed communities where members lived in dormitories and shared property and work, gaining new members through conversion and adoption. At their peak, in about 1830, American Shakers—officially the United Society of Believers in Christ's Second Appearing—may have numbered 6,000 people.

Ann Lee and her followers understood her to be the Second Coming of Christ. God, in their eyes, was both female and male, so because Christ was male, Christ's Second Coming would have to be in a female body. Another Protestant visionary who grew up in the Quaker tradition went beyond this, developing a persona as a prophet without gender. The Public Universal Friend (1752–1819) was born Jemima Wilkinson in a prominent Rhode Island family with many children. In 1776, she became ill with a high fever, and claimed to have died. Her body was now filled with a new spirit, the Public Universal Friend, who was neither male nor female and was charged by God to preach repentance to a sinful world. The Friend refused to answer to the name "Jemima" or the pronoun "she," and when asked about what we would today term "gender identity," the Friend simply said, "I am what I am." This may have been an allusion to the apostle Paul's similar words in the First Letter to the Corinthians (I Cor. 15:10: "by the grace of God I am what I am"), or an even more audacious allusion to God's response to Moses in Exodus (Exodus 3:14: "God said unto Moses, I am that I am").

Dressed in largely male clothing and accompanied by siblings, the Friend traveled and preached across several states, gathering a group of followers known as the Universal Friends. The Friend's teachings and theology were similar to those of the Quakers, with an emphasis on direct inspiration and social equality. Sexual abstinence was preferred, but not mandatory. The Friend's followers included a group of unmarried women known as the Faithful Sisterhood who took on important roles, but also married couples and unmarried men. Hostility grew, and the Universal Friends decided to form their own utopian community in western New York, naming it Jerusalem. The town expanded quickly, but after the death of the Friend in 1819, fewer of its residents were Universal Friends and the group had disappeared completely by the 1860s.

The Public Universal Friend challenged people's understandings of gender, but the Friend's religious ideas were not especially innovative. Radical Protestants since the sixteenth century had preached social equality and set up communities to put their ideas into practice. The American frontier in the eighteenth and nineteenth centuries saw many utopian communities founded by religious visionaries, most of them short-lived. Many of these had distinctive sexual and gender ideas and patterns. Along with the Shakers and Universal Friends, the Ephrata Cloister in Pennsylvania, established in 1732, preached the superiority of asceticism and celibacy; the Mormons, established in the 1830s, advocated polygamy; the Oneida Community, established in 1848, practiced group marriage and male continence. The Moravians, a pietist group you will meet in Chapter 6, segregated members by sex until they were married, and made decisions about possible marriages by drawing lots, that is, by pulling colored ballots out of a box. So the Shakers and Universal Friends were unusual compared to most Protestants, but well within what we could call the radical mainstream.

Many of the other visionaries in this chapter also fit within their own religious traditions more fully than they might seem to initially. The revelations of most Hispanic mystics supported Catholic doctrine, and, in fact, called for exactly what the Council of Trent advocated: stricter cloistering for nuns, higher standards of morality for laypeople, more prayer and good works for all. Kings, nobles, and high church officials looked to holy women for guidance and clues about the future, thus giving the women power, but most of their predictions were conservative rather than revolutionary. Even Kimpa Vita preached a message of returning to a unified Kongo, and was executed because she backed the wrong contender, not for what she was saying. The most common advice of French contemplatives, Puritan prophets, and American utopians was pray, repent, and live a more disciplined life.

Thus when we look at the *message* of most female visionaries, this often reinforced the teachings of whatever Christian denomination the women had grown up in rather than contesting these. But it was impossible for people at the time, and many since, to ignore the *messenger*. No matter how pious and conventional their instructions—Give to the poor! Care for the sick! Concern yourself less with worldly things! Pray for souls in purgatory! Prepare your soul for the coming Day of Judgment!—the fact that a woman was saying this made it threatening. Gaspar Navarro, Thomas Edwards, and Johann Feustking would have agreed on very little in terms of theology, but they would have fully agreed that most women who claimed to hear the voice of God or the Holy Spirit were arrogant, disobedient, obstinate, restless, unreasonable, and possibly demonic. Listening to them could be dangerous, no matter what they said and no matter how often they said it was simply God speaking through them. It took so little to turn the world upside down.

CHAPTER SIX

MISSIONARIES

While in jail I spoke about religion much more than I had out of it, with all the jailers and officials and their families and friends whom, with my permission, they brought to speak with me. And they listened nicely. And I didn't want to let the chance slip by, remembering the Holy Apostle who says that the word of God is not tied down.

Luisa de Carvajal, Spanish Catholic missionary

Turn to Him, who has everything. The Lord blesses and protects you and meets you and clothes you with mercy . . . the Lord shows us mercy, that we may turn ourselves over to Him. We know his great heart well, and He has also taught us that a great heart is patient.

Rebecca Protten, Afro-Caribbean Moravian teacher

Christianity was an expansive religion from its beginnings, carried by believers across much of Eurasia and North Africa, and in the sixteenth century into the Americas and more widely in Africa and Asia. Some of this expansion was the result of trade and migration, but much was the result of intentional evangelism. Women played an important role in the spread of Christianity, preaching and acting as missionaries, though their ability to do so was often challenged and restricted by male church authorities, who thought that women should not be engaged in public actions, even to spread the faith. Church officials were always happy to take women's financial support, however, and wealthy women regularly provided funding and supplies for missionary ventures.

The Protestant and Catholic Reformations led to a new type of missionary work: convincing those who were one type of Christian to become another, without necessarily leaving home or traveling far to do so. Protestant preachers and teachers were missionaries for their views, and a key aim of the Catholic Reformation was restoring parts of Europe to Catholicism. Members of the most dynamic religious order of the sixteenth century, the Jesuits, were just as active in Europe as they were in the colonies of Catholic powers.

The aim of missionaries is usually understood to be "conversion"—a word that is in many dictionary definitions of "missionary"—but this is a tricky and contested concept. Swift and dramatic conversion experiences have been prized in Christianity since biblical times, but for most people conversion is a process, not an event. Religious conversion involves changing outward behavior, but also changing internal beliefs and thoughts, a process impossible to see. Rulers and religious officials in the era of the Reformations recognized this, and worried about it. As you have read, Queen Isabel ordered Jews in Spain to convert or leave. Many were baptized, gave up Jewish devotional practices, and participated in Christian rituals and services. Thus they had officially converted, but the Inquisition still doubted them and accused many of incomplete conversions or of still being Jewish. People were also skeptical of converts from one type of Christianity to another, especially if they gained economically or socially by converting.

Some rulers chose not to worry about this. Queen Elizabeth decided that it was enough if people attended services of the Church of England. The Catholics and Protestant dissenters who got into trouble during her reign were those who refused to outwardly conform or who were involved in plots against her. This pragmatism may have been shaped by what had just happened in England, where the officially accepted religion switched from Catholic to Protestant to Catholic to Protestant within the space of several decades. Did this mean that people converted overnight in their heart of hearts from one to the other and then back again? Or that they did this in other parts of Europe when the ruler switched forms of Christianity, or a new ruler introduced a different form? Of course not. People (perhaps) accepted some of the new ideas and rejected others, gradually coming to terms with what was expected. Or they decided that religious beliefs and practices were less important than other aspects of life. Or they hid their beliefs, moved, or became martyrs.

These issues were even more pronounced when Christianity spread beyond Europe. In the Americas, Spanish conquerors and the missionaries who accompanied them sometimes ordered mass baptisms, along with ceremonies in which the conquered group gave its allegiance to the Spanish monarch. The Spaniards held up a cross and a flag, said some things in Latin and Spanish, and then counted the people in front of them as converts (and subjects).

The Franciscan, Dominican, and later Jesuit friars who carried out most of the missions to Indigenous people did attempt to convey more about Christian ideas and practices, sometimes learning local languages to do so. But people often blended these with their existing notions of religion and spirituality, transforming Christianity in the process, as you'll see in many examples in this chapter. Because of this, some scholars today have rejected the word "conversion," and instead talk about blending, mixing, negotiation, hybridity, syncretism, borrowing, or accommodation. They sometimes refer to this process of mixing as "creolization," taking this word from *Crioulo*, the mixture of Portuguese and African languages spoken first in the Atlantic islands. ("Creole" now means any language that has evolved as a mixture of languages, as well as a person of European, African, or mixed Eurafrican descent born in the Americas.) Other scholars say that not recognizing non-Europeans as converts denies their own understanding of themselves. Indigenous and mixed-heritage people in the Americas were not passive, but shaped Christian beliefs and practices. Some became missionaries themselves, as did enslaved and free Africans and Asians.

"Conversion" also came to have a slightly different meaning for some Christian groups. For Puritans, Methodists, Baptists, and others, especially evangelicals, a person's "conversion experience" was the point when they first or most strongly felt the power of God. This spiritual rebirth could be sudden or gradual, and it could involve joining a different group or simply developing more intense religious practices.

"Conversion" is not only complicated, it also carries a moral judgment. Trying to convert someone—to anything, not just a religion—means that you think their current situation is wrong, or at least could be improved. Otherwise, why convert them? For those who spread Christianity in the past there was little question about this, but today we recognize that missionary work led to pain and harm as it spread new beliefs and practices. Beginning in the late fifteenth century, Christian missionaries often operated within the context of colonial conquest and rule. Church officials and clergy not only taught the Christian faith, but also sought to wipe out Indigenous beliefs and practices by disrupting or destroying existing social and cultural institutions, often through violence. In the Americas, missions—along with other forms of European settlement—also brought diseases that ultimately killed millions of people. Unsurprisingly, along with adopting and adapting Christianity, many people resisted efforts to make them give up their religious traditions and culture. This resistance is also part of the story of missionaries in the early modern period.

Women were important in missionary work, though men tried to exclude them or diminish their role, both during their lifetimes and in the histories of missions that have been written since. Many of the women you met in the chapter on migrants were also missionaries. The English Quakers Mary Fisher, Ann Austin, and Elizabeth Hooton preached the Quaker message in Barbados, Boston, and beyond, despite imprisonment and deportation. The Spanish nuns Sor Jerónima de la Asunción and Sor Magdalena de Cristo crossed the Atlantic and Pacific to establish convents that would spread Catholic teachings through teaching, prayer, and example. The French Ursulines Marie of the Incarnation and Marguerite Bourgeoys established religious houses in Quebec that took in girls and women who were French, Indigenous, and of mixed heritage, some of whom took Christian teachings to their own communities. In this chapter you will meet other women who acted as missionaries or sought to do so, along with women who responded to evangelization by adopting, rejecting, and transforming Christian beliefs and practices.

CATHOLICS RISK PRISON

People attempting to convert others by something other than prayer or written works had to be in contact with them, which was increasingly difficult for Catholic women in the sixteenth and seventeenth centuries. At the Council of Trent (1545–1563), Catholic officials reaffirmed the necessity of cloister for all women religious and called for restrictions on laywomen's groups with an active role in the world. But extraordinary circumstances sometimes led church leadership to relax its restrictions, or at least to ignore women who preached and taught publicly, instead of imprisoning them, as it did Mary Ward.

One of these was Luisa de Carvajal y Mendoza (1566–1614), a superbly educated member of Spain's most powerful noble family. After a childhood and youth during which she was orphaned and then abused by her uncle, she opposed her family's wishes and neither married nor entered a convent. Instead she lived the life of a *beata* in the cities of Madrid and Valladolid, engaging in severe penitential practices and developing a close relationship with Jesuit confessors. In 1598, she took a vow of martyrdom, inspired by accounts of recent Catholic martyrs, especially Jesuit missionaries in England and Japan. She decided that England might be a place to accomplish this, and that her life goal was to reconvert English people to Catholicism, which fit with Jesuit ideals of heroic endeavors and with Spanish and Catholic Reformation global ambitions to spread the faith. She gained support for this idea from Spanish noblewomen, who later provided financial assistance for her venture as well.

In 1604, as part of a peace agreement between England and Spain, England's new king James I sent all Catholic priests jailed in England to the continent, or at least said he was going to do this. This left a void, and church officials in Spain and the Jesuit order gave tacit approval to Carvajal's venture. She went to London, a trip that took five months, and stayed first at a safe house outside the city, where she likely met some of the English recusant women you were introduced to in Chapter 2, such as Anne Vaux. In a letter to a friend, Carvajal admiringly recounts Vaux's testimony after being imprisoned for possible involvement in the Gunpowder Plot: "She laughed bravely at them [and] to more weighty

questions she responded very sensibly, and she pays no attention what-
soever to them, and so she has amazed them."[1]

In London, Carvajal learned English, and spoke openly about
converting to the Catholic faith in shops and streets. She gives a vivid
account of street-corner religious debates in a letter to Joseph Creswell,
the director of the English Jesuits in Spain and Portugal:

> I can tell Your Grace that I have walked between the cross and
> holy water, as they say there, because I have been in prison, and
> since it was in the public jail, it would be useless for me to keep
> silent about it. The reason was because, arriving one day at a store
> in Cheapside [a part of London], leaning on the door sill from
> outside, as is my custom, the occasion offered to ask one of the young
> attendants if he was Catholic presented itself, and he responded,
> "No, God forbid!" And I replied, "May God not permit that you not
> be, which is what matters for you." At this the mistress and master
> of the shop came over, and another youth and neighboring merchants,
> and a great chat about religion ensued. They asked a lot about the
> mass, about priests, about confession, but what we spent the most
> time on (over two hours) was whether the Roman religion was the
> only true one, and whether the Pope is the head of the Church, and
> whether St. Peter's keys have been left to them [the popes] forever in
> succession.
>
> Some listened with pleasure, others with fury, and so much that I
> sensed some danger, at least of being arrested. But I thought nothing
> of it, in exchange for setting that light before their eyes in the best
> way I could. . . .
>
> The mistress of the shop tried to stir everyone to anger, as did
> another infernal young man who was there, younger in age but with
> greater malice. The woman said it was a shame that they were toler-
> ating me and that, without a doubt, I was some Roman [Catholic]
> priest dressed like a woman so as to better persuade people of my
> religion. Our Lord saw fit that I speak the best English I've spoken
> since I've been in England, and they thought I was Scottish because
> of the way I spoke.[2]

Carvajal visited Catholic priests in jail, bringing them food and consolation, tried to find funding for young English Catholics who wished to enter convents or seminaries on the continent, and taught women and men Catholic doctrine. She became a key figure in the circulation of Catholic books into England, often using the diplomatic couriers of the Spanish ambassador to avoid having them confiscated. These included the *Life* of Teresa of Avila, which had been published in English in Antwerp in 1611, and which Carvajal describes as "very well translated."

Carvajal established a community of Catholic women in her home, one of whom was Mary Ward's aunt. (She and Mary Ward knew about each other but didn't meet.) She organized expeditions to graveyards to unearth severed body parts of Catholics who had been executed for their faith. She kept these in her house as what she called "guests," relics in the making, and then sent them to the continent. She wrote religious poetry and hundreds of letters, many of which have survived.

For her actions Carvajal was imprisoned twice, once briefly for public preaching and a second time for all her activities. Several of her companions were jailed as well. This did not slow her down, as she writes:

> While in jail I spoke about religion much more than I had out of it, with all the jailers and officials and their families and friends whom, with my permission, they brought to speak with me. And they listened nicely. And I didn't want to let the chance slip by, remembering the Holy Apostle who says that the word of God is not tied down . . . this for me is one of the greatest enchantments and delights I can find.[3]

Carvajal was not directly executed for her faith, but died from an illness after her second imprisonment while she was waiting at the Spanish embassy in London to be sent back to Spain. She was raised to the status of venerable, though she has never had the lobbying group needed to move her up the ladder to beatification or sainthood.

Her work did not end when Carvajal died, however, as the women in her community carried on. As the Spanish ambassador Diego de Sarmiento wrote to King Philip III of Spain:

Her companions have all been freed and are exercising freedom of conscience, without having been asked to take the Oath [of Supremacy], nor having restrictions put on them in matters of religion, which is a point that has cost me a lot of work and obliged me to speak about it with the King many times. And that was necessary because the emphasis that the Archbishop of Canterbury put on saying that they were founding monasteries here, and that they were nuns, and that they were converting people. And about this last item, he is right, and so they are doing even now, and this is the reason they do not wish to leave this kingdom. I have told them about the situation that the Marqués de Sieteiglesias has offered them [to give them dowries to enter convents in Spain]. They respond that they may perhaps accept that offer in the future, and with this in mind they are trying to learn Spanish, which right now not one of them understands.[4]

Exactly who her companions were is difficult to determine, as Carvajal was careful to use first names only in her letters to protect their identities. But they were clearly part of the network of English recusant women essential to the survival of Catholicism in England and, like Carvajal herself, active in the broader international Catholic community.

SHAPING LATIN AMERICAN CHRISTIANITY

The Catholic community spread to the Western hemisphere at the end of the fifteenth century, beginning in the Caribbean with the voyages of Christopher Columbus. In 1519, Hernando Cortés led an expeditionary force to Mexico, and two years later his soldiers and their Indigenous allies defeated the Aztec Empire. Cortés established the Viceroyalty of New Spain, which expanded to stretch from southwestern North America to northern South America and include some Spanish colonies in Asia. In 1532, Francisco Pizarro led a force that took over the Inca Empire, and a decade later the Viceroyalty of Peru was established to oversee most of the Spanish Empire in South America. Within these territories, Spanish officials and colonists set up various types of economic and administrative units that sought to extract the natural and agricultural wealth of the New World and provide resources for Spanish power. They attempted to organize the Indigenous population into tribute-paying units or groups for labor, which worked in some areas, but did not in many others because of resistance combined with dramatic depopulation brought on by disease.

In 1500, Portuguese ships on their way down the African coast to India drifted off course, and landed in eastern South America, which they named "Land of the Holy Cross." The Portuguese crown leased the territory to a merchant group, which began harvesting brazilwood, a tree whose heartwood yields a rich red dye the color of glowing coals— "*brasa*" in Portuguese—prized by clothmakers. Gradually the area became known as "Land of Brazil" on maps and documents, soon shortened simply to Brazil.

The first European women in the Americas (other than women who may have been in the Viking settlement in Canada) were a handful of women on Columbus's third voyage in 1498 and a handful who came with Hernando Cortés's conquest and the Spanish expeditions into South America. Like the women who accompanied armies in Europe, women who accompanied Spanish conquistadores found food, cooked, did laundry, and had sex with soldiers. Some of these women were enslaved but some came of their own accord, and soon higher-status women followed. One of the first European women in New Spain was Doña Marina Estrada, whose husband was the colony's first treasurer. She arrived in 1523, just two years after Cortés's conquest, and when her husband died in 1530, she chose to remain a widow and manage the financial interests of her family.

Colonial forces in Latin America and the Caribbean included Catholic missionaries and religious authorities who worked both to convert Indigenous people and to establish church structures for immigrants. As in Europe, the Catholic Church generally worked together with political authorities. Two years after Columbus's first voyage, the pope drew a line around the world in the Treaty of Tordesillas, dividing it between Spain and Portugal, and later granted special privileges—the *patronato*— to the Spanish and Portuguese crowns to control almost all aspects of religious life in the colonies. The first bishopric west of the Atlantic was set up in 1511 (Santo Domingo in the Caribbean), and by the

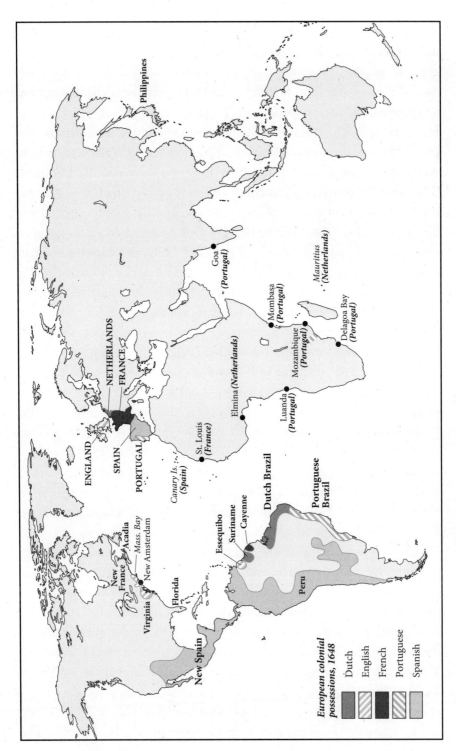

Map 5. *Colonial possessions of European states in 1648.*

ENGLAND

SPAIN

PORTUGAL

NETHERLANDS

FRANCE

Philippines

Goa
(Portugal)

Mauritius
(Netherlands)

Mombasa
(Portugal)

Delagoa Bay
(Portugal)

Mozambique
(Portugal)

Elmina *(Netherlands)*

Luanda
(Portugal)

St. Louis
(France)

Canary Is. ∴ :
(Spain)

New
France
Acadia

Mass. Bay

New Amsterdam

Virginia

Florida

Essequibo

Suriname

Cayenne

Dutch Brazil

Portuguese
Brazil

Peru

New Spain

*European colonial
possessions, 1648*

Dutch

English

French

Portuguese

Spanish

mid-sixteenth century there were bishops throughout the Caribbean and Mexico, and in Venezuela, Peru, Paraguay, and Brazil. Bishops oversaw missionary work, the establishment of parishes and church courts, the construction of churches, and the operation of the Inquisition.

Despite the pope's ruling, other European countries became colonizers as well. The Protestant Reformation ended the authority of the pope in half of Europe, and Protestant countries such as England and the Netherlands saw no reason to follow the pope's division of the world. They claimed territory for themselves based on their own voyages, and even Catholic countries such as France eventually simply ignored the Tordesillas Line. The French, British, Dutch, and Danish all came to rule islands or parts of islands in the Caribbean, and sometimes small colonies on the mainland of South and Central America, with ownership shifting as the result of war and treaties. European claims to territory were based much more on actual voyages, military force, and the establishment of colonies than on imaginary lines drawn by popes, though all European powers—and later the United States—agreed with the pope's assertion that the "doctrine of discovery" gave them the right to claim land in the Americas. English Protestant colonists built the first church in Jamestown, Virginia, in 1607, the year they arrived, and the first Protestant church in Bermuda, St. Peter's Church in St. George's, in 1612.

Soon after conquest, the Spanish began to bring enslaved Africans to work on plantations and in mines, and slightly later the Portuguese in Brazil did as well. In the Caribbean, most of the Indigenous population was wiped out in the first decades after the Spanish conquest through warfare, disease, and overwork, their labor replaced by that of enslaved people from Africa. By the end of the sixteenth century, people of African descent were the majority in the Caribbean, just as they were in Lima at the time that Rose of Lima and Ursula de Jesús lived there.

Beginning in the 1560s, Spanish ships began regular trade between the Philippines and Mexico, bringing in Asian people as well as products. The people were primarily from the Indian subcontinent or Southeast Asia but known collectively as *chinos*. Catarina de San Juan, the mystic you met in Chapter 5 who may have come from India originally, was only one of many enslaved and free Asians brought to Mexico to work. The

Catholic Church advocated for slave conversion, and the Spanish and Portuguese crowns ordered slave owners to baptize newly arrived enslaved people, provide them with chapels to worship, and allow them to attend Mass and marry in Christian ceremonies. Enslavers sometimes objected to giving time off from work for religious instruction or ceremonies, but most enslaved people in Iberian colonies were baptized, as they were in the French colonies established later as well.

Europeans brought their ideas about racial and other social differences with them to the Americas, where they shaped hierarchies throughout the colonial period and afterwards. The modern notion of "race" as a division of humans into a small number of groups based on continent or place of origin, skin color, facial features, and other physical or behavioral characteristics was created over time. Some scholars see its roots in the ancient or medieval world, and others see it as devised more recently. Today biologists and others who study the human species as a whole avoid using "race," as it has no scientific meaning, but, like other invented systems of difference, it has had (and continues to have) enormous power.

Spanish and Portuguese authorities were suspicious of any type of mixing, so hoped to keep Europeans, Africans, and Indigenous people apart in their American colonies. The gender balance among both European and African immigrants made this impossible, however, and authorities quickly gave up. Sexual relationships involving European and African men and Indigenous and African women produced a wide variety of mixed children. The response of colonial authorities was to create an ever more complex system of categories, called *castas*, for persons of mixed ancestry. They defined as many as fifteen or twenty different categories and combinations that were in theory based on place of birth, assumed geographic origin, and status of one's father and mother, with a specific name for each one: "*mestizo*," "*mulatto*," "*caboclo*," and so on. The *casta* system built on earlier Iberian notions of "purity of blood," in which descendants of Muslim and Jewish converts to Christianity were viewed as tainted, because their religious allegiance was carried in their blood. In the same way, Indigenous Americans' or Africans' loyalty to their traditional beliefs was seen as carried in the blood, so that the more non-European blood one had, the greater the danger.

Determining the proper *casta* in which to place actual people was not as easy as setting these out in theory, however. In practice, the category in which one was placed was to a large extent determined by how one looked, with lighter-skinned mixed-ancestry persons often accorded a higher rank than darker ones, even if they were siblings. Many historians have termed the social structure that developed in colonial Spanish and Portuguese America, including the Caribbean (and later in the French Caribbean) a "pigmentocracy" based largely on skin color, along with facial features and hair texture. Contemporaries always claimed that color was linked to honor, virtue, and family, so that one's social status—termed *calidad*—involved a moral as well as physical judgment. In reality, as intermarriage and other types of inter-ethnic sexual relations increased, people passed quite easily from one *casta* to another. The *casta* "system" was thus much less systematic than authorities had hoped. In theory, it was rooted in the embodied experiences of men, women, and children, but in reality it relied on people's judgment and imagination.

Status also frequently shifted over time. A person's ability to marry or inherit, enter a convent or the priesthood, or attend university relied on official determination of ancestral purity, so individuals not only passed as members of a higher group, but also sought to officially "whiten" their social status to obtain privileges in society. In many areas families of property and status bought a *gracias al sacar*—a royal exemption that allowed them to be considered descendants of Europeans, regardless of their ethnic appearance and ancestry.

Poorer people, and especially poorer and enslaved women, had much less ability to shape their fate. Indigenous and African women were forced from their homes to become sexual partners and laborers, traveling hundreds or thousands of miles to completely new settings. But even for them there were sometimes opportunities for social advance through family and other intimate connections, work, money, luck, or a combination of these. Some enslaved people negotiated or purchased their own freedom, and many free people of color flourished. Baptized people of all races, including those born out of wedlock or enslaved, had some legal rights in Catholic church law and Spanish legal codes, more than they had in British and Dutch colonies.

Christianity in colonial Latin America was just as complex and varied as colonial society. Many areas were totally untouched by church authority for centuries and Indigenous groups continued their original practices. Men and women—and in some places individuals understood to combine and/or transcend the gender binary—had positions as religious leaders and intermediaries with the spirit world.

In many parts of the viceroyalties of New Spain and Peru, missionaries traveled alone or in small groups, living with local people. They established settled missions, places where they gathered Indigenous people together into compact villages for conversion, taxpaying, cultural assimilation, and sometimes protection from slave-raiding. The first Spanish missions were in the sixteenth century in northern Mexico and Florida. By the seventeenth century missions existed from what is now northern California to Argentina, in some areas serving as the only real evidence of Spanish power. Converts to Christianity in missions were wards of the Spanish crown, and missionaries had great control over all aspects of their lives.

Indigenous or multi-ethnic people sometimes assisted European-background missionaries in their work, serving as go-betweens. Most of these were men, but women also occasionally served as translators for missionaries when they heard women's confessions and provided models of Christian behavior. As one Jesuit in Brazil remarked about his translator, "I believe she is the best confessor I have because she is so virtuous."[5] In New Spain, Jesuits established *haciendas*, large estates that raised crops and livestock, as well as missions. Here older enslaved women who could no longer work in the fields served as teachers and catechists, providing young children with basic instruction in Christian ideas and practices, including gendered norms of morality and family life.

Most of these women's names and details were never recorded, but occasionally fragments can be pieced together. A woman named in the records as Madalena, a Tocobaga woman from what is now the Tampa Bay area of Florida, was captured in 1539 by the Spanish conquistador Hernando de Soto's expedition on its way to the Mississippi River. Raids searching for gold and capturing people to enslave were common along the coasts of Florida, so the Tocobaga were familiar with Spanish aims and actions. De Soto sent her, along with several Tocobaga men, to his wife, Isabel de Bobadilla, in Havana in Cuba, where de Soto had the position as governor. Bobadilla had a large and busy household and was also the acting governor in de Soto's absence, just as the wives and sisters of male European rulers served as regents for them. Madalena worked in the household alongside other enslaved African, Muslim, and Indigenous people, learned Spanish, and participated in Christian prayers and rituals. Bobadilla took her along with other free and enslaved household servants to Spain, and after her death Madalena made her way back to Havana.

Here Madalena met the Dominican friar Luis Cáncer, who was planning a missionary venture in western Florida. She accompanied him as a translator in 1549, and, in Cáncer's account of his mission, told the people they met of his "intents and desires" to preach peacefully, assuring him in turn that, "They won't kill you. They are from my land, and this is from my language."[6] He reported that she offered a cross for a group of Tocobaga to kiss, which they did, and knelt as he read verses, which they also did. Exactly how she translated his words or explained these actions to the Tocobaga is impossible to know, just as it is impossible to know how she herself understood them. We know that several days later, Cáncer and the other Spaniards were killed by local people and the mission ended. Cáncer's report, finished by another friar after his death, portrays Madalena as a supporter of the mission, but she left no independent record of her own thoughts and beliefs. She did make it home after ten years of capture, enslavement, and migration, and then apparently stayed there, actions that perhaps indicate her views.

We know a bit more about another Indigenous woman who crossed the Atlantic and became a Christian, but in this case legends and myths rather than silence obscure our view. (No, not Pocahontas.) Guaibimpará was the daughter of a Tupinambá ruler in coastal Brazil, whose father married her in a ceremony that followed local customs to a shipwrecked Portuguese sailor, Diogo Álvares Correia, one of the first Europeans in this area, perhaps because he wished to make an alliance with the Portuguese. The Tupinambá gave Correia the name Caramuru, the name he is usually known by today. In 1528, the couple traveled to France, where Guaibimpará was baptized in the port of Saint-Malo as "Catherine of Brazil." Her baptismal sponsor was a local French noblewoman, Catherine de Granches, whose husband, Jacques Cartier, would later go on to explore much of Canada. The couple were married a second time, in a Christian ceremony, and then they returned to Brazil. They became influential in local politics and city-building, and their children married other prominent colonists.

In about 1535, Guaibimpará/Catherine founded a chapel dedicated to Our Lady of Grace, the first chapel to the Virgin Mary and one of the oldest Christian churches of any type in Brazil, in what is now the city of São Salvador da Bahia. The chapel became a place of pilgrimage, the pope donated relics that attracted even more pilgrims, and half a century later, when she was an elderly widow, Guaibimpará/Catherine donated the chapel and its lands to the Benedictine order in her will. There is now a church and monastery on the site, built in the eighteenth century, where Catherine is buried.

The story of the Tupinambá woman who built a chapel to the Virgin Mary in the early sixteenth century would seem to be remarkable enough, but in the seventeenth and eighteenth centuries more details were added to it. Jesuit chroniclers renamed her Paraguaçu, the name of a local river, which became the most common name she is known by today, usually with her Christian and married names added: Catherine Álvares Paraguaçu. They related that she had seen visions leading her to a discarded image of the Virgin Mary, which is what inspired her to build the chapel. An Augustinian poet added that the couple were actually married at the court of Catherine de' Medici in Paris, and that Guaibimpará/Catherine had foretold the seventeenth-century Dutch invasions of Brazil. Other stories told that she was deeply in love with Caramuru, so swam after his ship until he pulled her from the water. The couple became a symbol of ethnic mixture in Brazil, part of the country's notion of itself as a place without racial prejudice, with Guaibimpará/Catherine lauded as the mother of the nation and of Brazilian Catholicism.

Missionaries' letters and reports describe women who resisted their efforts, as well as those who accepted them. The memorial of Fray Alonso de Benavides, a Franciscan missionary in what is now New Mexico, for example, includes both opponents and supporters as it tells a story of miraculous intervention:

These Indians were well taught in church doctrine. And in the year just past of 1627, Our Lord confirmed His Holy Word with a miracle among them. As it happened, it was difficult for them to stop having so many women, as it was their custom before they were baptized. Each day, the friar preached to them the holy sacrament of matrimony, and the person who contradicted him most strongly was an old Indian sorceress. Under the pretext of going to the countryside for firewood, she took along four good Christian women, and married at that, all conforming to the good order of Our Holy Mother Church. And coming and going in their wood gathering, she was trying to persuade them not to continue with the kind of marriage our padre was teaching, saying how much better off a person was practicing her old heathenism.

These good Christians resisted this kind of talk. They were getting close to the pueblo again, and the sorceress was carrying on with her sermon. The sky was clear and serene, but a bolt from the blue struck that infernal instrument of the devil right in the middle of those good Christian women who had been resisting her evil creed. They were spared from the bolt, and quite confirmed in the truth of the holy sacrament of matrimony. The entire pueblo ran to the spot. Seeing the results of the thunderclap from heaven, everyone who had been secretly living in sin got married and began to believe mightily in everything the padre taught them. He, of course, made this episode the subject of a sermon.[7]

Missions became the locus of Christianity in much of Spanish America, but the pattern was different in the densely settled areas of Central America and the Andes. Here Christianization often began with a mass baptism, followed by teaching, church-building, and the establishment of institutions. Spanish religious authorities destroyed sacred written scriptures, objects, and buildings in Aztec, Maya, and other religious traditions, and initially regarded people who blended existing beliefs and practices with Christianity as incomplete converts or backsliders. Sporadic campaigns against what was termed "idolatry" or "diabolism" continued, but completely rooting out the existing religions would have required far more force than political authorities were willing or able to provide. Instead, what happened is that most Catholic authorities came to terms with local religion. They began to use local terms for theological concepts and created imagery that blended Christian figures with local deities. Some recognized that this co-option was an effective strategy rather than simply a matter of practicality. The understanding of Christianity that developed thus blended Indigenous and Christian teachings. In areas of Latin America with African populations, this blending also included African elements, as enslaved people carried religious beliefs and practices, as well as many other aspects of their cultures, with them when they crossed the Atlantic.

The best example of this blending is the Virgin Mary. Missionaries promoted the veneration of the Virgin Mary through paintings and statuary, along with sermons, catechisms, plays, prayers, and hymns describing the events of Mary's life written and presented in local languages by missionaries and Indigenous converts. Immigrants to Spanish America honored her as well. Stories and paintings of Mary emphasized her role as a nurturing mother, but also as an eternal virgin, whose own conception had been "immaculate," free from the normal sin accompanying sex. Devotion to Mary's Immaculate Conception, so important to Queen Isabel of Castile and to the Spanish bilocating nun María de Agreda you met in Chapter 5, spread in the Spanish Americas as well as in Spain. University students, confraternities, and even artisans' guilds often took special vows to defend the doctrine of the Immaculate Conception, highlighting Mary's sexless and sinless nature.

Among Indigenous people in many areas, however, Mary took on aspects of pre-conquest goddesses. Among the Maya of the Yucatán, she came to incorporate aspects of the fire goddess and the moon goddess; like the moon goddess, Mary "the Queen, the Virgin, the miraculous one descended . . . [on a] cord from heaven" to help humans who sought her assistance.[8] The powers of this hybrid deity, Virgin Mary Moon Goddess, also derived from her status as a "virgin," though this term had a different meaning for Indigenous people than it did for Spanish Catholics, for it symbolized her connection with cosmic female forces rather than her status as a non-sexual being.

The most famous representation of Mary in the Spanish New World is that of the Virgin of Guadalupe, whose shrine the Spanish nuns on their way to the Philippines visited. Depictions of the Virgin of Guadalupe blended in what many view as Indigenous elements, including the color of Mary's clothing, the stars that decorate it, and the way her belt is tied. (See Plate XIV.) The hill where the apparition of Mary was said to have occurred in 1531 may originally have been the site of a shrine to one of the Aztec mother-goddesses. Friars and Indigenous converts teaching about Mary used the Nahuatl word "Tonantzin," which means "Our Lady" or "Our Sacred Mother," to refer to her, a word also applied to Aztec goddesses. Some church officials criticized this as idolatry and trying to hide Indigenous beliefs in Christian garb, but others noted that European Christians used similar phrases for Mary in their own languages.

Women and men visiting the shrine no doubt varied in their understanding of the Virgin of Guadalupe, just like the millions of visitors since. Many images of her—in churches, homes, places of business, clothing, jewelry, and tattoos—show her as clearly Indigenous or *mestiza*, with brown skin. Some go further. The Chicana artist Alma López depicted Guadalupe dressed only in strands of roses in a photo-based digital print. This led to a huge controversy involving prayer vigils, protest rallies, and death threats at the museum where it was first exhibited in 2001, and at others where it has been shown since. López and other artists have justified their work by noting that the Virgin of Guadalupe began as a symbol with multiple meanings as people interpreted her in whatever way they thought most empowering, so they are simply continuing the tradition of synthesis and *mestizaje*.

The individuals who established missions and held church offices were all men, but women also spread Catholic teachings independently through the education of girls. Mexico's first bishop, Juan de Zumárraga, established a *beaterio* (a religious lay community) called La Madre de Dios in 1531, just a decade after Spanish forces and their Indigenous allies had conquered the Aztecs. He hoped its residents would instruct the daughters of elite Aztecs in the Christian faith, a plan that did not work very well. A decade later the first convent in the Americas, La Concepción in Mexico City, was founded under his direction, and some of the residents of the *beaterio* moved there and became professed nuns. Beatriz da Silva had founded the Conceptionist order in Spain to educate young women, so the aims of the order fit with those of the bishop. Other convents of the Conceptionist and other orders soon followed, first in the cities of New Spain, and then in the cities of Peru, Guatemala, Cuba, and other colonies. The first convent opened in Brazil in 1677.

A few of these convents were discalced, following the strict rules advocated by St. Teresa and others in which women adhered closely to their vows of poverty and obedience, living communally, eating simple meals, praying, and engaging in manual work. These tended to stay small, as their austerity limited their appeal. Most convents in the Americas were "calced," that is, their residents did not have to give up their material possessions or servants, and they housed many laywomen and girls as well as novices and nuns. These included girls in the convent for an education before marriage, young unmarried women whose families lacked the dowry for what the family regarded as an advantageous marriage, young women whose families thought they were too wild, orphans, out-of-wedlock daughters of the city's elite, married women whose husbands had abandoned them, wealthy widows, and free and enslaved servants. Nuns in many calced convents owned their own "cells," actually apartments with a kitchen and several rooms, shared by servants who did the cooking and cleaning and perhaps by other family members.

Professed nuns were supposed to be of European birth or background, but given the fluidity of racial categories, women of mixed descent were sometimes accepted as nuns. Enslaved and free servants and lay sisters were often of Indigenous, African, or *mestizo* background, so convents were sites of racial mixture and hierarchy, reflecting the society around them. They were also large and numerous: in the seventeenth century one-fifth of the female population of Lima, Peru, lived in convents, which were also the largest property owners in the city. We used to think of convents as marginal institutions and to pity the poor women sent to them, but they were central actors on the colonial stage. Nuns became leading guarantors of their city's social structure by making loans, managing property, and educating girls. They helped create a colonial order in which economic and spiritual interests were fused.

The Conceptionist Convent of Jesús María in Mexico City, one of the largest and wealthiest in New Spain, is a good example of a calced convent. Established in 1581, it housed eighty-four religious women ranging from novices to nuns by 1588, including Micaela de los Angeles, the out-of-wedlock daughter of King Philip II of Spain, who had been brought to New Spain by her uncle in 1572 when she was two. Philip granted the convent royal patronage, which included scholarships for women from elite families who had fallen on hard times so were unable to pay the dowry required by the convent. The convent also housed many servants, slaves, and family members of the nuns, thus a total of several hundred women.

The Hieronymite Convent of Santa Paula, another calced convent in Mexico City, was the home of probably the most famous woman in colonial Latin America, the scholar, poet, playwright, scientist, and composer Sor Juana Inés de la Cruz (1648–1695). Sor Juana was the out-of-wedlock daughter of a Spanish father and a Spanish-background mother, whose intelligence and drive emerged when she was a child. She inherited her maternal grandfather's library, and from this largely taught herself many subjects, including Latin and Nahuatl, the Indigenous language of central Mexico. She caught the attention of the Spanish viceroy and vicereine (the wife of the viceroy) and became a lady-in-waiting at their court, but decided that the only way she could continue her studies was to reject marriage and enter a convent. She briefly tried a Discalced Carmelite house, found this too strict, and in 1669 entered Santa Paula, with a dowry given by her grandfather. She moved her books into her apartment in the convent and bought more, eventually building the largest library in Mexico. Here she also hosted a discussion circle of women interested in new ideas, including several vicereines.

Sor Juana began writing poetry, plays, music, and philosophy, most of which has not survived, though much does, published in Spain thanks to the patronage of one of the vicereines, the Countess Paredes. Some of these bring in Indigenous characters and themes along with Spanish, biblical, and classical ones. A song about the Virgin of Guadalupe, for example, partly written in Nahuatl, also refers to an Aztec goddess. Sor Juana's religious drama, *The Divine Narcissus*, develops allegories for Christ and the Virgin Mary, using both classical and Indigenous elements. Religious dramas (*autos sacramentales*) featuring music, dance, dialogue, and action, were used by Spanish missionaries in their efforts at conversion, and they were also popular in Spain. Sor Juana's, the only *auto sacramental* written by a woman to survive, was commissioned for presentation in Madrid.

Sor Juana also wrote a short introductory play for this, called a *loa*, an allegory of the conquest of the peoples of the Americas that features two Indigenous characters, Occident (i.e. the West) and America, and two Spanish ones, Religion and Zeal. The *loa* opens with a celebration of the Festival of the God of Seeds by a group of ceremoniously dressed Indigenous people, including Occident, a man, and America, a woman. Religion, a Spanish noblewoman, is appalled at the "idolatry," and encourages the celebrants to convert. They think she is crazy, and Zeal, a Spanish captain and the husband of Religion, orders his soldiers to attack them. Religion intervenes when Zeal is ready to kill them all, saying, "your charge, to conquer her by force, / but mine to vanquish her with words . . . you must not, cannot kill them: for I am by nature benign / and I do not want them to die / but to convert, and then to live."[9]

The characters engage in discussion about their religious beliefs, and Religion highlights parallels between the Nahua God of Seeds and the Christian god: "The productive Providence . . . of the only true God . . . gives the plants their vegetative soul," she explains. When Occident asks whether Religion's god is made of "matter as fine and fair as the red blood shed and offered in sacrifice" in Aztec ceremonies, Religion responds excitedly with an explanation of the Catholic doctrine of transubstantiation, a doctrine Protestants rejected:

> His divine majesty
> is infinite, not
> material; but His blessed
> humanity, bloodless in the
> holy sacrifice of the Mass
> makes use of pure white seeds of wheat
> that then is transformed into His
> very flesh, His very blood
> and His most precious blood, pure
> and innocent and pristine that,
> offered on the altar of the

Holy Cross, is the salvation
and redemption of the world.[10]

Religion suggests they will understand more once they are baptized and have watched the play that follows, to which America and Occident agree, and they all settle in to do this.

Sor Juana's *loa* may seem to be a conventional portrayal of the superiority of Catholic beliefs to Indigenous (and Protestant) ones, but in portraying Indigenous people sympathetically and equating their faith to some degree with Catholicism, she gives dignity to Indigenous beliefs. Sor Juana is not a missionary in the traditional sense, but perhaps we can see her as a missionary communicating positive aspects of the New World to the Old. She recognizes this at the end of the *loa*, when Zeal asks Religion whether it is improper to perform something written in Mexico in Madrid, and Religion says, no, because "for an intelligent species no distances are a hindrance / and no oceans an obstacle." "Writing it," she adds, "is the result of obedience, not the child of audacity."[11]

Sor Juana may have viewed her writing as "the result of obedience," but her Jesuit confessor thought otherwise. He disapproved of women's education and argued that Sor Juana's dedication to her studies jeopardized her salvation. In 1681 she wrote him a letter, pointing first to learned women of the past: "Did not St. Catherine, St. Gertrude and my mother St. Paula study without harming their lofty contemplations, and was the latter's travail in the founding of convents impeded by her knowledge even of Greek? By having learned Hebrew? By having been instructed by my Father St. Jerome to understand and interpret Holy Writ, as the Saint himself tell us?"[12] (Sor Juana refers to St. Paula, the studious fourth-century colleague of the church father St. Jerome and the founder of a convent in Bethlehem, as "her mother" because Paula is viewed as the co-patron of the Hieronymite order.) She asked him directly:

But who has prohibited women private and individual studies? Do they not have a rational soul like men? Why should it [a woman's soul] then not enjoy within them the privilege of enlightenment in an education? Is it not as capable of earning God's glory and grace as yours? Why should it not be capable of such news and science, a trifle? What divine revelation, what determination of the Church, what dictate of reason made for us such a severe law?[13]

Sor Juana defended women's education a decade later more publicly, in response to a 1691 letter criticizing her by the bishop of Puebla, who wrote under the female pseudonym Sister Philotea, though everyone knew who the author was. Sor Juana's response, *Respuesta a Sor Filotea de la Cruz* (*Reply to Sister Philotea*) combines her life story, the examples of many learned women from the Bible and history, and the writings of the church fathers to make her case: "In this way I proceeded, always directing the steps of my study to the summit of sacred theology, as I have said; and to reach it, I thought it necessary to ascend by the steps of human sciences and arts, because how is one to understand the style of the queen of the sciences without knowing that of the handmaidens?"[14] (Theology was referred to as the "queen of the sciences" at that time.) St. Paul did not forbid women to study, write, and teach, she wrote, but only to preach publicly. Educating women also makes practical sense:

> Oh, how much harm could be averted in our republic if older women were as learned as Leta [St. Paula's daughter-in-law, whose daughter, also named Paula, would eventually lead her grandmother's convent] and knew how to teach as Saint Paul and my Father Saint Jerome advise! Since they do not, if some parents wish to give their daughters more instruction than usual, necessity and the lack of learned older women obliges them to have male tutors teach their daughters how to read, write, count, play an instrument, and other skills, which results in a good amount of harm. . . . For this reason, many parents choose to leave their daughters unlettered and uneducated rather than expose them to so notable a danger as familiarity with men, which could be avoided if there were learned older women, as Saint Paul desires, and instruction would be handed down from one female to another as occurs in the teaching of needlework and other customary skills.[15]

The bishop of Puebla did not deign to answer her, but because of this controversy Sor Juana was forced to give up her books and musical and scientific instruments and ordered to concentrate on religious and charitable activities. She was required to sign statements of penance and self-condemnation, one of which is signed "Yo, la Peor de Todas" ("I, the worst of them all"). She devoted herself to caring for the sick and died nursing other nuns stricken by the plague in 1695, though she also seems to have quietly returned to her intellectual pursuits and had begun rebuilding her library.

Sor Juana was well known during her lifetime and in the century that followed, dubbed "The Tenth Muse" for her poetry and prose. She was rediscovered in the 1970s and 1980s, celebrated as an early feminist for her views on women's abilities and her boldness in discussing these in public. She has since been the inspiration for films, plays, novels, television series, and other works, and she appears on the Mexican 200 peso note. The convent where she spent the last half of her life is now the University of the Cloister of Sor Juana, offering Bachelor's and Master's degrees, mostly in the humanities.

Sor Juana may have portrayed Indigenous people as capable of making religious choices, but many Catholic clergy infantilized them and treated them as irrational and sinful. This was particularly so with women, who clergy assumed would never be able to fulfill vows of chastity and obedience, so should not become professed nuns. In some cities, however, Indigenous Christians established *beaterios*, where Indigenous women lived simply, prayed, and performed religious observances. Women's behavior in these became an argument for opening full-blown convents. Antonio Pérez, a priest in Mexico City, noted that the women in the *beaterios* were already living like nuns even though they took no actual vows, which "increases my confusion . . . seeing young girls who have no obligation to fulfill the greatest perfection, living with such total perfection."[16]

The first cloistered convent for Indigenous nuns, Corpus Christi in Mexico City, finally opened in 1728. The women admitted had to be full-blooded, not *mestizas*, and have their virtue attested by the nuns or chaplains of convents in which they had previously worked as lay sisters or servants. An anonymous statement written by one of the first nuns about their founding mother Sister Maria Petra of St. Francis described the severe penitential practices she taught them, including carrying a heavy cross around the choir, but also noted that while they were still lay sisters "she would teach us to read in Latin and to pray the Divine Office . . . [so that] once we entered the convent, we could already do our singing." One of the priests assigned to the convent "wanted to force us to vote for the Spanish novices so that they could profess in the convent. We did not want that because our patron's idea was that the convent be only for Indian women," and the convent remained open to Indigenous women only.[17]

In 1753, the Jesuits founded the Colegio de Guadalupe, a school where a small number of Indigenous elite women instructed other girls and women from various ethnic groups in, as a Jesuit observer commented, "Christian doctrine, reading, writing, sewing, embroidery and other feminine skills."[18] These subjects—strikingly similar to those that Protestant authorities in Europe wanted women to teach girls in schools there—may seem benign and traditional, but the fact that they included Christian doctrine meant that Indigenous women had a role in a Jesuit-approved institution in Mexico that they did nowhere in Europe.

It is harder to learn about laywomen's religious lives in colonial Latin America than it is those of nuns and *beatas*, but we can find some traces. European, Indigenous, and African Christians formed confraternities for men and women, almost always racially separate and sometimes divided by occupation or parish. In some cities of New Spain, Asian *chinos* had their own confraternities as well, as did certain *castas*. The confraternities had various purposes: Some sponsored religious festivities, built altars for devotional celebrations, or carried out public penance such as flagellation in honor of certain saints or sacraments. Others provided charity for the poor, or arranged hospital care and funerals for their members, thus serving as a sort of fictive family. Confraternities also shaped marital arrangements, as they frequently gave dowries to poor girls and women who wished to marry if they judged them "honorable" and the potential husband acceptable.

People of all social groups also erected altars or small wooden structures called *retablos* in their homes, in which they placed images of the saints, the Virgin Mary, or Jesus. Some of these were permanent, and some were ephemeral, erected for specific feast days, such as All Saints' Day. Family members then lit candles, set out food and flowers, and provided gifts for saints and deceased family members. They also engaged in rituals in front of their household altar. In seventeenth-century Mexico, women especially favored what were called "oratorios," private rituals to the saints involving music, dancing, and food.

The Inquisition approved of venerating the saints, but not of oratorios, viewing them as a ceremony at which "women and men went to eat and drink in excess, to play games, sing and dance with great lewdness." In 1647, for example, it charged a woman named Petrona, "a mestiza married to an Indian," with hosting an oratorio at her employer's house at which "many mulattoes, blacks, and mestizos danced."[19] The participants venerated an image of St. Anthony of Padua that they then carried to Mass at several churches. Other women were also charged with organizing oratorios devoted to St. Anthony, a popular saint in Portugal, Spain, and the Spanish colonies as well as for Kimpa Vita and her followers in western Africa, as you read in Chapter 5. Anthony came to be invoked especially by women who wished to marry or become pregnant. Through rituals such as these, laywomen applied the sacred system of the Catholic Church to their own needs and concerns.

ASIAN CHRISTIANS ASSIST AND RESIST

Catholicism came into Asia from several directions: across the Indian Ocean to Ceylon, where the Portuguese established a colony in 1505 and then colonies in other Asian ports, and across the Pacific to the Philippines, where the Spanish established a permanent colony in 1565. From these colonies, Catholic missionaries traveled to areas not under European control, such as China, Japan, and Vietnam. During the seventeenth century, the Dutch East India Company (Verenigde Oost-Indische Compagnie in Dutch, generally abbreviated as VOC) began both to take over Portuguese centers and to establish their own. The VOC founded colonies on Ceylon, at Batavia on the island of Java, and then in other parts of Asia, along with South Africa. In the eighteenth century, the British East India Company established itself as a major power in parts of India. In all these colonies and trading centers, religious personnel were part of the European presence.

In the Philippines, members of religious orders were at the forefront of both missionary work and political control, as they were in Latin

America, although different religious orders varied slightly in their approaches. For most missionaries, there was to be no toleration of local religion. They punished local religious leaders, termed *baylans* or *catalonans*, who were generally married older women, regarded as to some degree beyond gender because they were no longer able to have children. *Catalonans* communicated with both male and female spirits and served as a bridge to the supernatural, typically through trance and rituals involving sacred objects. Thus missionaries cut down sacred groves of trees and trained boys to find the objects used in Indigenous rituals to desecrate and destroy them. Priests Christianized childbirth and funeral rituals, offering holy water, rosaries, and pictures of the saints and the Virgin Mary to assist people through difficult times instead of the traditional rituals and objects.

Catalonans sometimes resisted. In 1587, the Jesuit missionary Pedro Chirino complained about a "fire of idolatry" set by "a band of worthless women of the *Catalonas* . . . [who] in secret maintain a tyrannical hold upon the village by various means and plots."[20] In another letter, he admitted that *catalonans* included prominent women: "This woman [a *catalonan*] most stirred up the fire on account of the power that she wielded, not only on account of the sagacity which she certainly possessed, but by her influence and reputation in the village. Not only was she herself of high family, but she was very well connected; and had several children who were married and thus related to the most prominent families in the village."[21]

As in the Americas, local women assisted missionary ventures in the Philippines as well as resisting them. Most of their names are unrecorded, but occasionally letters and accounts provide them. Magdalena Bacuyo, an elderly elite woman who had become a Christian, coaxed her grandson Salangsang, a leader of the Kagayanon people on the island of Mindanao (a large island in the southern Philippines), into receiving two members of the Augustinian Recollect order in the 1620s. She told the missionaries that the Kagayanon people would "become good Christians if they listen to your advice and your words."[22] She made the arrangements for the voyage there, including finding an armed escort. The venture ultimately thrived. Salangsang and many Kagayanon were baptized, built a chapel and house for the missionaries, and defended them against armed attacks.

Despite such assistance, Spanish church officials were doubtful about Indigenous women's piety and devotion. The first convent for Spanish and Spanish-background women was founded in 1620 by Sor Jerónima de la Asunción, the nun you met in Chapter 3, but not until 1697 did it admit a Filipino woman, and that only because of a royal order. The Jesuits sponsored the establishment of several small *beaterios*, but only in 1721 was an actual convent opened especially for Indigenous women. Even after this, most Filipino women who lived in religious communities continued to be servants or lay sisters rather than professed nuns. Laywomen also joined confraternities, which often supported the public rituals of larger men's confraternities and engaged in charity.

In East Asia, Catholic missionaries came to Japan in 1549, as you have read in earlier chapters, and slightly later to the Portuguese colony of Macao, on the Asian mainland, from where they traveled into China. Jesuits in particular realized they would need to learn Chinese to be successful in China itself, and several did. They went to the imperial capital at Beijing, where they were impressed by Chinese culture and learning, especially Confucianism, and Chinese officials were equally impressed by them. Instead of trying to stamp out local beliefs, the Jesuits accommodated, modifying rituals and even judging certain Chinese practices, such as the veneration of ancestors, as compatible with Christianity. In the later seventeenth century missionaries traveled to many parts of China beyond Beijing, so that in some cities there were significant Christian communities.

Catholic baptism at the time involved more than the use of water: the priest also touched the converts' bare skin with salt, oil, and the priest's saliva, and breathed into their nostrils. Such close physical contact between an unrelated man and woman was unacceptable in many Asian cultures, and missionaries modified this. They also held confession in a large room, with a mat suspended between the priest and his female confessant. A prominent male Chinese Christian stood at the other end of the room, so that he could observe, though not hear. (This was certainly as private as most European confessions at the time; they often took place in the open in a crowded church, for the confessional box did not become widely used until the eighteenth century.)

To facilitate rituals and services involving women, Jesuits sought, in their words, "to create a few chapels in the homes of some Christians

268

where women can be baptized, mass can be said, and talks can be given to them."[23] Wealthy female converts facilitated the establishment of these separate women's chapels or congregations in some Chinese cities. Prayers and services were so common in one of these, wrote a Jesuit missionary in 1660, that the household "appeared more a convent of nuns and religious than the family and household of a noble, secular lady."[24] The women in charge of the congregations organized their meetings and admitted new members. They often invited non-Christian relatives, neighbors, and friends to attend, including children, thus helping to transmit Christian teachings beyond their immediate household and across generations. Jesuit letters report that women sometimes sought baptism after meeting with a women's congregation, that is, without having ever met a priest or missionary. Women took Christian books and objects into non-Christian households when they married, serving as domestic missionaries, and sometimes converted their husbands. Less wealthy women also served as itinerant catechists, traveling from village to village or to various house-holds within a city, leading prayers and discussions.

As they had in Europe and in European colonies, beginning in the 1620s Jesuits in China founded confraternities for laymen and women, generally dedicated to the Virgin Mary. The confraternities gathered together several times a year to hear Mass, make a confession, and take communion. Many met more often on their own without a priest to pray and worship. Whether in a household or a slightly larger group, women's communal piety among Chinese Christians was primarily directed by women.

Wealthy Asian women supported missionary and congregational activities with their influence and cash. Isabel Reigota (?–1698), the daughter of a Portuguese father and Japanese mother, left Japan for Macao as a young woman because of the persecution of Christians. She made money in the sandalwood trade, and provided major contributions for missions in Japan, China, Vietnam, and Cambodia. Justa Zhao converted to Christianity in Beijing, and in the 1650s and 1660s provided funds for Jesuit missionaries there and later for the renovation of a church in Yangzhou.

Candida Xu (1607–1680), a wealthy third-generation Chinese Christian, provided more money to Christian groups in and around

Shanghai than any other person. Her household was engaged in the production of silk textiles, and she used the profits for charitable and religious purposes. She gave donations to poor Chinese Christians, provided funds for printing devotional books, helped establish an orphanage, and provided support for churches in communities across China. Traveling with her son, she oversaw the establishment of churches thousands of miles from her home. According to Jesuit reports, she compared her travels and actions to those of missionaries, who "traveled so many miles [*li*] for the salvation of the Chinese and for the glory of the true God. . . . Am I to fear [a journey of] nine thousand miles in honor of God and for the eternal salvation of my people?"[25] The Virgin Mary had indicated her support, she said, by sending a vision to one of her domestic servants that she was to travel to far western China where there were few Christians. Xu was the subject of a biography, *The Story of a Christian Lady in China*, written by a French Jesuit and translated into other languages, which Jesuits hoped would inspire noblewomen in Europe to follow her example and give money. She and other Catholic women also sent embroidered silk altar hangings and other gifts to Europe to decorate Jesuit churches there.

Wealthy European women responded to such appeals. Catholic noblewomen in Madrid, Antwerp, and Paris sent money to support the Jesuit China mission. The German noblewoman Maria Theresia von Fugger-Wellenburg (1690–1762) read Jesuit mission reports, met several Jesuit missionaries in person on their way to Asia, and later supported them financially over decades. She was particularly taken by accounts that she had read of abandoned infants in China and efforts by Jesuits and Chinese converts to baptize them. Writing to Florian Bahr, one of the Jesuits she had met, for more details about this "matter that has touched my heart beyond all measure," she commented, "You see the concerns of a woman, which extend even to the end of the world."[26] She arranged to have payments sent for the baptism of abandoned children, and when she became head lady-in-waiting to the empress of the Holy Roman Empire, convinced her to send funds to China for this purpose as well.

Through French Jesuits with whom she corresponded, Maria Theresia sent books, devotional objects, musical instruments, and medicine to Jesuits in Vietnam, one of whom asked her to become his "most love-worthy

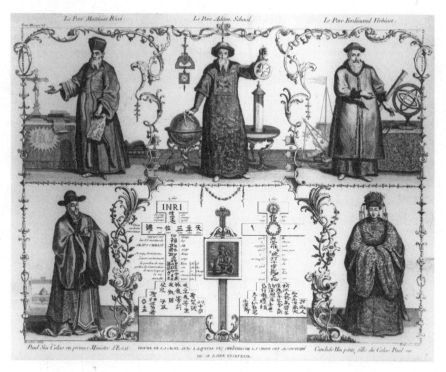

Le Pere Matthieu Ricci.   *Le Pere Adam Schaal.*   *Le Pere Ferdinand Verbiest.*

Paul Siu Colao ou premier Ministre d'Estat.   *FIGURE DE LA CROIX AVEC LAQUELLE LES CHRETIENS DE LA CHINE ONT ACCOUTUMÉ DE SE FAIRE ENSEVELIR.*   *Candide Hiu petite fille du Colao Paul siu*

7. *This seventeenth-century engraving by an unknown artist for a European audience depicts individuals important to the Jesuit mission in China. Candida Xu is at the lower right, her grandfather the scientist and Christian convert Xu Guangqi is at the top in the middle, and the other figures are European Jesuits who went to China: Matteo Ricci, Johann Adam Schall von Bell, and Ferdinand Verbiest.*

mother," to whom he would be a "most obedient and thankful son."[27] She agreed, commenting in a letter "that I will not refuse this, but hope always to have the strength to prove myself a worthy mother in advice and action."[28] The Jesuits in turn sent exotic gifts, effusive thanks, and pleas for more money and supplies, and used her example to inspire devotion (and donations) among other well-off women.

The Jesuits first came to the southern part of Vietnam, known as Cochinchina, in 1615, and to the northern part, known as Tonkin, in 1626. Members of other orders followed. People at all social levels were baptized, especially women, including the relatives of rulers and other members of the noble elite. When Sor Magdalena de Cristo and her group of nuns were shipwrecked in Vietnam in 1644 and met the queen—an encounter described in Chapter 3—this was not the first time the women of the royal court had heard Christian teachings, though it was the first time they had heard them from women. Missionaries in Vietnam praised the Christian wives of powerful men as models of devotion and good works, valiant even during periods of persecution, which alternated with periods of toleration. Women supported missionaries and chapels financially, constructed hospitals and schools, and organized religious and charitable groups, using family wealth or the profit they had made in trade.

Minh Duc Vuong Thai Phi, baptized as Marie-Madeleine (1568–1649), the great aunt of the Cochinchinese ruler, was the most important of these royal converts. She supported missionaries, built a hospital and chapel, and convinced several other family members to convert. During a period of persecution, according to Jesuit accounts, she even made a speech to fellow Christians:

> Do you not realize, my brothers, that brave soldiers should boldly put their lives at risk for their lord and king, being assured that the king will reward them? So too should we put our lives at risk for the just purposes of our God, to defend his holy law. . . . Without doubt he will repay us, not with some temporal and perishable reward but with the glory that never ends. Do you not see how our masters, the Fathers of the Company [the Jesuits] remain firm and constant in maintaining the holy law of our God. We should imitate them without ever weakening.[29]

Jesuits called women who defended them "courageous Amazons," models of determination and devotion to their fellow Christians in Vietnam and to Europeans reading missionary accounts.

The Vatican refused to ordain Indigenous men as priests, but it did allow the training of local catechists who could teach but not perform the sacraments. Officially these were all men, but women also acted as teachers and catechists, particularly in more isolated areas where visits by priests were rare. Missionaries praised their devotion, with one writing in 1639: "Our Lord having moved some of these women to desire more perpetual things, they have already asked to offer to the priest their obedience in anything he orders them to do, to leave what they have in their villages, and live on the alms of Christians, doing works of charity, preaching to women who wish to receive the Law in their houses, and teaching Christians who are as yet uncultured, beseeching them in sermons."[30] Missionaries reported powerful religious zeal among them, including one young woman who pressed a medallion of the Sacred Heart of Jesus that had been heated in the fire against her chest, "imprinting her body with this sacred image."[31]

In some places, devout women chose to gather in religious communities, living, as one Jesuit reported, "in common with a fidelity and edification that ceded nothing to women religious in Europe."[32] They carried out religious devotions, ministered to the poor and the sick, and engaged in work that allowed the community to survive. These communities were similar in many ways to the Buddhist convents that had long been in Vietnam, although they attracted young women along with the older widows who more commonly became Buddhist nuns. Young women's deciding to remain celibate and live in a community could put them at odds with their families, as this meant the women would not produce the sons needed to carry out rituals honoring family ancestors properly. Parents who had converted sometimes supported their daughters in this choice of celibacy over marriage, though others objected. As the Jesuit missionary Alexandre de Rhodes (1591–1660) described one young woman, "she conceived a love for the purity of her body against her parents' and the gentleman's wishes."[33]

As in Europe, male clergy were uneasy with women living in religious communities without formal rules, and in 1670 one of the French missionaries in Vietnam established the Amantes de la Croix (Lovers of the Cross), a religious order in which women took vows of poverty, chastity, and obedience. Amantes houses were given sets of regulations that specified the residents "must remain cloistered so that they maintain all the principles and be an example of holy righteousness for one another's spirit." But this cloister was not to be as strict as that in most European convents, as the women were also to "live and work to support one another in the flesh." Women who needed "to work and/or trade because they are in want" were to be "permitted to leave for fifteen days at a time."[34] Women in Vietnam had long been major traders in cloth, spices, and other goods, activities that did not necessarily end when a woman joined an Amantes house. Regulations also specified that residents were to meditate, chant, and pray, particularly for the souls of non-Christian Vietnamese, thus giving them a specific role in the missionary process. They were also to practice reading so that they could read the Catholic catechism and other religious works in Vietnamese, an educational opportunity that was unusual for women not from high social classes.

In traditional Vietnamese religion, women often served as spirit mediums, delivering prophetic messages and carrying out rituals to avoid misfortune and illness. Jesuit missionaries interpreted this as demonic possession, and Alexandre de Rhodes dubbed such women "pythonesses," taking this term from the women who interpreted ancient Greek oracles. As they did in cases of possession in Europe, missionaries carried out exorcisms, and sometimes the women converted and were baptized. The women's former association with demons made people think they had special power, however, and people sometimes turned to such women, rather than a priest, when they next needed a demon expelled. Former pythonesses commanding evil spirits to do their bidding was not quite what the Jesuits had in mind when they exorcised these women and baptized them as Christians, but spiritual power often takes unexpected forms.

Catholic missionaries in China and Vietnam accommodated to many existing beliefs in the seventeenth century, but in the first half of the eighteenth century this policy was reversed. Papal representatives and the pope himself ordered all missionaries to follow Roman practice and stop any distinctive rituals. Not surprisingly, the pace of conversion slowed, and some converts gave up their allegiance to Christianity.

In Dutch colonies, the missionaries were Protestant, and the "state" was a private company, the VOC, not the government of the Netherlands. The directors of the VOC thought it important to provide religious personnel for their own employees and to combat Catholicism in formerly Portuguese areas, but it kept these clergy strictly under VOC control.

Patterns of conversion varied widely in VOC colonies. In the Cape Colony of South Africa, the VOC was completely uninterested in converting either Indigenous people or enslaved migrants, and very few non-Europeans became Christians. In many Asian VOC trading posts, conversion to Protestant Christianity was almost entirely the result of intermarriage, so quite limited. Only on Ceylon (now Sri Lanka), Amboina (an island now in Indonesia), and Formosa (now Taiwan) were aggressive preaching and teaching campaigns led by a few ministers successful in gaining significant numbers of Indigenous converts. In Formosa the Dutch pastor George Candidius (1597–1647) held baptisms and church services in local languages, and advocated marriage with local women as a way not only to win converts but also give missionaries access to female religious rituals.

Formosa's Indigenous people played important roles in creating new Christian institutions and practices. For example, several Dutch military victories and an outbreak of smallpox that both the Dutch and the Indigenous Sirayan people attributed to the "Dutch god" led local inhabitants to destroy their religious objects, agree to be baptized, and support the construction of churches and schools. A delegation of headmen promised (as reported by Dutch authorities) that "henceforth the people were to desist from all lewdness and fornication; that the women when pregnant should no longer practise abortion; and that polygamy, which is most shamefully practised, should be done away with. Further, that the men should cover their nakedness, and henceforth live as Christians and not as beasts."[35] The headmen had clearly recognized that conversion involved sexual, bodily, and marital practices as well as notions of the divine. Some couples did marry in Christian ceremonies and a few local men became teachers, but divorce and multiple wives continued, as Indigenous converts filtered and blended Christian teachings with their own cultural values and social structures.

In India, the British East India Company also functioned in large part as an independent political power. The Anglican Society for the Promoting of Christian Knowledge (SPCK) was founded in 1698, but in India and throughout the British Empire the ministers that it sent were far more interested in increasing levels of religious observance among Europeans or gaining members from rival churches than they were in preaching to non-Europeans.

Women in Dutch and English colonies in Asia included Eurasians, the daughters of marital and non-marital relationships between Portuguese men and local women. These women were often Catholic, and Protestant church authorities worried about the women retaining their loyalty to

Catholicism, raising their children as Catholics, and perhaps even converting their husbands. Thus although they often tolerated Catholicism in general, they required marriages between a Protestant and a Catholic to be celebrated in a Protestant church and demanded a promise from the spouses that the children would be raised Protestant.

For example, in the late seventeenth century, Protestant ministers and officials in the English colony of Fort St. George on the east coast of India became alarmed that merchants and soldiers were taking wives and sexual partners from among Eurasian families in the nearby Portuguese colony of St. Thome. Children from these families were being baptized as Catholic by French and Portuguese friars, which the English Protestant clergy and officials saw as a threat to maintaining both religious and imperial boundaries. Instead, officials favored marriage with fully Indigenous women, and in 1687 backed this with money:

> The marriage of our soldiers to the native women of Fort St. George is a matter of such consequence to posterity that we shall be content to encourage it with some expense, and are thinking for the future to appoint a Pagoda [4 rupees of Indian currency] to be paid to the mother of any child that shall hereafter be born of any such future marriage upon the day the child is Christened.[36]

In the minds of English officials, the Eurasian women's Catholicism was a greater threat to English Protestant identity than the darker skin color or racial background of local women. Reformation disputes were easily exported to European colonies.

BLENDING BELIEFS AND PRACTICES IN NORTH AMERICA

French missionaries came to the French colonies of North America beginning in 1610, first among settled, agricultural groups such as the Hurons and later among the more nomadic peoples of the Great Lakes and the Mississippi Valley. Jesuits in particular learned local languages and lived and traveled with potential converts. They used every occasion to preach and teach, including funerals, councils, and visits to the sick, and employed imagery that fit with local traditions, often acting like shamans by curing illnesses and interpreting dreams. The conversion process was not simply an oral one, for missionaries also used pictures, chants, plays, music, bells, and holy objects such as amulets, crucifixes, and altar vessels. Rituals were more important than theology, with daily prayers and seasonal festivals.

Male converts became "prayer-captains" (*dogiques*) and a few Native American women became nuns or lay sisters in the convents established in the small cities of eastern French Canada you read about in Chapter 3. Missionaries also organized communities of converts, with churches, schools, and religious confraternities. In some places, Indigenous people formed Christian communities on their own near French settlements as refuges from war, disease, hunger, and the alcohol-induced violence that was destroying many Native American communities.

Indigenous women responded to French missionaries in a variety of ways. Many were strong opponents, as they recognized that accepting Christianity could bring a loss of status, an end to long-held spiritual practices and traditions, and changes in family structure as missionaries favored European-style patriarchal families rather than the more egalitarian ones common among Native American groups. According to Jesuit reports, male *dogiques* attempted to force women to comply with Christian norms, commenting, "it is you women . . . who are the cause of all our misfortunes—it is you who keep the demons among us. . . . You are lazy about going to prayers; when you pass the cross, you never salute it; you wish to be independent. Now know that you will obey your husbands; and you young people, you will obey your parents and our Captains; and, if any fail to do so, we have concluded to give them nothing to eat."[37] Such haranguing made male *dogiques* particularly unpopular, and the office was often taken over by older women, the clan mothers who had long been the core of Iroquoian society.

Other women accepted Catholic ideas enthusiastically. Marie-Barbe Attoncion d'Onotais (1656–?) and Marie-Thérèse Gannensagous (1665–?), two Iroquoian women, were the first Indigenous women in the religious communities started by Marguerite Bourgeoys in Montreal. Gannensagous remained at the small outpost "Mountain Mission" on Montreal Island, where she was a teacher and catechist for the several hundred Algonquins, Iroquois, Hurons, and Nipissings who lived there. D'Onotais moved to the larger main house in Montreal, where she taught girls. Both women also worked on the farm Bourgeoys had established to provide food for the community, bringing the agricultural knowledge and skills that were part of women's sphere among the Iroquois to a new setting.

Marie Rouensa (whose Indigenous name was Aramepinchone) (1678?– 1725), the daughter of a prominent leader of the Kaskaskia in what is now Illinois, refused to marry the French trader her father wanted her to marry because he was a known opponent of church aims. The Jesuit missionary Jacques Gravier supported her refusal, noting that "God did not command her not to marry, but also that she could not be forced into doing so; that she alone was mistress to do the one or the other."[38] She was also supported by a group of at least fifty women and girls, who barricaded themselves in a church in defiance of the male leaders of the Kaskaskia. The situation was resolved when Marie Rouensa agreed to the marriage providing both her father and the French trader agreed to become Christian. Their child was the first to be baptized in what later became Illinois (in 1695, at Peoria).

This marriage and Marie's second marriage to another French trader became the models for subsequent marriages between French men and Indigenous women in the Illinois area. Christian spouses chose godparents for their children from among other converts, creating Catholic kin networks cemented together by both French and Indigenous traditions, which happened in other parts of New France as well. Native Christians continued to define clan membership through the female line, so that individuals had both a Christian name and a clan name inherited through their mother's family.

Some converts adopted more extreme Catholic practices, including grueling asceticism and self-mortification. A group of Mohawk and Iroquois young women in the Jesuit community of Kahnawake near Montreal, for example, refused to marry, carried out long fasts, whipped themselves with branches, and burned themselves with glowing coals. "In the depth of winter," reported the Jesuit Claude Chauchetière, a missionary at Kahnawake, "two of them made a hole in the ice and threw themselves into the water, where they remained during the time that it would take to say the rosary slowly and deliberately."[39] Fasting and flagellation were penitential practices that were well known among European Christians, but voluntary exposure to cold and burning were not. The young women may have adopted these from earlier Iroquois rituals of healing and war preparation, a good example of the way local and imported practices merged in Indigenous Christianity. As with Rose of Lima, the women's penitential practices were sometimes seen as excessive by male priests, who reported that the women even went into the woods with hunting parties to dive into the winter ice without interference.

One of these women was Catherine Tekakwitha (1656–1680), the daughter of an Algonquin mother and a Mohawk father who had moved to Kahnawake after her village had been destroyed in warfare and her parents had died from smallpox, which also left her scarred. Her name represented her double identity: she was Tekakwitha as a member of the Turtle clan of the Mohawk, and became Catherine at her baptism, in memory—like so many other Catholic women in this book—of the Italian saint and mystic Catherine of Siena. (Later she also became known as Kateri, the Mohawk form of Catherine.) Like her namesake, she died at a young age perhaps in part because of her austerities. Chauchetière became convinced that she was a saint whose rosary and grave had healing properties. He and Pierre Cholenec, another Jesuit colleague who had been Tekakwitha's confessor, wrote long texts describing her virtues and the many miracles that occurred because of prayers asking for her assistance or visits to her grave. For this they relied on the words of two older Iroquois Christian women who had known her, Anastasia Tegonhatsiongo and Marie-Thérèse Tegaiagueneta. A local cult developed among French Catholics, although both Indigenous Christians and the higher-ups in the Jesuit order were not persuaded about her miraculous healing powers or sanctity.

Recognizing how important virginity was to ideals of female saintliness, Cholenec increasingly emphasized this aspect of her life, declaring, "What made our Catherine more blessed than all the rest and placed her in a higher rank, not only than the other Indians of the Sault, but than all the Indians who have embraced the faith throughout New France, was this great and glorious title of virgin. It was to have been the first in this new world who, by a special inspiration of the Holy Ghost, consecrated her virginity to Our Lord."[40] Cholenec's biography was published in 1715, with "first virgin of the Iroquois" as part of the title, though Tekakwitha was in fact not an Iroquois. (Other early works call her "Lily of the Mohawks," using a traditional European symbol for purity but at least getting her ancestry correct.) Several years later a Spanish translation was published in Mexico City as part of the successful campaign to open a convent specifically for Indigenous nuns. Tekakwitha's life was proof, said the translator, that Native American women could be sexually chaste.

Tekakwitha's hagiographers hoped to make her an official as well as locally honored saint, but this was a slow process. She was made venerable in 1943, beatified in 1980, and canonized in 2012, when the Congregation for the Causes of Saints and Pope Benedict XVI certified a second miracle through her intercession. The last step happened largely through the pressure of the Tekakwitha Conference, an organization of Native American Catholics, and she became the first North American Native American woman to be made a saint. The cathedral in Sante Fe, New Mexico, nearly 2,000 miles from where Tekakwitha lived and died, has a larger-than-life-size bronze statue of her by the sculptor Estella Loretto, erected in 2003. (See Plate XV.)

Missionary work among Native Americans was much slower in getting started and much less extensive in British North America than it was in French North America. The Puritan pastor John Eliot established what he termed "praying towns" for converts in Massachusetts beginning in the 1650s, where Native Americans were to learn European agriculture along with Scripture and form congregations and families modeled on those of their Puritan neighbors. Missionaries were most interested in winning male converts, who were to instruct their families, so schools for Native American boys were an essential part of these praying towns. Many Massachusett and Wampanoag men became schoolmasters, and some became missionaries, preaching and catechizing their own communities and other groups.

More Native Americans adopted Christian practices as a result of the First Great Awakening of the mid-eighteenth century, and then asserted some cultural autonomy by establishing their own churches, schools, and even a few settlements. As was true among white settlers, Native

American women affiliated themselves with Protestant churches—through adult and infant baptism, Christian marriage ceremonies, and full membership in communion—at about twice the rate of men. Mothers and grandmothers brought children to be baptized, in part because this might give them access to Euro-American education, but also because both Native and Euro-American Christians believed that the ritual of baptism itself gave the children physical and spiritual protection, even though ministers tried to dissuade them of this notion.

Some women converts refused to give up aspects of their culture, however, rejecting attempts, as missionaries put it, to "reduce them to civility." Mary Fowler Occom, for example, a Montaukett convert married to the internationally known Native American minister Simon Occom, continued to wear traditional clothing, prepare Indigenous foods, and answer her husband in her native language, though she could speak English well. Other women tried Christianity, but decided it was not for them. Sarah Simon and her siblings were Narragansetts from Rhode Island and students at Eleazar Wheelock's boarding school for Native American students in Connecticut in the 1760s. Her brother became a licensed minister, but Sarah decided after a spiritual crisis that she needed to return home. Writing to Wheelock—in the only self-authored reflections on religion by a colonial Indigenous woman to have survived—she says, "I have been this some time back thinking upon things of Religion, and I think thay do not look so plain to me as I have seen them."[41]

Some Native American women evangelized, but there are no surviving sources about them. Male Native American preachers and teachers have left letters, sermons, and diaries, and are described in many types of sources written by white Protestant leaders. Most of those leaders did not approve of women acting as missionaries, so do not mention Indigenous women who might have done so. Protestant opinion about women missionaries would change in the later nineteenth century, when mainstream Protestants began to send married couples and even a few unmarried women into the mission field, but this came too late to recover the stories of earlier Native American women evangelists.

The Protestant colonies of the Caribbean (and occasionally the north coast of South America) included those under British, Dutch, and Danish control in the seventeenth and eighteenth centuries. The

Indigenous population had already been reduced to a remnant, and colonizers seeking to expand agricultural production, especially in sugar, brought in enslaved Africans. More than 3 million Africans were transported to the Caribbean during the eighteenth century alone in the transatlantic slave trade. Christian churches in Protestant colonies were largely controlled by planters, who saw conversion as incompatible with slavery. They worried that baptism might encourage enslaved people to seek earthly freedom, as many laws and documents at the time made distinctions between "Christians" and "slaves."

Occasionally enslaved people were baptized in Protestant churches, and a few did use this as part of their arguments for freedom. An enslaved woman of mixed descent named Elizabeth Key in colonial Virginia sued for her freedom in 1654 based partly on her baptism and won her case, with the court stating, "shee hath bin long since Christened, Col. Higginson being her God father and that by report shee is able to give a very good account of her fayth."[42] Doll Allen, another young enslaved woman of mixed heritage in Bermuda, petitioned for the right to buy her freedom in 1658 based on her father/owner's status as a free white English man and on her Christian identity, noting, "it hath pleased God to sett a distinction between her and heathen Negros by providence [in] [a]lotting her birth among Christians and making her free of the Ordinances [of C]hrist." She had followed these "ordinances," that is, religious practices of Protestant Christianity, "from her Cradle unto fifteene yeares of age" living with "the priviledge of Christian people."[43] In contrast to Elizabeth Key, Allen was not successful, as the notion that the legal status of a child was based on that of its mother was already well established in Bermuda. Her petition suggests, however, that enslaved Christians saw their religious allegiance as a key part of their identity and saw themselves as part of the Christian community.

Cases such as this, plus the growing number of enslaved and free Black Christians in British colonies, led to laws passed throughout British American colonies beginning in the 1660s stating clearly that baptism did not bring freedom. These laws also affirmed that the children of enslaved women would themselves be enslaved, reversing normal English practice, in which legal status followed the father. Beginning with a 1697 law in the British Caribbean colony of Barbados, laws in

British colonies gradually began to use the word "white" rather than "Christian" to refer to people of European background, defining difference racially rather than religiously.

The shift from "Christian" to "white" also happened in laws and cases about unlawful sex. In contrast to Asia and to French North America, where intermarriage was tolerated or even encouraged, partly as a means of Christianization, British and Dutch colonies in the Americas forbade it. The first laws prohibiting sex between groups—1638 in New Amsterdam and 1662 in Virginia—distinguished between "Christian" and "Negroe," but this language soon shifted. A 1691 Virginia law forbade marriage between an "English or other white man or woman" and a "negroe, mulatto, or Indian man or woman." Such laws were passed in all the southern colonies in North America and also in Pennsylvania and Massachusetts between 1700 and 1750. (They were struck down by the U.S. Supreme Court in 1967 but remained on the books in some states for decades after that; the last of such "miscegenation" laws was rescinded by Alabama voters in a statewide referendum in 2000.)

Thus, in contrast to the hierarchy of racial categories found in Catholic Spanish, Portuguese, and French colonies, the Protestant British North American and Caribbean colonies, and later the United States, developed a dichotomous system, in which in theory one drop of "Black blood" made one Black, though in practice lighter-skinned mixed-ancestry individuals may have passed over without notice into the white world. Only in New England were marriages between enslaved people legally recognized. Protestant churches in the southern colonies and the Caribbean made little effort to promote the recognition of slave marriages or assure that enslaved people would be able to attend services, as Catholic officials did in Latin America.

The number of enslaved and free Africans who sought baptism and joined Christian churches increased during and after the religious revival of the First Great Awakening, though only a few were accepted as full church members. Because of discrimination, Black people in many places around the Atlantic began to establish independent Black Protestant churches in the late eighteenth century, such as the Bethel African Methodist Episcopal Church in Philadelphia, founded in 1793. In these, church members and clergy developed new and distinctive patterns of worship, forms of Christian expression, and institutional structures, providing spiritual sustenance and community.

THE GLOBAL MORAVIANS

Protestants were later than Catholics to develop missionary endeavors, but by the seventeenth century Quaker women preached throughout England and the English colonies in the New World and occasionally elsewhere, as you have read in earlier chapters. In the eighteenth century they were joined by Moravians, who traveled as missionaries throughout the Atlantic world, sometimes working as a team with their husbands, but sometimes independently. The Moravians were never a large group when compared to the Methodists or the Baptists, but they had a global reach from their beginning.

To understand the Moravians you need some backstory, as their origins actually go back a century before the Protestant Reformation. Among the migrants you met in Chapter 3 were radical Protestants who moved to Moravia and nearby Bohemia—now part of the Czech Republic—home to Hussites, followers of the fifteenth-century Czech reformer Jan Hus, who developed ideas similar to those of Luther a century later. He denied papal authority, called for translations of the Bible into the local Czech language, supported clerical marriage, and declared indulgences useless. Hus gained many followers, and after he was burned at the stake for heresy at the Council of Constance in 1415, his followers were successful at defeating the combined armies of the pope and the emperor many times. In the 1430s, the emperor agreed to recognize the Hussite Church, which became the dominant church in Bohemia. A group of Hus's followers, called the Unity of Brethren or Bohemian Brethren, developed more radical ideas similar to those of other radical Protestants later, rejecting the idea of a state church and sometimes rejecting private property, the saying of loyalty oaths, and warfare. Bohemia and Moravia became areas of refuge for many types of Protestants.

These territories were under the authority of the Catholic Habsburgs, however. In the late sixteenth century they brought the Jesuits to Bohemia to preach and open schools, and they closed all Protestant schools. Protestant noblemen revolted against the emperor in 1618 in what became the Thirty Years' War, and in Bohemia the Protestants lost. The Habsburgs executed or expelled many Protestant nobles, replacing them with loyal Catholics. Protestant worship went underground, surviving in places far from centers of power, including rural parts of Bohemia and Moravia.

In 1722, Henriette Catharina von Gersdorf (1648–1726), a religious poet and advocate of pietism—that movement of strong personal religious devotion you read about in Chapter 2—brought in Brethren as religious refugees to work her estate at Berthelsdorf in eastern Saxony, just over the border from Bohemia. Here she also hosted pietist Lutheran missionaries who had worked in the Danish colony of Tranquebar in India and in Greenland. She also oversaw the education of her orphaned grandson, sending him to study with pietist theologians at German universities. That grandson was Count Nicolas Ludwig von Zinzendorf (1700–1760), who encouraged more Brethren to immigrate and establish the village of Herrnhut (which means "under the care of the Lord") according to their religious ideas on a corner of the estate.

In August 1727, Susannah Kühnel, an eleven-year-old girl in Herrnhut whose mother had recently died, had a spiritual experience while praying and crying in her father's garden that led her to stop eating for several days. Other children also experienced a spiritual awakening, and several days later the congregation of Brethren gathered for communion did as well, responding by praying, crying, and singing hymns. They later interpreted this as a visit of the Holy Spirit similar to Pentecost as described in the Book of Acts. Zinzendorf supported this spiritual revival, and expanded the ideas of the Herrnhuters, revitalizing the tradition in what he originally wanted to be simply a group within the Lutheran Church that encouraged deeper religious sensibilities, as all pietists did. Instead, the group became a separate body, formally the Unity of Brethen (Unitas Fratrum in Latin) but in English usually just called the Moravian Church.

Zinzendorf's wife, Erdmuthe Dorothea (1700–1756), born countess of Reuss-Ebersdorf, had similar pietist sensibilities, largely encouraged by *her* mother, Erdmuthe Benigna of Solms-Laubach (1670–1732), who also taught her about women's important roles running states. (Solms-Laubach and Reuss-Ebersdorf were both small independent territories within the Holy Roman Empire.) Erdmuthe Dorothea put her spiritual and practical talents to use, especially during the periods when her husband was banished from Saxony. She handled the financial security and day-to-day operations of the community at Herrnhut and later at new communities several hundred miles away at Herrnhaag and Marienborn in Hesse, using her dowry and family money to do so. She visited pietist groups around Europe whenever her bearing and raising twelve children allowed, and oversaw Moravian missionary work in Denmark and Livonia, thus moving beyond the patronage that many well-off women engaged in to action.

Meanwhile her husband traveled to the Americas and England to set up Moravian congregations. The Moravians eventually established missions across Europe from Ireland to Silesia, and then beyond to the islands of the Caribbean, Suriname in northern South America, West and South Africa, and the British colonies of North America from Labrador to Georgia.

Zinzendorf's ideas about gender and sexuality provided opportunities for women's independent activities wherever the Moravians went. Zinzendorf wanted to lessen extra-marital contacts between male and female believers, as he recognized the emotional overlap between religious and sexual passions and thought that women would be better spiritual guides for other women than would men. Under his leadership, the Moravians organized men and women into separate "choirs" based on gender, marital status, and age, each with its own leaders, records, worship, work patterns, and sometimes living arrangements. Thus, as long as Zinzendorf was alive, women headed choirs, served as elders and deacons and ordained other women into these offices, gave sermons, taught, evaluated the spiritual condition of women before communion, helped serve communion to women, sat on governing councils in Moravian communities, and attended regional and general synods of members. From the late 1720s to the 1760s, between 100 and 150 women held offices that required their attendance at synods, a significant number given that Moravians most likely numbered only a few thousand.

Moravians were thus segregated by sex until marriage, and decisions on marriage partners were made by lot in established communities. A man seeking a wife came to the Elders' Conference, the group of all adult communicants, which proposed a possible spouse. Three colored ballots standing for "yes," "no," and "wait" were placed in a box, and one was drawn, which was regarded as "the Savior's decision." Prospective spouses and their families had to consent to the match, but the ultimate decision rested with the lottery. Where the number of Moravians was small, spouses were chosen less formally, but the decision was made by the community, not the individuals, as was true about so much of Moravian life.

Moravian women traveled as missionaries throughout the Atlantic world, sometimes working as a team with their husbands, but sometimes independently, in communities that included Europeans, Africans, and Indigenous people. Maria Barbara Knoll (1720–1770), for example, left her Lutheran family to join the Moravians at Marienborn as a young woman, married a man she had never met, whom church leaders had selected to serve as a physician in the mission of the Dutch colony of Suriname, and went with him from Suriname to the Danish colony of St. Thomas in the Caribbean and then to Pennsylvania. They left the Moravians to join the (theoretically) celibate cloister at Ephrata, where she and many other women developed close personal and sexual relations with its leader. After this, she and her husband reconciled and moved to Savannah, and then to a pietist Lutheran community at Ebenezer in Georgia, where both worked as medical practitioners until they died in the 1770s. In all these places, Knoll herself did not preach, but she provided spiritual support to other women and nursed colony residents and their servants and slaves, exchanging knowledge of local plants and remedies with Indigenous people and enslaved Africans in doing so.

When Maria Knoll and her husband stopped in St. Thomas, they joined a Moravian mission that had been there since the 1730s, when German Moravian missionaries had come to the Danish colony to begin the first sustained effort in the Americas to convert enslaved Africans to Christianity. The missionaries had lukewarm official support from the Danish West India-Guinea Company, the chartered company that dominated the slave trade on St. Thomas, and they did not directly speak out against slavery. In fact, after a few years on St. Thomas, several missionaries purchased a small plantation, including nine slaves. But they did view enslaved people as spiritual equals and they taught some to read and write.

Missionaries also appointed baptized Blacks, including one woman, as "helpers" to lead small groups in prayer and discussion. Male and female slave owners responded by ripping up and burning books. Converts were beaten, and a small group were imprisoned and interrogated. Count Zinzendorf himself arrived unexpectedly on the island in 1739 and arranged for their release. He tried to convince the planters that the Moravian mission was not a threat to slavery, even preaching to a large crowd of Afro-Caribbeans that Christian baptism brought spiritual freedom, but not manumission, and that they should obey their masters. His sermon only led to more violence.

Black leaders of the Moravians on St. Thomas decided to write petitions to the Danish king and queen on behalf of converts, a risky and courageous act. One of these, written in Dutch Creole by a group that included three men and three women, informed the Danish king about the book burnings and the beatings, and said that white settlers were calling the baptism of Africans a "baptism of dogs." They were willing to suffer martyrdom for their beliefs, they wrote: "We would gladly place our heads under the axe in defense of our congregation and for the sake of Lord Jesus."[44]

A second petition was written by a woman originally named Damma or Marotta, born to Catholic parents in the Popo Kingdom of West Africa, where she also learned several different African religious systems. She was captured, enslaved, and taken in the 1690s to St. Thomas. She was freed in the 1730s, when she was in her seventies, and became acquainted with the growing Moravian community. She joined the Moravian Church, and was baptized Magdalena, taking the name from the Danish queen Sophia Magdalene, originally a princess in the German state of Brandenburg-Kulmbach, who herself had strong pietist leanings. Marotta/Magdalena became an elder and her son joined the Moravians as well.

In a petition addressed to Queen Sophia Magdalene, written in her mother tongue, Aja-Ayizo, and translated into Dutch Creole, Marotta/Magdalena asserted her identity as a Christian and as an African: "Great Queen! . . . I am very sad in my heart that the Black women on St. Thomas are not allowed to serve the Lord Jesus. . . . If the Queen thinks it fitting, please pray to the Lord Jesus for us and let her intercede with the King to allow Baas Martin [the Moravian missionary Friedrich

Martin] to preach the Lord's word. . . . May the Lord save you and bless you, along with your whole family. I will pray to the Lord Jesus for you. In the name of over 250 black women, who love Lord Jesus, written by Marotta, now Madlena of Poppo in Africa."[45] Recognizing the publicity value of these petitions, Zinzendorf later published them in a collection of Moravian writings, along with his own farewell sermon. They represent quite different views of the relationship between slavery and Christianity.

Marotta/Magdalena was not the only woman from St. Thomas to reach across the Atlantic after becoming a Moravian. The best-known Moravian missionary of African background was Rebecca Protten (1718–1780), a woman of African and European descent born into slavery in the Caribbean. She was taken to St. Thomas and sold to a family of sugar planters, who gave her the name Rebecca, introduced her to Protestant Christianity, and eventually freed her. She learned to read and write from Moravian missionaries, and began to walk the roads of the island, preaching in slave quarters and at nightly meetings, drawing from her own experience and her reading of the Bible. Friedrich Martin reported that she was "very accomplished in the teaching of God. She has done the work of the Savior by teaching African women and speaking about that which the Holy Spirit himself has shown her."[46] While on St. Thomas she married a German Moravian missionary and had a daughter, an interracial marriage that became another flashpoint with the authorities. Both she and her husband were among those imprisoned and, after Zinzendorf arranged their release, they were exiled as subversives for preaching and for teaching people to read, accused of inciting rebellion.

The family sailed to Germany, planning to go to Herrnhut, but Rebecca's husband became sick and died in a small village on the way. One of the other Moravian missionaries traveling with them described the deathbed scene in great detail in his account of the journey, including words spoken by Rebecca as she tried to console her husband: "his wife answered that he should not admit such thoughts, or doubt his belief in the Savior, who began this journey with us and would see it through, and that though his body was weak the Savior would give him strength."[47]

Rebecca made it to Herrnhut, and then to the Moravian community at Herrnhaag/Marienborn, where her daughter also died. In 1746 she married a second time. Her husband was Christian Jacob Protten (1715–1769), a Euro-African scholar and missionary who had been born in Christiansborg, a slave-trading colony in the Danish Gold Coast, what is now Ghana. The son of a Danish soldier and a Ga mother from a prominent family, Protten went to a local school for children of mixed descent, and was sent to Denmark for further education. He attended the University of Copenhagen, met Count von Zinzendorf, and moved to Herrnhaag. Protten was apparently a difficult man, prone to bouts of what was then called "melancholy" and anger, particularly at what he regarded as demeaning treatment of him for his African background and skin color. He was also a skilled linguist, translating Luther's Small Catechism into Ga and Fante, the two Ghanaian languages, and writing the first grammar of these languages for those who wanted to learn them.

The Moravian community was expelled from Herrnhaag/Marienborn in 1750 when the new ruler of the territory decided he did not approve of groups that would not swear allegiance to him or the Lutheran state church. Rebecca and Christian Protten moved back to Herrnhut. They took their infant daughter Anna Maria with them, though she died when she was only three, the second of Rebecca's children to be buried in Germany. (See Plate XVI.) Zinzendorf sent Christian Protten around the Atlantic as a Moravian missionary: first to the Gold Coast, back to Herrnhut, then to St. Thomas, back to Herrnhut, to the Gold Coast again, where he met up with his mother and other members of his family, and back to Herrnhut. During most of his travels, Rebecca stayed in Herrnhut, and the two occasionally communicated by letter. In one of the very few letters of hers to survive, Rebecca attempted to raise her second husband's spirits with encouraging words, just as she had with her first husband:

> You know well that I love you and that I will never forget it. That I promise, but, poor me, what will your poor heart do in these times. Turn to Him, who has everything. The Lord blesses and protects you and meets you and clothes you with mercy. I received your last letter, from 12 May 1759, with joy and with sorrow. Dear heart, what should I say? My heart, the Lord shows us mercy, that we may turn ourselves

over to Him. We know his great heart well, and He has also taught us that a great heart is patient.[48]

None of Christian Protten's missions were very successful, and in 1765 he returned to the Gold Coast again, this time with Rebecca. The two established a boarding school for pupils of mixed descent. Protten died several years later and Rebecca hoped to go back to St. Thomas, but her health was poor, so she stayed in Africa, where she died in 1780, at sixty-two.

During her lifetime, other Moravians recognized that Rebecca Protten was central to the mission on St. Thomas, though after she died, she was largely forgotten for centuries, as were so many of the women you have met in this book. She has been rediscovered in the last few decades, viewed as a key figure in the creation of Afro-Atlantic Christianity in the Americas.

Moravians settled in North America about the same time they established their mission on St. Thomas, first in Savannah in 1735 and then in larger numbers in New York and Pennsylvania in the 1740s. They followed paths set by earlier German immigrants, whom the Moravians hoped to convert to their own more pietist version of Protestant Christianity. Zinzendorf himself came to Pennsylvania in 1742 hoping to make himself the head of a united Moravian-Lutheran Church. He made contact with Native American leaders at the trade town of Shamokin, where branches of the Susquehanna River intersected and people from many different Native groups lived. After several years of negotiations, the Moravians were allowed to preach to Native American groups if they also supplied blacksmiths. Moravians established missions among the Mahicans and Lenape (Delaware), building houses, churches, and schools, and expecting converts to live in European-style houses and to give up warfare. When the Lenape were forced by the British and then the American government to move to what became Ohio and Ontario, Moravian missionaries accompanied them.

A Mahican woman who also spoke Iroquois translated at the first negotiations at Shamokin, and though her name was not recorded, this same woman later spoke with Jeanette Mack, a Moravian woman who had learned several Native American languages, about the destiny of her recently deceased daughter's soul. Mack gave her materials to build a

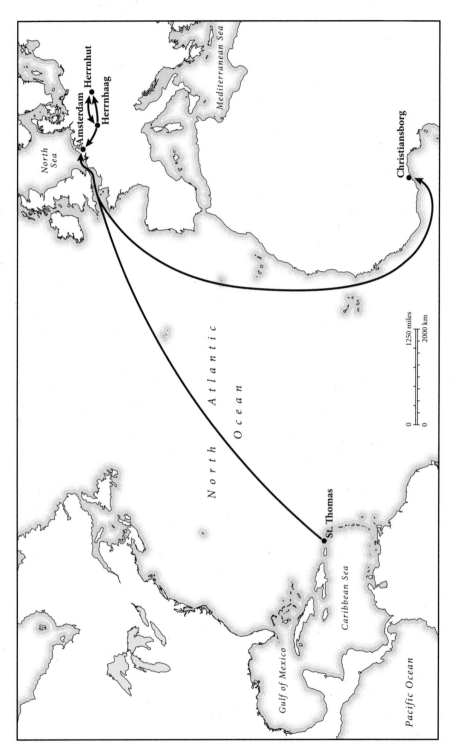

Map 6. Rebecca Protten's travels.

coffin, and the Mahican woman in turn gave Mack a tin container in remembrance of the little girl.

Although this woman did not convert—she filled her daughter's coffin with materials normal in Mahican burials, not Christian ones—other Native American women did, or at least decided to accept baptism, often through the efforts of Moravian women, who taught in schools, conducted religious services, helped in childbirth, blessed infants, and dressed the dead in Indian communities. Between 1742 and 1764, several hundred Lenape and Mahican women in Pennsylvania were baptized, more than the number of men. Even male Moravian missionaries openly admitted this was the result of their wives' efforts. Gottlob Büttner, for example, reported in 1742 that Native American women "love my wife much and are Glad of all opportunities to speak with her," and, after peering through cracks in a wall at the separate service she held for them, commented that they "were all much moved, and sighed, and fell on each other's necks."[49] Johann Jungmann noted that his wife Margarethe "was very practiced in the Indian languages, so that she could speak with the Mahikan and Delawares quite fluently. Nothing could move her heart more than when she saw or heard a soul concerned for our Saviour."[50]

Moravians believed that converts would be stronger in their faith if they lived together under the watchful eye of Europeans, just as did Catholic missionaries in Spanish colonies. But in contrast to Catholic missions, where there was generally no formal role for Indigenous women, baptized Native American women became elders (*Arbeiter Schwestern*) in Native congregations, where they blessed children, heard other Native women's professions of faith, and proselytized. After Moravians introduced the practice of godparenting, German and Native American women became joint godmothers for the children of converts. Native converts did not set up independent single and widowed women's choirs with separate living spaces, but occasionally married Christian Native women found refuge from domestic quarrels in those established in European Moravian communities.

Wherever they lived and traveled, Moravian use of female, maternal, and sensual imagery for Christ and the Holy Spirit provided women with ways to express their personal piety unusual within Protestant traditions. Moravian devotion to the blood and wounds of Christ, expressed in sensual language about blood flowing from the side wound and believers crawling inside this to bathe or be baptized in the blood, was powerful to Native American men and women, for whom blood and wounds also had deep meaning. Missionaries' letters and reports speak of Native American women who were "hungry after the Savior's blood" and saw this blood as both a spiritual and physical healing agent.[51] Their dreams and visions, and those of Native men, told as part of the life stories about spiritual longing and crisis that were related after baptism, were written down, distributed, and read by Moravians and others in Pennsylvania and beyond. Thus, as Native Americans accommodated their spiritual language somewhat to Moravian ideas—or the missionaries recorded them as doing so—German and English audiences read about vision quests, hunting magic, and miraculous healings, which fit well with their own worldview, in which prophecies, apparitions, and portents were regularly reported and interpreted. To Moravians and other pietists who read these, the similarities among these life stories were evidence of God's global providence and the coming kingdom of God.

After Zinzendorf's death in 1760, several general synods quickly ended women's independent spiritual and governance responsibilities and put women's choirs under male caretakers, as they tried to make Moravians seem less threatening to orthodox Lutherans. Johanna Pietsch (1726–1788), the niece of Anna Nitschmann—another leading female figure of the first generation and Zinzendorf's secret second wife—watched this undoing as she traveled in Germany, the Netherlands, England, and Pennsylvania, commenting that "the settlements and choirs had now lost their lead sheep," which gave her "anxious thoughts" and "inexpressible pain," and over which she "cried many, many tears."[52]

In North America, this change in policy coincided with increasing conflicts among Native nations and between Britain and France as they consolidated their power and increased settlements on the colonial frontier. These conflicts fed off one another and resulted in the Seven Years' War (1756–1763), often called the French and Indian War in the United States, a conflict in which the British and French both had Native American allies. Moravian pacifism and unwillingness to take loyalty oaths meant they were regarded with suspicion by all sides, and missionary communities were subject to raids. Moravians and their

Native converts were later caught in the middle of the American War of Independence (1776–1781) as well. Many Native American Christians moved away from Moravian mission towns and resettled among non-Christian Native groups, too far to allow the web of relations that had been built up among European and Native American women to continue much past the 1770s.

Moravian women were more literate than those in most other immigrant groups and were expected to record their spiritual path in written memoirs to be shared with the congregation. It seems appropriate to end this book with one of these, the memoir of Margarethe Jungmann (1721–1793), a woman who connects with almost every other chapter. She was not a monarch, but she was a mother (and grandmother) and a migrant, had mystical experiences, and nearly died several times on her missions to Native Americans. She left the memoir written in her own hand.

Born in Germany, Margarethe and her family moved to Pennsylvania when she was five, where her pietist father led them in twice-daily family worship and prayer. "This often brought me into great fear and perplexity, for, I thought, I should never become so pious. . . . However, whenever I read the history of the dear Saviour's Passion in the New Testament, I felt so well in my heart that I was sometimes almost in an ecstasy."[53] But her "uneasiness and anxiety returned . . . and I gave myself no peace" until she heard Zinzendorf preach when he arrived in Philadelphia in 1741. His words "penetrated deep into my heart," and she decided to join the Moravians, a move initially opposed by her father, but to which he ultimately gave his approval.

Several months after Margarethe joined the major Moravian community at Bethlehem in Pennsylvania, a husband was chosen for her. "A few days later, it was decided that we should go among the Indians at Schekomeko," the first Moravian missionary venture among the Mahicans, in upstate New York. "Now I found myself placed in a situation of utmost poverty. . . . But I learned the language of the Indians very quickly and soon gained a love for them and was loved by them in return; and this cheered me up again and made my course a great deal easier." Her husband died when she was six months pregnant, and her son died three weeks after being born. The remaining Moravians decided to move back to Bethlehem but were arrested on the way by British authorities under suspicion of treason and faced a hostile mob. As Margarethe comments with her usual understatement: "That was once again a testing time for me. At that time the Saviour's ways were still almost impenetrable to me, and I hardly knew what I should think about what had happened."

Six months after the death of her first husband, Margarethe was married again, to Johann Jungmann, a marriage that was to last forty-eight years, although she could hardly have imagined this at the time. The couple set off to a Lenape congregation at Gnadenhütten in Pennsylvania, where they stayed six years and Margarethe heard the voice of Jesus, which she describes as "the most blessed moment of my life." Back to Bethlehem, then off to Pachgatgoch in upstate New York, "until the war of that time [the Seven Years' War] caused great confusion among our Indian brothers and sisters." Back to Bethlehem, where they ran a soap manufactory for several years, and Margarethe was made a deacon.

Off to Languntotenek in western Pennsylvania, a trip during which Margarethe fell from a horse "so dangerous that my dear husband did not know whether I would come back to life again or not, for I lay a considerable time as if dead." Then further west, joining other Moravian missionaries and Lenape converts who had established the first white settlement in what is now Ohio, at Schoenbrunn in 1772, on land given to them by the Lenape along the Tuscarawas River. The couple lived in different Moravian communities in Ohio until the outbreak of the American Revolution, a war "that caused much unease among us," and led them to decide it was "unsafe for us to remain here any longer because I was the only white sister there." They were nearly killed in a flood and by soldiers when heading east to Bethlehem, and arrived "weak, sick, and exhausted." But a few years later, when Margarethe was sixty, "we were willing and ready to venture there again . . . in the hope of concluding our lives with the dear Indian Congregation, to which I felt a particularly strong attachment." This time they ended up in what is now Michigan, where they stayed several years until Margarethe's failing health led them back to Bethlehem, where she died in 1793 at the age of seventy-two. The song composed for and sung at her funeral highlights her work among Native Americans: she "sees in the companies on high /

The Mohicans, and Wampanos / The Delawares and Shawanos / Who have gone home blessedly."

After mentioning the death of her first child, Margarethe's memoir says very little about her own children, but we know from her second husband's memoir that she had eight children with him who survived, and that one of her daughters died while serving as a missionary on St. Thomas. Thus, as she was traveling on the muddy paths and flooding creeks of the American wilderness, and suffering from hunger, illness, and injuries, Margarethe was often pregnant or nursing, although she never comments on this. On their many returns to Bethlehem, the couple left children behind and visited the ones they had left previously. Two of her sons decided to leave the Moravian congregation, "a fact that cost her," as her husband wrote, "many tears because she cared deeply about the welfare of her children." She had eleven grandchildren by the time that she died, and "heartily hoped that these would flourish."

Margarethe's grandchildren did flourish, and so did the Moravian Church. Today there are more than a million Moravians worldwide, more than half of them in Tanzania and about a quarter in Latin America and the Caribbean. The paths and sea-lanes that Rebecca Protten and Margarethe Jungmann traveled still take Moravians around the world.

The Protestant Christianity of Rebecca Protten or Margarethe Jungmann was of course very different from the Catholic Christianity of Luisa de Carvajal, Guaibimpará/Catherine, or Candida Xu. Over the centuries in which these women lived, hundreds of thousands of people were killed or forced to move, had their homes and villages destroyed, or saw their families split apart because of those differences and the political aims that became attached to them. The expansion of Christianity through missionary work took the verbal, written, and actual battles between Protestants and Catholics onto a global stage.

The women in this chapter were not immune from these deep divisions but helped shape them. Luisa de Carvajal set off for England *because* she could be martyred there, not despite this. Margarethe Jungmann was so upset that her sons were no longer part of the Moravian community that, according to her husband, she "said to the Saviour, 'you know, I would give up everything except you and the Congregation'" to have them rejoin. Most likely they were worshipping with other Protestants, but to Margarethe, that was not close enough. Catholic noblewomen such as Maria Theresia von Fugger-Wellenburg supported Jesuits with their money and influence, well aware that wealthy Protestant noblewomen, such as the pietists you met in Chapter 2, were doing the same for Protestant missionaries.

The women in this chapter were also not immune from the suppression and destruction of Indigenous beliefs, spiritual practices, buildings, objects, and people that accompanied the spread of Christianity. In Sor Juana's *loa*, Religion stops her husband Zeal from killing America and those celebrating the Festival of Seeds with her, but asserts that her goal is "to vanquish her [America] with words," still a violent process. The verses sung at Margarethe Jungmann's funeral proudly proclaim that in heaven "Each and every Indian nation / will sing to God with elation / . . . she will see / Standing majestically, / Whole hordes slaughtered for the Lamb."

But the women in this chapter also helped shape and transform Christianity. They were not passive recipients of what male missionaries taught, but actively created new religious meanings for Christian symbols, practices, and rituals. In Mexico City, Petrona and her friends venerated St. Anthony by carrying his image to Masses, but also by dancing, singing, and feasting in his honor. In the Yucatán, Maya women honored Virgin Mary Moon Goddess. In the Illinois area, Marie Rouensa and other Kaskaskia women created networks of godparents among Native American and European Christians, drawing on both French and Kaskaskia traditions. In China, Isabel Reigota and Candida Xu invested money they had made in missions, inspiring elite European women to invest their money as well. In Peru, Vietnam, New France, St. Thomas, Pennsylvania, and many other places, Christianity provided opportunities for intense expressions of personal piety that women made their own. Christianity colonized them, but they also colonized Christianity.

EPILOGUE

In this book, I seek to place women at the center of the story of the Reformations and the spread of Christianity around the world. I hope the hundreds of women you have met along the way have convinced you that they belong there. "Church mothers," to use Katharina Zell's self-description, were everywhere. Their stories have often been unearthed by academic historians, part of the explosion of women's history over the last fifty years. But many have been recovered by women within the faith traditions they embodied, who are erecting statues, naming schools, and building institutions in their honor. Others are questioning their legacies, as they seek to understand their actions but do not condone them, or are building on these legacies to create new opportunities.

The developments traced in every chapter continued long past the eighteenth century, and many continue today. There are still women among the dynastic monarchs in Europe, and some remain the official head of their state churches, though their role is mostly ceremonial. Among her many titles, the queen of the United Kingdom Elizabeth II bore the same one Elizabeth I did: "Defender of the Faith and Supreme Governor of the Church of England." At her coronation in 1953, Elizabeth II swore to "maintain and preserve" the churches "established by the laws" in England and Scotland. Because of this, she had to be a member of the Church of England, as do all future British monarchs.

The 2013 Succession to the Crown Act, which made royal daughters and sons equal in terms of succession to the throne, revoked the 1701 law that had disqualified those who married Roman Catholics from inheriting the throne. (The older law had not mentioned other religions, so the newer one did not need to either.) It also limited those who had to seek royal approval for their marriage to the first six persons in line to the throne rather than a much broader group, reflecting the modern idea that the choice of a spouse should be up to the individual rather than being a matter of dynastic politics, as it was for the women you met in Chapter 1. Supporters of the Act noted approvingly that it "removed centuries of discrimination on both religious and gender grounds."

The many roles highlighted in the chapter on mothers have endured, and to these more have been added. Pastors' wives continue to assist their husbands and demonstrate their faith, just as Katharina von Bora did, but many women have increasingly understood their spiritual calling to be broader. Some aim for an equal role in church leadership. They have gained the ability to become ordained clergy in many Protestant denominations and are seeking to do so in others. Today women make up between 20 and 30 per cent of the total ordained clergy in the United States, more than 30 per cent in England, and more than 50 per cent in Denmark and Sweden.

Within Catholicism, women continue to head women's religious houses and orders, while the Women's Ordination Conference and similar groups are pushing for women's ordination. Roman Catholic Women Priests, an international movement, decided to stop waiting for permission, and in 2002 found bishops within the Church who would ordain women. Today womenpriests (the movement usually runs the words together) can be found in churches in Europe, North and South America, and South Africa, though they prefer to be called "Reverend" rather than "Mother." Laywomen remain just as essential to the maintenance of Catholicism as they were in seventeenth-century England or eighteenth-century France: Catholic lay ministers outnumber priests in the U.S., and 80 per cent of them are women.

This expansion of women's role is not always welcome, of course. Very few women head major churches, encountering what many have termed the "stained-glass ceiling." Non-denominational evangelical churches, including huge megachurches, have an almost completely male network of leadership, though the wives of their charismatic leaders often appear, smiling, as "helpmeets" at their sides. In 2008, the Vatican excommunicated the women priests and the bishops who ordained them. Women lay ministers in Catholic churches are often unpaid or paid very poorly, and rarely receive the housing, meals, and other benefits that priests do. In 2023, the Southern Baptist Convention—the largest Protestant Christian denomination in the United States—voted to expel two churches that allowed women pastors and restricted all pastoral and elder roles only to men. None of this would probably surprise Marie Dentière, Katharina Zell, Susanna Wesley, the Methodist preacher Elizabeth, Katherina Rem, or Angélique Arnauld, all of whom were told by those around them that their words and actions were unsuitable for women.

Individual, family, and mass migration for religious reasons did not end in the eighteenth century. In 2022, the United Nations High Commission for Refugees estimated there were over 80 million people displaced from their homelands for various reasons worldwide. Many of these were from countries that engage in what it termed "systematic and ongoing persecution of various religious communities," or from places where religious, ethnic, and national identities intertwine in a deadly mixture. Three-quarters of refugees and internally displaced people (those who have fled their homes but are still in their country) are women and children, as vulnerable to violence during times of migration, displacement, and war as they were 500 years ago.

In less grim continuities from the chapter on migrants, Mary Ward's Institute ultimately received approval in 1877, and in 1909 she was allowed to be publicly recognized as the Institute's founder. Today there are two groups that view her as their founder, the Institute of the Blessed Virgin Mary (IBVM) and the Congregation of Jesus (CJ). There are more than 2,000 sisters in 40 countries around the world, who emphasize education and social care in their actions. In 2009, the Church proclaimed Mary Ward venerable, four centuries after she had been charged with heresy and her Institute suppressed. The two groups that describe themselves as "Mary Ward women" are currently working on moving her further up the ladder to sainthood.

Among Protestants, Quaker women have continued to travel, preach, and make trouble. They were central to the women's rights, abolitionist, and prison reform movements of the nineteenth century, and to efforts for peace, social justice, and human rights in the twentieth and twenty-first centuries. Today IBVM and CJ sisters and Quaker women work to improve the treatment of refugees and asylum seekers, reflecting their spiritual principles and their own histories of migration and exile.

Women continue to be arrested and killed for ideas and actions authorities view as religious and political dissent. The young Iranian Kurdish woman Mahsa Amini was arrested in 2022 by the morality police in Iran for wearing her head-covering "inappropriately" and died while in government detention. Her death set off protests in Iran and around the world under the slogan "woman, life, freedom," transforming what had been a small act into something much larger. Iranian authorities have responded to these protests with brutal crackdowns in which hundreds of people have been killed and with prohibitions of even private memorial services, but actions continue. Today the stories of women who have suffered and died for opposing authoritarian policies are more likely to be told through films and digital media than in giant martyrologies, but the idea that they can inspire—and thus are dangerous—remains.

Women martyrs from Reformation times are also finally receiving more official acknowledgment. Almost immediately after the discovery of Japanese "hidden Christians" in the nineteenth century, the Catholic Church began recognizing and celebrating Japanese martyrs. Twenty-six European friars and male Japanese lay teachers who had been executed in Nagasaki in 1597 had already been beatified, and in 1862 they were canonized. Another 205 martyrs were beatified in 1867, a group that included 14 women. Pope John Paul II beatified a group of twenty-six martyrs in 1981 and canonized them as saints two years later. This group included two women executed in 1634, St. Magdalena of Nagasaki and St. Ōmura Marína, both of whom had been interpreters and assistants to missionaries.

In 2008, after a long campaign by Japanese bishops, Pope Benedict XVI beatified another 188 martyrs in a ceremony held in a Nagasaki baseball stadium. This group was primarily Japanese lay Christians, including entire families. Of this group, sixty-three were women and girls, and the Japanese bishops used the occasion to make a statement about the importance of laypeople, especially women: "We have realized that, without these women, the Church in Japan today would not exist. We should see the Beatification of these female martyrs as a message of hope and consolation for all women of this country, whatever faith they are."[1] Officially the group is known as "Father Peter Kibe and his companions," however, thus identified by one of the few clergy in it rather than as a group of laywomen and men. The ceremony was not accompanied by any actual measures designed to enhance the role of women in Japanese Christianity, so its "message of hope and consolation for all women" was limited to words.

Protestants don't have saints, but they do have heroes. Mary Dyer and Anne Hutchinson have become emblems of religious liberty and toleration. You can buy inspirational posters with quotations and images of them online, and there is a medicinal herb garden dedicated to the two women near where they lived in Rhode Island. There is a statue of Dyer by Sylvia Shaw Judson on the grounds of the Massachusetts State House in Boston, with copies at the Friends Center in Philadelphia and at Earlham College. (See Plate XVII.)

There is a statue of Anne Hutchinson on the grounds of the Massachusetts State House as well, erected over some objections in 1922, and she was pardoned by the state of Massachusetts in 1987. The official dedication of the statue was not until 2005, at which point the First Church of Boston also restored Hutchinson to membership after having "cast her out" in 1638, praising "her personal strength and enduring spiritual insight," and noting that "it is time for her Church to remove the yoke upon her memory." Security measures because of the 9/11 attacks restricted access to the statue, however. Other than during special ceremonies, it is now only visible at a distance, behind fencing, an ironic touch.

Christian women and girls continued to report hearing or seeing God, Christ, the Virgin Mary, Divine Wisdom, the Holy Spirit, saints, angels, and other spiritual beings long after the eighteenth century. Apparitions of the Virgin Mary are the best known of these, and include some approved by the papacy, such as Our Lady of Lourdes, an apparition reported by the teenaged Bernadette Soubirous in southern France in 1858; Our Lady of Champion, an apparition reported by Adele Brise, a young Belgian immigrant in Champion, Wisconsin in 1859; Our Lady of Fátima in Portugal, an apparition reported by three children in 1917; and Our Lady of Medjugorje, an apparition reported by six children in Bosnia-Herzegovina in 1981.

Today the sanctuary of Lourdes is one of the most-visited shrines in the world, drawing millions of pilgrims a year, and replicas of the grotto where Mary reportedly appeared have been built in hundreds of places. There are novels, films, television mini-series, songs, operas, and plays about Bernadette Soubirous, and relics from her corpse have traveled the world. Soubirous left no writings of her own, so even more than most of the women in the chapter on mystics, church officials, authors, composers, and directors have been able to imagine her any way they choose.

Many more recent women visionaries in Christianity and other religious traditions *do* shape their own message. They write books and blogs, produce YouTube videos, and appear in person. Their messages are diverse, but you can access them directly and decide what you think, rather than having these filtered by others as were those from women visionaries in the past.

Finally, Christianity has continued to spread because of intentional missionary work as well as migration, and women have been key parts of this. The Institute of the Blessed Virgin Mary is only one of many women's religious orders and congregations with an international reach, and tens of thousands of women serve as Catholic lay missionaries. In the nineteenth and twentieth centuries, Protestant organizations and churches sent both married couples and single women as missionaries, and in the twenty-first this has continued. In fact, a joke among those concerned about such issues is that two-thirds of missionaries today are married couples, one-third are single women, and the rest are single men. (You do the math.) Actual numbers are not much different—perhaps 10 or at most 20 per cent of the unmarried missionaries are men. Even among the Church of Jesus Christ of the Latter Day Saints (the Mormons), women now make up nearly one-third of all missionaries, a number that has tripled in the last decade. Christian churches with conservative gender politics tend to view missionary work, as well as the ministry, largely as the province of men. Among them there is much hand-wringing about the "disturbing trend" toward women's predominance in missionary work, and discussions of how to attract men.

Despite attempts to go back to some imagined golden age, Christianity now has a very different shape than it did in Reformation times and will change even more soon. According to the Pew Research Center, in 2015 more than 40 per cent of the world's Protestant Christians lived in Africa, a share that is expected to grow to 53 per cent by 2050. Less than 15 per cent lived in Europe, a share that will shrink to less than 10 per cent by 2050. Fifty-six million Protestants lived in the United States, the country with the most Protestants, but 53 million lived in Nigeria. Given population growth rates in the U.S. and Nigeria, Nigeria will soon be the country with the largest number of Protestants and is already sending missionaries to Europe and North America.

According to the Vatican, roughly 21 per cent of the world's Catholic Christians lived in Europe in 2020, roughly 9 per cent in North America, and roughly 39 per cent in Latin America, percentages that will also shrink in the coming decades, as the number of Catholics grows in Asia and Africa. Catholic nuns and lay missionaries now move from Africa, Asia, and Latin America to Europe and North America for ministry, study, and evangelization rather than the other way around.

The global nature of today's and tomorrow's Christianity can be seen in the celebrations that marked the 500th anniversary of the Protestant Reformation in 2017. The Lutheran World Federation and the Catholic Church began a year of joint celebrations of the Reformation in October 2016 with an Argentinian pope traveling to Lund, Sweden, to co-lead an event with the head of the Lutheran World Federation, Bishop Munib Younan of Jordan. "What unites us is far greater than what divides us," they said in their joint statement, "and we emphatically reject all hatred and violence, past and present, especially that expressed in the name of religion. . . . God summons us to be close to all those who yearn for dignity, justice, peace and reconciliation . . . and to be faithful heralds of God's boundless love for all humanity."[2] Some of that hatred and violence is an inheritance of the religious Reformations and the way those Reformations were spread across the globe. It is good to understand this, which I hope I have helped you do through this book. But after 500 years, it is also good to give this up. The first two Christian rulers in Europe to grant religious toleration in their territories after the Reformations were women, Queen Isabella of Hungary and Jeanne d'Albret, queen of Navarre. They can serve as fine models moving forward.

ACKNOWLEDGMENTS

This book draws on the research and publications of hundreds of scholars in many fields and has been shaped by conversations with colleagues, students, and friends over many decades. It is dedicated to the memory of Miriam Usher Chrisman and Natalie Zemon Davis, two founders of the field I was fortunate to get to know when I was a graduate student. As I was writing, I received advice on specific issues from Yasemin Altun, Barbara Andaya, Susan Broomhall, Julie Campbell, Pamela Hammonds, Melissa Hyde, Grethe Jacobsen, Anne Larsen, Elizabeth Lehfeldt, Mary Lindemann, Bronagh McShane, Svante Norrhem, Allyson Poska, Meredith Ray, Elizabeth Rhodes, Simon Siemianowski, Mihoko Suzuki, John L. Thompson, Mara Wade, Elsbeth Whitney, Gerhild Scholz Williams, many members of the Early Modern Women listserve, and the anonymous readers for Yale University Press. Julie Drew, Krista Grensavitch, Gwynne Kennedy, Mary Delgado, Jodi Bilinkoff, and Jon Sensbach read all or parts of the book in draft and provided me with invaluable suggestions for improvement and clarification, as did the Evanston discussion group Saturday Morning Sisters. I have known Heather McCallum, my editor at Yale University Press, for close to three decades. She championed my earlier book with Yale, *The Marvelous Hairy Girls: The Gonzales Sisters and Their Worlds*, and has done the same with this one.

NOTES

PREFACE

1. Gottfried Arnold, *Unpartheiische Kirchen und Ketzerhistorie: Von Anfang des Neuen Testaments biß auf das Jahr Christi 1688* (Frankfurt: Fritschens sel. Erber, 1729) and Johann Feustking, *Gynaeceum Haeretico Fanaticum* (Frankfurt and Leipzig, 1704). The quotations are from the very long title pages. My translation.
2. Barbara Newman, "On the Ethics of Feminist Historiography," *Exemplaria: A Journal of Theory in Medieval and Renaissance Studies* 2, no. 2 (1990): 702–706, quote on p. 702.

1 MONARCHS

1. Answer of the Queen to the addresses of both Houses of Parliament delivered to Mr Speaker Thomas Williams, 28 January 1563 (SP 12/27 f.143r–144v), at https://www.nationalarchives.gov.uk/education/resources/elizabeth-monarchy/answer-of-the-queen/ (spelling modernized).
2. Quoted and trans. in Elizabeth Lehfeldt, "Ruling Sexuality: The Political Legitimacy of Isabel of Castile," *Renaissance Quarterly* 53, no. 1 (2000): 44.
3. Joaquim Veríssimo Serrão, ed., *Documentos inéditos para a história do reinado de D. Sebastião* (Coimbra: Universidade de Coimbra, 1958), 46–47. Trans. Darlene Abreu-Ferreira.
4. *The Shepheards Calendar*, quoted in Peter McClure and Robin Headlam Wells, "Elizabeth I as a Second Virgin Mary," *Renaissance Studies* 4, no. 1 (1990): 57.
5. Victoria Smith, "Perspectives on Female Monarchy," in *Gender and Political Culture in Early Modern Europe*, ed. James Daybell and Svante Norrhem (London: Routledge, 2016), 148–149.
6. Anne Somerset, *Queen Anne: The Politics of Passion* (London: HarperCollins, 2012), 21.
7. Quoted and trans. in Nancy Roelker, *Queen of Navarre: Jeanne d'Albret* (Cambridge, MA: Harvard University Press, 1968), 216.

8. Quoted and trans. in Roland Bainton, *Women of the Reformation in France and England* (Minneapolis, MN: Augsburg Publishing House, 1973), 65.
9. *The History of the Life of Katherine de Medici, Queen Mother and Regent of France* (London, 1693).
10. Quoted and trans. in Roland Bainton, *Women of the Reformation: From Spain to Scandinavia* (Minneapolis, MN: Augsburg Publishing House, 1977), 226.
11. Elisabeth of Braunschweig-Lüneburg, *Ein Christlicher Sendebrieff* [. . .] (Hannover, 1545), n.p. My translation.
12. Quoted and trans. in Tryntje Helfferich, *The Iron Princess: Amalia Elisabeth and the Thirty Years' War* (Cambridge, MA: Harvard University Press, 2013), 124.

2 MOTHERS

1. Quoted and trans. in Gerald Strauss, "The Social Function of Schools in the Lutheran Reformation in Germany," *History of Education Quarterly* 28 (1988): 198.
2. Quoted and trans. in Jeanette Smith, "Katharina von Bora through Five Centuries: A Historiography," *Sixteenth Century Journal* 30 (1999): 770–771.
3. Quoted and trans. in Susan C. Karant-Nunn and Merry E. Wiesner-Hanks, eds., *Luther on Women: A Sourcebook* (Cambridge: Cambridge University Press, 2003), 193.
4. Eusebius Engelhard [Michael Kuen], *Lucifer Wittenbergensis, oder, Der Morgen-Stern von Wittemberg. Das ist: Vollständiger Lebens-Lauff Catharinae von Bore, Des vermaynten Ehe-Weibs D. Martini Lutheri* (Landsperg, 1747; 2nd ed., 1749). My translation.
5. *Luther's Lives: Two Contemporary Accounts of Martin Luther*, trans. and annotated by Elizabeth Vandiver, Ralph Keen, and Thomas D. Frazel (Manchester: Manchester University Press, 2003), 16.
6. Quoted and trans. in Karant-Nunn and Wiesner-Hanks, eds., *Luther on Women*, 203, 204, 205.
7. Quotations from Anne Llewellyn Barstow, "An Ambiguous Legacy: Anglican Clergy Wives after the Reformation," in *Women in New Worlds: Historical Perspectives on the Wesleyan Tradition*, vol. 2, ed. Rosemary Skinner Keller, Louise L. Queen, and Hilah F. Thomas (Nashville, TN: Abingdon, 1982), 100, 102.
8. Quoted in Robert Stupperich, "Die Frau in der Publizistik der Reformation," *Archiv für Kulturgeschichte* 37 (1927): 226. My translation.
9. Quoted and trans. in Paul A. Russell, *Lay Theology in the Reformation: Popular Pamphleteers in Southwest Germany 1521–1525* (Cambridge: Cambridge University Press, 1986), 203.
10. Argula von Grumbach, "To the University of Ingolstadt," in *Argula von Grumbach: A Woman's Voice in the Reformation*, ed. Peter Matheson (Edinburgh: T. & T. Clark, 1995), 90.
11. Jeanne de Jussie, *Petite chronique*, quoted and trans. in Marie Dentière, *Epistle to Marguerite de Navarre and Preface to a Sermon by John Calvin*, ed. and trans. Mary B. McKinley (Chicago: University of Chicago Press, 2004), 8–9.
12. Dentière, *Epistle to Marguerite de Navarre*, 55–56, 79.
13. John Calvin, *Letters of John Calvin*, quoted and trans. in Dentière, *Epistle to Marguerite de Navarre*, 19.

14. Katharina Schütz Zell, *Church Mother: The Writings of a Protestant Reformer in Sixteenth-Century Germany*, ed. and trans. Elsie Anne McKee (Chicago: University of Chicago Press, 2006), 70, 73, 77.

15. Ibid., 78, 80, 82.

16. Ibid., 51, 56.

17. Ibid., 224, 225, 226.

18. Quoted in Otto Winckelmann, *Das Fürsorgewesen der Stadt Strassburg*. Two parts in one volume (Leipzig: Heinsius, 1922), 2:76. My translation.

19. Quoted and trans. in Merry E. Wiesner, "Katherine Zell's *Ein Brieff an die ganze Bürgerschaft der Statt Strassburg* as Autobiography and Theology," *Colloquia Germanica: Internationale Zeitschrift für Germanistik* 28, no. 3/4 (1995): 248.

20. Quoted and trans. in Amanda C. Pipkin, *Dissenting Daughters: Reformed Women in the Dutch Republic, 1572–1725* (New York: Oxford University Press, 2022), 82.

21. A.C. Southern, *An Elizabethan recusant house, comprising the life of the Lady Magdalen Viscountess Montague (1538–1608)*, quoted in Laurence Lux-Sterritt, " 'Virgo becomes Virago': Women in the Accounts of Seventeenth-Century English Catholic Missionaries," *Recusant History*, 30, no. 4 (Oct. 2011): 537–553, quote on p. 542.

22. William Palmes, S.J., *The Life of Mrs Dorothy Lawson*, quoted in Ellen A. Macek, "Devout Recusant Women, Advice Manuals, and the Creation of Holy Households Under Siege," in *Devout Laywomen in the Early Modern World*, ed. Alison Weber (London: Routledge, 2016), 239–240.

23. Henry Foley, *Record of the English Province* (London, 1877–83), iv, 110, in Lux-Sterritt, "Virgo becomes Virago," 545.

24. Ibid., 546.

25. Quoted in Henry Jefferies, "Women and the Reformation in Tudor Ireland," *Journal of Ecclesiastical History* 73 (2022): 543.

26. Ibid.

27. Quoted in Clodagh Tait, "Progress, Challenges and Opportunities in Early Modern Gender History, c.1550–1720," *Irish Historical Studies* 46 (2022): 248.

28. Quoted in Jefferies, "Women and the Reformation," 545.

29. Quoted in Bronagh Ann McShane, *The Roles and Representations of Women in Religious Change and Conflict in Leinster and South-East Munster, c.1560–c.1641*, PhD dissertation, National University of Ireland Maynooth (2015), 87, 88.

30. Johanna Eleonora Petersen, *The Life of Lady Johanna Eleonora Petersen, Written by Herself*, ed. and trans. Barbara Becker-Cantarino (Chicago: University of Chicago Press, 2005), 26.

31. Ibid., 98.

32. J.H. Hennes, *Aus Friedrich Leopold von Stolberg's Jugendjahren. Nach Briefen der Familie und andern handschiftlichen Nachrichten* (Frankfurt, 1876), 7–8. My translation.

33. Susanna Wesley's letters reprinted in John Whitehead, *The Life of Rev. John Wesley*, 2 vols. (London: Couchman, 1793–96), vol. 1, 47–49, 54.

34. Letter reprinted in Paul W. Chilcote, *She Offered Them Christ: The Legacy of Women Preachers in Early Methodism* (Nashville, TN: Abingdon, 1993), 78–79.

35. Quoted in Monique Scheer, "German 'Shouting Methodists': Religious Emotion as a Transatlantic Cultural Practice," *Emotions and Christian Missions: Historical Perspectives*, ed. Karen Vallgårda, Claire Mclisky, and Daniel Midena (London: Palgrave, 2015), 53, 54.

36. Quotations from Sylvia R. Frey and Betty Wood, *Come Shouting to Zion: African American Protestantism in the American South and British Caribbean to 1830* (Chapel Hill, NC: University of North Carolina Press, 1998), 104, 105, 106, 171.

37. "Elizabeth," in Bert James Loewenberg and Ruth Bogin, eds., *Black Women in Nineteenth-Century American Life* (University Park, PA: Pennsylvania State University Press, 1976), 130–133.

38. Merry Wiesner-Hanks and Joan Skocir, ed. and trans., *Convents Confront the Reformation: Catholic and Protestant Nuns in Germany* (Milwaukee, WI: Marquette University Press, 1998), 29–31.

39. Quoted and trans. in Marjorie Elizabeth Plummer, "Anna Jacobäa Fuggerin (1547–1587) and St. Katharina Convent in Augsburg," in *Women Reformers in Early Modern Europe: Profiles, Texts, and Contexts*, ed. Kirsi I. Stjerna (Minneapolis, MN: Fortress Press, 2022), 335, 336.

40. Caritas Pirckheimer, *Denkwürdigkeiten*, quoted and trans. in Gwendolyn Bryant, "The Nuremberg Abbess: Caritas Pirckheimer," in *Women Writers of the Renaissance and Reformation*, ed. Katharina M. Wilson (Athens, GA: University of Georgia Press, 1987), 298, 300–301.

41. Quoted in Franz Schrader, *Ringen, Untergang und Überleben der katholischen Klöster in den Hochstiften Magdeburg und Halberstadt von der Reformation bis zum Westfälischen Frieden*, Katholisches Leben und Kirchenreform im Zeitalter der Glaubensspaltung, 37 (Münster: Aschendorff, 1977), 74. My translation.

42. Quoted in Johann Karl Seidemann, *Dr. Jacob Schenk, der vermeintlicher Antinomer, Freibergs Reformator* (Leipzig: C. Hinrichs'sche, 1875), Appendix 7, 193. My translation.

43. Mary C. Erler, *Reading and Writing during the Dissolution: Monks, Friars, and Nuns 1530–1558* (Cambridge: Cambridge University Press, 2013), 168.

44. María de San José, *Avisos y máximas para el gobierno de las religiosas*, quoted and trans. in Elizabeth Lehfeldt, " 'Contrary to Reason': The Absence of Enclosure in Early Modern Convents," *Early Modern Women: An Interdisciplinary Journal* 18, no. 1 (Fall 2023): 15.

45. Quoted and trans. in Querciolo Mazzonis, "The Company of St. Ursula in Counter-Reformation Italy," in *Devout Laywomen*, ed. Weber, 58.

46. Quoted in Elizabeth Rapley, *The Dévotes: Women and Church in Seventeenth-Century France* (Montreal: McGill-Queen's University Press, 1990), 92.

47. Quoted in Jo Ann Kay McNamara, *Sisters in Arms: Catholic Nuns through Two Millennia* (Cambridge, MA: Harvard University Press, 1996), 524.

48. Galawdewos, *The Life and Struggles of Our Mother Walatta Petros: A Seventeenth-Century African Biography of an Ethiopian Woman*, ed. and trans. Wendy Laura Belcher and Michael Kleiner (Princeton, NJ: Princeton University Press, 2015), 122.

49. Ibid., 116.

3 MIGRANTS

1. Inquisition records, quoted and trans. in Gretchen Starr-LeBeau, *In the Shadow of the Virgin: Inquisitors, Friars, and Conversos in Guadalupe, Spain* (Princeton, NJ: Princeton University Press, 2003), 73.

2. Inquisition records, quoted and trans. in Richard L. Kagan and Abigail Dyer, ed. and trans., *Inquisitorial Inquiries: Brief Lives of Secret Jews and Other Heretics*, 2nd ed. (Baltimore, MD: Johns Hopkins University Press, 2011), 188.

3. Ibid., 193.
4. Ibid., 200.
5. Inquisition records, quoted and trans. in Mary Elizabeth Perry, *The Handless Maiden: Moriscos and the Politics of Religion in Early Modern Spain* (Princeton, NJ: Princeton University Press, 2005), 48.
6. Hurtado de Mendoza, *La guerra de Granada*, quoted and trans. in Perry, *Handless Maiden*, 111.
7. Ibid., 110.
8. Inquisition records, quoted and trans. in Perry, *Handless Maiden*, 130.
9. Inquisition records, Archivo General de la Nación, Mexico City, Mexico, quoted and trans. in Karoline P. Cook, *Forbidden Passages: Muslims and Moriscos in Colonial Spanish America* (Philadelphia, PA: University of Pennsylvania Press, 2016), 83.
10. Ibid., 85.
11. Inquisition records, quoted and trans. in Perry, *Handless Maiden*, 156.
12. Inquisition records, quoted and trans. in Matthew Carr, *Blood and Faith: The Purging of Muslim Spain*, rev. ed. (London: Hurst & Company, 2017), 292.
13. Inquisition records, quoted and trans. in Perry, *Handless Maiden*, 169.
14. Ibid., 171.
15. Quoted and trans. in C. Arnold Snyder and Linda A. Hubert Hecht, eds., *Profiles of Anabaptist Women: Sixteenth-Century Reforming Pioneers* (Toronto: Canadian Corporation for Studies in Religion, 1996), 135.
16. Quoted and trans. in Maria Bogucka, *Women in Early Modern Polish Society, against the European Background* (Aldershot: Ashgate, 2004), 67.
17. Gottfried Arnold, *Unpartheiische Kirchen und Ketzerhistorie . . .* (Frankfurt: Fritschens sel. Erber, 1729), 106. My translation.
18. Quoted in Sylvia Brown, "The Radical Travels of Mary Fisher: Walking and Writing in the Universal Light," in *Women, Gender, and Radical Religion in Early Modern Europe*, ed. Sylvia Brown (Leiden: Brill, 2007), 43.
19. George Bishop, *New England Judged by the Spirit of the Lord* (London, 1660), 7, 12–13.
20. Elizabeth Hooton, unpublished manuscript 1663, quoted in Susanna Calkins, "Colonial Whips, Royal Writs and the Quaker Challenge: Elizabeth Hooton's Voyages through New England in the Seventeenth Century," *Journeys: The International Journal of Travel and Travel Writing* 5, no. 2 (2004): 82.
21. *Quaker Faith and Practice*, 5th ed., ch. 19, p. 27: https://qfp.quaker.org.uk/chapter/19/
22. Letter quoted in Brown, "Radical Travels," 61.
23. Reprinted in Charles Francis Adams, *Antinomianism in the Colony of Massachusetts Bay, 1636–1638* (Boston, MA: The Prince Society, 1894), 175.
24. Emery Battis, *Saints and Sectaries: Anne Hutchinson and the Antinomian Controversy in the Massachusetts Bay Colony* (Chapel Hill, NC: University of North Carolina Press, 1962), 242.
25. Eve LaPlante, *American Jezebel: The Uncommon Life of Anne Hutchinson, the Woman Who Defied the Puritans* (San Francisco: HarperCollins, 2004), 218.
26. Charlotte Arbaleste Duplessis-Mornay, *Memoirs* (1584–1606), in Charlotte Arbaleste Duplessis-Mornay, Anne de Chaufepié, and Anne Marguerite Petit Du Noyer, *The Huguenot Experience of Persecution and Exile: Three Women's Stories*, ed. Colette H. Winn; trans. Lauren King and Colette H. Winn (Toronto: Iter Press, 2019), 46, 49.

27. Penny Roberts, "Emotion, Exclusion, Exile: The Huguenot Experience during the French Religious Wars," in *Feeling Exclusion: Religious Conflict, Exile and Emotion in Early Modern Europe*, ed. Giovanni Tarantino and Charles Zika (London: Routledge, 2019), 18.

28. Quotations from Susan Broomhall, "Cross-Channel Affections: Pressure and Persuasion in Letters to Calvinist Refugees in England, 1569–1570," in *Feeling Exclusion*, ed. Tarantino and Zika, 33, 37–38.

29. Anne de Chaufepié, *Journal* (1689), quoted and trans. in *The Huguenot Experience of Persecution and Exile*, ed. Winn, 76.

30. Anne Marguerite Petit Du Noyer, *Memoirs* (1703–1710), quoted and trans. in *The Huguenot Experience of Persecution and Exile*, ed. Winn, 88.

31. Quoted and trans. in Carolyn Lougee Chappell, "'The Pains I Took to Save My/His Family': Escape Accounts by a Huguenot Mother and Daughter after the Revocation of the Edict of Nantes," *French Historical Studies* 22, no. 1 (Winter 1999): 1–64, quotes pp. 43, 44, 45.

32. Ibid., 54, 56, 57, 58, 59, 60.

33. Quoted in James E. Kelly, *English Convents in Catholic Europe, c. 1600–1800* (Cambridge: Cambridge University Press, 2020), 18.

34. Quoted in Claire Walker, "The Experience of Exile in Early Modern English Convents," *Parergon* 34, no. 2 (2017): 159–177, quote on p. 176.

35. Quoted in Marie B. Rowlands, "Recusant Women 1560–1640," in *Women in English Society, 1500–1800*, ed. Mary Prior (London and New York: Methuen, 1985), 173.

36. Quoted in Rapley, *The Dévotes*, 29.

37. Ibid., 31.

38. Bull of Suppression (1631), quoted and trans. in Mary Wright, IBVM, *Mary Ward's Institute: The Struggle for Identity* (Sydney: Crossing Press, 1997), 191.

39. Quoted and trans. in Sarah E. Owens, *Nuns Navigating the Spanish Empire* (Albuquerque, NM: University of New Mexico Press, 2017), 55.

40. Ibid., 57.

41. Francisco Colín, *Labor evangélica* (1663), quoted and trans. in Haruko Nawata Ward, "Jesuits, Too: Jesuits, Women Catechists, and Jezebels in Christian-Century Japan," in *The Jesuits II: Cultures, Sciences, and the Arts, 1540–1773*, ed. John W. O'Malley et al. (Toronto: University of Toronto Press, 2006), 647.

42. Juan de Salazer, Jesuit annual letter, 1634–35, quoted and trans. in Haruko Nawata Ward, "Women Apostles in Early Modern Japan," in *Devout Laywomen*, ed. Weber, 316.

43. Quoted and trans. in Sarah E. Owens, "Religious Spaces in the Far East: Women's Travel and Writing in Manila and Macao," in *Challenging Women's Agency and Activism in Early Modernity*, ed. Merry E. Wiesner-Hanks (Amsterdam: Amsterdam University Press, 2021), 276.

44. Ibid.

45. Jeanne-Françoise Juchereau de St. Ignace and Marie Andrée Duplessis de Ste. Hélène, *Les Annales de Hôtel-Dieu de Quebec, 1636–1716* (Quebec, 1939), quoted and trans. in Natalie Zemon Davis, "Iroquois Women, European Women," in *Women, "Race," and Writing in the Early Modern Period*, ed. Margo Hendricks and Patricia Parker (London: Routledge, 1994), 255–256.

46. Marguerite Bourgeoys (1695), *The Writings of Marguerite Bourgeoys*, trans. M.V. Cotter (Montreal: Congrégation de Notre-Dame, 1976), 49, 52.

4 MARTYRS

1. Florimund de Raemond, *L'Histoire de la Naissance, progrez, et decadence de l'Hérésie de ce siècle* (1611), quoted and trans. in Nikki Shepardson, "Gender and the Rhetoric of Martyrdom in Jean Crespin's *Histoire de vrays tesmoins*," *Sixteenth Century Journal* 35 (2004): 155–174, quote on p. 155.
2. Quoted and trans. in *"Elisabeth's Manly Courage": Testimonials and Songs by and about Martyred Anabaptist Women*, ed. and trans. Hermina Joldersma and Louis Grijp (Milwaukee, WI: Marquette University Press, 2001), 43, 45.
3. Ibid., 18.
4. Ibid., 161, 163.
5. Ibid., 26.
6. Ibid., 143, 149, 151.
7. Ibid., 103.
8. Ibid., 65.
9. Ibid., 175, 177.
10. Ibid., 189.
11. Ibid., 17.
12. All quotations from *First examinacyon of Anne Askewe; Lattre examinacyon of Anne Askewe* [London, *c*. 1560].
13. Robert Parsons, quoted in Megan L. Hickerson, "Gospelling Sisters 'Goinge Up and Downe': John Foxe and Disorderly Women," *Sixteenth Century Journal* 35, no. 4 (Winter 2004): 1035–1051, quote on pp. 1039–1040.
14. All quotations from John Foxe, *Actes and Monuments of these Latter and Perillous Days, Touching Matters of the Church* (London, 1583).
15. Jesuit reports, quoted in Robert E. Scully, S.J., "The Lives of Anne Line: Vowed Laywoman, Recusant Martyr, and Elizabethan Saint," in *Devout Laywomen*, ed. Weber, 285.
16. *Passages in the Lives of Helen Alexander and James Currie of Pentland*, quoted in Dolly MacKinnon, "She Suffered for Christ Jesus' Sake: The Scottish Covenanters' Emotional Strategies to Combat Religious Persecution (1685–1714)," in *Feeling Exclusion*, ed. Tarantino and Zika, 176.
17. Haruko Nawata Ward, "Women and Kirishitanban Literature: Translation, Gender, and Theology in Early Modern Japan," *Early Modern Women: An Interdisciplinary Journal* 7 (2012): 271–281.
18. Bernardino de Avila Girón, *Relación de Reino de Nippon*, quoted and trans. in George Elison, *Deus Destroyed: The Image of Christianity in Early Modern Japan* (Cambridge, MA: Harvard University Press, 1973), 217.
19. C.R. Boxer, "Hosokawa Tadaoki and the Jesuits, 1587–1645," in C.R. Boxer, *Portuguese Merchants and Missionaries in Feudal Japan, 1543–1640* (Aldershot: Ashgate, 1986), IV: 89.
20. Quoted and trans. in Haruko Nawata Ward, *Women Religious Leaders in Japan's Christian Century* (Farnham: Ashgate, 2009), 262.
21. *Mulier fortis*, quoted and trans. in A. Louise Cole, "The Birth of a Martyr: The Metamorphosis of Hosokawa Tama Gracia," *Sixteenth Century Journal* 42, no. 4 (2021): 857–880, quotes on pp. 875, 876.
22. *Malleus maleficarum* (1486), quoted and trans. in Alan C. Kors and Edward Peters, eds., *Witchcraft in Europe 1100–1700: A Documentary History*, 2nd ed. (Philadelphia, PA: University of Pennsylvania Press, 2001), 181, 183, 184, 188.

23. Quoted in Christina Larner, *Enemies of God: The Witch Hunt in Scotland* (Baltimore, MD: Johns Hopkins University Press, 1981), 95.
24. Quoted in Christina Larner, *Witchcraft and Religion: The Politics of Popular Belief* (London: Basil Blackwell, 1984), 85.
25. Quoted in Kors and Peters, eds., *Witchcraft in Europe*, 359–367.
26. Margaret Cavendish, *Philosophical Letters* (1664), 228, 298.
27. Elizabeth Cary, Lady Falkland, *The Tragedy of Mariam: The Fair Queen of Jewry with The Lady Falkland: Her Life by one of her daughters*, ed. Barry Weller and Margaret W. Ferguson (Berkeley, CA: University of California Press, 1994), 187.
28. *De sagis*, quoted and trans. in Gerhild Scholz Williams, "On Finding Words: Witchcraft and the Discourses of Dissidence and Discovery," in *The Graph of Sex and the German Text: Gendered Culture in Early Modern Germany 1500–1700*, ed. Lynne Tatlock and Christiane Bohnert (Amsterdam: Rodolpi, 1994), 55.

5 MYSTICS

1. Quoted and trans. in McNamara, *Sisters in Arms*, 507.
2. Thomas Edwards, *Gangraena* (London, 1646). The quotation is from the long subtitle.
3. *The Life of Saint Teresa of Ávila by Herself*, trans. J.M. Cohen (London: Penguin, 1957), 210.
4. Ibid., 71.
5. *The Way of Perfection*, quoted and trans. in Alison Weber, *Teresa of Avila and the Rhetoric of Femininity* (Princeton, NJ: Princeton University Press, 1990), 41.
6. *The Way of Perfection*, quoted and trans. in Jodi Bilinkoff, *The Avila of St. Teresa: Religious Reform in a Sixteenth-Century City* (Ithaca, NY: Cornell University Press, 1989), 136.
7. Quoted and trans. in Weber, *Teresa of Avila*, 3–4.
8. Diego Pérez de Valdivia, *Aviso de gente recogida* (1585), quoted and trans. in Stephen Haliczer, *Sexuality in the Confessional: A Sacrament Profaned* (New York: Oxford University Press, 1996), 111.
9. The quotations are from the trial record, quoted and trans. in Jodi Bilinkoff, "A Spanish Prophetess and Her Patrons: The Case of María de Santo Domingo," *Sixteenth Century Journal* 23 (1992): 21–34, quotes on pp. 27, 24.
10. Quotations from the Inquisition record, trans. in Gillian T.W. Ahlgren, "Francisca de los Apóstoles: A Visionary Voice for Reform in Sixteenth-Century Toledo," in *Women in the Inquisition: Spain and the New World*, ed. Mary Giles (Baltimore, MD: Johns Hopkins University Press, 1998), 120, 131, 132.
11. *The Souls of Purgatory: The Spiritual Diary of a Seventeenth-Century Afro-Peruvian Mystic, Ursula de Jesús*, ed. and trans. Nancy E. van Deusen (Albuquerque, NM: University of New Mexico Press, 2004), 82.
12. Ibid., 91.
13. Alonso Ramos, *Primera Parte de los Prodigios de la Omnipotencia . . .* (1689), quoted and trans. in Kathleen Myers, "Testimony for Canonization or Proof of Blasphemy? The New Spanish Inquisition and the Hagiographic Biography of Catarina de San Juan," in *Women in the Inquisition*, ed. Giles, 281.
14. Jeanne Guyon, *Selected Writings*, trans. and ed. Dianne Guenin-Lelle and Ronney Mourad (New York: Paulist Press, 2012), 57, 58–59, 61–62.

15. Quotations from Antoinette Bourignon, *Le Temoignage de Verité*, trans. in Joyce Irwin, "Anna Maria von Schurman and Antoinette Bourignon: Contrasting Examples of Seventeenth-Century Pietism," *Church History* 60, no. 3 (1991): 313, 314.

16. John Thornton, *The Kongolese Saint Anthony: Dona Beatriz Kimpa Vita and the Antonian Movement, 1684–1706* (Cambridge: Cambridge University Press, 1998).

17. Gottfried Arnold, *Unpartheiische Kirchen und Ketzerhistorie: Von Anfang des Neuen Testaments biß auf das Jahr Christi 1688* (Frankfurt am Main, 1729), 1108. My translation.

18. Pierre Jurieu, *The Reflections of the reverend and learned Monsieur Jurieu upon the strange and miraculous exstasies of Isabel Vincent, the shepherdess of Saou in Dauphiné . . .* (London: R. Baldwin, 1689).

19. Johann Feustking, *Gynaeceum Haeretico Fanaticum* (Frankfurt and Leipzig, 1704). Title page. My translation.

20. Quotes from Feustking, *Gynaeceum*, 65, 110, 349. My translations.

21. Henry Jessey, *The Exceeding Riches of Grace Advanced by the Spirit of Grace, in an Empty Nothing Creature, Viz. Mris [sic] Sarah Wight* (London, 1647), 31, 22.

22. Ibid., 123–124.

23. Anna Trapnel, *The Cry of a Stone: Or a Relation of Something Spoken in Whitehall, by Anna Trapnel, Being in the Visions of God* (London, 1654), 3.

24. Anna Trapnel, *Anna Trapnel's Report and Plea; or, a Narrative of Her Journey from London into Cornwall*, ed. Hilary Hinds (Toronto: Iter Press, 2016), 70.

25. Ibid., 80.

26. Mary Cary, *A New and More Exact Mappe or Description of New Jerusalem's Glory, When Jesus Christ and His Saints with Him Shall Reign on Earth a Thousand Years, and Possess all Kingdoms* (London, 1651), 289–290.

27. Eleanor Davies, *Bethlehem, Signifying the House of Bread: Or War* (1652) in *Prophetic Writings of Lady Eleanor Davies*, ed. Esther Cope (New York: Oxford University Press, 1995), 370, 371.

28. Jane Lead, *A Fountain of Gardens, or, a Spiritual Diary of the Wonderful Experiences of a Christian Soul, under the Conduct of Heavenly Wisdom* (London, 1697–1701), 1:18, 21.

29. Ibid., 1:34.

6 MISSIONARIES

1. Luisa de Carvajal, letter to Magdalena de San Jerónimo (1606), quoted and trans. in Elizabeth Rhodes, *This Tight Embrace: Luisa de Carvajal y Mendoza (1566–1614)* (Milwaukee, WI: Marquette University Press, 2000), 239.

2. Quoted and trans. in Rhodes, *This Tight Embrace*, 265.

3. Quoted and trans. in ibid., 267, 279.

4. Quoted and trans. in ibid., 30.

5. Quoted and trans. in Alida Metcalf, "Women as Go-Betweens? Patterns in Sixteenth-Century Brazil," in *Gender, Race, and Religion in the Colonization of the Americas*, ed. Nora E. Jaffary (Burlington, VT: Ashgate, 2007), 25.

6. Quoted and trans. in Scott Cave, "Madalena: The Entangled History of One Indigenous Floridian in the Atlantic World," *The Americas* 74, no. 2 (2017): 196–197.

7. *A Harvest of Reluctant Souls: The Memorial of Fray Alonso de Benavides, 1630*, trans. and ed. Baker H. Morrow (Niwot, CO: University Press of Colorado, 1996), 31–32.

8. Pete Sigal, *From Moon Goddesses to Virgins: The Colonization of Yucatecan Maya Sexual Desire* (Austin, TX: University of Texas Press, 2000), 120.

9. Sor Juana Inés de la Cruz, *Selected Works*, trans. Edith Grossman (New York: W.W. Norton, 2014), 125–126.

10. Ibid., 130, 132–133.

11. Ibid., 138.

12. Quoted and trans. in Stephanie Kirk, "The Gendering of Knowledge in New Spain: Enclosure, Women's Education, and Writing," in *The Routledge Research Companion to the Works of Sor Juana Inés de la Cruz*, ed. Emilie L. Bergmann and Stacey Schlau (London: Routledge, 2017), 23.

13. Project Vox team (2021), "Sor Juana Ines de la Cruz," Project Vox, Duke University Libraries. https://projectvox.org/sor-juana-1648-1695/

14. Sor Juana Inés de la Cruz, *Selected Works*, 165.

15. Ibid., 193–194.

16. Quoted and trans. in Elisa Sampson Vera Tudela, "Fashioning a *Cacique* Nun: From Saints' Lives to Indian Lives in the Spanish Americas," *Gender and History* 9 (1997): 187.

17. Quoted and trans. in Mónica Díaz, *Indigenous Writings from the Convent: Negotiating Ethnic Autonomy in Colonial Mexico* (Tucson, AZ: University of Arizona Press, 2010), 164, 165.

18. Juan Mayora, *Relación de la vida, y virtudes del P. Antonio Herdoñana* (Mexico City, 1758), 35, quoted and trans. in Simon Siemianowski, "Language as an Object of Cultural Translation? Negotiating Communication in the Multilingual Mission in New Spain (1670–1770)," PhD dissertation, University of Tübingen, forthcoming.

19. Inquisition records, quoted and trans. in Linda A. Curcio-Nagy, "Rose de Escante's Private Party: Popular Female Religiosity in Colonial Mexico City," in *Women and the Inquisition*, ed. Giles, 256, 257.

20. Quoted and trans. in Carolyn Brewer, *Shamanism, Catholicism, and Gender Relations in Colonial Philippines, 1521–1685* (Aldershot: Ashgate, 2004), 109.

21. Ibid., 173.

22. Quoted and trans. in Oona Paredes, *A Mountain of Difference: The Lumad in Early Colonial Mindanao* (Ithaca, NY: Southeast Asia Program Publications, 2013), 72.

23. Quoted and trans. in Liam Matthew Brockey, *Journey to the East: The Jesuit Mission to China 1579–1724* (Cambridge, MA: Harvard University Press, 2008), 333.

24. Quoted and trans. in Liam Matthew Brockey, "Flowers of Faith in an Emporium of Vices: The 'Portuguese' Jesuit Church in Seventeenth Century Peking," *Monumenta Serica* 53 (2005): 61.

25. Quoted and trans. in Nadine Amsler, *Jesuits and Matriarchs: Domestic Worship in Early Modern China* (Seattle: University of Washington Press, 2018), 149.

26. Letter from Maria Theresia to Florian Bahr, S.J., October 31, 1740, quoted and trans. in R. Po-Chia Hsia, *Noble Patronage and Jesuit Missions: Maria Theresia von Fugger-Wellenburg (1690–1762) and Jesuit Missionaries in China and Vietnam* (Rome: Institutum Historicum Societatis Iesu, 2006), 113.

27. Letter from Johannes Koffler, S.J., to Maria Theresia, October 28, 1755. In Hsia, *Noble Patronage*, 297. My translation.

28. Letter from Maria Theresia to Johannes Koffler, S.J., September 14, 1756. In Hsia, *Noble Patronage*, 304. My translation.

29. Quoted and trans. in Keith Luria, "Narrating Women's Catholic Conversions in Seventeenth-Century Vietnam," in *Conversions: Gender and Religious Change in Early Modern Europe*, ed. Simon Ditchfield and Helen Smith (Manchester: Manchester University Press, 2018), 203.

30. Quoted and trans. in Tara Alberts, *Conflict and Conversion: Catholicism in Southeast Asia, 1500–1700* (Oxford: Oxford University Press, 2013), 174.

31. Quoted and trans. in Barbara Andaya, *The Flaming Womb: Repositioning Women in Early Modern Southeast Asia* (Honolulu: University of Hawai'i Press, 2006), 99.

32. Ibid., 205.

33. Quoted and trans. in Luria, "Narrating Women's Catholic Conversions," 204.

34. Quoted and trans. in Nhung Tuyet Tran, "Les Amantes de la Croix: An Early Modern Vietnamese Sisterhood," in *Le Việt Nam au féminin / Việt Nam: Women's Realities*, ed. Gisèle Bousquet and Nora Taylor (Paris: Les Indes Savantes, 2005), 56, 57.

35. Quoted and trans. in Chiu Hsin-hui, *The Colonial "Civilizing Process" in Dutch Formosa, 1624–1662* (Amsterdam: Brill, 2008), 195.

36. Quoted in Stephen Neill, *A History of Christianity in India: The Beginnings to AD 1707* (Cambridge: Cambridge University Press, 1984), 372.

37. Reuben Gold Thwaites, ed., *Jesuit Relations and Allied Documents* (Cleveland, OH: Burrows Brothers, 1896–1901), vol. 18, 105–107.

38. Thwaites, *Jesuit Relations*, vol. 64, 195.

39. Quoted and trans. in Allan Greer, *Mohawk Saint: Catherine Tekakwitha and the Jesuits* (New York: Oxford, 2005), 116.

40. Quoted and trans. in Greer, *Mohawk Saint*, 176.

41. Quoted in Hilary E. Wyss, "Mary Occom and Sarah Simon: Gender and Native Literacy in Colonial New England," *New England Quarterly* 79, no. 3 (2006): 408.

42. Quoted in Rebecca Anne Goetz, *The Baptism of Early Virginia: How Christianity Created Race* (Baltimore, MD: Johns Hopkins University Press, 2012), 102.

43. General Court, Bermuda (1652), quoted in Heather Miyano Kopelson, *Faithful Bodies: Performing Religion and Race in the Puritan Atlantic* (New York: New York University Press, 2014), 203–204.

44. Quoted in Katharine Gerbner, *Christian Slavery: Conversion and Race in the Protestant Atlantic World* (Philadelphia, PA: University of Pennsylvania Press, 2018), 181.

45. Ray A. Kea, "From Catholicism to Moravian Pietism: The World of Marotta/Magdalena, a Woman of Popo and St. Thomas," in *The Creation of the British Atlantic World*, ed. Elizabeth Mancke and Carole Shammas (Baltimore, MD: Johns Hopkins University Press, 2005), 136.

46. Quoted and trans. in Jon F. Sensbach, *Rebecca's Revival: Creating Black Christianity in the Atlantic World* (Cambridge, MA: Harvard University Press, 2005), 46.

47. In ibid., 159.

48. In ibid., 212.

49. Quoted in Jane T. Merritt, *At the Crossroads: Indians and Empires on a Mid-Atlantic Frontier, 1700–1763* (Chapel Hill, NC: University of North Carolina Press, 2003), 103.

50. Quoted and trans. in Katherine M. Faull, ed., *Moravian Women's Memoirs: Their Related Lives, 1750–1820* (Syracuse, NY: Syracuse University Press, 1997), 55.

51. Merritt, *At the Crossroads*, 113.

52. Autobiography of Anna Johanna Pietsch Seidel, quoted and trans. in Beverly P. Smaby, "'No one should lust after power . . . women least of all': Dismantling Female Leadership among Eighteenth-Century Moravians," in *Pious Pursuits: German Moravians in the Atlantic World*, ed. Michele Gillespie and Robert Beachy (New York: Berghahn Books, 2007), 164, 173.

53. Faull, *Moravian Women's Memoirs*, 49–57.

EPILOGUE

1. http://www.fides.org/en/news/19317-ASIA_JAPAN_Beatification_of_188_ Japanese_martyrs_example_for_the_lay_faithful_and_opportunity_to_show_ the_importance_of_the_woman_s_role_in_the_Church
2. https://www.lutheranworld.org/sites/default/files/joint_commemoration_ joint_statement_final_en.pdf

FURTHER READING

There are inspirational biographies written for adults and for young people of a few of the better-known women in this book, including Katharina von Bora, Teresa of Avila, Rose of Lima, and Susanna Wesley. They present their subjects as models to emulate, and often include material drawn from traditions that have developed about these women as well as from the historical records. The same is true of many websites and blogs, so I have not included these.

Among historians, the study of women and the Reformations really began with Roland Bainton's three volumes of short biographies, *Women of the Reformation* (Minneapolis, MN: Fortress Press, 1971, 1973, 1977), still useful and still in print half a century later. Most of the women in them are Protestants, as are most of the women in Kirsi I. Stjerna, ed., *Women Reformers in Early Modern Europe: Profiles, Texts and Contexts* (Minneapolis, MN: Fortress Press, 2022). Kirsi Stjerna, *Women and the Reformation* (London: Blackwell, 2009), written for students, focuses on nine Protestant women from across Europe, though it also discusses the effects of the Protestant Reformation on women's lives. There are no corresponding books on women in the Catholic Reformation written for general readers, or on women in seventeenth- and eighteenth-century Christianity.

By contrast, there has been a huge outpouring of scholarly work on women and Christianity in this era published over the last several decades. The books below are only a tiny share of this. These are generally available in academic and larger public libraries, or sometimes quite cheaply as used books through online booksellers or in bookstores. Some of the newer of these are available as e-books, or even as audiobooks, and some of these are Open Access, so they don't cost anything to listen to or view online. The notes, which contain only references to material I have quoted directly, will point you to more studies, including editions and translations of original sources. In publishing works by women, the series The Other Voice in Early Modern Europe, first published by the University of Chicago Press and more recently by the University of Toronto Press, has been especially important.

For a look at all aspects of women's lives in this era, see my *Women and Gender in Early Modern Europe*, 4th ed. (Cambridge: Cambridge University Press, 2019), and for a survey, see my *Early Modern Europe, 1450–1789*, 3rd ed. (Cambridge: Cambridge University Press, 2020). Both include chapters on the colonial world. Ulinka Rublack, *Reformation Europe*, 2nd ed. (Cambridge: Cambridge University Press, 2017) puts theological ideas in their cultural contexts. Jennifer Hornyak Wojciechowski, *Women and the Christian Story: A Global History* (Minneapolis, MN: Fortress Press, 2022) provides an engaging and balanced overview of women in Christian history.

MONARCHS

For general information on women rulers, see Sharon L. Jansen, *The Monstrous Regiment of Women: Female Rulers in Early Modern Europe* (New York: Palgrave, 2002); William Monter, *The Rise of Female Kings in Europe 1300–1800* (New Haven, CT: Yale University Press, 2012); and Sarah Gristwood, *Game of Queens: The Women Who Made Sixteenth-Century Europe* (New York: Basic Books, 2016).

On Isabel of Castile, see Peggy K. Liss, *Isabel the Queen* (New York: Oxford University Press, 1992) and Barbara Weissberger, *Isabel Rules: Constructing Queenship, Wielding Power* (Minneapolis, MN: University of Minnesota Press, 2003). Magdalena Sanchez, *The Empress, the Queen and the Nun: Women and Power at the Court of Philip III of Spain* (Baltimore, MD: Johns Hopkins University Press, 1998) traces the ways three royal women used piety, childbearing, and marriage arrangements to influence political decisions. Silvia Z. Mitchell, *Queen, Mother, and Stateswoman: Mariana of Austria and the Government of Spain* (University Park, PA: Pennsylvania State University Press, 2018) discusses one of Spain's most important regents.

There are hundreds of books about the Tudor queens of England, ranging from biographies for young adult readers to giant scholarly tomes on every aspect of their reigns. Theresa Earenfight, *Catherine of Aragon: Infanta of Spain, Queen of England* (State College, PA: Penn State University Press, 2021) is an innovative biography that draws on Spanish sources and the objects that Catherine owned. Anna Whitelock, *Mary Tudor: England's First Queen* (London: Bloomsbury, 2010) presents Mary as a determined and complex figure. Carole Levin, *The Reign and Life of Queen Elizabeth I* (London: Palgrave Macmillan, 2003) is a lively and accessible overview. On the Stuart queens, see Susan Doran, *Mary Queen of Scots: An Illustrated Life* (London: British Library, 2007) and Nadine Akkerman, *Elizabeth Stuart: Queen of Hearts* (Oxford: Oxford University Press, 2021).

For the network of Protestant royal women in France, see Barbara Stephenson, *The Power and Patronage of Marguerite de Navarre* (Burlington, VT: Ashgate, 2004) and Nancy Lyman Roelker, *Queen of Navarre, Jeanne d'Albret: 1528–1572* (Cambridge, MA: Harvard University Press, 1968). Leonie Frieda, *Catherine de Medici: Renaissance Queen of France* (New York: HarperCollins, 2006) and Nancy Goldstone, *The Rival Queens: Catherine de' Medici, Her Daughter Marguerite de Valois, and the Betrayal that Ignited a Kingdom* (New York: Back Bay Books, 2016) tell the story of family and religious conflict involving France's most powerful Catholic queen.

There are no biographies in English of the northern and eastern European women rulers mentioned in the book, but Maria Bogucka, *Women in Early Modern Polish Society, Against the European Background* (London: Routledge, 2004) offers a general study of women in Poland. On the Habsburgs, see Charles R. Steen, *Margaret of Parma: A Life* (Leiden: Brill, 2013); Anne J. Cruz and Maria Galli Stampino, eds., *Early Modern Habsburg*

Women: Transnational Contexts, Cultural Conflicts, Dynastic Continuities (Farnham: Ashgate, 2013); and Rubén González Cuerva, *Maria of Austria, Holy Roman Empress (1528–1603): Dynastic Networker* (London: Routledge, 2021). Barbara Stollberg-Rilinger, *Maria Theresa: The Habsburg Empress in Her Time*, trans. Robert Savage (Princeton, NJ: Princeton University Press, 2022) is a sweeping work that examines the dynamic ruler along with eighteenth-century society.

MOTHERS

John Witte, Jr., *From Sacrament to Contract: Marriage, Religion, and Law in the Western Tradition*, 2nd ed. (Louisville, KY: Westminster John Knox Press, 2012) provides an overview of Christian ideas and laws about marriage. Joel F. Harrington, *Reordering Marriage and Society in Reformation Germany* (Cambridge: Cambridge University Press, 1995) examines the impact of the Reformation on the ideal and practice of marriage. On clerical marriage, see Marjorie Elizabeth Plummer, *From Priest's Whore to Pastor's Wife: Clerical Marriage and the Process of Reform in the Early German Reformation* (Farnham: Ashgate, 2012); Helen L. Parish, *Clerical Marriage and the English Reformation: Precedent, Policy and Practice* (London: Routledge, 2017); and Anne Thompson, *Parish Clergy Wives in Elizabethan England* (Leiden: Brill, 2019).

Very few sources for the life of Katharina von Bora survive, so many biographies, beginning with those of the sixteenth century, just make things up. Ruth A. Tucker, *Katie Luther, First Lady of the Reformation: The Unconventional Life of Katharina von Bora* (Grand Rapids, MI: Zondervan, 2017) is a sympathetic study that admits the limitations of her evidence and puts Katharina within the context of other women who supported the Protestant Reformation. Ian Siggins, *Luther and His Mother* (Minneapolis, MN: Fortress Press, 1981) is a brief look at the role Margarethe Luther played in Martin's development.

The writings of many Protestant "church mothers" have been translated into English, with introductions that discuss their lives. These include Peter Matheson, ed. and trans., *Argula von Grumbach: A Woman's Voice in the Reformation* (Edinburgh: T. & T. Clark, 1995); Marie Dentière, *Epistle to Marguerite de Navarre and Preface to a Sermon by John Calvin*, ed. and trans. Mary B. McKinley (Chicago: University of Chicago Press, 2004); and Katharina Schütz Zell, *Church Mother: The Writings of a Protestant Reformer in Sixteenth-Century Germany*, ed. and trans. Elsie McKee (Chicago: University of Chicago Press, 2006). On women's religious writing more generally, see Kate Narveson, *Bible Readers and Lay Writers in Early Modern England: Gender and Self-Definition in an Emergent Writing Culture* (Farnham: Ashgate, 2012) and Amanda C. Pipkin, *Dissenting Daughters: Reformed Women in the Dutch Republic, 1572–1725* (New York: Oxford University Press, 2022).

There is no book-length study of recusant women, though there are many articles, dissertations, and chapters in collections, such as Marie B. Rowlands, "Recusant Women, 1560–1640," in *Women in English Society, 1500–1800*, ed. Mary Prior (London and New York: Methuen, 1985), 149–180, and Sarah L. Bastow, "'Worth Nothing, but Very Wilful'; Catholic Recusant Women of Yorkshire, 1536–1642," *British Catholic History* 25, no. 4 (October 2001): 591–603. Patricia Crawford, *Women and Religion in England: 1500–1720* (Routledge: London, 1993) provides a good overview of Catholics and Protestants.

Most of the research on pietist women is published in German, but there are several essays on women and gender in Jonathan Strom, Hartmut Lehmann and James van Horn Melton, eds., *Pietism in Germany and North America 1680–1820* (Burlington, VT: Ashgate, 2009). *The Life of Lady Johanna Eleonora Petersen, Written by Herself*, ed. and trans. Barbara Becker-Cantarino (Chicago: University of Chicago Press, 2005) is a translation of Johanna Eleonora Petersen's autobiography with a good introduction.

For Methodists and other early evangelicals, see Paul W. Chilcote, *She Offered Them Christ: The Legacy of Women Preachers in Early Methodism* (Nashville, TN: Abingdon Press, 1993); Phyllis Mack, *Heart Religion in the British Enlightenment: Gender and Emotion in Early Methodism* (Cambridge: Cambridge University Press, 2011); Sarah Apetrei, *Women, Feminism and Religion in Early Enlightenment England* (Cambridge: Cambridge University Press, 2013); and William Gibson and Joanne Begiato, *Sex and the Church in the Long Eighteenth Century: Religion, Enlightenment, and the Sexual Revolution* (London: I.B. Tauris, 2017).

On evangelicals in North America, see Susan Juster, *Disorderly Women: Sexual Politics and Evangelicalism in Revolutionary New England* (Ithaca, NY: Cornell University Press, 1994); Catherine A. Brekus, *Strangers and Pilgrims: Female Preaching in America, 1740–1845* (Chapel Hill, NC: University of North Carolina Press, 1998) and *Sarah Osborn's World: The Rise of Evangelical Christianity in Early America* (New Haven, CT: Yale University Press, 2013). Sylvia R. Frey and Betty Wood, *Come Shouting to Zion: African American Protestantism in the American South and British Caribbean to 1830* (Chapel Hill, NC: University of North Carolina Press, 1998) includes fascinating details about Black women preachers and the development of Afro-Atlantic Christianity.

For changes in convents during the era of the Catholic Reformation, see Ulrike Strasser, *State of Virginity: Gender, Religion, and Politics in an Early Modern Catholic State* (Ann Arbor, MI: University of Michigan Press, 2004); Elizabeth Lehfeldt, *Women and Religion in Golden-Age Spain: The Permeable Cloister* (Burlington, VT: Ashgate, 2006); Silvia Evangelisti, *Nuns: A History of Convent Life* (Oxford: Oxford University Press, 2007); and Barbara R. Woshinsky, *Imagining Women's Conventual Spaces in France, 1600–1800* (Aldershot: Ashgate, 2010).

Merry Wiesner-Hanks and Joan Skocir, ed. and trans., *Convents Confront the Reformation: Catholic and Protestant Nuns in Germany* (Milwaukee, WI: Marquette University Press, 1998); Amy Leonard, *Nails in the Wall: Catholic Nuns in Reformation Germany* (Chicago: University of Chicago Press, 2005); and Marjorie Elizabeth Plummer, *Stripping the Veil: Convent Reform, Protestant Nuns, and Female Devotional Life in Sixteenth-Century Germany* (Oxford: Oxford University Press, 2022) focus on the effects of the Protestant Reformation on nuns.

The efforts of Catholic religious women to create an active life in the world have been examined in Elizabeth Rapley, *The Dévotes: Women and Church in Seventeenth-Century France* (Montreal and Kingston: McGill-Queen's University Press, 1990); Susan Dinan, *Women and Poor Relief in Seventeenth-Century France: The Early History of the Daughters of Charity* (Burlington, VT: Ashgate, 2006); Barbara Diefendorf, *From Penitence to Charity: Pious Women and the Catholic Reformation in Paris* (Oxford: Oxford University Press, 2006); Querciolo Mazzonis, *Spirituality, Gender, and the Self in Renaissance Italy: Angela Merici and the Company of St. Ursula (1474–1540)* (Washington, DC: Catholic University Press, 2007); Emily Clark, *Masterless Mistresses: The New Orleans Ursulines and the Development of a New World Society, 1727–1834* (Durham, NC: University of North Carolina Press, 2007); and Alison Weber, ed., *Devout Laywomen in the Early Modern World* (London: Routledge, 2016).

Alexander Sedgwick, *The Travails of Conscience: The Arnauld Family and the Ancien Régime* (Cambridge, MA: Harvard University Press, 1998) explores the religious ideas of Angélique and Agnés Arnauld, and the effects these had on their family and French politics. The story of Walatta Petros is told in Galawdewos, *The Life and Struggles of Our Mother Walatta Petros: A Seventeenth-Century African Biography of an Ethiopian Woman*, trans. and ed. Wendy Laura Belcher and Michael Kleiner (Princeton, NJ: Princeton University Press, 2015).

MIGRANTS

Nicholas Terpstra, *Religious Refugees in the Early Modern World: An Alternative History of the Reformation* (Cambridge: Cambridge University Press, 2015) is an essential study of people driven from their homes for religious reasons.

Mary E. Giles, ed., *Women in the Inquisition: Spain and the New World* (Baltimore, MD: Johns Hopkins University Press, 1999) includes essays on many women forced to move because of the Inquisition. Renée Levine Melammed, *Heretics or Daughters of Israel: The Crypto-Jewish Women of Castile* (Oxford: Oxford University Press, 1999) examines Jewish women and *conversas*. Dolores Sloan, *The Sephardic Jews of Spain and Portugal: Survival of an Imperiled Culture in the Fifteenth and Sixteenth Centuries* (Jefferson, NC: McFarland Press, 2009) and Julia R. Lieberman, ed., *Sephardi Family Life in the Early Modern Diaspora* (Waltham, MA: Brandeis University Press, 2011) examine Sephardic exile communities. Cecil Roth, *Doña Gracia of the House of Nasi* (Philadelphia, PA: Jewish Publication Society, 1948) and Marianna D. Birnbaum, *The Long Journey of Gracia Mendes* (Budapest: Central European University Press, 2003) tell the story of the remarkable Gracia Mendes Nasi.

Matthew Carr, *Blood and Faith: The Purging of Muslim Spain*, rev. ed. (London: Hurst & Company, 2017) chronicles the expulsion of the Muslims. On Muslim women, see Mary Elizabeth Perry, *The Handless Maiden: Moriscos and the Politics of Religion in Early Modern Spain* (Princeton, NJ: Princeton University Press, 2005).

On Anabaptists and other radicals, see C. Arnold Snyder and Linda A. Heubert Hecht, eds., *Profiles of Anabaptist Women: Sixteenth-Century Reforming Pioneers* (Waterloo, Ontario: Wilfried Laurier University Press, 1996); Sylvia Brown, ed., *Women, Gender, and Radical Religion in Early Modern Europe* (Leiden: Brill, 2007); and Mirjiam van Veen et al., eds., *Sisters: Myth and Reality of Anabaptists, Mennonite and Doopsgezind Women, ca. 1525–1900* (Leiden: Brill, 2014).

Quaker women have been well studied: Bonnelyn Young Kunze, *Margaret Fell and the Rise of Quakerism* (Stanford, CA: Stanford University Press, 1994); Catherine M. Wilcox, *Theology and Women's Ministry in Seventeenth-Century English Quakerism: Handmaids of the Lord* (London: E. Mellen, 1995); Rebecca Larson, *Daughters of Light: Quaker Women Preaching and Prophesying in the Colonies and Abroad, 1700–1775* (Chapel Hill, NC: University of North Carolina Press, 2000); Judith Jennings, *Gender, Religion and Radicalism in the Long Eighteenth Century: The "Ingenious Quaker" and Her Connections* (Burlington, VT: Ashgate, 2006); Michele Lise Tarter and Catie Gill, eds., *New Critical Studies on Early Quaker Women, 1650–1800* (Oxford: Oxford University Press, 2018); Naomi Pullin, *Female Friends and the Making of Transatlantic Quakerism, 1650–1750* (Cambridge: Cambridge University Press, 2018).

Quaker women wrote more than women in any other Protestant group, and their writings have seen modern editions and reprints, including Teresa Feroli and Margaret Olofson Thickstun, eds., *Witness, Warning and Prophecy: Quaker Women's Writing, 1655–1700* (Toronto: Iter Press, 2017); Jane Donawerth and Rebecca M. Lush, eds., *Margaret Fell: Women's Speaking Justified and Other Pamphlets* (Toronto: Iter Press, 2018). Eve LaPlante, *American Jezebel: The Uncommon Life of Anne Hutchinson, the Woman Who Defied the Puritans* (San Francisco: HarperCollins, 2004) is an excellent biography of Anne Hutchinson.

Charlotte Arbaleste Duplessis-Mornay, Anne de Chaufepié, and Anne Marguerite Petit Du Noyer, *The Huguenot Experience of Persecution and Exile: Three Women's Stories*, ed. Colette H. Winn, trans. Lauren King and Colette H. Winn (Toronto, Ontario: Iter Press, 2019) includes memoirs of Huguenot women, with a broad introduction. Susan Broomhall, *Women and Religion in Sixteenth-Century France* (London: Palgrave Macmillan, 2007) provides an overview of Catholic and Protestant women in France.

On English and Irish nuns who moved to Europe, see Claire Walker, *Gender and Politics in Early Modern Europe: English Convents in France and the Low Countries* (London: Palgrave Macmillan, 2002); James E. Kelly, *English Convents in Catholic Europe, c. 1600–1800* (Cambridge: Cambridge University Press, 2020); Andrea Knox, *Irish Women on the Move: Migration and Mission in Spain, 1499–1700* (Oxford: Oxford University Press, 2020); and Bronagh Ann McShane, *Irish Women in Religious Orders, 1530–1700: Suppression, Migration and Reintegration* (London: Woodbridge, 2022). On Mary Ward, see Mary Wright, IBVM, *Mary Ward's Institute: The Struggle for Identity* (Sydney: Crossing Press, 1997) and Laurence Lux-Sterritt, *Redefining Female Religious Life: French Ursulines and English Ladies in Seventeenth-Century Catholicism* (Burlington, VT: Ashgate, 2005).

Sarah E. Owens, *Nuns Navigating the Spanish Empire* (Albuquerque, NM: University of New Mexico Press, 2017) tells the story of the Spanish nuns who traveled to Asia. Haruko Nawata Ward, *Women Religious Leaders in Japan's Christian Century, 1549–1650* (London: Routledge, 2016) is an in-depth look at women's religious activities in the "Christian Century" in Japan, including Buddhist and Shinto leaders as well as Christian teachers, catechists, and martyrs.

MARTYRS

Brad S. Gregory, *Salvation at Stake: Christian Martyrdom in Early Modern Europe* (Cambridge, MA: Harvard University Press, 2001) offers a broad comparative analysis of Protestant and Catholic martyrs, including women.

The *Martyrs Mirror* is available in an inexpensive modern edition in English, in all its 1,000+ pages: Thieleman J. van Braght, *Martyrs Mirror: The Story of Seventeen Centuries of Christian Martyrdom from the Time of Christ to A.D. 1660* (Harrisonburg, VA: Herald Press, 1938). Hermina Joldersma and Louis Grijp, ed. and trans., *"Elisabeth's Manly Courage": Testimonials and Songs by and about Martyred Anabaptist Women* (Milwaukee, WI: Marquette University Press, 2001) has original sources with a good introduction.

On English women martyrs, see Megan L. Hickerson, *Making Women Martyrs in Tudor England* (London: Palgrave, 2005) and Peter Lake and Michael Questier, *The Trials of Margaret Clitherow: Persecution, Martyrdom and the Politics of Sanctity in Elizabethan England* (Bloomsbury: London, 2011). Elaine V. Beilin, ed., *The Examinations of Anne Askew* (New York: Oxford University Press, 1996) is a modern edition.

If you have access to an academic library that subscribes to ProQuest, you can read John Foxe's *Acts and Monuments* in its sixteenth-century editions through the Early English Books Online program. These will have the original gory woodcuts. There are several modern paperback books claiming to be Foxe's Book of Martyrs, often self-published, but these include only small parts of Foxe, and generally "update" the text by including more recent Christian martyrs that fit with the author's own ideals and beliefs. Buyer beware!

Susan Broomhall, *Evangelising Korean Women in the Early Modern World: The Power of Body and Text* (York: ARC Humanities Press, 2023) examines Korean Christian women and how their experiences have been remembered.

Brian P. Levack, *The Witch-Hunt in Early Modern Europe*, 4th ed. (London: Longman, 2015) is an up-to-date general study. Deborah Willis, *Malevolent Nurture: Witch-Hunting and Maternal Power in Early Modern England* (Ithaca, NY: Cornell University Press, 1995) examines the links between witchcraft and motherhood. Diane Purkiss, *The Witch in History: Early Modern and Twentieth-Century Representations* (London: Routledge, 1996) provides a thorough and often witty analysis of contemporary representations of witches and the academic study of witchcraft. Marion Gibson has written eight good books on various aspects of witchcraft, including *Witchcraft: The Basics* (London: Routledge, 2018).

MYSTICS

Stephen Haliczer, *Between Exaltation and Infamy: Female Mystics in Golden-Age Spain* (Oxford: Oxford University Press, 2002) is a solid general study. Stacey Schlau, *Gendered Crime and Punishment: Women and/in the Hispanic Inquisitions* (Leiden: Brill, 2013) includes many visionaries. Electa Arenal and Stacey Schlau, *Untold Sisters: Hispanic Nuns in Their Own Works* (Albuquerque, NM: University of New Mexico Press, 1989) provides long selections in both Spanish and English from the works of many Spanish and New World nuns, as well as interpretations of their writings.

On St. Teresa, see Jodi Bilinkoff, *The Avila of St. Theresa*, new ed. (Ithaca, NY: Cornell University Press, 2015); Alison Weber, *Teresa of Avila and the Rhetoric of Femininity* (Princeton, NJ: Princeton University Press, 1990); and Carole Slade, *Saint Teresa of Avila: Author of a Heroic Life* (Berkeley, CA: University of California Press, 1995). Francisca de los Apóstoles, *The Inquisition of Francisca: A Sixteenth-Century Visionary on Trial*, ed. and trans. Gillian T.W. Ahlgren (Chicago: University of Chicago Press, 2005) presents records from the trial of the visionary *beata*. Anna M. Nogar, *Quill and Cross in the Borderlands: Sor María de Ágreda and the Lady in Blue, 1628 to the Present* (South Bend, IN: University of Notre Dame Press, 2018) examines the life and legacy of the bilocating nun.

The best recent study of Rose of Lima and her followers is Frank Graziano, *Wounds of Love: The Mystical Marriage of Saint Rose of Lima* (New York: Oxford University Press, 2004). On other New World visionaries and saints, see Allan Greer and Jodi Bilinkoff, eds., *Colonial Saints: Discovering the Holy in the Americas, 1500–1800* (New York: Routledge, 2003); Nancy E. van Deusen, *Embodying the Sacred: Women Mystics in Seventeenth-Century Lima* (Durham, NC: Duke University Press, 2017); and Nancy Van Deusen, *The Souls of Purgatory: The Spiritual Diary of a Seventeenth-Century Afro-Peruvian Mystic, Ursula de Jesus* (Albuquerque, NM: University of New Mexico Press, 2004).

Marie-Florine Bruneau, *French Mystics Confront the Modern World: Marie de l'Incarnation (1599–1672) and Madame Guyon (1648–1717)* (Albany: SUNY Press, 1998) compares Madame Guyon and Marie de l'Incarnation, discussed in Chapter 6.

John Thornton, *The Kongolese Saint Anthony: Dona Beatriz Kimpa Vita and the Antonian Movement, 1684–1706* (Cambridge: Cambridge University Press, 1998) tells the story of this remarkable African visionary. On African Christianity more broadly, see John Thornton, *Africa and Africans in the Making of the Atlantic World, 1400–1800*, 2nd ed. (Cambridge: Cambridge University Press, 1998) and James Sweet, *Recreating Africa: Culture, Kinship and Religion in the African-Portuguese World, 1441–1770* (Chapel Hill, NC: University of North Carolina Press, 2003).

The scholarship on German Protestant visionaries is almost all in German. By contrast, there are many studies of English women prophets, especially during the

English Civil War, including: Phyllis Mack, *Visionary Women: Ecstatic Prophecy in Seventeenth-Century England* (Berkeley, CA: University of California Press, 1993); Alison Plowden, *Our Women All on Fire: The Women of the English Civil War* (London: Sutton Books, 1999); Diane Watt, *Sectaries of God: Women Prophets in Late Medieval and Early Modern England* (Rochester, NY: Boydell & Brewer, 1997); Elizabeth Bouldin, *Women Prophets and Radical Protestantism in the British Atlantic World, 1640–1730* (Cambridge: Cambridge University Press, 2015).

On Eleanor Davies, see Esther S. Cope, *Handmaid of the Holy Spirit: Dame Eleanor Davies, Never So Mad a Ladie* (Ann Arbor, MI: University of Michigan Press, 1993) and Eleanor Davies, *Prophetic Writings of Lady Eleanor Davies* (New York: Oxford University Press, 1995).

Julie Hirst, *Jane Lead: Biography of a Seventeenth-Century Mystic* (Aldershot: Ashgate, 2005) and Ariel Hessayon, ed., *Jane Lead and Her Transnational Legacy* (London: Palgrave Macmillan, 2016) examine Jane Lead and her impact. Jean Humez, *Mother's First-Born Daughters: Early Shaker Writings on Women and Religion* (Bloomington, IN: Indiana University Press, 1993) is a good collection of original sources, and Glendyne R. Wergland, *Sisters in the Faith: Shaker Women, 1780–1890* (Amherst, MA: University of Massachusetts Press, 2011) is a study of Shaker communities after the death of Ann Lee. Paul B. Moyer, *The Public Universal Friend: Jemima Wilkinson and Religious Enthusiasm in Revolutionary America* (Ithaca, NY: Cornell University Press, 2011) analyzes the prophet's ministry.

MISSIONARIES

My *Christianity and Sexuality in the Early Modern World: Regulating Desire, Reforming Practice*, 3rd ed. (London: Routledge and Kegan Paul, 2020) is a global overview of the impact of the spread of Christianity on gender and sexuality. Collections of articles that discuss women and religion in many colonial places include: Susan E. Dinan and Debra Meters, eds., *Women and Religion in Old and New Worlds* (London: Routledge, 2001); Daniella Kostroun and Lisa Vollendorf, eds., *Women, Religion and the Atlantic World, 1600–1800* (Toronto: University of Toronto Press, 2009); Emily Clark and Mary Laven, eds., *Women and Religion in the Atlantic Age* (Farnham: Ashgate, 2013); Simon Ditchfield and Helen Smiths, eds., *Conversions: Gender and Religious Change in Early Modern Europe* (Manchester: Manchester University Press, 2018).

On Luisa de Carvajal, see Elizabeth Rhodes, ed. and trans., *"This Tight Embrace": Luisa de Carvajal y Mendoza* (Milwaukee, WI: Marquette University Press, 2000) and Glyn Redworth, *The She-Apostle: The Extraordinary Life and Death of Luisa de Carvajal* (Oxford: Oxford University Press, 2008).

The first study to examine women in Spanish colonization, still valuable, is C.R. Boxer, *Mary and Misogyny: Women in Iberian Expansion Overseas, 1415–1815* (New York: Oxford University Press, 1975). More recent overviews include Susan Socolow, *The Women of Colonial Latin America* (Cambridge: Cambridge University Press, 2000) and Sarah E. Owens and Jane E. Mangan, eds., *Women of the Iberian Atlantic* (Baton Rouge, LA: Louisiana State University Press, 2012). Nora E. Jaffary and Jane E. Mangan, eds., *Women in Colonial Latin America, 1526 to 1806: Texts and Contexts* (Indianapolis, IN: Hackett, 2018) has translations of original sources. Nora E. Jaffary, ed., *Gender, Race, and Religion in the Colonization of the Americas* (Burlington, VT: Ashgate, 2007) and María Elena Martínez, *Genealogical Fictions: Limpieza de Sangre, Religion, and Gender in Colonial Mexico* (Stanford, CA: Stanford University Press, 2011) consider the role of gender and religion in the construction of racial hierarchies.

Irene Silverblatt, *Moon, Sun and Witches: Gender Ideologies and Class in Inca and Colonial Peru* (Princeton, NJ: Princeton University Press, 1987); Ramón A. Gutiérrez, *When Jesus Came, the Corn Mothers Went Away: Marriage, Sexuality, and Power in New Mexico 1500–1846* (Stanford, CA: Stanford University Press, 1991); Pete Sigal, *From Moon Goddesses to Virgins: The Colonization of Yucatecan Maya Sexual Desire* (Austin, TX: University of Texas Press, 2000); and Virginia M. Bouvier, *Women and the Conquest of California, 1542–1840: Codes of Silence* (Tucson, AZ: University of Arizona Press, 2001) examine the impact of Spanish colonization on Indigenous religion and gender. Caroline Dodds Pennock, *On Savage Shores: How Indigenous Americans Discovered Europe* (New York: Alfred A. Knopf, 2023) includes the story of Guaibimpará/Catherine and her chapel.

On devotion to the Virgin Mary in Mexico, see Louise M. Burkhart, *Before Guadalupe: The Virgin Mary in Early Colonial Nahuatl Literature* (Austin, TX: University of Texas Press for Institute of Mesoamerican Studies, SUNY, Albany, 2001) and David A. Brading, *Mexican Phoenix: Our Lady of Guadalupe: Image and Tradition* (Cambridge: Cambridge University Press, 2001).

On colonial convents, see Kathryn Burns, *Colonial Habits: Convents and the Spiritual Economy of Cuzco, Peru* (Durham, NC: Duke University Press, 1999) and Stephanie Kirk, *Convent Life in Colonial Mexico: A Tale of Two Communities* (Gainesville, FL: University Press of Florida, 2007). Sor Juana de la Cruz has sparked so much scholarship in many languages that there is now a collection simply about this: Emilie L. Bergmann and Stace Schlau, eds., *The Routledge Research Companion to the Works of Sor Juana Inés de la Cruz* (London: Routledge, 2017).

On women and Christianity in Asia, see: Carolyn Brewer, *Shamanism, Catholicism, and Gender Relations in Colonial Philippines, 1521–1685* (Aldershot: Ashgate, 2004); Ines G. Zupanov, *Missionary Tropics: The Catholic Frontier in India (16th–17th Centuries)* (Ann Arbor, MI: University of Michigan Press, 2005); Barbara Andaya, *The Flaming Womb: Repositioning Women in Early Modern Southeast Asia* (Honolulu, HI: University of Hawai'i Press, 2006); Tara Alberts, *Conflict and Conversion: Catholicism in Southeast Asia, 1500–1700* (Oxford: University of Oxford Press, 2013); Nadine Amsler, *Jesuits and Matriarchs: Domestic Worship in Early Modern China* (Seattle, WA: University of Washington Press, 2018).

Carol Devens, *Countering Colonization: Native American Women and Great Lakes Missions, 1630–1900* (Berkeley, CA: University of California Press, 1992); Susan Sleeper-Smith, *Indian Women and French Men: Rethinking Cultural Encounter in the Western Great Lakes* (Amherst, MA: University of Massachusetts Press, 2001); and Lisa J.M. Poirier, *Religion, Gender, and Kinship in Colonial New France* (Syracuse, NY: Syracuse University Press, 2016) discuss relations between Indigenous women and missionaries in French North America, and Gunlog Fur, *A Nation of Women: Gender and Colonial Encounters among the Delaware Indians* (Philadelphia, PA: University of Pennsylvania Press, 2012) in British North America. Allan Greer, *Mohawk Saint: Catherine Tekakwitha and the Jesuits* (New York: Oxford University Press, 2004) is an insightful study of this first North American Indigenous woman made a saint.

Natalie Zemon Davis, *Women on the Margins: Three Seventeenth-Century Lives* (Cambridge, MA: Harvard University Press, 1995) compares three women, the Jewish merchant Glickl bah Judah Leib, the Protestant scientist Maria Sibylla Marian, and the Catholic abbess Marie of the Incarnation. Two books by Patricia Simpson look at the life of the remarkable Marguerite Bourgeoys: *Marguerite Bourgeoys and Montreal* and *Marguerite Bourgeoys and the Congregation of Notre Dame* (Montreal and Kingston: McGill-Queen's University Press, 1997 and 2005).

On women in British North America, Mary Beth Norton, *Separated by Their Sex: Women in Public and Private in the Colonial Atlantic World* (Ithaca, NY: Cornell University Press, 2014) is an excellent overview. Marilyn J. Westerkamp, *Women and Religion in Early America, 1600–1850: The Puritan and Evangelical Traditions* (New York: Routledge, 1999) and Leslie J. Lindenauer, *Piety and Power: Gender and Religious Culture in the American Colonies* (New York: Routledge, 2001) focus on gender and religion.

On Christian Native Americans, see Joel W. Martin and Mark A. Nicholas, *Native Americans, Christianity, and the Reshaping of the American Religious Landscape* (Chapel Hill, NC: University of North Carolina Press, 2010) and Linford D. Fisher, *The Indian Great Awakening: Religion and the Shaping of Native Cultures in Early America* (New York: Oxford University Press, 2012). Rebecca Anne Goetz, *The Baptism of Early Virginia: How Christianity Created Race* (Baltimore, MD: Johns Hopkins University Press, 2012); Heather Miyano Kopelson, *Faithful Bodies: Performing Religion and Race in the Puritan Atlantic* (New York: New York University Press, 2014); and Katharine Gerbner, *Christian Slavery: Conversion and Race in the Protestant Atlantic World* (Philadelphia, PA: University of Pennsylvania Press, 2018) focus on the role of Protestant Christianity in creating notions of race in the Americas.

Aaron Spencer Fogleman, *Jesus Is Female: Moravians and the Challenge of Radical Religion in Early America* (Philadelphia, PA: University of Pennsylvania Press, 2007) and Paul Peucker, *Marriage and the Crisis of Moravian Piety in the Eighteenth Century* (University Park, PA: Pennsylvania State University Press, 2015) provide good introductions to Moravian ideas, and Michele Gillespie and Robert Beachy, eds., *Pious Pursuits: German Moravians in the Atlantic World* (New York: Berghahn Books, 2007) to their actions. For Barbara Knoll, see Aaron Spencer Fogleman, *Two Troubled Souls: An Eighteenth-Century Couple's Spiritual Journey in the Atlantic World* (Chapel Hill, NC: University of North Carolina Press, 2013), and for Rebecca Protten, see Jon F. Sensbach, *Rebecca's Revival: Creating Black Christianity in the Atlantic World* (Cambridge, MA: Harvard University Press, 2005). For Moravian women in Pennsylvania, see Jane T. Merritt, *At the Crossroads: Indians and Empires on a Mid-Atlantic Frontier, 1700–1763* (Chapel Hill, NC: University of North Carolina Press, 2003). Katherine M. Faull, ed. and trans., *Moravian Women's Memoirs: Their Related Lives, 1750–1820* (Syracuse, NY: Syracuse University Press, 1997) has fascinating original sources.

INDEX

Society for the Promoting of Christian Knowledge, 275
songs and hymns, 2, 31, 48–9, 76, 82, 163–4, 224
Sophia, electress of Hanover, 22
Sophia Jagiellon, princess of Poland, 28
Sophia Magdalene, queen of Denmark, 288
Sophie of Mecklenburg-Güstrow, queen consort of Denmark-Norway, 31
Soto, Hernando de, Spanish explorer, 253–4
Soubirous, Bernadette, French Catholic visionary and saint, 304
Southern Baptist Convention, 301
Spain, 4–10, 102–12, 201–15
Spenser, Edmund, English poet, 16
state churches, Protestant, 3, 18, 20, 70–1, 132, 200, 299
Stolberg, Anna von, German Protestant abbess, 88
Stolberg, Christiane Charlotte Friederike, German pietist, 73
Stolberg, Katherine, German Protestant writer, 73
Stono Rebellion, 225
Strasbourg, 51, 56–60, 114, 132
Stuart, Henry, Lord Darnley, Scottish nobleman, 19
Süleyman the Magnificent, Ottoman sultan, 105
Suriname, 286, 287
Susenyos, king of Ethiopia, 96
Sweden, 29–30, 50, 86, 120, 195, 221, 300, 305

Tama Gracia, Japanese convert and noblewoman, 184–6
Tamil people, 73
Teellinck, Susanna and Cornelia, Dutch Protestant writers, 61
Tegaiagueneta, Marie-Thérèse, Iroquois Christian convert, 279
Tegonhatsiongo, Anastasia, Iroquois Christian convert, 279
Tekakwitha, Catherine (Kateri), Algonquin-Mohawk convert and saint, xv, 279–80, Plate XV

Teresa of Avila, Spanish mystic, reformer, and saint, xii, 90, 95, 198, 201–7, 209, 217, 218, 219, 246, 259, Plates I, XI
third-order groups (tertiaries), 91, 199, 207, 212
Thirty Years' War, 22, 29, 30, 34, 83, 101, 117, 119, 226, 285
Throckmorton, Nicholas, Protestant English ambassador, 18
Tordesillas, Treaty of, 248, 250
Tranquebar, 73–4, 285
Trapnel, Anna, English prophet, xv, 198, 233, 235
Trunchfield, Joan, English Protestant martyr, 177

Ukraine, 117
University of the Cloister of Sor Juana, 264
Urban VIII, pope, 91, 145
Ursula de Jesús, Afro-Peruvian visionary, 213–15
Ursula of Münsterberg, German Protestant nun, 86
Ursulines, 41, 91–2, 154–5, 220, 243

Vadstena convent, 86
Vaux, Anne, English Catholic recusant, 65–6, 244
Vaux, Elizabeth, English Catholic recusant, 65–6
Velázquez, Diego, Spanish painter, 147, Plate IX
Vermigli, Peter Martyr, Italian Protestant reformer, 51
Vernon, Margaret, English Catholic prioress, 88–9
Vetterin, Anna, German visionary, 227
Victoria, queen of the United Kingdom, 22
Vietnam, 154, 269–74, 298
Villena, Isabel de, Spanish abbess and author, 7
Vincent, Isabeau, French Protestant visionary, 227–8
Virgin Mary Moon Goddess, 257, 298
Virgin of Guadalupe, 148–9, 257–8, 260, Plate XIV